P9-DMI-800

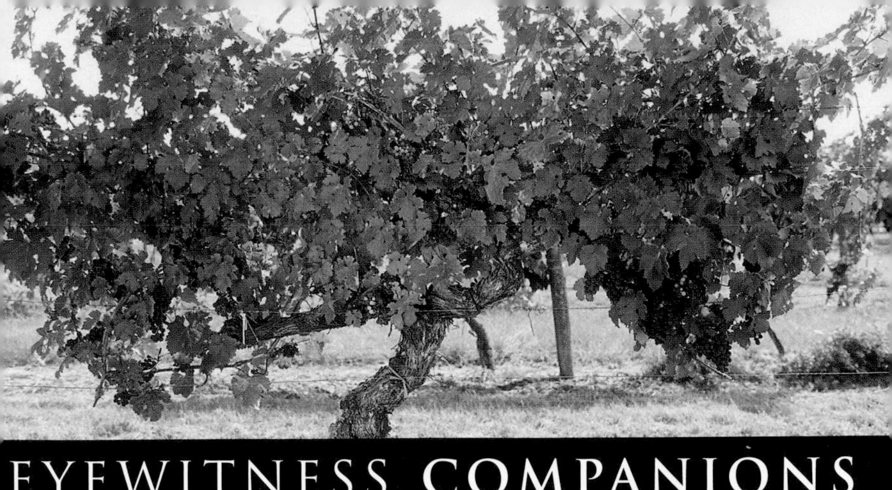

EYEWITNESS COMPANIONS

French Wine

ROBERT JOSEPH

LONDON, NEW YORK,
MUNICH, MELBOURNE, DELHI

Senior Editor	Claire Nottage
Senior Art Editor	Anne Fisher
Managing Editor	Deirdre Headon
Managing Art Editor	Marianne Markham
DTP Designer	Louise Waller
Production Controller	Mandy Inness

Produced for Dorling Kindersley by Departure Lounge

Editor	Debbie Woska
Designer	Janis Utton

Robert Joseph's team

Kitty Johnson, Jane Boyce, Richard Royds

First American Edition 1999
This revised edition 2005
Published in the United States by
DK Publishing, Inc.
375 Hudson Street
New York, New York 10014

06 07 08 09 10 9 8 7 6 5 4 3 2

A Cataloging-in-Publication record for this book is available from the Library of Congress.

ISBN 0-7566-1520-8

Reproduced by Colourscan
Printed in China by LREX

Discover more at
www.dk.com

CONTENTS

How to Use this Guide

Whether you are a wine buff or simply enjoy drinking a glass of wine with a meal, this comprehensive guide will provide you with all the information you need on the world of French wines.

Highlights of the introductory section include an informative outline of the history of wine, detailed information on how wine is made, step-by-step instructions in the art of wine tasting, a useful guide to starting a cellar, and handy hints for cooking with wine.

The bulk of the book is divided alphabetically into the 10 wine-making regions of France, with full-color photographs throughout. Each regional chapter opens with an introduction to the region as a whole, followed by a driving tour that encompasses some of the region's highlights. The pages that follow provide an insight into Robert Joseph's choices of wine among the region's appellations, and include a selection of recommended producers, examples of good vintages, ideal wine and food partnerships, and tasting tips.

Because wine and food are so inextricably linked, each chapter includes a mouth-watering introduction to the local dishes, together with a separate box on the various cheeses made in the region, which invariably pair very well with the local wines.

As you delve into the world of French wines, this book will be useful both at home and on your travels through the vineyards of France.

THE WINE-PRODUCING REGIONS

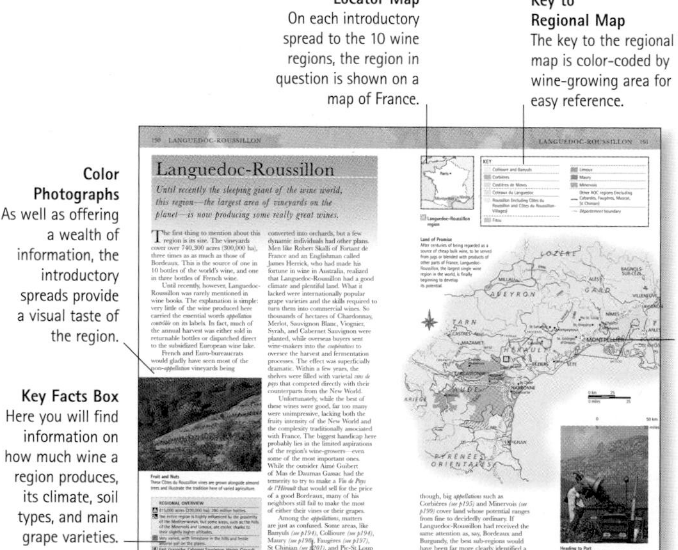

Description of Region
The introductory spreads provide background information on each wine-producing region as a whole.

THE REGIONAL TOURS

TOUR SYMBOLS
Tasting possible
Places to eat
Tourist information
★ Site of interest
Tour route
Viewpoint

Locator Map
This locator map pinpoints the part of the region covered by the driving tour.

Driving Tour Map
A suggested route for a driving tour of the region is plotted on this map.

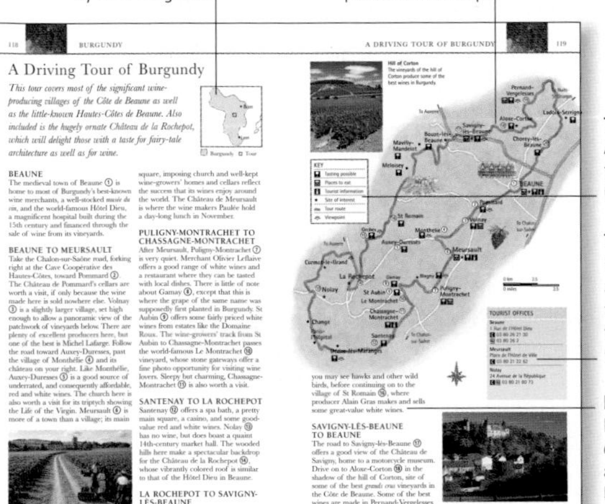

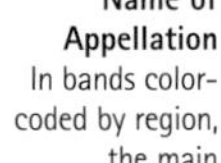

Tour Symbols
A key explains the symbols used (above) on the map.

Touring Tips Box
Here you will find addresses and telephone numbers for the local tourist offices.

Description of Tour
Here you will find details of the sites and places covered by the driving tour.

THE INDIVIDUAL APPELLATIONS

Name of Appellation
In bands color-coded by region, the main *appellations* appear in alphabetical order.

Description of Appellation
This text describes the *appellation* and the styles and qualities of its wines.

Locator Map
The locator map pinpoints the *appellation* on a map of the region.

Illustrated Wine
An important wine from the *appellation* is shown.

Key Facts Box
This fact box systematically provides further information about the *appellation.*

KEY FACTS SYMBOLS

- Quality designation, ranked from least good to best
- Top villages and/or vineyards
- Yield
- Climate
- Soil
- Grape varieties, for red, white, and rosé
- Wine style(s)
- Producers or top wines (Champagne)
- Associated producers (Champagne only)
- Recommended dish
- Key vintages, in descending order
- Longevity for red, white, and rosé

Foreword

I FIRST FELL IN LOVE with the wines of France as an adolescent while exploring the cellar of my parents' country hotel. Wine, I imagined then, came in four colors—red, white, pink and brown—and in various levels of sweetness. Pulling a few corks, however, I discovered an extraordinary range of flavors concealed behind the green and clear glass of the bottles.

There was young, red Burgundy, its raspberry tang contrasting with the gamey flavor of older vintages. There was flinty Chablis and nutty Meursault, red Bordeaux full of black currants from the Médoc and full of plums from St Émilion. I discovered notes of gooseberry in Sancerre and spring flowers in wine from Condrieu in the Rhône Valley.

I continued my education on youthful trips to France with the help of a book or two and many generous wine-makers. Both well-known and lesser-known wines, including Jurançon, Château Chalon, and Banyuls, gave me a combined course in geography and history. I discovered the tastes of different grape varieties and the effects of changing soils, climates, and vintages. Even more important, both then and later when I was living in Burgundy, I learned about the vital role of the wine-maker in the alchemy that transforms a simple fruit into a drink that can somehow touch the emotions and linger for decades in the memory of the drinker.

The story of a wine cannot be fully understood without proper reference to the place where it is made, the people who make it, and the local food with which it is drunk. Celebrating all of these things in this book, I have chosen some of France's best-known wines—and some of the least known—from the merchant's shelf and restaurant wine list, and endeavored to set them in a context that makes the most sense of their flavor and style.

As well as exploring the flavors and styles of French wines, I have also drawn attention to some of the pitfalls that you may encounter when you come to buy your own wine. Critics now agree that the famous French system of *appellations contrôlées* is in urgent need of a thorough overhaul. The name of a region on a wine label provides no guarantee of its quality—so while one bottle of Champagne or Bordeaux may be a delight, the next may be a disaster. A supposedly basic Burgundy made by a skilled and diligent wine-maker often tastes much better than an expensive wine made to less exacting standards using grapes from a neighboring *grand cru appellation*. Besides its inadequacy as an indicator of quality, the *appellation* system can also be extremely confusing. Cheverny and Cour-Cheverny, for example, are both white wines, made in the same place but from different grape varieties, resulting in wines with completely different flavors. Further, the wines made in Rully taste nothing like the wines made in Reuilly, and likewise, the wines made in Pouilly-Fumé, Pouilly-sur-Loire, and Pouilly-Fuissé have very little in common beyond the first part of their name.

With so many problems like these, it is easy to understand why a growing number of people choose wine that is labeled simply by grape variety, such as Chardonnay, Cabernet Sauvignon, or Merlot. By doing so, however, they are missing out on the enormous range of subtle flavors that set wine apart from almost anything else you can drink. The myriad variables of the French climate, micro-climates, soils, grapes, wine-makers, and wine-making traditions come together to create an ever-changing maze of different wines, each with its own unique flavors. Despite, and perhaps because of, its complexity, France's long wine-making tradition still offers surprises and delights to match, and often surpass, those of any other wine-producing country in the world.

My aim in this book is to provide you with a few paths through the exciting maze of French wine, and a few detours around its potential pitfalls. More important, perhaps, I want to provide you with the confidence and the knowledge that will enable you to anticipate the qualities of almost any French wine that you may encounter. I hope you enjoy reading this book half as much as I have enjoyed researching and writing it.

Robert Joseph

Introducing FRENCH WINES

The History of Wine

The Old Testament acknowledges the pleasure and the power of the drink derived from fermented grapes, but it was the Greeks, the Romans, and, most particularly, the French who perfected the art of wine-making.

For those of us who now heed medical warnings about the minimum and maximum weekly consumption of wine, it is worth pausing to recall that, for most of man's history, wine tended to be the safest, healthiest drink available. It was finding water pure enough to drink that was the luxury.

To listen to some of France's more chauvinist wine growers, it would be easy to believe that it was their ancestors who first had the notion of turning grapes into wine. In fact, while it was the French who most successfully developed the art of wine-making and created what are now regarded as the world's most famous wines, credit for the actual invention must go elsewhere. The biblical legend says that it was Noah who first drank wine. According to the Bible, soon after Noah's boat had come aground in the country that we now know as Turkey, he noticed the giddy antics of a goat that had been eating overripe, partially fermented grapes.

Noah's Art
According to the Old Testament, Noah was the first person ever to make wine. This 14th-century relief by Andrea Pisano records the aftermath.

Port of Bordeaux
Monet's 1871 painting of the busy port of Bordeaux, depicting the forest of masts belonging to cargo vessels, shows the potential for trade at this time.

Encouraged by the sight, he planted a vineyard and, to the shame of his sons, Noah "drank of the wine and was drunk, and became uncovered in his tent." If this story is to be believed, not only was Noah the first wine-maker, he was also the first person ever to get drunk. Wine is also featured elsewhere in the Bible. In one case, Lot's two daughters are described as making their father, with whom they are hiding in a cave, drink wine on two successive nights so that they could "lay with him" and "preserve [his] lineage." Wine evidently had other uses, too: Abraham, Lot's contemporary, is described as being blessed and given bread and wine by a priest called Melchezidek.

The Persians, however, tell a very different story. For them, the person who invented wine was not Noah, but a sad princess who was intent on doing away with herself. Assuming that a jar full of frothing grape juice was poisonous, she drank what she believed to be a deadly dose. The pleasurable effects that immediately followed, and indeed her survival, must have come as quite a surprise to the young princess. Sadly, her reaction to the world's first hangover has gone unrecorded.

SURVIVAL OF THE COOLEST

Whatever story you prefer, it cannot have taken long for man to discover that grape juice, given half a chance, ferments into something alcoholic, and that, with a bit of luck, the beverage may even be pleasant to drink. At the same time, experience would have taught him that fermented grape juice, though generally more robust and

Wine as an Aphrodisiac
Rubens' highly imaginative painting of Lot and his daughters shows the two women getting their apparently willing father drunk in order to continue the family with his assistance.

longer-lived than in its natural state, is vulnerable to bacteria that have the ability to convert it into vinegar. We now know that these bacteria are most active at warmer temperatures so, in the absence of the refrigeration and sulfur dioxide that are used today to protect wine against these bacteria, there is no question that the wines with the greatest chance of remaining drinkable from one vintage to the next would have been the ones produced and stored in regions that were relatively cool.

From the earliest vintages made in what is now called the Middle East, the story of wine can be traced alongside the history of most of the civilized world. Archaeological discoveries suggest that wine has been made in Egypt for at least 3,000 years and, according to records, Marco Polo enjoyed wine that was imported into China from Persia in the 1400s. The Romans were very serious about their wine-drinking and laid down the best vintages for as long as 100 years. They are known to have planted vines even in Britain. However, archaeological finds suggest that then, as now, imported wine was more popular.

When European emigrants traveled to the New World, they took both wines and vines with them, so that by the late 19th century it was clear that nothing could stand in the way of the production and gradual spread of wine around the world.

Persians
Wine has always been a symbol of civilized, courtly life, as in this painting of a Persian prince drinking wine in his harem.

THE HISTORY OF FRENCH WINE

Monks, emperors, and revolutionaries all shaped France's wine industry. However, more recently, it has been ravaged by disease and jolted by competition from younger countries and the demands of supermarkets.

We have no way of knowing exactly when anyone enjoyed the first mouthful of wine produced from French grapes that were grown on French soil, but we can be pretty sure that there was plenty of wine being drunk in France more than 500 years before the birth of Christ. Some of the first drinkers would have been the Phoenicians and the Greeks in their trading posts on the Mediterranean coast. The climate of this region, the presence of indigenous vines, and the difficulties of transporting wine in amphorae from their homelands meant that it was inevitable that the newcomers would soon turn their hands to the production of wine. By the time the Romans occupied the northern part of the country in the first century AD, vines were growing and wine was being made in many of the regions that have since become synonymous with wine. The men who made these wines were often members of tribes that took to the ways of the Romans and continued to make and trade wine following the collapse of the Roman Empire. From the outset, the vine growers sought out pieces of land where the grapes stood the greatest chance of reaching full ripeness. According to local legend, the 9th-century French emperor Charlemagne chose a particular slope on the hill of Corton, in Burgundy *(see pp112–159)*, on which to plant a vineyard. He is said to have noticed that, thanks to regular exposure to sunlight, the snows on that slope were always the first to thaw.

The Observant Charlemagne
The Emperor Charlemagne is said to have spent much time selecting promising new sites for vineyards.

PAVING THE WAY

The churches and monasteries, which were established between the 10th and 13th centuries throughout France, played a crucial role in the further development of wine-making both in this country and beyond. However, France is a fairly large country, and

Medieval Harvest
The colorful scene depicted on this tapestry is somewhat idealized, since the 15th-century French nobility did not really stage mass invasions of the harvest in their best clothes.

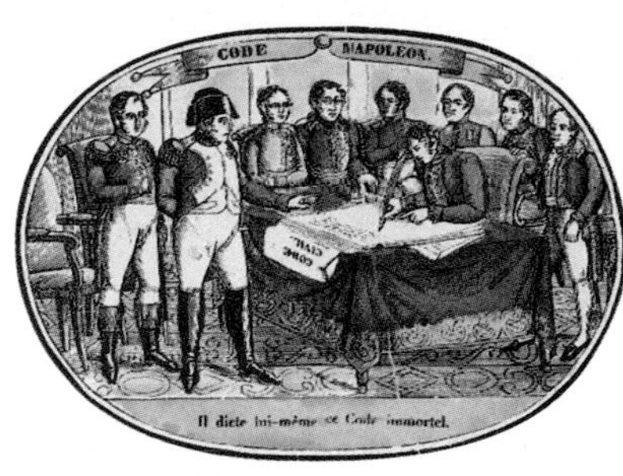

Napoleonic Inheritance
Here Napoleon is pictured signing the Code Napoléon, the law that splits every inheritance, including any vineyards, equally between all the heirs.

the difficulties of transporting wine over poor roads limited the markets that the wine could reach. Places with river access, such as Alsace *(see pp64–79)*, and sea ports, such as Bordeaux *(see pp80–111)*, clearly had the greatest advantage.

The arrival of the cork in around 1650 further increased the popularity of wine. In the 1780s, the French Revolution removed the church from the industry. Vineyards that had once been owned by the monasteries were sold off to the middle classes and even to peasants. In 1804, the Code Napoléon was introduced, stating that all heirs, regardless of their age or sex, would share any inheritance, including vineyards, equally between them.

A BREAK FROM TRADITION

The resulting fragmentation of the vineyards, coupled with the arrival of a new breed of landowners, opened the way for merchants whose role lay in blending and selling the wines of numerous small producers. The merchants also benefited from access to new markets as a result of better roads, canals, and railroads.

A century after the revolution, France's wine industry was thrown into turmoil by the vine diseases mildew and oidium and, worst of all, the phylloxera louse, which affected almost every vine. The vineyards that were replanted—or, to be more precise, grafted with phylloxera-resistant vines—were often very different from the ones that had gone before. Once-famous vineyards shrank, once-familiar grape varieties disappeared, and, between the two world wars, fraudulent labeling was rife. This latter practice was countered in the 1930s when the *appellation contrôlée* legislation was introduced.

During the second half of the 20th century, unprecedented competition from producers in the New World resulted in extensive research into the "how" and "why" of vine-growing and wine-making. As the evolution of French wine accelerated, previously neglected vineyards in the south of the country were given a new lease of life.

If the way in which wine is made has changed as a result of increased competition, so has the way in which it is bought and drunk. The recent rapid growth in the number of supermarkets in France has encouraged wine-drinkers to try wines from other regions. Most French wine-drinkers now drink less, but better, wine than they did in the past. However, many young French people do not drink wine at all, which helps to explain why many French wine-makers now have to be much more focused on selling their wines overseas.

Supermarket Revolution
Today, we buy wine with an ease that was undreamed of by the Romans or Charlemagne, and at far lower prices for the quality offered.

How Wine is Made

Wine-making is both one of the simplest and one of the most complex activities known to man. It brings together the skills of the farmer, the horticulturist, the cook, the chemist, and, occasionally, the artist.

The French language has no commonly used translation for "wine-maker" or "winery," terms that are used frequently throughout the English-speaking world. In French, the person who turns grapes into wine is known as the *vigneron* or *viticulteur*—words that refer to the growing of grapes in the vineyard rather than the process of converting the harvested fruit into wine. As far as the word "winery" is concerned, even a state-of-the-art, fully computerized establishment is still usually known in France as a *cave*, or a cellar, when it could be mistaken by passersby for a semi-conductor factory.

Château Carbonnieux
Bottling at the château is a relatively new idea. Before World War II, it was common for wine to be shipped in bulk for bottling by merchants.

In France, traditionally at least, outside of Bordeaux, Champagne, and Alsace, the most visible words on a wine label refer to the place where the grapes were grown. The name of the producer appears only in small print. In the New World, by contrast, it is the wine maker or winery—"the brand"—that takes center stage.

DIFFERENCE OF OPINION

These differences reveal the French producers' sense of tradition and their belief that wine is, as they say, "made in the vineyard." Few New World producers would disagree with this view, but in the US and Australia, the emphasis has often been on what happens to grapes at the winery. In the 1990s, the two attitudes collided when, unhappy with the wine they were getting from some French regions, British retailers sent "flying wine-makers," who were often Australian or had been trained in Australia, to the *coopératives* in France to make the wine for them.

BOTTLING IT UP

Historically, grape-growers could not afford wooden presses, barrels, and fermenting vats, so they had little to do with the making of wine. Grapes went to the monastery or château that served as a central processing plant. Even when, as in Burgundy, individual estates did make their own wine, they usually sold it on to merchants and *négociants* who blended and bottled it for them.

The New Way
Modern wineries, like this one at Château Haut-Brion in Bordeaux, make use of stainless-steel vats.

Wine Press
Basket presses are still used in Champagne because they extract less color. Old ones, like this, are operated by hand.

Today, Burgundies bottled at the *domaine* are becoming increasingly popular and represent a growing proportion of the region's wine. But even in Bordeaux, where châteaux have maintained their good reputations for centuries, the idea of the wine-maker, rather than a merchant, bottling the wine only dates back to the end of World War II.

SMALL IS BEAUTIFUL

The 1970s and 1980s brought the arrival of New World competition and of a new generation of *vignerons* who had learned their skills in college. Unlike their parents, they know how things are done in other regions of France and often have experience of working in Australia or California. They prefer to deal with customers worldwide than to be restricted to a local merchant or *coopérative,* and they want to see their own labels on their bottles. Even 20 years ago, it was a rare Champagne that was not produced by a big merchant or *coopérative.* Today, however, it is as though every other cottage in the region houses a grower with wine to sell, and a sign advertising the fact.

Competition among *vignerons* is fierce. They know the value of a good rating from an influential critic, and are aware that skillful grape-growing is only the first step on the journey to success. They appreciate that the way in which they treat those grapes will have a crucial influence on the quality and flavor of the wine. A wine may be made in the vineyard, but it can be improved immensely—or ruined completely—by the way it is handled in the *cave.*

The Old Way
Wine presses like this one were built to last for centuries. Until recently, wine-making techniques had altered very little over the years.

GRAPE VARIETIES

The character of any wine is influenced by the soil, the climate, and the art of the wine-maker, but nothing will dictate its flavor more than the variety, or varieties, of grape from which it is made.

Stringent rules applied over the centuries have decreed precisely which varieties of grape might be planted where, but in spite of these, wine-growers in France obstinately continued to experiment with new grape varieties. All that was brought to an end, however, with the establishment of a country-wide *appellation contrôlée* system set up in 1935 to control the origin and quality of French wines. Pomerol *(see p103)*, for example, which produced white wine before 1935, is now a red-only zone; the only area of choice left open to its wine growers is the precise proportion of the Merlot, Cabernet Franc, and Cabernet Sauvignon grapes that they grow. In regions such as Burgundy *(see pp112–59)*, where only one grape variety is used in each style of wine, all the wine growers can choose is the specific clone, or group of clones, with which to replant their vineyards. The *appellation* rules have undoubtedly, and laudably, helped to protect the individuality of France's best-known wines and encouraged the adoption of traditional French grape varieties in the New World. Less positively, however, they have also effectively halted experimentation in French vineyards, sadly stopping vinous evolution in its tracks.

Gewürztraminer
This eccentric pink-skinned grape produces wonderfully perfumed white wines.

Fortunately, there are some welcome exceptions to this state of affairs. In southern France, for example, recent moves have been made to acknowledge the improvement that judicious change can bring to wines. Quality has improved following a reduction in the use of traditional, rather dull grape varieties, such as Carignan, and the introduction of proven alternatives, such as Syrah and Mourvèdre. Other regions, such as Muscadet, could benefit from similarly innovative thinking.

Merlot and Cabernet Sauvignon
These two Bordeaux grape varieties need very different soils. Merlot *(below left)* likes clay, while Cabernet Sauvignon *(below right)* prefers gravel.

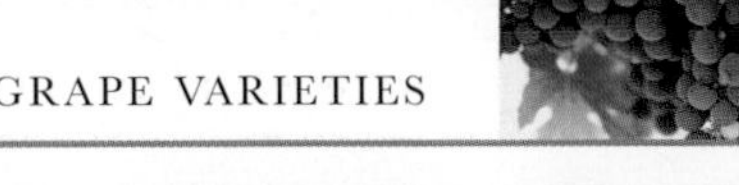

Cabernet Franc
At home in the Loire Valley and in red Bordeaux blends.

Gamay
This grape is at its best in the granite soil of Beaujolais.

Pinot Noir
Used to make both red Burgundy and Champagne.

Syrah
The top grape of the Rhône Valley—also known as Shiraz.

TOP RED GRAPES

Carignan The traditional grape variety of southern French regions such as Minervois, Corbières, and—in particular—Fitou. Old Carignan vines, when carefully used, can produce delicious, rich, earthy wines. Overproduction, however, tends to lead to dullness.

Cabernet Franc This grape is Cabernet Sauvignon's more vibrantly black-curranty kid brother. Cabernet Franc is best known as a crucial component of most red Bordeaux blends—most famously, it contributes considerably to the quality of Vieux Château Certan and Châteaux Cheval Blanc wines. However, it is not only a blending tool, as it also flies solo in the Loire Valley, in *appellations* such as Chinon, Bourgueil, and Saumur-Champigny.

Cabernet Sauvignon The mainstay of the Médoc and Graves *appellations* in Bordeaux, this black-curranty, green-peppery, sometimes even minty grape grows well on gravelly soil, and usually performs at its best in blends with Merlot, Cabernet Franc, and Syrah— though this last marriage is rarely found except in Provence and *vins de pays* wines.

Gamay The only grape used to make Beaujolais, this variety benefits from that region's combination of granite soil and use of the *maceration carbonique* technique to produce bright, cherryish wines. Gamay is also grown in the Loire Valley and southwest France, but the wines it makes there are usually less interesting.

Grenache The peppery grape of Côtes du Rhone (and Châteauneuf du Pape) also performs well in blends in Languedoc-Roussillon and can also produce good Rhône Valley and Provence Rosé.

Malbec Once overlooked even in its traditional heartland of Cahors (and consequently more or less banished from the Bordeaux blend), this spicy variety is now attracting attention elsewhere in France. It is now proving a success in the wines of Bergerac, but less so in those of the Loire Valley— where it is known as Cot.

Merlot A global superstar thanks to its plummy fruit, soft texture (it is less tannic than either of the two Cabernets) and association with big-name wines like Château Pétrus. Whether blended with Cabernet Franc (for example, in St Émilion and Pomerol) or used straight as it is in the south, it can sometimes also produce very dull, weedy wine.

Pinot Noir Some people consider this the greatest red grape of all. It is single-handedly responsible for all great red Burgundy, as well as some enjoyable reds and rosés that are produced in the Loire Valley. Expect to find raspberry and cherry fruit backed up by gentle tannins.

Syrah This is the smoky, spicy, blackberryish grape found in the Rhône Valley *appellations* of Côte Rôtie and Hermitage. It also produces delicious results in Pic St Loup and other parts of Languedoc-Roussillon. The same grape variety is widely known in the New World as Shiraz.

TOP WHITE GRAPES

Chardonnay Synonymous with white wine for many people these days, this versatile grape can produce a huge range of wine styles. The list covers everything from stony-dry, unoaked Chablis to buttery, nutty examples from Meursault, a little farther south, and fruit-salady, woody wines made in the southern part of the country under the Vin de Pays d'Oc label.

Chenin Blanc Appley, honeyed, and waxy, this Loire Valley grape variety is capable of producing both bone-dry and medium-dry wines, as well as lusciously sweet ones like Vouvray that can last for decades. Acidity can be very high when young, however. Chenin Blanc also gives good results in sparkling wine.

Gewürztraminer Famous for its lychee and parma violet character, this Alsace grape also produces both dry and sweet wines, and has an easily recognizable, unusually oily texture.

Gros Manseng Best known for its use in the wines of Jurançon, where it is blended with Petit Manseng, Gros Manseng is now also being used in Vin de Pays des Côtes de Gascogne.

Marsanne Lemony and rich, this Rhône grape makes wines at their best young, or after six or seven years.

Muscat This variety gives truly grapey-tasting wine. There are several strains, the best being Muscat Blanc à Petits Grains. Alsace makes fine dry examples; sweet, fortified ones come from the Rhône Valley and southern France.

Petit Manseng At its best in the Jurançon *appellation* of Southwest France, where it is blended with its lesser relative, Gros Manseng, to produce floral dry and sweeter wines.

Pinot Blanc An Alsace variety that is like a less fruity Chardonnay. Almost always unoaked, it makes creamy dry wines with a brazil-nut character.

Pinot Gris The grape known in Italy as Pinot Grigio produces peary, gently spicy wines in Alsace. These are most interesting when off-dry or sweet.

Riesling The greatest white grape, widely grown in Alsace, Riesling makes terrific dry and lusciously sweet wines with a richer texture than most examples from the German side of the Rhine.

Roussanne This partner to Marsanne contributes to dry white wines such as Hermitage and white Côtes du Rhône.

Sauvignon Blanc A fresh, zingy variety with black-curranty, gooseberryish flavors is at its best as a dry, unoaked varietal from the Loire Valley (Sancerre and Pouilly Fumé) or as a barrel-fermented Bordeaux, perhaps blended with a little Sémillon. Lighter, unoaked Bordeaux Blanc (or Entre Deux Mers) and *vins de pays* are less exciting.

Sémillon A rich, peachy, honeyed grape that shines (with the help of some Sauvignon Blanc) in sweet white Bordeaux.

Viognier The extraordinarily floral, apricoty grape used in Condrieu and a growing number of *vins de pays* from southern France. It produces good dry and sweet wines.

Chardonnay
The grape that is used to make both white Burgundy and Champagne.

Chenin Blanc
Rarely seen outside the Loire, this appley grape makes long-lived wines.

Riesling
One of the great Alsatian grapes; now, sadly, less fashionable than in the past.

Sémillon
The classic peachy, honeyed grape of Sauternes and Barsac in Bordeaux.

OTHER GRAPES

ALIGOTÉ An acidic white grape variety grown in Burgundy, where it is used to produce often ordinary but sometimes good white wine, especially in the village of Bouzeron. It is best known for its role in Kir, a cocktail in which it is mixed with black-currant liqueur.

CHASSELAS This once-popular non-aromatic white variety is still used in Alsace and Pouilly-sur-Loire, although it has largely been supplanted by Sauvignon Blanc. Chasselas usually proves better for eating than making wine.

CINSAULT A full-bodied and increasingly widely used component of many red wines, Cinsault is most often found in the southern part of the Rhône Valley and throughout southern France.

COLOMBARD A basic appley grape variety that is used primarily for making Vin de Pays des Côtes de Gascogne in Southwest France.

FER This tough, tannic grape is used in the southwest of France to produce wines like Madiran.

GROS PLANT Gros Plant is an undeniably undistinguished grape variety that is used to produce the dry, acidic white wine of the same name in the Loire Valley. It can make a passable accompaniment to oysters if no Muscadet is available.

MELON DE BOURGOGNE A non-aromatic white variety that can produce attractively lemony wines, Melon de Bourgogne is used exclusively for Muscadet.

MOURVÈDRE This blackberry-flavored component of Rhône Valley reds is another grape grown in southern France, particularly in the Provençal *appellation* of Bandol.

MUSCADELLE A spicy white grape variety that is used—albeit in small doses—in white Bordeaux wines and now occasionally also finds its way into examples of southern France's Vins de Pays d'Oc.

PETIT VERDOT Traditionally a spicy ingredient of red Bordeaux, Petit Verdot is now being used on its own in the New World.

PINOT MEUNIER This black-skinned cousin of Pinot Noir is far more widely used in the wines of Champagne than producers generally admit. It is rarely used to make still wines.

SYLVANER A non-aromatic white grape used in Alsace. Good examples can be excellent, but earthiness is often a problem.

TANNAT This tough red grape variety is widely planted in the Madiran *appellation* in Southwest France. It is now also being used in Uruguay.

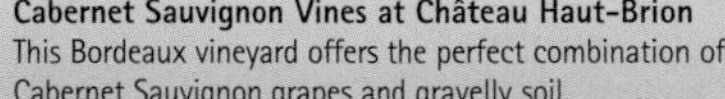

Cabernet Sauvignon Vines at Château Haut-Brion
This Bordeaux vineyard offers the perfect combination of Cabernet Sauvignon grapes and gravelly soil.

CLIMATE, SOIL AND VINEYARDS

The individual flavor of every wine is created by a combination of factors. A subtle variation of soil or microclimate can make wines produced in neighboring vineyards taste quite different.

If the French language has no translation for the English term "wine-maker," it has in *terroir* a far more valuable and untranslatable word of its own, which is now being used throughout the wine-making world. The classic definition of this term was offered by Bruno Prats, former owner of Château Cos d'Estournel in Bordeaux. For Prats, *terroir* is "the combination of the climate, the soil, and the landscape" that forms the character of a vineyard and its wines. At its simplest, *terroir* could be used to refer to a chalky hillside in a cool region, but it can also be far more precise. As Prats continues, "the night and day temperatures, the distribution of rainfall, hours of sunlight, the slope and drainage... All these factors react together in each part of the vineyard."

Blood from Stones
Châteauneuf-du-Pape's pebbles store and reflect heat, a process that contributes to the rich flavor of its wines.

So, although the literal meaning of the word *terroir* is simply "soil," it actually encompasses far more than that. The climate, or to be more precise the specific combination of macro- and microclimate, is a vital component of *terroir*. The macroclimate is the weather of a whole region—for example, the sea-influenced and moderate conditions of Bordeaux, or the more extreme, continental conditions of Burgundy. The microclimate refers instead to prevailing conditions and the geographical location of a specific vineyard: the altitude of the vineyard and the proximity of hills, forests, rivers, lakes or the sea. The site's exposure, orientation, and gradient also play a part in determining its microclimate.

ASPECTS OF THE TERROIR

Vines grown on south-facing slopes get more sunshine and, as a result, ripen much better than those that are grown on flat land. While hills and woods can offer a protective "rain shadow" against storms, they can also provide shelter from winds that would otherwise blow away the pockets of cold air in which frost develops. A nearby lake or river can increase humidity, which in turn raises the likelihood of both the desirable noble rot *(see p109)* and the undesirable gray rot developing.

The soil in which vines are grown has three sets of properties. The first, texture, is

Healthy Chill
While frost can cause problems in spring, cold weather in winter helps to keep vines dormant and ensures that their sap is kept down in the roots.

determined by the size of the particles that make up the soil. Vines can be grown in soil that is either as fine as sand or as lumpy as pebbles. However, if the particles are not to be blown or washed away by the wind or rain, they must be glued together by clay. Some soils contain more clay than others, with the clay itself varying in nature. The second property, the soil's structure, determines the way in which clay bonds particles of soil together and how water is retained in the soil or drained away. This depends also on the amount and nature of organic matter, the level of sodium and calcium and the nature of the clay. Soil's third property, its degree of acidity, determines how acidic the wine will be.

View from the Terraces
The earliest wine-makers discovered that, although vines planted on steep hillside slopes ripened better, they were hard to tend and pick. To solve the problem, they soon began to lay out their vineyards on terraces.

THE PRINCIPAL SOILS OF FRANCE

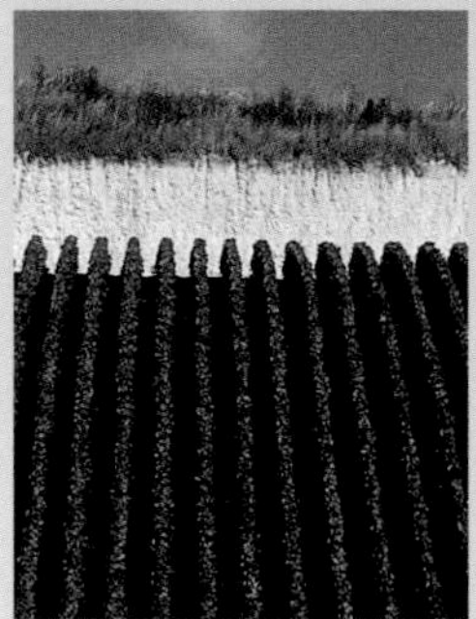

Chalking It Up
Champagne and other dry white wines benefit from chalky soil like this.

Priceless Gravel
Bordeaux's gravelly soil is perfect for growing Cabernet Sauvignon.

ALLUVIAL Potentially fertile, sandy, silty, gravelly soil laid down by rivers. At its best in the Médoc.

ARGILLACEOUS Catch-all term for sedimentary clay, siltstones, marl or shale. *Argilo-calcaire* means a combination of clay and limestone.

CLAY Acidic, malleable, argillaceous compound that holds water well and drains poorly. Important as subsoil in Pomerol, where it is well suited to the Merlot grape.

GRANITE Both a quartz-rich, hard rock and the alkaline, easy-draining, low-fertility soil of the best vineyards of Beaujolais and the northern Rhône.

GRAVEL Easy-draining, low-fertility, pebbly topsoil that is at its best in Bordeaux and Châteauneuf-du-Pape, where it retains the heat of the sun.

LIMESTONE Alkaline, easy-draining rock, mainly consisting of calcium carbonates. Best suited to white wines.

LOAM A crumbly mixture of clay, silt and sand. Generally too fertile for fine wine.

MARL Acidic mixture of limestone and clay that is at its best in the Côte d'Or, the Rhône, and the Jura.

SAND Sandy soil has the advantage of deterring the phylloxera louse and the disadvantage of draining too easily and storing no nutrients.

SANDSTONE Variable sedimentary rock that can be composed either of quartz or of calcium carbonate.

SCHIST Crystalline rock that can be split into layers. Found beneath the soil of Alsace and in the Côte Rôtie. Rich in magnesium and potassium.

SHALE Crumbly, quite fertile, sedimentary rock.

SILT Quite fertile, poor-draining river deposit.

SLATE Crystalline rock formed from clay, mudstone and shale, to be found beneath the topsoil of Pouilly Fumé and parts of southern Beaujolais; known in French as *schiste*.

TUFA/TUFFEAU Easy-draining limestone soil found in the Loire Valley.

GRAPE-GROWING AND HARVESTING

Wherever the vineyard and whatever the variety of vine or style of wine, the grapes develop according to an inexorable timetable, dictating precisely what the wine-grower will be doing at any given time of the year.

JANUARY Despite low temperatures, wine-growers are out pruning their vines. Traditionally, pruning was begun on the 22nd, the feast day of St. Vincent, patron saint of wine growers.

FEBRUARY A quiet month in the vineyards once the pruning is finished. There is, however, plenty of work to be done on the new wine maturing in the cellars.

MARCH Most wine-growers have finished pruning and will now be tilling the soil in order to aerate it and remove weeds. In some areas, depending on soil type and local climate, late March sees bud-break, the first sign of new growth on the woody vine.

Pruning
Trimming back the vines for spring growth is a laborious and often chilly process, but it is a job that must be done before the new season begins.

Flowers
The flowering of the vine is an exciting time of the season, providing a first glimpse of the future crop. Poor weather at this stage can cause major problems later.

APRIL Rapid growth of leaves, shoots, and embryo bunches follows bud-break. The embryo bunches, which will eventually flower and become grapes, are the first indication of the size and date of the coming harvest. Cool temperatures or rain at this crucial time may cause *millerandage*, the formation of seedless grapes that will never grow to maturity. A spell of especially warm sunshine, on the other hand, will encourage the vine's sap to feed the leaves rather than the embryo grapes, often leading to *coulure*, in which the embryos fail to develop, and fall off the plant.

MAY Oil stoves and windmills are often used at this time of year to protect the vulnerable leafy vines from frost. The soil is fertilized and tilled to remove weeds, and many growers spray the vines against mildew and oidium fungus.

JUNE This is the month in which the vines pollinate, fertilize, and flower. Dry, warm weather now allows the vines to flower rapidly, and the grapes on each bunch to grow simultaneously. Changeable weather produces bunches with berries of uneven ripeness—so-called "hens and chickens." After flowering, some shoots are trained to the wires and others are removed. Spraying against oidium continues.

JULY As the vines respond to the warm weather, each fertilized berry in the embryo bunches becomes a recognizable tiny grape. This process is called "fruit set." Some grape varieties, such as

Merlot, set less successfully than others. The wine-grower removes some of the bunches at this stage in order to concentrate the vines' energy into the remaining fruit. Spraying against oidium continues in the vineyard, and growers may also clear the ground of weeds.

AUGUST This is the time for *véraison*, a series of important chemical changes marked by the changing color of the grape skins. The fruit's sugar content increases dramatically at this stage. It is a critical moment for the vines: a bad storm followed by warm weather provides perfect conditions for rot, one of the reasons why growers increasingly remove some foliage to allow air to circulate and sunlight to reach the grapes. Drought conditions now will slow the ripening process. In exceptionally hot years like 2003, harvesting of white grapes may even begin at the end of this month.

SEPTEMBER Quality-conscious growers will be trimming the vines tightly and possibly performing a *vendange verte*, or green harvest: removing a proportion of the potential crop in order to concentrate the vines' energies. Drought conditions can still pose a danger to the ripening grapes. Likewise, rain or even hail at this time of year may expose the fruit to the risk of rot. Depending on the region, the weather conditions, and the grape variety, the grape harvest is usually begun in late September, although there is a growing trend of delaying picking until the grapes are as ripe as possible.

Véraison
Another crucial stage in the vineyard, when warm weather accelerates sugar accumulation and chemical changes lead black grapes to develop their color.

OCTOBER In most regions, grapes are still being picked. In some years and in areas where late-harvest wines are made, the harvest may just be beginning. Once the crop is in and the grapes have been pressed, the skin, stalks, and seeds, known collectively as the *marc*, are spread among the vines, often together with a combination of manure and chemical fertilizer.

NOVEMBER As cold weather returns, the sap retreats into the vines' root systems. The vineyard is tidied up and the feet of the vines are buried with soil in preparation for the rigors of winter.

DECEMBER Many of France's wine growers are busy shipping wines to customers in time for Christmas. A few may now begin some early pruning in the vineyards, as the annual cycle begins once again.

Harvest
While machines are widely used to pick grapes, most quality-conscious producers still prefer to harvest their crop by hand.

HOW RED WINE IS MADE

Human skill will always be the essential key to transforming grapes into a fine and typical wine, whether the equipment and techniques used are highly traditional or ultra-modern, very simple or highly sophisticated.

Once the wine-grower has determined the moment when the grapes are as ripe as possible, while retaining sufficient acidity, they can be harvested, either manually or by machine. Many people believe that harvesting by hand makes for higher quality, but machine harvesting, in which the grapes are shaken from the vines, has the advantage that it may be conducted both in daylight and at night.

Machine Picking
Mechanical harvesters are highly efficient, picking grapes quickly, 24 hours a day.

FERMENTATION

Quality-conscious producers remove rotten grapes, either in the vineyard or at the *cuverie*. Stalks are also removed at this stage to avoid the harsh tannic character they might give the finished wine. The fruit is then lightly crushed and transferred into a stainless steel tank, the *cuve*, or a wooden vat, the *foudre*. The grapes are now left to macerate, or soften, for two or three days. Fermentation is kicked off using either cultured yeasts or yeasts that occur naturally on the grapes. The fruit may be heated or juice—known as must—that is already fermenting may be added. To prevent the floating skins and seeds from drying out, the must is pumped over them, or they are pushed down with wooden paddles in a process known as *pigeage*. Some wine-makers now use rotary fermenters similar to sealed cement mixers, although some critics argue that these cause excessive astringency. For successful fermentation, the fruit must be kept at 77–86°F (25–30°C). Soft, fruity wine such as Beaujolais *(see pp126–7)* is made by a process known as *macération carbonique*, which involves fermenting the grapes uncrushed.

Harvesting Black Grapes
The key to making good wine lies in the quality of the grapes. Quality-conscious producers take pains to sort the grapes in the vineyard or on conveyor belts at the *cuverie*, discarding any that are either underripe or rotten.

New Wine Barrels
Good-quality red wines are generally matured in casks, many of which will be made of new French oak, which give the wine a vanilla character that tends to win praise from critics.

ADJUSTING THE MIXTURE

The alcoholic strength of the wine may be increased—in some regions—by adding sugar, or chaptalizing, during fermentation. Likewise, acidity may be increased by adding tartaric acid, a substance that occurs naturally in the grape. Legislation restricts both chaptalization and acidification, but is often ignored. If the mixture is too watery, some of the part-fermented pink juice is drawn off, concentrating the remainder. The drawn-off juice may become wine that is sold as rosé.

AFTER FERMENTATION

Fermentation is complete when all the sugar has been converted into alcohol. The wine may now be left to macerate on the skins for a period of between one and four weeks, during which time the color will deepen and the tannins soften. The free-run juice, the *vin de goutte*, is then drawn off and the solids transferred to a press, which extracts from them tougher, darker press wine—*vin de presse*. Depending on the vintage, some or all of this will be blended into the final wine. Following fermentation, red wine will almost always be allowed to undergo a natural process called malolactic fermentation, in which appley malic acid is transformed into the creamier lactic acid.

Some wine, such as Beaujolais and basic *vin de pays*, is intended to be drunk young, but most high-quality wine will now be matured for up to 18 months in wooden casks. Increasingly, in recent years, some or all of the casks tend to be made of new oak from forests in the heart of France. When used carefully, new oak can add complexity, while giving the wine an appealing vanilla character that often wins favor from critics and wine-drinkers used to woody wines from the New World. It can, however, easily overpower other, subtler flavors.

RACKING AND FINING

Sulfur dioxide is used to protect the wine against bacteria throughout the wine-making process. If not managed carefully, though, it can combine with hydrogen to produce the stink-bomb smell and flavor of hydrogen sulfide, or foul-smelling mercaptans, which are hydrogen sulfide and alcohol compounds. Racking the wine—transferring it from one cask to another to aerate it—should prevent this.

Before bottling, the wine is likely to be fined or clarified with powdered clay or lightly beaten egg whites to remove cloudiness. It may also be filtered to remove sediment, though many producers now prefer to bottle their wine unfiltered, and possibly even unfined, to preserve as much of its subtlety and flavor as possible.

Egg White
When added to the wine, beaten egg whites drag suspended solids with them as they fall to the bottom of the cask.

HOW WHITE WINE IS MADE

Many factors can influence the more delicate flavors associated with white wines, and many wine-makers believe that producing a really good white presents the ultimate challenge.

While the skins of black grapes provide the tannins that give red wine its longevity and are responsible for the color of the finished red wine, the skins of white grapes have little or no role to play in finished white wine. For various reasons, it is far trickier to make white wine that tastes good than it is to make a drinkable red wine. First, the thinner skins of most white grape varieties increase the risk of harmful rot in the vineyard. It is also easy for white grapes to become oxidized or "cooked" if they are left out in the sun after picking, as happens at many southern *cuveries*. Some producers reduce the risk by using machines to pick the grapes at night, but quality-conscious growers still prefer to harvest by hand.

Sorting the Grapes
Thin-skinned white grapes require careful sorting to eliminate rotten and oxidized fruit.

THE HARVEST

Picking white grapes too early will give the wine a green character, while harvesting too late makes for dull wine. In some regions, however, grapes are deliberately allowed to overripen, developing as much natural sugar as possible in the hope that they will become covered by the sought-after fungus *Botrytis cinerea* *(see p109)*, or noble rot. This fungus concentrates the flavors of the grape and adds a dried-apricot character of its own. Noble rot, however, only occurs in humid conditions in which undesirable gray rot is also a risk. For this reason, makers of sweet botrytized wines have to take special care to select only grapes with the right kind of rot.

SULFURING AND PRESSING

One of the best ways to avoid oxidation and unwanted rot is to use sulfur dioxide, which works both as an antiseptic and as an antioxidant. Sulfur is as necessary in a *cuverie* as soap is in a kitchen, but in excess, it is as unwelcome in a wine as detergent in a sauce. Nowadays,

Harvesting the Grapes
These grapes being harvested in Riquewihr, Alsace, will be used to make rich, aromatic, and slightly sweet white wines.

Rosé
Made from the juice of black grapes, like red wine, but produced in the same way as white, rosé owes its delicate color to restricted contact with the black grape skins.

in any case, most producers also use cooling equipment that helps to keep bacteria at bay.

Having arrived at the *cuverie*, white grapes often pass into the press uncrushed and still attached to their stalks. Alternatively, in the case of less aromatic grape varieties, the wine-maker may crush the grapes and leave them for several days in a vat or a cement-mixer-like tank called a *Vinimatic*, which extracts the aromatics stored in the skins before the grapes are pressed. Once the grapes have been pressed, the juice will be separated from the seeds and skins. The juice may be chilled, fined, or filtered at this point, but many producers of quality white wines believe that these procedures remove flavor and richness from the wine.

FERMENTATION

Fermentation, using natural or cultured yeasts, now follows—either in stainless steel tanks or in wooden barrels. Fermentation takes place at anything from 41° to 86°F (5–30°C) and can take weeks or even months. Low temperatures produce light, crisp wines with a pear character. Warmer temperatures produce richer, fatter-textured wines with less specific flavors. After fermentation, dry white wines such as Burgundy and Bordeaux will be allowed—and if necessary, encouraged with cultured yeasts—to undergo a naturally occurring biochemical process known as malolactic fermentation, in which appley malic acid is transformed into richer lactic acid. For sweeter wines that benefit from the freshness of the malic acid, malolactic fermentation is prevented by adding sulfur.

Light-bodied, fruity wines will now be fined, filtered, and bottled, often within a few months of the harvest. Finer wines will be matured for up to 18 months, probably in oak barrels. Filtering may then take place. Sulfur dioxide, ideally in as small a quantity as possible, will be added before bottling to protect the wine from oxidation as it matures. The drier and more alcoholic the wine, the less sulfur will be needed. Late-harvest wines get larger doses to protect them from refermenting.

ROSÉ WINES

Champagne rosé is unique in that it is made by mixing red and white wine. All other French rosé wines are made from black grape juice that is drawn off before the skins have had time to give it much color. In every other respect, rosé wine is produced in the same way as white. It rarely goes into new oak barrels, however.

Vats and Barrels
Modern producers such as the Château de Meursault in Burgundy use a combination of stainless steel vats and new oak barrels for fermenting and maturing their wines.

SPARKLING AND FORTIFIED WINES

Many areas of France produce excellent sparkling wines, including, of course, the world-famous region of Champagne. Also of interest are the various fortified wines known as vins doux naturels.

Both the simplest of cola drinks and the finest Champagnes contain bubbles of dissolved carbon dioxide. To make cola, the carbon dioxide is injected directly into the drink. The same method can also be used in wine-making, but it will not produce a wine of any quality or longevity. Four different methods are used to produce fine sparkling wine, all of which create carbon dioxide naturally during fermentation.

Champagne Yeast
Yeast is the secret ingredient that puts the bubbles into sparkling wine, causing it to ferment in the bottle.

MÉTHODE RURALE

The most traditional method is the now-rare *méthode rurale*, which involves bottling the wine during its initial fermentation like cider or beer. The carbon dioxide released as fermentation continues has nowhere to go and so remains dissolved in the wine. One wine produced by this method is the sweet Clairette de Die Méthode Dioise Ancestrale, from the northern Rhône. Fine dry wines are also made by this method in Gaillac in southwest France, where it is known as the *méthode gaillaçoise*.

MÉTHODE TRADITIONELLE

More widely used for the production of high-quality wines than the *méthode rurale* is the *méthode traditionelle*. In wines made using this method, a second fermentation is induced in the bottle. To achieve this, the wine-maker adds a *liqueur de tirage*, a blend of wine, sugar, and yeast, to the wine after the initial fermentation has taken place and just before bottling. As in the *méthode rurale*, the carbon dioxide cannot escape and so remains dissolved in the wine. Unlike in the *méthode rurale*, however, the wine also acquires a distinctive flavor from the yeast solids that are used to kick off the second fermentation. These are broken down in a process known as autolysis, which gives the finished wine the yeasty or biscuity character that is the hallmark of the *méthode traditionelle*. The bottles are then aged for between one and four years, depending on the region and the style of wine. The longer the aging period, the stronger the biscuity flavor.

To avoid leaving a gritty deposit at the bottom of your glass, the dead yeast must be removed once the second fermentation and ageing is complete. This is achieved by

Mechanical Remuage
Even in the most illustrious Champagne houses, machines have taken over the laborious task of *remuage*.

Manual Remuage
Only a few Champagne and sparkling wine producers still perform the skilled and lengthy task of *remuage* by hand.

a process called riddling or *remuage*: by manually or mechanically turning and shaking the gradually upturned bottle, the yeast solids are made to slide down into the neck of the bottle, where they are collected in a thimblelike container beneath the stopper.

Eventually the yeast is removed in a process called *dégorgement*: the wine close to the cap is frozen and the stopper, usually a beer-bottle cap, is removed. The pressure that has built up in the wine propels the icy yeast out of the bottle, leaving the remaining wine clear. The bottle is now topped up and a blend of wine and sugar syrup, known as the *liqueur d'expédition*, is added. Finally, the bottle is resealed with a traditional Champagne cork.

OTHER METHODS

The remaining two methods are simplifications of the *méthode traditionelle*, and neither of them is used to make *appellation contrôlée* wine. In the transfer method, instead of undergoing *remuage*, the wine and yeast are transferred into a tank before being filtered and rebottled. The *cuve close* method is similar to the transfer method, except that the second fermentation takes place in a sealed tank instead of in the bottle.

FORTIFIED WINES

Less famous than port, sherry, Marsala, and Madeira, France's fortified wines, or *vins doux naturels*, deserve a larger share of the spotlight. The principle behind the production of all fortified wines is the same: the fermentation of the juice of very ripe white or black grapes is interrupted by the addition of neutral grape spirit. This raises the alcohol content of the vat above 15 percent, the point at which the yeasts that transform sugar into alcohol can no longer function, and thus halts fermentation. French wines made in this way, such as the famous Muscat de Beaumes-de-Venise *(see p259)*, are by definition sweet and fruity. They are usually fairly simple in character and rarely improve with age.

One exception is Banyuls *(see p194)*, the most southerly *appellation* in France. Red Banyuls is the wine that chauvinistic French experts like to compare to vintage port. Like that Portuguese wine, the best examples develop complexity with age and can mature for up to 40 years in the bottle. But truly great Banyuls is rare. Other fortified wines that can be worth aging are well-made *rancio* wines such as Rasteau *(see p260)* in the southern Rhône. To be labeled *rancio*, fortified wine must be stored in oak casks and exposed to heat (often sunshine) and oxygen for at least two years, during which time the wine develops its distinctive nutty, tangy, *rancio* flavor.

Champagne Corks
Made from separate layers of cork of varying flexibility, the corks used for sparkling wines develop their mushroom shape in the bottle. The older the wine, the straighter the cork.

Reading the Label

Understanding the label is essential to choosing wines successfully. French labels can be some of the most informative, and unfortunately also some of the most confusing, in the world.

Fraudulent labeling by wine merchants was not uncommon at the beginning of the 20th century, and since that time the French authorities have done their utmost to lay down labeling legislation designed to protect the consumer. The most vaunted and visible part of this legislation is the system of *appellation contrôlée*, or controlled appellation *(see pp36–7)*. However, before putting the *appellation contrôlée* system under the magnifying glass, it is useful to understand the other pieces of information that appear on French wine labels.

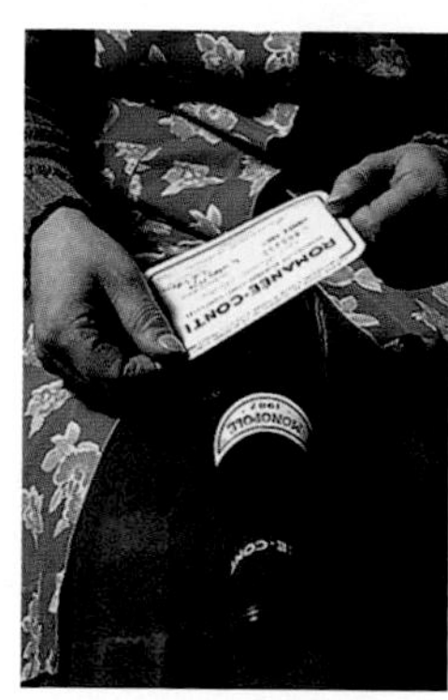

Proof of Identity
Producers on even the smallest family-run estates must comply with labelling requirements, which vary depending on the country to which the wines are exported.

The label on the front of every bottle, whether it is classified as a basic *vin de pays* *(see pp276–279)*, a *vin délimité de qualité supérieure* or *VDQS* *(see p35)* or an *appellation d'origine contrôlée*, is legally required to include certain pieces of information: first, the bottle volume, usually 37.5 cl, 75 cl, or 150 cl; second, the name and address of the bottler, who may or may not also be the producer. Unhelpfully, this information sometimes appears in code, as *JFV à 5600*, for example, or may be one of a number of pseudonyms adopted to help sell the same wine to a variety of customers. A third piece of information that is required by law is the place where the wine was made. Any wine that fails to reveal its geographic origins can be labeled only as a lowly *vin de table* and, as such, is denied the right to declare either a vintage or a grape variety. Finally, the alcoholic strength, which is usually between 10.5 and 15 percent, and classification (*vin de table, vin de pays, VDQS* or *appellation d'origine contrôlée*) must be given.

Other information that can often be found on the label, although it is not required by law, includes a brand name, such as Mouton Cadet, Malesan, or Piat d'Or; the name of a particular vineyard, such as Clos du Mesnil, or of an individual *cuvée*, such as Cuvée Laurence; an indication of whether

Alsace
This is the only major region in France to specify the grape variety on its labels. Other areas, such as Bordeaux and Burgundy, are now beginning to do likewise, probably in answer to competition from the New World.

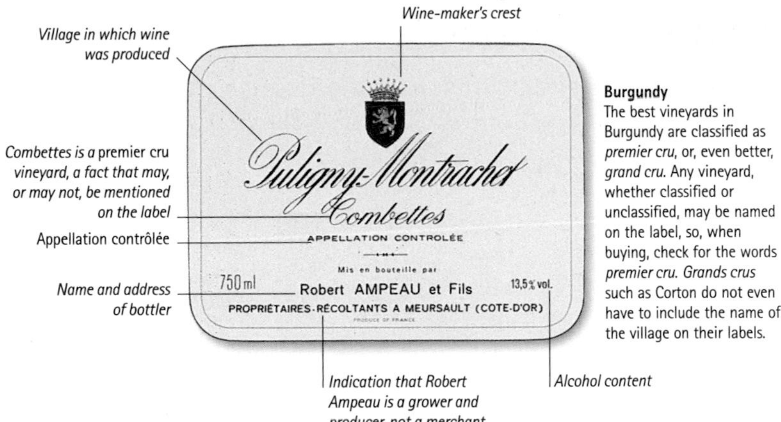

Burgundy
The best vineyards in Burgundy are classified as *premier cru*, or, even better, *grand cru*. Any vineyard, whether classified or unclassified, may be named on the label, so, when buying, check for the words *premier cru*. *Grands crus* such as Corton do not even have to include the name of the village on their labels.

or not the wine was bottled on the estate; and finally, the vintage in which the wine was made.

LOCAL CLASSIFICATIONS

In addition to the terms discussed above, different regions also use various local systems of classification. To illustrate this point, I have chosen labels from three different regions, Alsace *(see pp64–79)*, Burgundy *(see pp112–159)*, and Bordeaux *(see pp80–111)*. In Alsace, the grape variety nearly always appears on the label, and, in addition, 50 or so of the best vineyards are classified as *grand cru*. In Bordeaux and Burgundy, on the other hand, classifications of the best estates and vineyards are confusingly varied, including *cru bourgeois, cru classé, premier cru, grand cru, grand cru classé* and *premier grand cru classé*. In the case of these wines, the grape variety almost never features on the label. It is also important to be aware of a number of grand-sounding words that often appear on labels, but which should be taken with a large pinch of salt. *Grand Vin de France, Cuvée Prestige* and *Réserve Speciale*, for example, are all legally meaningless terms. Almost unbelievably, any Bordeaux producer who wants to use the words "Grand Vin" can do so—provided they don't use the shortest, cheapest bottles for it. Likewise, while *vieilles vignes* or "old vines" suggests especially rich wines, no one has ever defined how old a vine must be to qualify as *vieille*. Finally, while a wine labeled *elévé en fûts de chêne* will have spent time in an oak barrel, there is no way of knowing the age of the barrel, important since old and young oak affect the wine differently.

Bordeaux
Labels on the wines of Bordeaux vary quite widely, depending on the individual *appellation*. St Émilion has its very own unique system of classification, as do the *appellations* of the Médoc (including Pauillac, shown here), while the châteaux of Pomerol use no system of classification.

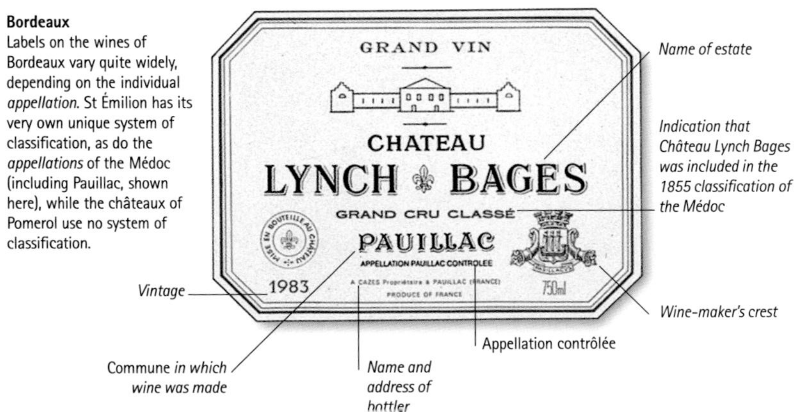

WINES FOR EVERYDAY DRINKING

The majority of French vineyards produce wines that fall outside the prestigious appellation contrôlée *classification system, but which can still offer enormous enjoyment and interest.*

All French wines are classified according to a pyramid system that was designed as a guide to quality. There are four categories: the bottom layer consists of *vin de table*; next, *vin de pays*; then *vin délimité de qualité supérieure* (VDQS); and finally *appellation contrôlée.*

Growing in Stature
At the time when this excellent wine was produced, the Corbières region was classified as *vin délimité de qualité supérieure* or *VDQS*, but Corbières now enjoys *appellation contrôlée* status.

VIN DE TABLE

Covering 22 percent of French wines, this is the most basic of the French quality designations. There are no rules as to how *vin de table* should be produced; the only stipulation is that no grape variety or place of origin may be stated on the front label. *Vin de table* is rarely of great quality, although the classification does occasionally include good wines that fall foul of restrictive *appellation* rules. Examples include the innovative, sweet Pouilly-Fumé *(see p220)* made by Didier Dagueneau, one of the best wine-makers in the Loire Valley, and Rebelle, the award-winning red blend produced by the Bordeaux firm of Dulong.

VIN DE PAYS

The next layer in the pyramid of categories is made up of 150 or so *vin de pays* or "country wine" *appellations*, which were introduced in 1973 in order to promote regional wines. Unlike the *vin de table* category, this classification allows producers to specify an area of origin for each wine, and also to state which production methods were used. In addition, they are permitted to print the name of the dominant grape variety on the label—a privilege that is denied not only to *vins de table* but also to most *appellation contrôlée* wines.

This fast-evolving category was not designed to cater to anything better than decent daily-drinking fare, and the fact that the best *vins de pays* now demand higher prices than some *appellation contrôlée* wines is something that many supporters of the *appellation contrôlée* system still find very hard to swallow. To achieve this state of affairs, ambitious producers such as Aimé

Vin de Table
A label from a great Alsace producer that flirts with illegality. According to the (crazy) rules, a French *vin de table* cannot carry a vintage, and there is indeed no year mentioned here—but the "Z002" might provide a hint. Hopefully a relaxation of the laws will make such efforts unnecessary.

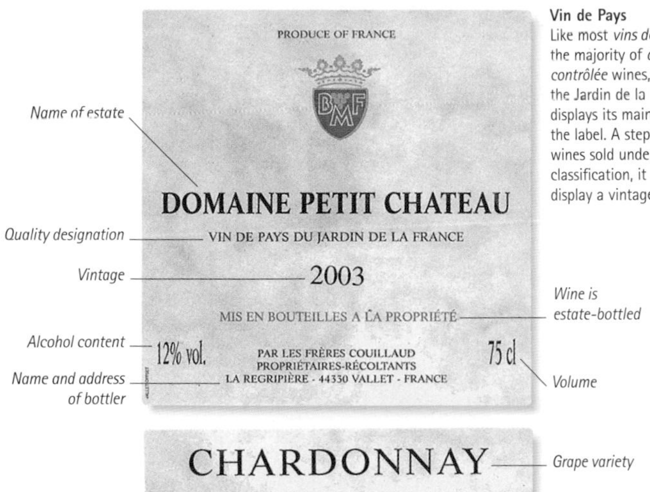

Vin de Pays
Like most *vins de pays*, but unlike the majority of *appellation contrôlée* wines, this example, from the Jardin de la France region, displays its main grape variety on the label. A step up from the basic wines sold under the *vin de table* classification, it is also allowed to display a vintage.

Guibert of Mas de Daumas Gassac in the Hérault *(see p278)* and Robert Skalli of Skalli Fortant de France in Languedoc-Roussillon have applied skill and care in the production of their *vins de pays* to match that of the better producers of *appellation contrôlée* wines. Accounting for a quarter of French wine production, the success of *vins de pays* has led to the strange situation where grapes from *appellation contrôlée* vineyards in Minervois *(see p199)* and Corbières *(see p195)*, for example, are being used, for the time being at least, to make wines that will be sold as *vins de pays*, rather than under their *appellation*. The *vin de pays* producers now successfully lobby to prevent any changes to other parts of the French *appellation* system.

VDQS

Squeezed in between the *vin de pays* and *appellation contrôlée* classifications is the much smaller category of *vin délimité de qualité supérieur* or *VDQS*, which was officially due to have been phased out some years ago. Many *VDQS*-designated areas—including, most recently, Sauvignon de St Bris, which is now known simply as St Bris *(see p155)*—are now being promoted to *appellation contrôlée* status, but new ones are still being created to replace them. This inevitably adds to the existing confusion. Possibly the best explanation for this seemingly ludicrous situation is that the *VDQS* wines are not of sufficient interest to either the *appellation contrôlée* or the *vin de pays* authorities.

Vin Délimité de Qualité Supérieur
This category is the perfect illustration of the need to rethink the French *appellation* system. This halfway-house includes wines like the Loire Valley's Gros Plant that are much more ordinary than many *vins de pays*, and examples like Tursan that can easily outclass lesser efforts from nearby *appellations contrôlées*. Worse still, producers of *VDQS* are given very little encouragement to produce good results because of the expectation for prices of these wines to be low.

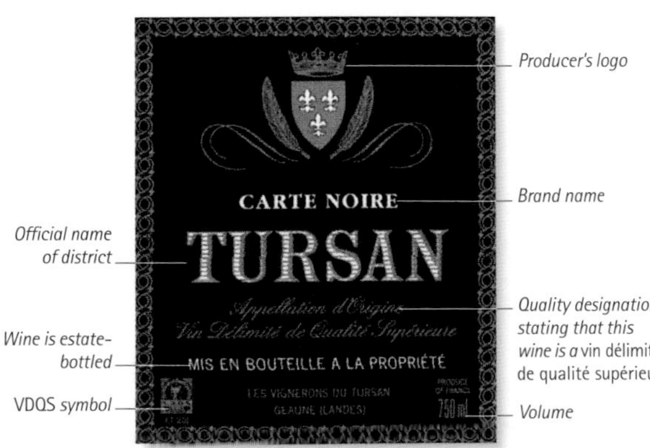

APPELLATION D'ORIGINE CONTRÔLÉE

Around 40 percent of all French wines are included in the appellation d'origine contrôlée *system, which guarantees their style and geographical origin, though not their quality—and which is now proving controversial.*

Since its creation in 1935, the system of *appellation d'origine contrôlée*, or controlled appellation, has included all of France's best-known wines and has been widely copied around the world. The system was devised to protect honest producers and their customers by ensuring that the wine in every bottle corresponds to what is claimed on its label.

Making the Rules
Based in Paris, the INAO, or Institut National des Appellations d'Origine, promotes and regulates the production of many French wines and a variety of other regional food products, including more than 30 cheeses.

Today, as in 1935, the words *appellation contrôlée* aim to provide a guarantee of origin, style, and quality. In reality, most wine-makers agree that, despite valiant efforts, the system often fails in a task fraught with pitfalls. On the plus side, the presence of an *appellation d'origine contrôlée* label will, despite a certain amount of illegal transfer of wine from one region to another, generally guarantee that a wine comes from the region, *commune*, or vineyard on the label. In addition, it will almost certainly guarantee the grape variety or varieties that have been used, as each *appellation* has its own list of permitted varieties. Even here, however, there are quirks in the system. More than 99 percent of the white wines of Burgundy *(see pp112–159)*, for example, are made from the Chardonnay grape, so wines made from the equally legal Pinot Blanc come as a surprise. In the same way, most wines from the *appellation* of Minervois *(see p199)* are, like many southern French reds, made from a blend of grape varieties. Some producers, however, perhaps seeking to copy wines made in Australia and the Rhône Valley *(see pp238–263)*, have

Young Vines in Muscadet
Only Melon de Bourgogne grapes can be used to make wines sold as *appellation contrôlée* Muscadet. Legal restrictions on grape varieties help consumers to know what to expect from the wines of a particular *appellation*.

found a legal loophole that allows them to make their wines purely from the Syrah grape, giving them a completely different flavor. Grape variety aside, while the *appellation d'origine contrôlée* rules do help to identify the style of a wine, they often do so in a rather irregular fashion. Didier Dagueneau's luscious, sweet, late-harvest Pouilly-Fumé *(see p220)*, for instance, is illegal, while there are plenty of producers in Vouvray *(see p226)* and Alsace *(see pp64–79)* who make sweet wines that are perfectly legal and often delicious, but that one would expect, from the label, to be dry.

Hidden Quality
Although they do not have *appellation contrôlée* status, the long-lived, top-class red and white *vins de pays* produced at Mas de Daumas Gassac in Languedoc-Roussillon sell for higher prices than many well-known Bordeaux.

FLAWS IN THE SYSTEM

Further confusion is created by the arcane legislation governing the way in which *premiers crus* vineyards are identified. Take, for example, the Charmes vineyard in Meursault *(see p145)*, which enjoys *premier cru* status. Producers there can label their wines either as *appellation contrôlée* Meursault Charmes Premier Cru or as *appellation contrôlée* Meursault Charmes. Down the road from Charmes is the non-*premier cru* Clos de la Barre vineyard, whose wines may be labeled either as *appellation contrôlée* Meursault or as *appellation contrôlée* Meursault Clos de la Barre. So, if you were confronted with two bottles, one Meursault Charmes and the other Meursault Clos de la Barre, how would you know which was from the *premier cru* vineyard? It's simple: according to *appellation* rules, unless the wine is from a *premier cru* vineyard, the vineyard name must be printed in characters no more than half the height of the ones used for the village name. Easy! These difficulties, however, are minor in comparison with the worst failing of the system, which lies in the way it oversees quality. To carry the term *appellation contrôlée* on its label, every wine must undergo a blind tasting. The first flaw here is that the tasting is carried out by local experts who have been known to be rather generous in assessing the wines of their friends. Much more crucially, the tasting always takes place before the wine is bottled, often even before it is sold in bulk to a merchant, who will blend it with other wines. In other words, there is no reason to believe that the wine you are drinking is the one that was given its *appellation* by the tasting panel.

In 2004, confronted by growing competition from the New World—and a falling market share in countries like the US and the UK—the authorities finally began to acknowledge the need for change. Unfortunately, there is no evidence that this will be achieved in a coherent and effective way, thanks to blinkered thinking and political lobbying by *vin de pays* producers.

Wine Pioneers
In 1923, Baron Leroy *(above right)* sowed the seeds of what became the national *appellation contrôlée* system. This was put into practice by men such as Joseph Capus *(above left)*, known as the "godfather" of the *appellation* laws.

Wine Tasting

Of all the specialized skills that man has acquired over the centuries, few have been more regularly—and more justifiably—lampooned by cartoonists than that of the wine taster.

You can see the cartoonists' point. What, after all, is the connection between drinking and enjoying wine, and all that very serious-looking swirling, sniffing, and spitting? We in the West draw lines between the different ways in which we perceive and experience things. On one level, we see, hear, eat, and drink, while on another we watch, listen and taste. The difference is plain: sometimes we apply more of our brain to the task. A person may buy an expensive concert ticket and listen intently to Miles Davis, Mahler, or Mick Jagger, but will, on another occasion, use the same music as the background to a social event. Every day, all around the world, billions of mouthfuls of food and drink are eaten and drunk. How often will their flavors really make a lasting impact on the brains of the eaters and drinkers?

Memory lies at the heart of the appreciation of almost anything. We may like or enjoy something on a first encounter, but we are bound to be setting it in the context of previous experiences, and of tastes and prejudices we have developed over the years. Wine tasting consists of briefly concentrating on a glass of wine sufficiently to be able to compare its characteristics with those of other wines you have tasted. Does it taste the same, better, or worse than similar examples you can remember? If the flavor is unfamiliar, do you like it? The following procedure, which will not look impolite in a restaurant, will help you to develop your tasting skills.

SEE

When analyzing a wine, first look at it. Whatever the style or age, it should be transparent and bright. Any cloudiness—unless it is simply caused by disturbing the deposit in a red wine—reveals a fault. A wine's color, and the depth of that color, indicates the wine's age, while the way in which the liquid flows down the inside of the glass will reveal its richness.

Beaujolais
This youthful Beaujolais, with its almost violet color that runs right to the rim, is typical of young red wine from almost any region or grape variety.

Burgundy
Burgundy can be recognized by its brick-red color. This one is three years old and already going slightly pale at the rim—a feature that will be more marked in a very mature wine.

Color and Clarity
Is the wine bright and transparent? Youthful, or beginning to turn brown? The appearance of a wine will tell you a great deal about its age and health.

The Smell
Does it smell clean? And of what, precisely? Is the aroma simple or complex? To an experienced nose, a few sniffs can reveal much about a wine's origin and quality.

Body and Texture
Is the wine light and delicate, or richly full-bodied? Fat or thin? The texture provides more clues about the grape variety and ripeness of the vintage.

The Flavor
Does it taste of fruit? Is it spicy, gamey, or vegetal? Is there a single flavor or complex layers of flavors? Does the taste fade quickly or linger?

SNIFF

Swirl the wine around the glass, take a good sniff, then concentrate on what you have smelled. Does the wine seem light or intense? Fresh and clean, or musty, dirty, or vinegary? Does it smell of fruits, spices, flowers, or vegetables? Fix that smell or mixture of smells in your memory, and you will be surprised how quickly you begin to acquire the skill of guessing at the identity of a wine without having to read the label.

SIP

Wine tasters sip slowly, allowing the liquid to reveal as many layers of flavor as it has to reveal. In the past, they focused on the tongue and its receptors for salt, sugar, sourness, and bitterness; now they pay more attention to aroma. To increase the effect of the oxygen, they aerate the wine by sucking air between their teeth and through the liquid. Along with the warming effect of the mouth, this will bring out flavors you might otherwise never notice.

SPIT OR SWALLOW

Spitting is a good idea if you have many wines to taste and do not want to ingest too much alcohol. Concentrate on the flavor—if any—that the wine has left behind. One of the greatest differences between really fine wine and the ordinary stuff lies in the quality and longevity of the "finish" or aftertaste.

Sauternes
A three-year-old botrytized wine like this example from Sauternes, if made in a good vintage, will have a lovely golden color that gets deeper with age.

Riesling
A two-year-old dry Riesling from the Alsace region will have the delicate color of pale straw. Over the course of a decade, however, this wine, too, will turn gold.

JUDGING QUALITY

Having learned the mechanics of tasting wine, the next stage is to focus your new skills on the task of judging the quality of a wine, and, just as importantly, its potential for improvement in the future.

Assuming that a wine possesses attractive and well-balanced flavors, the feature that sets a fine wine apart from the rest is its complexity. While plenty of wines are like a melody played on a single instrument, the greatest wines have the many-layered quality of a full-blown symphony.

As it ages, the appearance of any wine will change. Try holding your glass tipped away from you against a white background, and look at the far edge of the liquid. The older the wine, the paler and more watery the edge will appear. The color of the wine itself will give you more clues to its age, with reds beginning life as violet, changing to ruby, then to brick and finally to brown. Whites change from green-gold to gold and then to bronze. Smell and flavor also evolve. The wine loses the simple primary characteristics derived from its grape variety and the way in which it was fermented and matured before bottling. These are replaced with the more complex secondary smells and flavors that develop only during its time in the bottle.

Most wines nowadays are drunk while primary characteristics are still evident. Some wines, such as Beaujolais *(see pp126–7)*, Muscadet *(see p219)* and Vins de Pays d'Oc *(see p279)*, are actually at their best at this stage. Drinking great reds and whites in their youth, however, can be compared to going to watch a play in rehearsal rather than on its opening night.

Future Stars
Here, young wine of the previous year's vintage is tasted. Even expert tasters can make misjudgments at this stage.

FORECASTING THE FUTURE

In order to judge a wine's future potential, you should look for various characteristics. Does it smell and taste fresh? Like sprightly old people, good wines can retain an element of their freshness throughout life. Unfortunately, a wine that seems

Still Going Strong
Few wines have the quality needed to survive for more than 80 years. This one, from Château Margaux in Bordeaux, is one of the greats.

dull or stale today is likely to be even more so tomorrow. Does it have enough flavor to survive a few more years in the bottle? A light, delicate wine may taste good now, but after storage it may be thin and watery. There is also the matter of balance. A red wine will need a certain amount of tannin (its harshness balances the fruitiness of black grapes), and a white needs acidity to keep any tendency to sweetness in check. Neither tannin nor acid is good in excess, however, and it can be tricky to forecast changes in the balance between them as the wine ages.

When tasting young claret, it is difficult to assess the amount and the quality of the fruit behind the tannin. Critics who ranked the intensely tannic 1970 red Bordeaux as great when they first tasted it dismissed 1982 Bordeaux as being too short of tannin to be worth keeping. Both these assessments were proved wrong. The 1970 retained its toughness throughout its life and was rarely an enjoyable drink. The 1982 vintage, like an athlete with hidden reserves of strength, turned out to have more tannin than had seemed to be the case.

PATTERNS OF CHANGE

Another challenge confronting the wine taster is the unpredictable way in which different wines evolve. Some grape varieties and some regions produce wines that consistently evolve much faster, or slower, than some others. Wines made from the Viognier grape in the Rhône Valley *appellation* of Condrieu *(see p252)*, for example, age faster than than those made from the Riesling variety in Alsace *(see pp64–79)*. White Rhône Valley wines made from the Marsanne and Roussanne grapes go into decline for a few years after bottling, and then develop more interesting flavors when they reach seven years old.

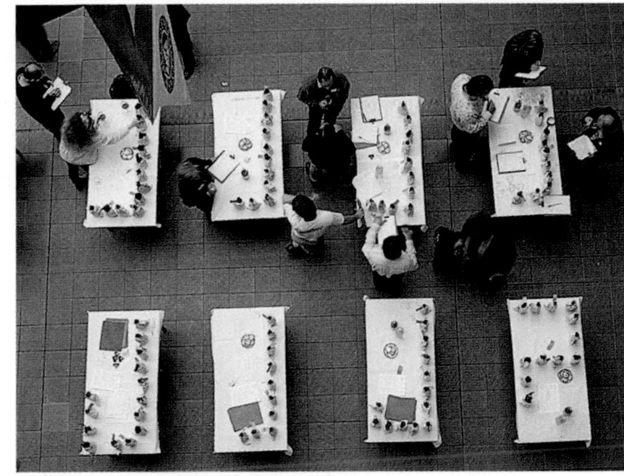

Wine Competitions
Tasting wines "blind" *(see below)* against each other, as shown here at the annual international Wine Challenge event, occasionally brings unexpected results.

The wines of Bordeaux, too, tend to decline for a year or so at various stages of their development. Unlike with the Rhône whites, however, this trait varies from one vintage to another. The wines of 1985 went through no such sulk, for instance, while good examples of the 1966 vintage have been known to return from apparent death on more than one occasion. Red Burgundy, which contains less tannin than many other red wines, can fade from fruity drinkability to watery fragility in the space of six months. The weightier red wines of Bordeaux generally take rather longer to lose their appeal, but can quite often end their days with a mouth-drying, tannic edge. Decanting and airing a wine in the glass can—to a certain extent—mimic the way a wine will evolve in the cellar.

Blind Tasting
At a blind tasting, the tasters do not know the identity of the wines, and must judge purely by their impressions. Here, the labels are hidden by napkins.

The Language of Wine

Every generation and every country—and almost every region—develops its own vocabulary for the challenging task of describing wine.

Translating the flavor of a wine into words is as difficult as trying to describe a symphony or a painting. Language is clearly not the ideal medium in which to convey physical sensations. That said, in describing a wine, one is trying to define three aspects of its character. First, there is the smell and the flavor, often best evoked by reference to familiar fruits, spices, and herbs.

Next, there is the style and texture. Is it tannic like stewed tea, or flabby like a dull Golden Delicious apple? Is it thin or concentrated? Last, although inextricably bound up in the description of flavor and style, there is the question of whether it is actually enjoyable to drink. Is it immature, at its peak or past its best? Is it clean or dirty? Simple or complex?

A GALLIC GLOSSARY

ACETIC Wine with a vinegary taste caused by bacteria that produce acetic acid.
AMYLIQUE The pear-drop character of wine that has been fermented at a low temperature.
ANIMAL The character of some mature reds and examples of the Syrah grape. May also indicate a wine-making fault.
ÂPRE Describes a bitter, harshly tannic wine.
AROMATIQUE The spicy or perfumed character of wines made from aromatic grape varieties such as Gewürztraminer.
ARÔME Term used to describe the fresh, grapey smells of a young unbottled wine.
AUSTERE An acidic white wine or a tannic red one.
BALANCED A wine whose component flavors are in harmony.
BARRIQUE An oak barrel, usually new.
BISCUITY The rich flavor of mature white Bourgogne and Champagne.
BOISÉ A woody-flavored wine.
BOUCHON (GOÛT DE) Corked.
BOUQUET The smell of a maturing wine, as opposed to the *arôme* of a younger wine. Can also refer to the smell of a wine generally.
BUTTERY Describes the character of wines such as a good white Burgundy.
CAPITEUX Describes an overly alcoholic wine.
CHALEUREUX Suggests a richly flavored red wine with a high alcohol content.
CHAPTALISÉ Wine whose alcoholic strength has been increased by the addition of sugar during fermentation.
CHARNU A less pronounced version of chaleureux.
CHARPENTÉ A full-flavored but slightly over-tannic red wine that will improve with keeping.
CHÊNE Oak—probably new.
CIGAR BOX The cedar-wood character of maturing red Bordeaux.
CLOSED Wine whose smell and flavor are hard to discern. Such wines may open out with time and exposure to the air.
COMPLET Complex and balanced.
COMPLEX Wine with more than one flavor.
CORKED Describes a musty-tasting wine, caused by a mold-infected cork. This fault affects three to six percent of bottles of wine to a lesser or greater extent. Sadly, after inventing screwcaps for wine, French producers have been slower than their New World counterparts to exploit them.
CORSÉ Similar to charnu and chaleureux.
DÉPOUILLÉ A faded, flavorless wine.
DILUTE/*DILUÉ* Wine lacking concentration because of overcropping or a rainy harvest.
ELEGANT A subtle, well-balanced wine.
ÉTOFFÉ Muscular, full-bodied wine with aging potential.
ÉVENTÉ A wine that is past its best.
FAT Flavorsome wine made from ripe fruit.
FÉMININ Delicate, light wine.
FINISH The flavor that lingers in the mouth after the wine has been swallowed.
FLABBY Wine lacking acidity, which will deteriorate further with time.
FONDU A mature wine that is in its prime.
FRIAND Wine, of any age, with a good fruity balance of ripeness and acidity.
FUMÉ Smoky. The term is used differently in the New World, where it refers to oaky wines.
GOBS OF FRUIT American description for a fruit-packed, new-style red.
GREEN A wine made from unripe grapes. Often the result of a cool summer or overcropping.

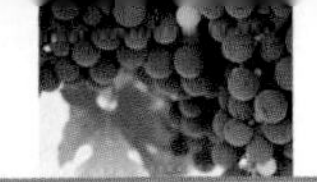

Does the flavor vanish quickly or linger in the mouth? Descriptions of wines have ranged from Michelangelo's Italian wine that "kisses, licks, bites, thrusts and stings," through a wine described by one nameless drinker as "like the little Lord Jesus slipping down your throat in velvet pantaloons," to wines with "silky," "satiny," or even "lacy" textures. In North America, reference is frequently made to such technical terms as "malolactic fermentation" and "skin contact." The following list is a personal attempt to bring together some of the most commonly used French, US, and British terminology.

Myriad Styles
There are many, many styles of wine, and describing the unique taste and character of each one is a fine art.

HOT Similar to *capiteux*. A wine with too much alcohol for its flavor.
HYDROGEN SULFIDE If wine is insufficiently aired in the cellar, the sulfur, added as an antioxidant when the wine is bottled, can turn into hydrogen sulfide, giving the wine a very unpleasant rotten-egg odor.
LONG A wine with a lingering flavor.
LOUCHE A wine that is cloudy, usually as a result of bacterial spoilage.
MEATY A wine with a texture so dense that you almost imagine you could chew it.
MERCAPTAN A foul-smelling chemical compound, produced once the wine is bottled when hydrogen sulfide reacts with alcohol.
MOISI A musty smell, usually caused by dirty casks or tanks.
NOBLE ROT/*POURRITURE NOBLE* This benevolent fungus grows on white grapes, adding a unique flavor to sweet white wines.
NOSE A wine's "nose" is its smell, including both its *árome* and its bouquet.
PÂTEUX Describes a flabby, sweet white wine lacking in acidity.
PÉTILLANT Similar in meaning to *crémant*, this describes a slightly sparkling wine. An even lighter sparkle is described as *perlant*.
PIERRE-À-FUSIL Meaning "gun-flint," this term is used to describe the steely character of some wines made from Sauvignon Blanc grapes.
POURRI Describes wines made from grapes that have been spoiled by harmful rot.
PUISSANT A wine with plenty of flavor and a high alcohol content.
RANCIO Refers to a fortified wine or *vin doux naturel* that has been stored in oak casks for at least two years, often exposed to direct sunlight. This oxidizes the wine and gives it a much-prized sherrylike character that is especially popular in the Roussillon area.
RICH English equivalent of *puissant*.
ROBE The appearance (literally, "dress") of a wine.
RÔTI Describes the roasted character of wines made from nobly rotten grapes.
SHORT Describes a wine whose flavor fades fast.
SOYEUX Refers to a wine that is silky in texture and easy to drink.
STALKY This refers to a wine spoiled by the woody flavor of grape stalks.
STRUCTURE A wine's structure is made up of various components, including tannin, acidity, sugar, and fruitiness, in relation to its alcohol content.
SULFUR Used throughout the wine-making process as an antiseptic and an antioxidant, sulfur is cough-inducing when used excessively, especially in sweet white wines.
TANNIC Used to describe a tough red wine with the mouth-puckering character of strong, cold tea.
VEGETAL Vegetal smell and flavor of a wine made from unripe grapes.
VIF Lively, light.
VOLATILE ACIDS Acids that evaporate at low temperatures. One of the most important volatile acids is acetic acid, which, in excess, gives wine an unpleasant vinegary character.
VOLUPTUOUS Refers to wine that is rich and flavorsome with a high alcohol content.
YEASTY The characteristic flavor of good Champagne, and of traditional Muscadet bottled *sur lie*—that is, without racking or filtering.

Serving Wine

Over the centuries, wine has been drunk out of a variety of glasses, ranging from heavy beakers to delicate crystal flutes. Nowadays, glasses are even designed to bring out the best in particular wines.

Wine by Candlelight
The secret of decanting lies in standing the bottle upright for at least 24 hours beforehand. Then, with a candle or flashlight, simply pour until you see the first specks of deposit.

Among the best wine-drinking experiences I have ever had were drinking Champagne directly from the bottle in a cornfield with a woman with whom I was madly in love, and sipping a 50-year-old red Burgundy from a hotel toothbrush mug. On neither of these occasions was the wine served in the ideal glass, at the correct temperature, or with the appropriate dish, but that was more than compensated for by the setting, the company, and the flavor. Had I been drinking either of these wines at home, however, I would have taken the trouble to serve them in glasses that helped to bring out their potential. The Austrian glass manufacturer Georg Riedel has, with inventive genius, proven that by altering the form of the glass, he can subtly but perceptibly bring out the flavors of different kinds of wines. So his red Bordeaux, red Burgundy, and red Rhône glasses all have their own distinctive shape, as do those designed for an ever-growing range of other regions. If you are a fan of a particular wine, there is a lot to be said for indulging in a full set of Riedel glasses. Possessing a range of ideal glasses, however, is not unlike having an array of kitchen knives, in that you can, in fact, accomplish almost everything you want with three or four really good ones. My own most frequently used quartet consists of a large red wine glass, a long-stemmed, smaller glass for white wines, a flute for Champagne, and a small, but not too small, glass for port and sweet white wines.

Whatever glass you use, it should conform to the following criteria if it is to bring out the wine's best qualities. It should be made of clear crystal and be large enough to contain a reasonable

Basic Glasses
These four glasses, made from clear crystal, will see you through most wine drinking occasions.

amount of wine when only a third- to half-full. The circumference of the rim should be quite a bit smaller than that of the bowl, while the bowl itself should be taller than it is wide. In other words, no wine glass is more poorly designed for the task than the traditional "saucer" Champagne glass that is said to have been modeled on Marie Antoinette's breasts. This glass's wide brim allows both the aroma and the bubbles to escape from the glass.

DECANTING WINE

The business of decanting wines and allowing them to "breathe" is a controversial one. In my opinion, opening a bottle a few hours before serving it is almost pointless, since the surface area that is in contact with the air is far too small. Decanting wines, however, achieves two purposes. First, in the case of older red wines, it offers a means of separating the wine from the deposit that has settled at the bottom of the bottle. Second, decanting is an effective way to "open out" and soften young reds, whites, and even sparkling wines, provided that the wine is allowed to spread across the surface of the glass as it flows into the decanter. Young wines can be decanted two or three hours before serving, but older wines are best decanted as late as possible, since forcible exposure to air in a decanter after decades in a bottle can be tiring for a mature wine. Never forget that a wine may continue to evolve in the glass after decanting.

According to tradition, at dinner, light wines should come before full-bodied examples, whites before reds, young before old and dry before sweet. The wines should also improve with every course. So what should you do if the white Burgundy is finer than the red that it precedes, or if, as is highly likely, the mature Bordeaux you have saved for the cheese is more delicate than the Hermitage that you served with the venison? As with every other form of etiquette, the best rule to follow is common sense. You will do a fair wine no favors by serving it after a great one, unless that fair wine happens to be the perfect partner for the dish with which it is to be drunk. Treat a series of wines as you do a set of paintings, giving each the space and setting it needs to be enjoyed at its best.

Screwpull Corkscrew — American-style Ah-So Corkscrew — Walter's Friend

Choosing a Corkscrew
While no corkscrew does the job better than the "Screwpull," the American "Ah-So" is useful for old corks, and the "Waiter's Friend" is another reliable alternative. Whatever corkscrew you choose, make sure its screw is in the form of an open spiral.

SERVING TEMPERATURES

A dry white wine served too cold will have hardly any taste, while a red served too warm will be like soup. To chill wine, put it in a bucket full of water and ice for 10 minutes before serving. Wines that are too cold can be warmed in tepid water.

Wine	Temperature
Light, dry, and semisweet white wines such as Vouvray	43–48°F (6–9°C)
Rosé, Champagne, aromatic white wines such as Riesling, and fuller-bodied ones such as Sancerre and basic Chablis	46–52°F (8–11°C)
Richer white Burgundies and Bordeaux, and light reds such as Loires and Beaujolais	52–55°F (11–13°C)
Younger red Burgundy and Rhônes and older Bordeaux	57–61°F (14–16°C)
Older red Burgundy, tannic young Bordeaux, and Rhône reds	61–64°F (16–18°C)

Food and Wine

It is no accident that a region's wines go so well with its food; wine-makers first supply their own tables. To get the perfect match, always try to think of the wine as a secondary sauce for the dish.

When it comes to matching wine to food, and vice versa, there are two very different schools of thought. On the one hand, there is what could be called the doctrinal approach of traditional *sommeliers*, who prescribe specific partnerships of wine and food as if they were holy writs. On the other, there is the laissez-faire approach that suggests there are no rules and that the choice is down to personal taste.

In my experience, neither approach is as useful as a readiness to learn from both common sense and the experiences of others. It is only natural that over the years, wine-growers have more often than not produced styles of wine to suit the types of food that are laid on their tables. Burgundy *(see pp112–159)* is the source of some of France's best beef and chicken, while the Médoc *(see p99)* is more famous for its lamb;

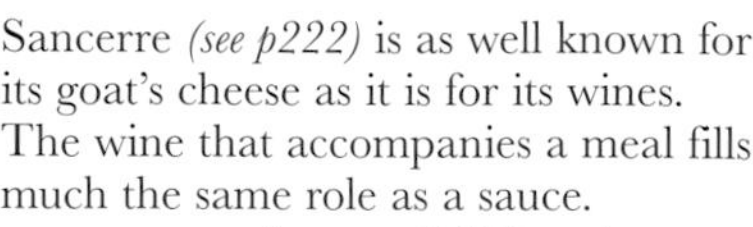

Sancerre *(see p222)* is as well known for its goat's cheese as it is for its wines. The wine that accompanies a meal fills much the same role as a sauce.

Wine and Cheese
Not all wines go with all types of cheese. Sauvignon Blanc is the perfect accompaniment to goats' cheese like this Chavignol.

A powerful Hermitage *(see p258)* will do no more favors for a dish of sweetbreads than *sauce poivrade* (cracked pepper sauce) will, and a Muscadet will be as overshadowed by venison as a creamy sauce would be. So, when choosing a wine to go with a dish, consider the intensity of its flavor. Next, bear in mind the flavor itself. Gamey dishes such as venison are complemented by spicy sauces such as *sauce poivrade* and by spicy wines like Hermitage. Fruity dishes, such as *sole Véronique*, which contains grapes, call for fruity wines like Riesling and Muscat. The textures of both dish and wine are also important. One of the worst culinary marriages I have ever come across is the one between smoked salmon, which is an oily fish, and Gewürztraminer, a wine that has an oily texture. A crisp Sauvignon Blanc would be a far better match.

The Effects of Wine
Slow cooking with wine helps to tenderize a tough old bird *(below left)*, and gives mussels *(below right)* added flavor and aroma.

Tough, tannic red wines are a poor match for beef, which makes them taste harsher, so you'd be better off drinking Burgundy with the beef and saving your Bordeaux *(see p93)* for the lamb. If this incompatibility between beef and Bordeaux comes as a surprise, just try a good, young Médoc with an unpasteurized Brie and you'll find a partnership from hell. The creamy cheese makes the tannic wine taste positively metallic, and would be far better served with a soft red Burgundy or a dry white wine.

Rich dessert wines are often laced with the scents of the fruits that share the grapes' growing space, and make ideal matches for them. Whether dessert wines should accompany a meal's sweet ending or themselves be the dessert is a debatable point. An alternative to the usual dessert is to make one from wine—a gelatin dessert with Claret and red currants, for example, or a Champagne sherbet.

A Classic Match
With the delicate flavors of shellfish, only the most delicate of wines will do. Muscadet goes perfectly with most seafood.

COOKING WITH WINE

Wine is used for a wide range of purposes in the kitchen. Since Roman times, people have been making marinades from wine, olive oil, and herbs, using them to soften and flavor potentially tough meat. The best wines for this are simple, youthful, full-flavored reds from the Rhône valley *(see pp238–263)*, Bordeaux *(see pp80–111)* and southern France. Similarly, peaches improve with white Bordeaux *(see p93)*, strawberries with old red Bordeaux, and fruit salad with Muscat de Beaumes-de-Venise *(see p259)*. Fish can be poached in white wine and stock, while dishes like *coq au vin* and *boeuf Bourguignon* show what slow cooking in red wine can do for sinewy meat.

When it comes to choosing the wine you are going to use in the kitchen, be rigorous—if you wouldn't choose to drink it, you should avoid cooking with it. If you want a dish to taste of vinegar or sherry, use stuff from bottles bearing those exact words on their labels. By the same token, though, ignore classic recipes that instruct you to cook with the same expensive wine you plan to enjoy with the meal. Few people nowadays can afford even to drink the rare Grand Cru Chambertin very often, so using it in a chicken dish seems terribly extravagant. I would instead argue that a full-bodied Vin de Pays *(see pp276–79)* Pinot Noir, Mâcon Rouge, or any other soft, juicy red would be a perfectly acceptable alternative. Where a recipe specifies that red Bordeaux should be used, good Vin de Pays Cabernet Sauvignon will do more for the dish than a watery Bordeaux Rouge. Any dry sparkling wine can be used as a substitute for Champagne *(see pp160–177)*, as could a yeasty Muscadet *(see p219)*. If you do cook with wine, remember to add it to the pan early so that the alcohol has time to evaporate.

Adding Wine
Unless you are making a dish like sherry trifle, in which the alcohol is supposed to be apparent, don't add the wine right at the end of the cooking.

FOOD AND WINE GLOSSARY

The following partnerships are not necessarily ones with which every sommelier *will agree, but they all represent the fruits of my personal experiments and experience over the years.*

APPETIZERS

Caviar This delicacy and Champagne were made for each other.

Eggs Burgundians poach eggs in their red wine, and Beaujolais and young basic Burgundy can go well with omelets. Alternatively, I'd suggest *blanc de blancs* Champagne or white wine from Burgundy, the Loire valley, or Bordeaux.

Foie Gras The rich, "sweet" character of *foie gras* is delicious with Sauternes or any other top-quality late-harvest wine.

Terrine A good country terrine is best served with a rustic wine like a Madiran, a Fitou, a Provence rosé, a Côtes du Rhône, or a Beaujolais.

Melon This fruit does unexpected damage to the flavor of most wines. Quarts-de-Chaume or *vendange tardive* Riesling will fare better than most.

Salad A vinaigrette sauce will do no wine any good at all. If you must drink wine with your salad, try a basic white.

Wine and Cheese
Although many people believe that only red wine should be drunk with cheese, most creamy cheeses are better matched with white wines.

FISH AND SHELLFISH

River fish These flavorsome fish call for flavorsome wines. White Burgundy, Riesling d'Alsace, Sancerre, and dry white Bordeaux all work well, as does dry rosé and even young red Burgundy (the Burgundians go so far as to cook trout in it).

Sea fish The key here is subtle wines to complement the light flavors of the fish. Chablis, white Hermitage, dry Jurançon, Pinot Blanc, and dry white Bordeaux all work well with most sea fish.

Smoked fish The oily character of most smoked fish needs crisp wine, so forget the recommendation to drink Alsace Gewürztraminer with smoked salmon. This is also the one type of dish that calls for oaky white wine, such as modern Pessac-Léognan, Burgundy, and *vins de pays*.

Shellfish "Sweeter"-tasting shellfish such as crayfish, crab, lobster, and scallops go well with white Burgundy, Sancerre, dry Vouvray, Pinot Gris, or Riesling d'Alsace. Rosé Champagne and peppery Rhône rosés can also be delicious. Mussels are best partnered with Muscadet, Chablis, or Sauvignon de Touraine.

Oysters Chablis or Muscadet would be my choice here. Alternatively, you could opt for Champagne.

MEATS

Beef Everything depends on the way the dish is prepared. However, I believe that red Bordeaux is far less appropriate than red Burgundy or wines from the northern or southern Rhône.

Lamb Red Bordeaux is the best choice here, although red Loire like Chinon or Bourgueil can be good, as can Cahors.

Offal Liver and kidney dishes suit red Bordeaux (especially St Émilion and Pomerol) and Châteauneuf-du-Pape.

Game Red Burgundy is good here, too, but Rhône reds are better, as are the finer wines from southwestern regions such as Cahors and Madiran.

Chicken Avoid flavors that are either too strong or too subtle. Creamy chicken dishes need the bite of dry, fruity Sauvignon Blanc, dry Vouvray, or Alsace Riesling. A Chardonnay or an Alsace Riesling will work better if the chicken is simply roasted.

Duck The ideal wine here is red Burgundy, but a flavorsome Alsace Riesling or a fruity southern Rhône wine, such as a Châteauneuf du-Pape or Gigondas, will also work well.

SPICY DISHES

In India, wine has no traditional place. It can, therefore, be a challenge to select a wine to accompany a curry. Everything depends on the spiciness of the dish, but Gewürztraminer or fruity white Sancerre should work. Ginger is no friend to most wines, but seems best suited to Gewürztraminer or Clairette de Die Tradition.

VEGETABLES

Most vegetables can be enjoyed with any style of wine. Some, however, have strong flavors that should be taken into account. **Artichokes**, for example, are not always an easy match for wine. This flavorsome vegetable will make most reds taste metallic, especially when a Hollandaise sauce is involved. White or rosé Sancerre works well here, as does dry Tokay Pinot Gris, Cabernet d'Anjou, or rosé from the Jura or Burgundy regions. Dry white Loire Sauvignon is delicious with **asparagus**, as the wine can have an asparagus flavor of its own. Another option is unoaked Chablis or good Pouilly Fuissé. Whether they are stuffed or used in *ratatouille*, **eggplants** are well matched to reds from southern France and peppery Côtes du Rhône. The fatty character of **avocado** calls for crisp wines like Loire Sauvignon or Chablis. Pinot Gris is a good alternative. The licorice flavor of **fennel** can overpower many wines, so in this case I would choose a full-bodied Pouilly-Fumé.

CHEESES

The more appealing and varied the cheese board, the greater the risk of choosing an inappropriate wine. As a rule, tannic reds such as young Bordeaux are only worth drinking with a hard, savory cheese such as **Parmesan**. Smoky and slightly sweet cheeses like **Comté**, **Gruyère**, and **Emmenthal** go well with fruity Alsace wines such as Pinot Gris, Muscat, or Gewürztraminer, while blue cheeses such as **Roquefort** are delicious with late-harvest wines like Sauternes, medium sweet Jurançon, or Bonnezeaux. Creamy cheeses such as **Brillat Savarin**, **Brie**, and **Camembert** are horrible with many red wines, but perfect with whites such as Sancerre and Pouilly Fumé, both of which are also ideal with **goat's cheese**. Because of its lack of tannin, red Burgundy is better with creamy cheese than red Bordeaux or Rhône, but strong Burgundian cheeses like **Ami du Chambertin** will overwhelm a subtle, mature Burgundy. Champagne is a good match to all sorts of cheese, as is *vin jaune* from Arbois.

DESSERTS

Chocolate-based desserts The strong flavor of milk or semi-sweet chocolate is one of the most formidable enemies for most wines. The strongest contenders are Muscat *vins doux naturels* such as Beaumes-de-Venise and Banyuls. Clairette de Die Tradition can just about handle chocolate mousse, but any kind of Champagne is a bad idea.
Cream-based desserts The best sweet wines for these dishes are not the fruitiest. Try semi-sweet Jurançon, sweet white Bordeaux, or *riche* or *doux* Champagne.
Fruit-based desserts Fruit calls for fruit, so go for *vendange tardive* Riesling or Muscat *vin doux naturel*.

A Sweet Partnership
According to some rule books, all desserts deserve Sauternes, but there are numerous alternatives.

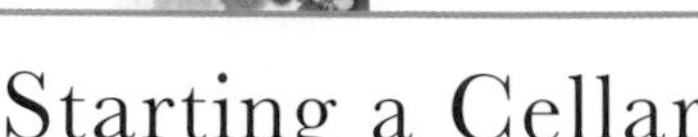

Starting a Cellar

For anyone with more than a passing interest in wine, stocking even a modest wine cellar is as rewarding as building up a collection of good books or music. But keeping track of your bottles calls for planning.

In an age when not all of us are lucky enough to live in a home with a basement, the term "cellar" has to be a broad one. For some, it is a rack beneath the stairs or in an unused fireplace; some opt for a Eurocave—a commercially made, temperature- and humidity-controlled cabinet; others use a converted refrigerator.

A cellar should enjoy a constant, cool temperature. Around 52°F (11°C) is ideal, but constancy is more important than coolness.

A cellar should be reasonably humid, to prevent corks from drying out: aim for 75–85 percent humidity. Drier cellars should be humidified, while ones that are too humid can be improved with a bit of gravel. This also greatly reduces the risk of bottles breaking when they are dropped. Fresh air should circulate reasonably freely through the cellar. And then, a cellar must be secure. There is little point in locking up your jewelry while leaving priceless bottles at the mercy of thieves. Don't neglect to insure the cellar, and to keep the insured value up to date. Finally, you need racks or bins—examples are illustrated on this page.

Wine Rack in a Private Cellar
Identification tags like these can prove very useful, provided both they and the ink used to write on them are humidity-proof.

ORGANIZATION

However good your cellar, it is in effect only the vinous equivalent of the shelves on which you store your books. It is just as frustrating to have to search for a bottle of Musigny as for your copy of *Les Misérables*. Once, in the days when most people drank only a dozen or so different wines, keeping track of them was quite simple. Today, with an ever-growing selection of new wines to discover, it is a lot trickier.

The system I use removes the need to group together wines of similar style and allows me to fill every hole in the rack while being able to lay my hands on the bottle I want almost instantly. I use a business spreadsheet, and identify the individual holes or bins with a system of numbers and letters. Numbers run horizontally, while letters run vertically. So, bottles of the same Nuits-St Georges bought

Château Cellar
Major producers like this one (Château Cos d'Estournel in Bordeaux) keep reference bottles of all their old vintages.

on different occasions might, for example, be found in B45, F82, and U12. The key to the system lies in a well-kept record of what went where. For this, a computer database is easy to use.

Anyone starting a cellar should aim to have four different sets of wines: current daily drinking, current "special occasion" bottles, and a set of examples of each for the future. Muscadet, most Pinot Blanc, and most basic red Côtes du Rhône are not worth laying down, for example, while most good red Bordeaux will improve after a few years in the cellar. Some wines are supposedly ready to drink when sold but are well worth maturing for a year or two: an example of this, in my experience, is good non-vintage Champagne.

I offer the 210-bottle selection below as a possible starting point; an alternative might be to halve all the quantities, resulting in a total of 105 bottles.

Hidden Treasure
This elegantly designed wine cellar is built into a spiral staircase and accessed by a trap door, conveniently close to the dining table.

LIST OF SUGGESTED WINES

Qty	Wine
6	Bottles of assorted, mature (or maturing) high-quality red Bordeaux.
6	Bottles of young, high-quality red Bordeaux.
12	*Cru bourgeois* or *petit-château* Bordeaux.
6	Northern Rhône reds: Hermitage, Côte Rôtie or Cornas.
6	Southern Rhône reds: Châteauneuf-du-Pape or Gigondas.
12	Good red Côtes du Rhône-Villages.
6	Good young red Burgundies such as Beaune, Volnay, or Vosne-Romanée.
6	Older examples of the above wines.
12	Bottles of red Burgundy.
4	Bottles of Chinon or Bourgueil.
4	Bottles of Fleurie.
12	Assorted Cahors, Minervois, and Côteaux d'Aix en Provence reds.
12	Good Vin de Pays reds.
6	Bottles of top white Burgundy: Chablis Grand Cru, Meursault, or Chassagne-Montrachet.
12	Bottles of white Burgundy or good Chablis.
4	Bottles of Alsace Riesling, Pinot Gris, or Gewürztraminer.
4	Bottles of good Alsace Pinot Blanc.
4	Bottles of Alsace Vendange Tardive.
6	Bottles of good Condrieu.
6	Bottles of Sancerre or Pouilly Fumé.
4	Bottles of Vouvray Sec.
4	Bottles of Vouvray Mousseux.
6	Bottles of Pessac-Léognan Blanc.
12	Bottles of good white Bordeaux (choose with particular care).
4	Bottles of young Condrieu.
4	Bottles of Sauternes or Barsac.
4	Bottles of Jurançon Sec.
12	Bottles of good white Vin de Pays Sauvignon or Chardonnay.
4	Bottles of Muscadet (useful for oysters).
6	Bottles of good non-vintage Champagne.
4	Bottles of vintage Champagne.

Investing in Wine

Every bottle of wine, like everything else we buy, comes at a price. In some cases, that price rises quite dramatically over time. In others, unfortunately but inevitably, it falls.

Most of the wine we buy is intended for drinking. Just try auctioning off, for example, a case of basic Côtes du Rhône. If, however, in 1993 you offered an auctioneer some 1982 Château Latour in the barrel, your profit might have been as high as 1,000 percent. Provided you buy the right bottles and take care of them, wine can be one of the best investments around.

Sale by Candlelight
At the Hospices de Beaune wine auctions, auctioneers do not use a hammer. Each time a new bid is placed on a wine, a candle is lit to indicate how much time is left for a new bid to be made.

Many producers feel that there is something unacceptable about speculating on wine. However, how many of them, when deciding the price of each year's wine, ignore the popularity of previous vintages at auction?

Unlike paintings, which can last forever, bottles of wine have a life-span that depends on the vintage and the quality of the vineyard and wine-making. It is as difficult to predict the longevity of a particular vintage as it is to foretell the success on the racecourse of a newly born foal. The 1983 Château Latour, for example, would have initially cost you around the same price as the 1982, but, like other wines of that vintage, is aging far more quickly and is now worth much less.

Until the early 1990s, the people who fueled the market by buying mature and maturing bottles at auction rarely strayed far beyond the wines of a few "blue chip" Bordeaux estates like Château Latour. This changed, however, both with the growth in popularity of pundits who "discover" and recommend "new" wines, and with the arrival on the scene of a wave of "new" wine buyers.

THE RISING STARS

Once buyers have filled their racks with "blue chip" wines, they move on to purchasing novelties that their friends don't have. So wines from the recently created Château le Pin, which produces only 25,000 bottles each year, are now worth more than the longer-established Château Margaux, which produces 10 times as many. Wines in limited

Value Judgment
The 200-year-old firm of Christie's may now belong to a Frenchman and sell wine throughout the globe, but it remains at the heart of the London wine trade.

Château le Pin
The values of the wines produced by this tiny, recently created estate have risen dramatically, but some observers expect them to fall again.

production from little-known châteaux in St Émilion and Pomerol, and *domaines* in Burgundy and the Rhône, also attract investors.

The long-term investment potential of these wines will, however, depend on whether they stand the test of time as well as the "blue chips." The one certainty is that, unless the world turns teetotal or top restaurants turn to offering only cola with their meals, the value of classic, fine wines will continue to rise. The only rules for wine-lovers who would like to benefit from this trend are to keep track of what influential commentators are saying about the vintages in your cellar, to take care of your wines, and to buy the ones that you enjoy drinking. At least then, if their performance is disappointing, you can always enjoy your liquid assets—which is more than can be said for underperforming stocks.

THE BLUE CHIP NAMES

BORDEAUX Château l'Angélus, Cheval Blanc, Cos d'Estournel, Ducru-Beaucaillou, Figeac, Grand-Puy-Lacoste, Gruaud-Larose, Haut-Brion, Lafite, Lafleur, Léoville Barton, Léoville-Las Cases, Lynch Bages, Margaux, la Mission-Haut-Brion, Montrose, Mouton-Rothschild, Palmer, Pape Clément, Pétrus, Pichon-Lalande, Pichon-Longueville, Rauzan Segla, Château Église Clinet, la Mondotte, le Pin, Valandraud.

BURGUNDY Drouhin, Marquis de Laguiche, Gros Frères, Hospices de Beaune (Drouhin and Jadot), Lafon, Leroy, Méo Camuzet, Romanée Conti (La Tâche, Romanée Conti, Romanée St Vivant), de Vogüe.

RHÔNE Chapoutier, Chave, Guigal, Jaboulet Aîné.

Test of Time
The value of the wines produced by individual châteaux can fluctuate. Recording the value of the 1982 vintage at auction, this chart, produced by wine merchants Bordeaux Index, shows that "blue chip" châteaux like Cheval Blanc and Pichon-Lalande are far more reliable than some humbler estates.

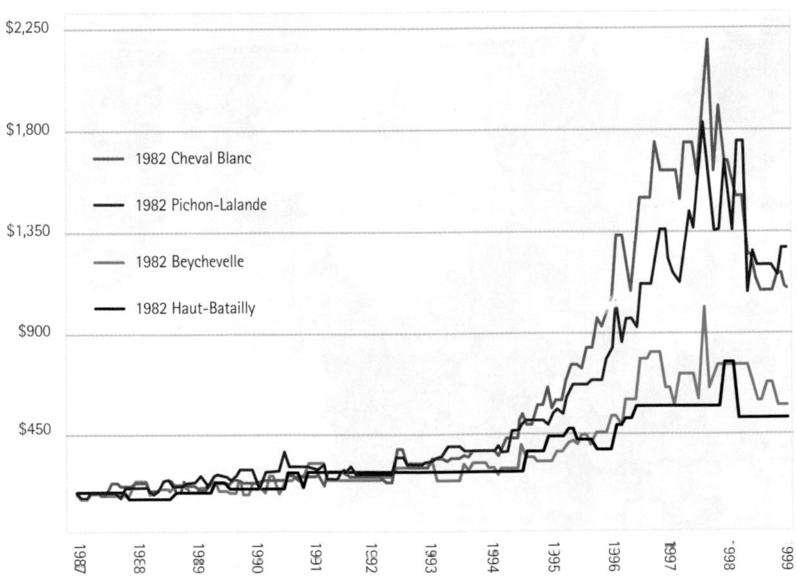

Vintages

Assessing the potential of a wine from a given year's grapes is never easy. Favored vintages may ultimately disappoint, while apparently average years can yield rare classics.

The Test of Time
Bottles of top-class wines from great vintages can survive the test of time if they are properly cellared.

Vintages are one of the aspects of wine that can confuse even the most experienced wine enthusiasts and professionals. Every year, in every region and every vineyard, nature provides a fresh set of challenges for the wine maker. Grapes on the vine, and wines in the bottle, often develop in unpredictable ways. Add to this the fact that wine enthusiasts differ in their definition of a perfectly mature wine, and it is clear that predicting the longevity of any wine is going to be tricky.

When using a vintage chart, it helps to bear in mind that it is the work of a broad brush. A chart cannot take account of the lucky or exceptionally skilful producer, nor can it encompass, at the other end of the spectrum, underperforming wine makers who fail to make the most of a good vintage. The example on the following pages is based on the performance of wines made by better-than-average producers. It indicates how good a particular vintage was and when wines made in that vintage are best drunk. For example, 1998 was a very good vintage for Margaux and bottles made by good châteaux from this year would be best drunk between 2004 and 2020.

Beauty or Beast?
From the earliest stages of the growing season to the time when the wine is fermenting in the vat or barrel, it is very hard to predict the quality and longevity of a wine.

The first key to understanding vintages lies in appreciating that they often vary from region to region (and even within the same region) and from wine style to wine style. So, while 1982 was a great year for Bordeaux's red wines, it was a mediocre vintage for Burgundy, on the other side of France. Years that suit the Merlot grape in Bordeaux, for example, are not always as kind to Cabernet Sauvignon. So, in 1998, it was easier to make good claret in the Merlot-filled vineyards of Pomerol and St Émilion than in their Cabernet Sauvignon-dominated neighbours of the Médoc. Similarly, vintages that provide ideal conditions for the development of the "noble rot" that is needed for sweet white wine are often years when it is hard to make good dry red wine.

There are different kinds of good and poor vintages. There are some years when the best wines are drinkable almost from the outset, while others from the same regions repay patience in their early life. So-called "bad" vintages may be unpalatably acidic, or simply lightweight and dilute. Some supposedly "lesser" vintages give a great deal of pleasure during their brief heyday, while so-called top-class vintages may never fulfil their initial promise.

Slumbering claret
These 1949 Bordeaux wines still taste fine today, yet the same château's 1950 vintage is now past its peak.

1949

FRENCH WINES VINTAGES

	2004	2003	2002	2001	2000	1999	1998	1997	1996	1995
ALSACE										
Vendange Tardive	– –	**** '07–'17	***** '07–'20	*** '06–'18	**** '05–'16	*** '05–'09	*** '05–'10	***** '05–'20	**** '99–'10	**** '97–'09
RED BORDEAUX										
Médoc	***	***** '07–'30	**** '06–'18	**** '06–'16	***** '05–'30	*** '05–'12	**** '04–'25	– –	***** '00–'20	**** '00–'18
Pessac-Léognan	**	**** '07–'25	**** '06–'15	**** '06–'16	***** '05–'25	**** '05–'12	**** '04–'20	– –	**** '02–'15	**** '01–'18
Pomerol/St-Émilion	***	**** '07–'27	*** '06–'10	**** '06–'12	**** '05–'25	*** '05–'12	***** '03–'28	– –	**** '01–'15	**** '02–'20
WHITE BORDEAUX										
Pessac-Léognan	****	*** '04–'09	**** '05–'17	***** '04–'17	***** '03–'20	**** '04–'16	**** '98–'12	**** '00–'10	– –	*** Now
Sauternes	***	***** '07–'30	**** '05–'25	***** '05–'30	**** '04–'25	***** '03–'25	**** '02–'25	**** '03–'22	– –	*** '00–'12
RED BURGUNDY										
Beaujolais Crus	**	**** '05–'10	*** '04–'06	**** Now	*** Now	**** Now	**** Now	**** Now	**** Now	***** Now
Côte de Beaune	***	***** '07–'15	***** '06–'15	**** '04–'11	*** '02–'09	***** '02–'11	***** '04–'10	**** '00–'12	**** '00–'10	**** '98–'12
Côte de Nuits	***	***** '07–'18	***** '07–'17	***** '04–'18	**** '02–'11	***** '02–'13	***** '04–'15	**** '01–'15	**** '01–'12	**** '00–'15
WHITE BURGUNDY										
Chablis	****	**** '06–'13	***** '06–'18	**** '05–'11	***** '05–'18	**** '05–'11	– –	**** '00–'07	***** '00–'12	***** '99–'10
Mâconnais	***	**** '06–'10	**** '05–'12	**** '05–'09	***** '05–'16	**** '05–'10	– –	**** '00–'06	**** '99–'10	**** '98–'07
Côte de Beaune	***	*** '06–'11	**** '06–'18	**** '05–'12	***** '05–'15	*** '05–'12	– –	**** '00–'10	***** '99–'15	**** '99–'10
CHAMPAGNE										
Vintage	****	*** '10–'16	**** '09–'30	** '06–'10	*** '07–'15	**** '06–'23	***** '05–'27	**** '05–'23	***** '05–'25	**** '05–'15
RED LOIRE										
Red Loire	***	***** '05–'15	**** '06–'21	**** '05–'12	*** '05–'10	*** '05–'08	**** '00–'10	***** '00–'15	***** '99–'14	**** Now
WHITE LOIRE										
Coteaux du Layon	***	***** '08–'25	***** '06–'22	**** '05–'12	*** '05–'09	**** '05–'10	*** '05–'15	***** '05–'22	***** '05–'21	***** '00–'22
THE RHÔNE VALLEY										
Northern Rhône red	****	**** '06–'18	** '05–'09	***** '05–'25	**** '05–'16	**** '05–'15	**** '05–'20	*** '00–'15	***** '05–'23	***** '00–'24
Southern Rhône red	****	***** '06–'15	** '05–'07	***** '05–'18	**** '05–'15	**** '05–'12	**** '05–'12	*** '00–'08	*** Now/ past it	**** '98–'12
Northern Rhône white	****	**** '05–'10	** '05–'06	***** '05–'12	**** '05–'11	**** '03–'10	**** '00–'07	**** Now	**** Now	*** Now

KEY
** Average   *** Good   **** Very good   ***** Excellent
'06–'10 Best drunk between 2006 and 2010   – – Not a good vintage

1994	1993	1992	1991	1990	1989	1988	1987	1986	1985	Other Good Vintages
– –	– –	– –	– –	***** '94–'16	**** '93–'06	**** '92–'06	– –	– –	– –	'85, '83, '81, '76, '69
– –	– –	– –	– –	***** '95–'20	***** '95–'20	**** '01–'16	– –	**** '96–'12	– –	'85, '82, '70, '61, '59, '55
– –	– –	– –	– –	***** '95–'15	***** '95–'15	**** '98–'10	– –	**** '95–'10	– –	'85, '82, '70, '64, '61
– –	– –	– –	– –	***** '02–'20	***** '94–'20	***** '05–'20	– –	– –	**** '90–'10	'82, '71, '70, '64, '61
– –	– –	– –	– –	**** Now	**** Now	**** Now	– –	– –	*** Now	'83, '82, '81
– –	– –	– –	– –	***** '95–'17	**** '93–'12	**** '93–'14	– –	– –	**** '90–'10	'83, '76, '75, '71, '70
– –	– –	– –	– –	*** Now	**** '91–'98	*** '09–'97	– –	– –	– –	'85, '78
– –	– –	– –	– –	***** '94–'11	*** '93–'11	***** '92–'11	– –	– –	– –	'85, '78, '71, '64
– –	– –	– –	– –	***** '95–'12	**** '95–'12	***** '93–'11	– –	– –	– –	'85, '78, '71, '64, '61
– –	– –	**** Now	– –	– –	**** Now	**** Now	– –	***** Now/ past it	– –	'85, '82, '79, '78
– –	– –	**** Now	– –	– –	**** Now/ past it	***** Now	– –	**** Now	– –	'85, '82, '79
– –	– –	**** Now	– –	– –	***** '91–'08	**** Now	– –	*** Now	– –	'85, '82, '79, '78, '73
– –	**** '00–'15	**** '99–'15	– –	***** '98–'20	– –	– –	– –	– –	– –	'88, '85, '83, '82, '79, '76
– –	– –	– –	– –	***** '93–'06	***** Now	– –	– –	– –	Now	'78, '71
**** '97–'09	– –	– –	– –	***** '95–'20	***** '94–'15	– –	– –	– –	– –	'78. '71, '64, '61
– –	– –	– –	***** – –	***** '95–'11	**** '95–'11	'94–'09	– –	– –	– –	'88, '86, '85, '83, '79, '78
– –	– –	– –	– –	Past best	***** '94–'06	***** '94–'08	– –	– –	– –	'81, '78, '70
– –	– –	– –	– –	***** '93–'06	***** '93–'06	**** Now	– –	– –	– –	'88, '86, '85, '83

Touring

France's wine-makers are surprisingly approachable, and many, including some of the most famous, welcome visitors to their cellars and are happy to pour—and sell—examples of their wine.

Bar à Vin
In the absence of a tasting room or the address of a recommended producer, your best first stop is a restaurant or *bar à vin* in which you can sample wines by the glass.

The pebbled vineyards of Châteauneuf-du-Pape, the chalky hills of Champagne, and the sheer slopes of the Rhône all look very different once you have tasted the wines they are instrumental in producing. The experience can be likened to watching a play performed live that you have only ever seen before on paper.

The timing of your visit to any wine region depends very much on what you are planning to do there. For a sightseeing vacation, the summer is a good choice: wine-makers will be delighted to welcome you into their cellars, though you may have to share a limited amount of space and attention with other tourists. Harvest time is likely to appeal to an avid photographer. No one who has watched pickers of all ages in the vineyards, and witnessed the picnics among the vines and the banquets in the cellars, will ever forget the experience. As a general rule, most French grapes are picked at some point between September 20 and October 15. However, timing your trip to coincide with the week or two of the harvest can be very tricky. Like sailors trimming their sails to the wind, wine-makers are often forced to reschedule the harvest according to the weather. If you are thinking of combining your tour with some wine-buying, bear in mind that people busy picking, pressing, and fermenting grapes are unlikely to have time for a leisurely chat over a barrel or bottle, which means that harvest time is not a good time to fill your cellar.

In my experience, to be sure of getting the warmest possible welcome from wine-growers, the best time to visit the cellars is midweek in January or February. Most growers will be glad of an excuse to spend time in the cellar, showing you wines, rather than among the freezing vines. In addition, you run far less risk than in the summer of being elbowed out of the way by a succession of other visitors.

VISITING THE CELLARS

In New World countries like the United States and Australia, wineries often offer tasting rooms and gift shops packed with branded glasses, corkscrews, T-shirts, hats, and posters. In the vast majority of French cellars, however, the person who welcomes you will be either the wine-maker or a member of his or her family. Of course, there are plenty of tourist-friendly cellars that advertise their presence at the side of the road, but, like the restaurants with the brightest neon signs, they are not always the best places in which to discover the wines that a region can offer.

It is important to remember that, when you visit the cellars of a small estate, you are entering a place that is not so much a shop or a showroom as a cross between the wine-maker's home and place of work. Most producers prefer to offer tastings by appointment,

Patron Saint of Wine Growers
In many wine-growing regions, producers show off their wines on the weekend following January 22, feast day of St. Vincent, the patron saint of wine-growers.

restricting them to hours that do not interfere with work time or with family time. Lunchtime, especially, is a bad part of the day to arrive. Interrupting a Gallic wine-grower who has sat down to enjoy his midday meal is less impolite than intruding on him at prayer, but not much.

One hazard to be wary of when visiting out of season is the "tired" bottle, one that has been opened some days earlier for the last people to visit the cellar. Always be politely honest about your impressions of the wines you are tasting so as to give the wine-grower an idea of your tastes. If you know anything at all about the region, its wines, and its vintages, then tactfully ensuring that your host is aware of that knowledge may persuade him or her to open another bottle or two for you to taste. As a rule, never purchase a wine from a producer who is not willing to let you taste at least a few of his bottles. Most producers will be happy to sell you anything from a single bottle to several cases or more. If you find nothing that you like, or you think the wines are overpriced, there is no need to feel pressured into buying. At the same time, it is important to avoid wasting the producer's time by outstaying your welcome in his cellar.

Living History
Artifacts and wine-making equipment from Greek, Roman, and medieval times appear in many museums in wine-producing areas. Together with old maps and written records, these help to put a region's wine into context.

The FRENCH WINE REGIONS

Wine Map of France

Within its hexagonal borders, France boasts an extraordinarily diverse collection of wine regions, each of which has its own, immediately recognizable style and flavor. The quality and character of these regions is dictated by the climate, soil, and tradition. Popularity, price, and prestige may have more to do with historical chance; once-modest wines have now overtaken others that were once served on royal tables.

KEY	pages
Alsace and Lorraine	58-69
Bordeaux	70-97
Burgundy	98-141
Champagne	142-155
Jura and Savoie	156-161
Languedoc-Roussillon	162-171
The Loire Valley	172-193
Provence and Corsica	194-199
The Rhône Valley	200-221
Southwest France	222-229
Département boundary	

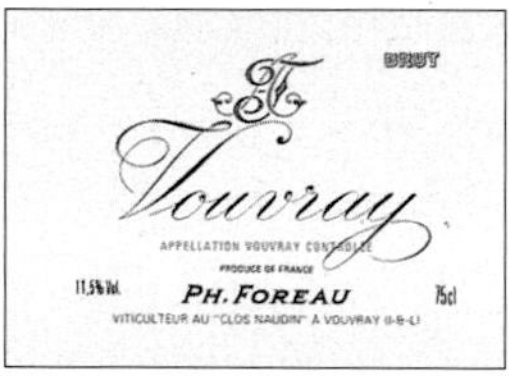

BRUT
Vouvray
APPELLATION VOUVRAY CONTRÔLÉE
11,5% Vol. PH. FOREAU 75cl

The Loire Valley is home to many of the world's best white and rosé wines.

The wines of southwest France offer some fine alternatives to Bordeaux.

0 km 100
0 miles 100

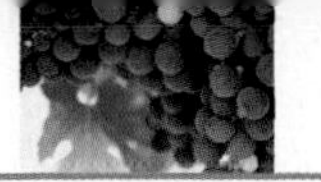

LILLE
NORD
AISNE
ARDENNES
REIMS
PARIS
MARNE
MEUSE
Metz
MOSELLE
BAS-RHIN
Nancy
STRASBOURG
MEURTHE-ET-MOSELLE
SEINE-ET-MARNE
AUBE
HAUTE-MARNE
VOSGES
HAUT-RHIN
Rhine
Mulhouse
YONNE
HAUTE-SAÔNE
TERRITOIRE-DE-BELFORT
CÔTE D'OR
Dijon
Saône
DOUBS
NIÈVRE
SAÔNE-ET-LOIRE
JURA
Lake Geneva
ALLIER
Mâcon
RHÔNE
LOIRE
AIN
HAUTE-SAVOIE
LYON
PUY-DE-DÔME
ST ÉTIENNE
ISÈRE
SAVOIE
GRENOBLE
HAUTE-LOIRE
Isère
Rhône
ARDÈCHE
HAUTES-ALPES
LOZÈRE
DRÔME
GARD
VAUCLUSE
ALPES-DE-HAUTE-PROVENCE
ALPES-MARITIMES
Nîmes
Durance
MONTPELLIER
HÉRAULT
BOUCHES-DU-RHÔNE
VAR
NICE
MARSEILLE
TOULON
Perpignan
A26
A2
A1
A4
A26
A6
A31
A36
A6
A40
A43
N75
A9
A8
A61
A71

Champagne still produces many of the world's top-quality bottles of bubbly.

The unique whites of Alsace and Lorraine are now regaining popularity.

When they are at their best, the wines of Burgundy are unequaled.

The vast Rhône Valley produces a huge quantity of delicious, warm, spicy reds.

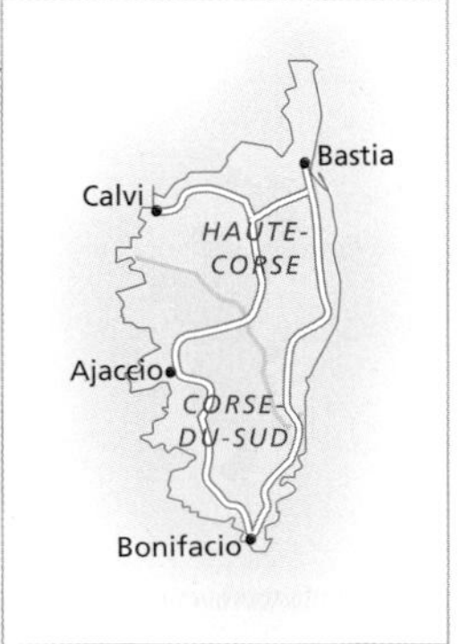

Alsace and Lorraine

Alsace and Lorraine

Alsace is, as its neighbor Lorraine once also used to be, the source of some of the world's most extraordinary white wines.

Alsatian Wine Merchant
Many of Alsace's wine merchants first opened their doors over 400 years ago.

Alsace stands apart from other French wine regions. Around 20 years ago, I remember judging a set of anonymous wines at a French competition, alongside wine-makers from Burgundy and Bordeaux. For one member of our team in particular, this was a daunting task. Having taken a perplexed few sniffs, and an even more confused sip, he spat out the first sample, spluttering the words, "*C'est pas du vin, c'est du parfum!*"("This isn't wine, it's perfume!"). For a man who was used to drinking Chardonnay, a wine made from the extraordinary Gewürztraminer grape, with its combined flavors of spice and perfume, simply made no sense. Fortunately, this was not my first exposure to Alsace's most characterful grape, but I could easily sympathize with the plight of that Burgundian.

Today, thankfully, most French wine-makers are far less insular when it comes to wine tasting. The relatively recent experience of being a territorial tug-of-love child between the Germans to the east and the French to the west has left the Alsatians with a language, cuisine, and wines that are part Germanic, part Gallic, and 100 percent Alsatian. This is the only significant wine-making region in France to devote itself almost exclusively to growing white grapes. It is also the only major *appellation contrôlée* to have embraced the notion of printing the names of the grapes from which its wines are made on the labels.

Almost All White
About 90 percent of the grapes grown in this region are white varieties. Most, like Gewürztraminer, have origins elsewhere, on the other side of the Rhine or in Italy.

So, while people buying white Burgundy may choose between wines produced from the same Chardonnay grape variety in the well-known *appellations* of Chassagne-Montrachet *(see p135)* or Puligny-Montrachet *(see p153)*, for example, the Alsace-wine-drinker is confronted with labels like Riesling d'Alsace, Gewürztraminer d'Alsace, or Tokay Pinot Gris d'Alsace. These three wines are made from very different grapes that are grown almost anywhere within an area of 32,000 acres (13,000 ha), covering very diverse soils and benefiting from very diverse climates. If you are lucky, the label might mention a *grand cru* vineyard, but, with over four dozen of these to remember, that could be of little help.

When buying Alsace, read the small print on the label and look for the name of a producer whose quality and style you trust. Although the same can be said for all wines, it is particularly important with Alsace.

REGIONAL OVERVIEW

- 33,300 acres (13,500 ha): 157 million bottles.
- Northern continental, with warm summers. The Vosges Mountains create a rain shadow and most vines are planted on slopes so they ripen well and allow generous yields.
- Very varied, with granite and sandstone on the slopes of the Vosges, limestone on the hills, and fertile soil on the plains.
- White: Pinot Blanc, Tokay-Pinot Gris, Muscat, Gewürztraminer, Sylvaner, Auxerrois, Pinot Noir.

Alsace and Lorraine regions

0 km 25
0 miles 25

KEY
Intensive wine-growing region
VDQS Vin de Moselle
VDQS Côtes de Toul
Département boundary
Delimited AOC region of Alsace

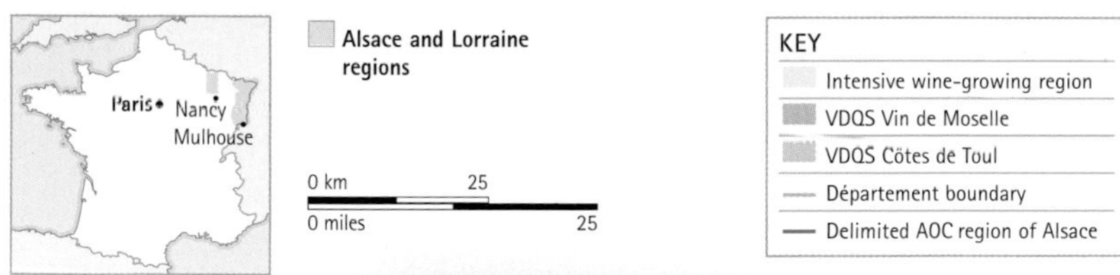

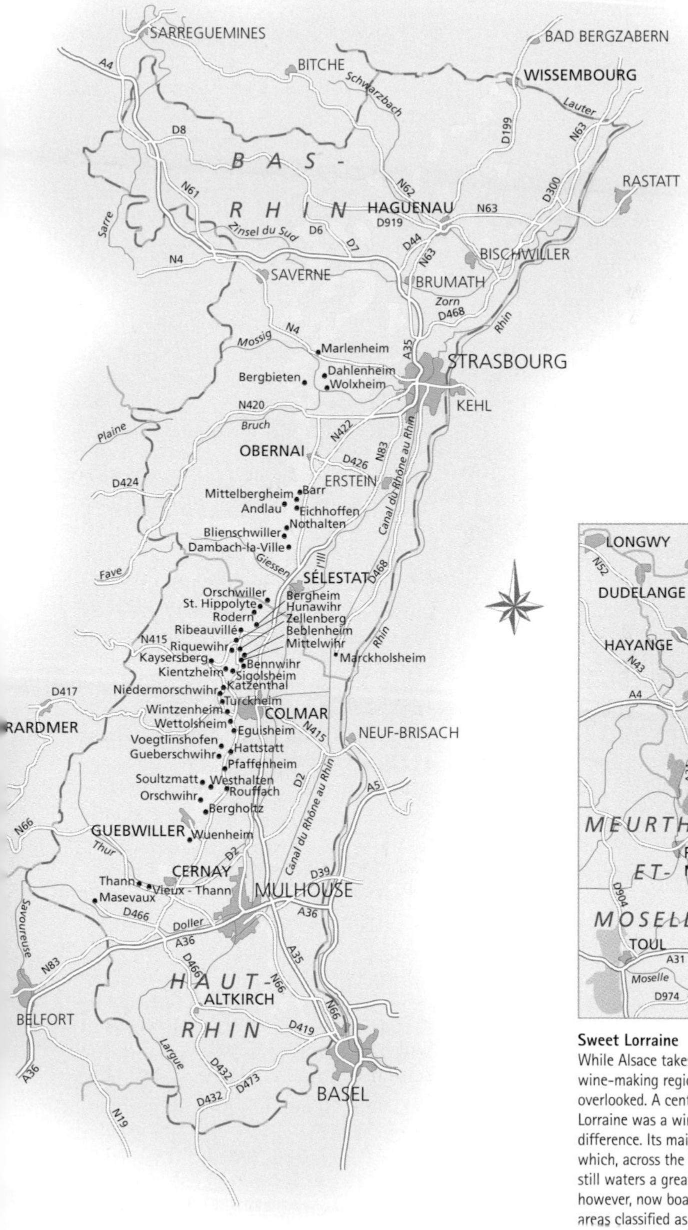

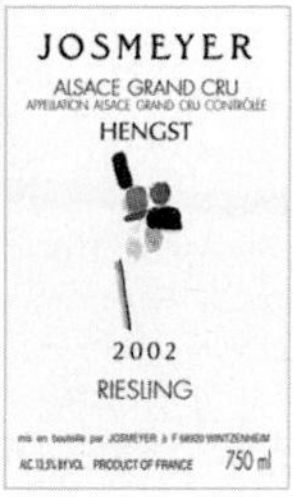

Josmeyer Riesling
Alsace is one of the only regions of France to focus attention on its grape varieties.

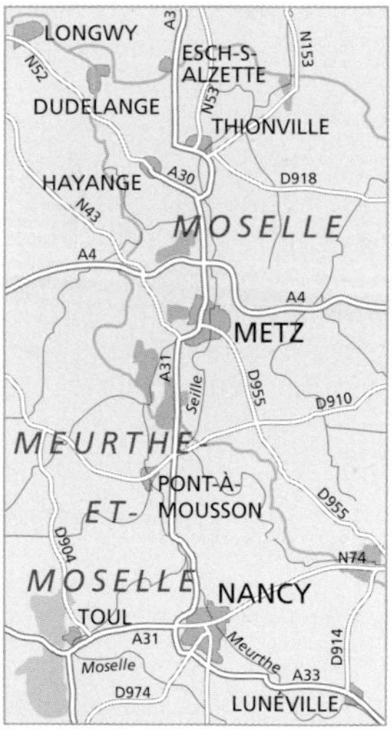

Sweet Lorraine
While Alsace takes the spotlight, the old wine-making region of Lorraine is often overlooked. A century ago, like Alsace, Lorraine was a wine region with a difference. Its main river is the Moselle, which, across the border in Germany, still waters a great wine region. Lorraine, however, now boasts little more than two areas classified as VDQS: Vin de Moselle and the Côtes de Toul.

The History of Alsace and Lorraine

Wine-making in the neighboring regions of Alsace and Lorraine dates back to Roman times, since when it has had its ups and downs. The trade in both regions became depressed in the 1870s. In Alsace, a renaissance was begun in the mid-20th century, whereas Lorraine has yet to see a return to the levels of trade it enjoyed in the 19th century.

The region of Alsace has been passed back and forth between France and Germany for perhaps as long as 2,000 years. The first time this is known to have happened was in the 1st century AD, when a Germanic tribe called the Suebi wrested the region from a Celtic people known as the Sequani.

The Romans under Julius Caesar reversed the situation. They ruled the region for the next 200 years, but in the 4th century another Germanic tribe, the Alemanni, overran Alsace. Later, in 496, the Alemanni in their turn were expelled from Alsace by the Franks—the ancestors of the modern French.

Vine-Growing in the 15th Century
Vine-growing and wine-making, as well as other tasks, meant that peasants in Alsace were employed throughout the year. This beautiful 15th-century tapestry shows them at work.

Fortunately for wine enthusiasts, when the Alsatians were not involved in these wars, they evidently had time to plant and grow vines. By 780 the ecclesiastical chronicler Adam the Monk was referring to wine-making as the most profitable of the region's activities.

The 843 Treaty of Verdun gave Charlemagne the right to share his pan-European empire between his three grandsons. The Alsace region was presented to Louis the German, who also received Germany, in order that, among other things, "he might have wine in his new kingdom." By the end of the 9th century, vines were tended and wine made in no fewer than 119 Alsatian villages.

Over the next 500 years, vine-growing extended to over 400 villages and some 300 abbeys. According to one of the region's best-known wine merchants, Johnny Hugel, in his book *Reasons for the Renaissance of Alsace Wines*, by 1481 exports had risen to the modern equivalent of nearly 80 million bottles: twice today's total.

VARIETY SHOWS

The first wine-grape variety to be grown in Alsace was probably Pinot Noir. This may have been introduced by the Romans for use in red wine.

A shift from red to white wine was already taking place during the 12th century. "Rissling," Traminer (Gewürztraminer), and Muscat seem to have been introduced before the 15th century. These were followed by Pinot Blanc, which was almost certainly imported from Burgundy. The Tokay Pinot Gris variety probably also originated there, although the locals prefer to believe that a heroic Alsatian general brought it back from campaigning in Hungary. Whatever the origins of Pinot Gris, Alsatian growers of the 16th century certainly had a sophisticated understanding of the varied potential offered by different grape varieties. They also knew plenty about the ways in which these grapes should be grown and harvested. At that time, the wine-making trade was governed by a body known as the

Wine Growers' Association of Riquewihr, which established rules to ensure that grapes were picked as late and as ripe as possible.

PROSPERITY, THEN DECLINE

Under Riquewihr rules, officially registered tasters—*Weinsticheren*—were given the task of rating wines as either *hüntsch* (which had to be drunk within Alsace) or *vin noble* (in German, *Edelwein*), the export variety. Sale outside Alsace was in the hands of such wine houses as Dopff, which opened in 1574 and whose name survives today in the firms Dopff au Moulin and Dopff & Irion. Among other existing exporters, Trimbach and Hugel began trading in 1626 and 1637, respectively.

These firms thrived, but the early heyday of Alsace's wine industry was brought to a halt during the Thirty Years' War of 1618–48. By the end of the 17th century, the number of *Weinsticheren* had halved and vineyards were being taken over by settlers from other parts of France, from Switzerland, the Tyrol, and Germany, who were given land for nothing by Louis XIV of France. The newcomers were often less quality-conscious than their predecessors, preferring to plant vines on flat, fertile land rather than the more rewarding but labor-intensive slopes. In spite of the royal edicts that were issued in 1731 and 1766 to protect them, Riesling, Muscat, and Traminer, as well as the Pinots, were steadily supplanted by the dull but productive Elbling, Chasselas, and Sylvaner grapes.

Le Petit Journal

SUPPLÉMENT ILLUSTRÉ

LA FÊTE DES VENDANGES EN ALSACE

1911 Harvest Festival
The costumes may have changed, but the task facing pickers in the 21st century has changed remarkably little.

RETURN TO FRENCH RULE

Following the French Revolution in 1790 and the resulting breakup of ecclesiastical estates, the Alsace region saw another enthusiastic bout of planting, which this time involved yet another substandard grape variety, Knipperlé. This soon comprised all but a fifth of the region's vines.

The banalization of Alsace's wines was exacerbated by the annexation of the region to Germany in 1871 and by the devastation caused by a set of virulent vine diseases and the spread of phylloxera. After World War I and Alsace's return to France, the area was, as Johnny Hugel recalls, in a sorry and very confused state.

"To change nationality is not only to change flags. It is also to enter into a different economic space. They move the customs offices, you lose all of your customers, and you are subjected to another set of viticultural rules ... in 1918, we didn't have a single customer in Paris." Even if there had been Parisian customers, it is questionable how fond they would have been of the wines that the region was then making.

The survival to this day of Alsace's wine industry, with its traditional standards, is largely the work of a set of unusually dynamic and quality-conscious *coopératives*.

Warring Neighbors
Although the war between France and Prussia was over 130 years ago, it is still remembered as one of the low points of Alsace's vinous history.

A Driving Tour of Alsace

This tour covers part of the Alsace Route du Vin, an official scenic route meandering over 108 miles (180 km) from Marlenheim to Thann. The tour takes in some of the region's most spectacular landscapes and prettiest villages and towns, many of which are reminiscent of tales from the Brothers Grimm.

Alsace & Lorraine □ Tour

COLMAR TO EGUISHEIM

Wandering around the cobbled streets of Colmar ①, past the clocks, ornate signs, and half-timbered, often pastel-colored buildings, is like listening to the overture before the opera that is the rest of Alsace. Like so many towns and villages in this region, Colmar is so idyllic that it looks as though it could have been put together by Walt Disney's designers. As elsewhere in Alsace, the best way to explore is on foot—the town is not made for cars. While in Colmar, make sure you visit the Petite Venise canal and the Maison Pfinster on the Rue des Marchands.

Rouffach ②, the southernmost port of call on your journey, is an old walled town with an impressive church that has been added to over the centuries and a 15th-century corn exchange. Husseren les Châteaux is nestled in the hills here, nearly 1,300 ft (400 m) above sea level, and is distinguishable by the Tours d'Eguisheim, three ruined towers that poke through the woodland like dinosaur teeth. Kuentz-Bas makes good wine here and in Eichberg Grand Cru, located in the nearby *commune* of Eguisheim ③, your next stop on this tour. An exquisite 15th-century town, Eguisheim's château once belonged to Pope Leo IX, who was born here. Bruno Sorg and Leon Beyer are the producers to visit, but the huge *coopérative* also makes good wines. Nearby Wintzenheim has a pair of ruined châteaux and the great Hengst Grand Cru vineyard, which makes great Gewürztraminer.

A Peaceful Retreat
Sentiers viticoles, lovely paths that run through the vineyards, complement the charm of Alsace's towns and villages.

TURCKHEIM TO RIQUEWIHR

Turckheim ④ offers the chance to sample and compare the wines of Zind Humbrecht, one of the best producers in Alsace, with those of the excellent Turckheim *coopérative.* Don't forget to look up at the roofs, where, with luck, you will see the white storks that nest here.

Albert Schweitzer, one of Alsace's most famous sons, was born in Kaysersberg ⑤, a village that sits astride the Weiss River. The long and prosperous history of wine-making here is evident in the beauty of its buildings and in the fact that there is a chapel whose statue of Christ is holding a bunch of grapes. The place of pilgrimage for wine-lovers, though, is Domaine Weinbach's cellar, where Laurence Faller makes exquisite Riesling.

The twin *communes* of Bennwihr ⑥ and Mittelwihr ⑦ are a triumph of restoration and reconstruction, following their near-destruction by war. Here, the often unloved Sylvaner grape variety gets almost as much tender loving care and attention as the buildings. Make sure your visit to Riquewihr ⑧ isn't in the summer, unless you enjoy rubbing shoulders with crowds of tourists. It was here that the merchants Hugel first opened their doors—and where they are still to be found. On your way through

Hunawihr, note the fortified church, the clock of which has hands that look like bunches of grapes.

RIBEAUVILLÉ TO MITTELBERGHEIM

Ribeauvillé (9) still feels like the wine capital of Alsace. Here you will find lovely old churches and ruined castles as well as plenty of fine restaurants, wine producers, and top-class *grands crus* vineyards. Your next stop, Bergheim (10), is known for its town hall and Porte Haute gateway, through which outlaws seeking sanctuary once fled. St Hippolyte's claim to fame lies in its stately town square and the quality of its Pinot Noir. The old watchtower is worth photographing, but save some film for the castle of Haut-Koenigsbourg that towers over the vineyards between Kintzheim and Châtenois.

Dambach-la-Ville (11) used to be known as Dambach-la-Vigne, and the importance of wine here is reflected in the 4th-century chapel to St. Sebastian that sits almost within the Frankstein Grand Cru vineyard. In Dambach itself, the half-timbered houses and flowering plants are so perfect that they look as though they are touched up daily. Andlau (12) is said to owe its situation to a bear that was sent by an angel to indicate the valley where a 9th-century abbey should be built, while Mittelbergheim (13), the historic "City of Wine," is arguably the most ornate and least changed of all the region's *communes*.

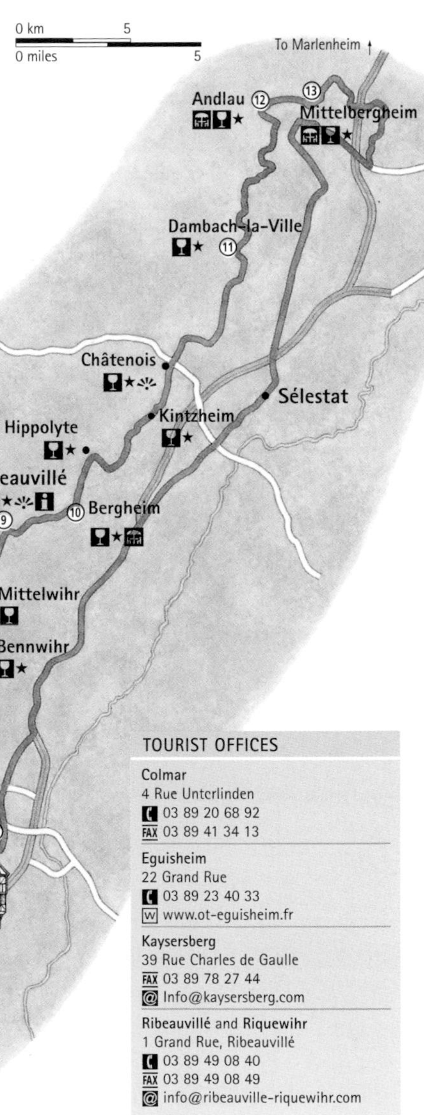

KEY

- Tasting possible
- Places to eat
- Tourist information
- ★ Site of interest
- Tour route
- Viewpoint

TOURIST OFFICES

Colmar
4 Rue Unterlinden
Tel 03 89 20 68 92
FAX 03 89 41 34 13

Eguisheim
22 Grand Rue
Tel 03 89 23 40 33
www.ot-eguisheim.fr

Kaysersberg
39 Rue Charles de Gaulle
FAX 03 89 78 27 44
@ Info@kaysersberg.com

Ribeauvillé and Riquewihr
1 Grand Rue, Ribeauvillé
Tel 03 89 49 08 40
FAX 03 89 49 08 49
@ info@ribeauville-riquewihr.com

The Food of Alsace and Lorraine

Nothing more vividly illustrates the geography and history of these two regions, sandwiched between France and Germany, than the food that is eaten here. Lovers of the way in which pork and pickles are served to the east of the Rhine River will relish several Alsatian dishes, while those favoring the freshwater fish recipes of the Loire will also find much to enjoy.

Pastry has always played a large part in the cuisine of both Alsace and Lorraine, ranging from the world-famous but, sadly, often bastardized quiche Lorraine to *flamme-küche,* an onion, bacon, and cream tart that is made, like pizza, using bread dough.

Traditional references to *le seigneur cochon*, the "lord pig," reveal how important pork is, especially in Alsace. Several of the ways in which this meat is prepared may be sampled by ordering a dish of *choucroute (Sauerkraut)*, which includes smoked and unsmoked pork, sausages, ham, and bacon. Of course, it is the cabbage that has given this dish its fame and its place of honor in the region's households. Every fall, after the wine harvest, a specialist *choucroute* cutter would go from door to door shredding the freshly picked cabbage before putting it in a barrel with salt, water, cumin, juniper berries, bay leaves and vine or cabbage leaves. The barrel was then covered with a cloth and a lid that was weighed down with a stone. When cut and stored in this fashion, the cabbage lasted all through the cold winter.

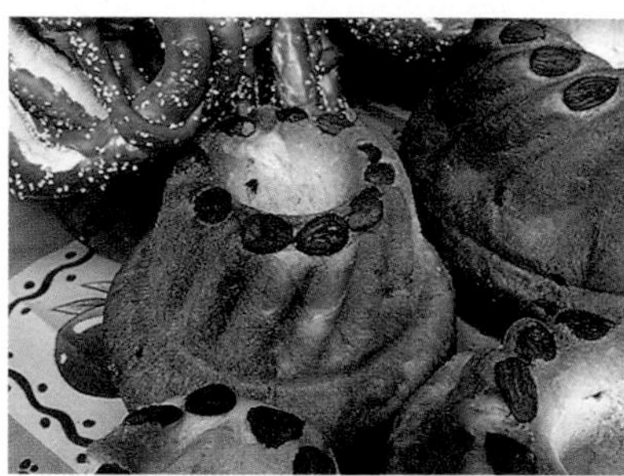

Pastries
Kugelhopf, the most beloved of Alsatian pastries, is a rich yeast cake with raisins and almonds. Made in fluted earthenware ring molds, this slightly sweet delicacy is intended to look like a medieval merchant's hat.

Choucroute Garnie
Pickled cabbage, like *Sauerkraut* in Germany, is made in wooden barrels filled with salt, cumin, juniper berries, and bay leaves. It is left for a month before being cooked slowly with pork, ham, sausages, and Alsace wine.

Pork is also used with other meats, such as veal in *tourte de la vallée de Munster*, and lamb and beef in *bäckeoffe* casserole. Over the years, the Jewish population of Alsace has promoted several alternatives to pork, the most successful being goose. The goose meat is smoked, while the liver is relished in the form of *foie gras*. Popular meats with stronger flavors include wild hare and boar, both hunted in the region's forests.

Porc aux Deux Pommes
Alsatian chefs have long appreciated and exploited the affinity that apples and the appley flavor of the Riesling grape both have for pork.

Fish is also abundant in this white-wine region. Older recipes feature salmon and lampreys from the Rhine and Ill rivers. Today, however, you are more likely to find perch, pike, tench, trout, and eel, which are cooked with fish stock and Riesling to make *matelote* stew.

Whatever the dish, there is a strong likelihood that spices, most notably cinnamon, cumin, caraway, coriander, and nutmeg, will have been used in its preparation. These spices are also used in the desserts and cakes that swell the Alsatian waistline. However, the famous *kugelhopf* cake, an exceptionally light tube cake, owes its flavor instead to raisins and almonds.

Tarte Alsacienne
This traditional dessert can be made using apples, apricots, or cherries, steeped in kirsch and sugar. Custard, flavored with cinnamon, is poured into the crust.

REGIONAL CHEESES

Given the flavorsome character of Alsace's wines, it is hardly surprising that the cheeses produced here tend to be pretty pungent, too. Originally, cheese was made by Alsatian monks for their own consumption. Today, inevitably, while there are still plenty of small cheese farms, a great deal of cheese is also made industrially. Factory-made, pasteurized Munster and Gérome, its cousin from Lorraine, have some of the character of the artisanal product, but they are far duller. It is worth seeking out a cheese from one of the few producers who display the fact that they are holders of the diploma of the Syndicat Interprofessionnel du Fromage Munster.

Munster
Produced in both Alsace and Lorraine, this smooth cheese is immediately recognizable by its pungent smell. In Alsace it is eaten with potatoes.

Trami d'Alsace
This soft, slightly creamy cheese is made from unpasteurized cow's milk and washed in Gewürztraminer. It has a strong smell and is quite spicy.

TRAVELING IN ALSACE

Arguably the most picturesque of France's wine regions, Alsace is also one of the best to visit during the cooler months. The hearty food here is certainly welcome after a brisk climb up some of the steeply sloping hills and, during the month of December, Christmas fairs bring even more magic to the fairy-tale villages.

HOTELS & RESTAURANTS

A selection of the region's best establishments, offering good local food and wine, and notable, characterful places to stay.

COLMAR

Le Maréchal, 4–6 Place des Six Montagnes Noires.
03 89 41 43 07
Right on the edge of the water, this 16th-century timbered hotel in the center of the town offers almost a surfeit of romantic Alsatian atmosphere. Book early.

Château de Barembach, 5 Rue du Maréchal de Lattre de Tassigny.
03 88 97 97 50
This is a lovely Renaissance château with grounds and tennis courts. The perfect place to relax after a long day of wine-tasting.

La Maison des Têtes, 19 Rue des Têtes.
03 89 24 43 43
Taking its name from the heads on its facade, this national monument offers good, hearty, traditional Alsatian cooking in a very central location.

EGUISHEIM

Caveau d'Eguisheim, 3 Place du Château St-Léon.
03 89 41 08 8
FAX 03 89 23 79 99
The *cooperative* that produces much of this *commune*'s wine also runs a pair of creditable restaurants. For a modern twist on traditional cuisine, go to the first floor. The press room offers more casual fare.

ILHAUSERN

L'Auberge de l'Il, 2 Rue de Collonges au Mont d'Or.
03 89 71 89 00
This 3-star gastronomic mecca offers traditional and modern takes on Alsace cuisine, alongside a great wine list.

MULHOUSE

Hotel du Parc, 26 Rue de la Sinne.
03 89 66 12 22
FAX 03 89 66 42 44
W www.hotelduparc-mulhouse.com
If you want to splurge on a really grand hotel, with food to match, this is the perfect place. Rooms come with reading/sitting areas for when it is too cold to laze in the park.

Winstub Henriette, 9 Rue Henriette.
03 89 46 27 83
FAX 03 89 70 81 02
A good, traditional "wine-pub" with fairly priced and well-prepared traditional dishes.

OBERNAI

A la Cour d'Alsace, le Jardin des Remparts, Le Caveau de Gall Winstub, 3 Rue de Gall.
03 88 95 07 00
FAX 03 88 95 19 21
A hotel, a courtyard bar and two restaurants are all squeezed into this old manor house and wine cellar. The cooking in both restaurants is classical and very fine—and appropriately priced.

RIQUEWIHR

La Grappe d'Or, 1 Rue des Ecuries.
FAX 03 89 47 89 52
A tiny, flower- and plant-festooned restaurant with very fair prices.

STRASBOURG

Le Festin de Lucullus, 18 Rue Ste-Hélène.
FAX 03 88 22 40 78
The chef here learned his craft from Michel Guerard, inventor of *Cuisine Minceur*. The food here is light, too, but with plenty of flavor. Meals are cheaper than chez Guerard, as is the list of carefully selected local wines.

TURCKHEIM

Auberge du Brand, 8 Grande Rue.
03 89 27 06 10
FAX 03 89 27 55 51
Named after the village's best vineyard, this is a half-timbered inn of the kind you'll have been photographing throughout the region. There are only nine rooms, so reserve well in advance. The restaurant is also good.

WINE SHOPS

Many of the region's wines are difficult to find back home, so don't leave without stocking up on your favorites.

HAGUENAU

Vins et Terroirs, 2 Rue Maréchal-Foch.
03 88 07 16 47
Winner of a "Coup de Coeur" from the readers and editors of *La Révue du Vin de France*.

STRASBOURG

Le Vinophile, 10 Rue d'Obernai.
03 88 22 14 06

Eating à l'Alsacienne
Alsace's restaurants offer some of the best cooking in France.

Michel Gris is one of France's very best wine retailers, with a range that covers all of his country's best vineyards. And he might also be worth asking for advice on concerts, as he doubles as a well-respected music critic.

MUSEUMS

Some producers offer vineyard or winery tours. Contact tourist offices *(see below)* for details.

KIENTZHEIM
Le Musée du Vignoble et des Vins d'Alsace, Château de la Confrérie St Etienne, 1 Grande Rue.
☎ 03 89 78 21 36
A good little museum in the heart of the wine region.

LAPOUTROIE
Le Musée des Eaux de Vie, 85 Rue du Général Dufieux.
☎ 03 89 47 50 26
FAX 03 89 47 22 24
The focus of this collection is on Alsace's fruit brandies.

STRASBOURG
Musée Alsacien, 23 Quai St-Nicolas.
☎ 03 88 35 55 36
Everything about Alsace is brought together in this museum in the regional capital.

WEBSITES

The main site for Alsace wines is www.vinsalsace.com, which also provides links to producers; www.ribeauville-riquewihr.com is a good source of local tourist information; alternatively, visit www.tourisme.fr to find out more about a specific town or village.

OTHER INFORMATION

Regional Wine Committee
12 Avenue de la Foire au Vin, Colmar.
☎ 03 89 20 16 20

Office du Tourisme du Pays de Ribeauvillé et Riquewihr, 1 Grand Rue, Ribeauvillé.
☎ 08 20 36 09 22
FAX 03 89 49 08 49
@ info@ribeauville-riquewihr.com

ANNUAL WINE EVENTS

During the spring, summer, and fall, the villages of Alsace have an enthusiasm for festivals and events of every kind that can only be matched by the efforts of the Rhône Valley. In the few weeks leading up to Christmas, however, nowhere else can compete with the festivities here. Indeed, some people say that December is the ideal time of year to visit Alsace's picturesque *communes*—because this is when the region's usual fairy-tale looks will have been made all the more magical by the addition of plentiful colored lights. Alsace's winter fairs often go on for several weeks, but the weekends are generally the best times to visit. Check with the Regional Wine Committee *(see Other Information)* for specific dates of events.

APRIL
Ammerschwihr wine fair
Osenbach snail fair

MAY
Molsheim and **Guebwiller** wine fairs
Rouffach Eco-Bio bread, wine and cheese fair
Kintzheim St. Urbain fair

JUNE
Colmar picnic in the vineyards
Voegtlinshofen wine fair

JULY
Dambach-la-Ville evening wine fair
Noalten, Hattstatt, Pfaffenheim, Barr, Eguisheim, Ribeauvillé, Rodern, and **Blienschwiller** wine fairs

JULY/AUGUST
St-Hippolyte, Wettolsheim, Mittlebergheim, and **Goxwwiller** wine fairs

AUGUST
Blienschwiller, Soultzmatt, Obermorschwihr, Bergheim, Turkheim, Andlau, and **Cleebourg** wine fairs
Epfig festival of wine, art, folklore, and *foie gras*
Colmar Alsace wine fair—the region's main annual wine event
Heiligenstein, Rorschwihr, Bennwihr, Obernai, Dambach-la-Ville, Zellenburg, and **Eguisheim** wine fairs
Scherwiller festival of Riesling and handicrafts

SEPTEMBER
Barr, Bergheim, Boersch, Cleebourg, Marlenheim, Molsheim, Obernai, Ribeauvillé, Strasbourg, Steinseltz, Wintzenheim, and **Wissembourg** harvest festivals

OCTOBER
Barr, Boersch, Steinseltz, Molsheim, Wintzenheim, Obernai, and **Marlenheim** harvest festivals
Strasbourg La Couronne d'Or harvest festival

NOVEMBER
Dachstein winter fair

NOVEMBER/DECEMBER
Strasbourg, Kayserberg, and **Colmar** winter fairs

DECEMBER
Riquewihr, Ribeauvillé, Rosheim, Obernai, Sélestat, and **Eguisheim** winter fairs.
Turckheim New Year's Eve celebration

EDELZWICKER

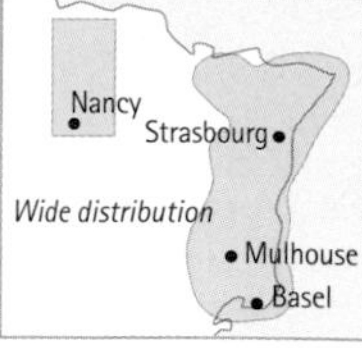

ALTHOUGH ALSACE WINE is commonly thought to be made from a single type of grape, the region has a strong tradition of blending. Blends of basic grape varieties were called *Zwicker* (a German word), while those made up of quality varieties were given the French name *gentil*. In 1871, when the Germans ruled Alsace, they tried to impose the term *Edelwein* in place of *gentil*. The Alsatians agreed only to the two terms *Edelzwicker* and *Zwicker*. In 1972 the French authorities banned the use of *Zwicker*, so that today all blended Alsace wine, regardless of variety, is called *Edelzwicker*. Most of it is such ordinary wine that the more quality-conscious producers label their blends "Gentil," "Réserve," or "Côtes du," followed by the name of the relevant *commune*. Unfortunately, some downright poor wines are also sold under these labels.

Rolly Gassmann
Rolly Gassmann's Edelzwicker is a cut above most: it is less expensive than examples of single varieties from Gassmann and other producers but still very stylish.

Visitors Welcome
Many cellars welcome visitors, and in Alsace even the top growers often keep a shop where you can taste and buy wine that is hard to find elsewhere.

- This wine is produced throughout the Alsace region.
- Traditional, simple, fruity, dry white wine.
- Jean-Baptiste Adam, Marcel Deiss, Jean-Pierre Dirler, Hugel, Kreydenweiss, Kuehn, Rolly Gassman, Cave de Ribeauvillé, Schlumberger, Louis Sipp, Pierre Sparr.
- Roast haunch of pork with pistachios.
- 2003, 2002, 2001.
- 2–3 years.

GEWÜRZTRAMINER

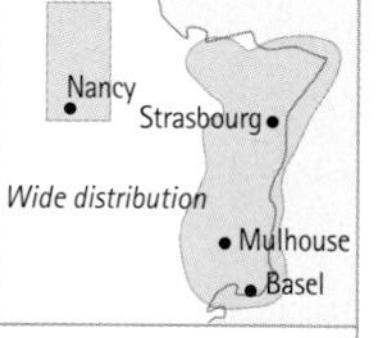

THE TERM "GEWÜRZTRAMINER" refers to a grape variety that used to be known as "Traminer." The Alsatians themselves may believe that Riesling makes the finer, longer-lived wines, but even the best of these never begin to compete with this instantly recognizable, pink-skinned grape when it comes to seductiveness and excitement. The character of Alsace Gewürztraminer varies enormously, depending on the site in which it is grown, the ripeness at which it is picked, and the skills and techniques of the wine-makers. In the hands of careful producers such as Faller, Ostertag, Trimbach, and Zind Humbrecht, using low-cropped grapes that have grown in the soil of the best *grands crus* vineyards, Gewürztraminer can produce dry and luscious, late-harvested wines that have all the irresistible exotic aroma and appeal of the finest perfumes.

Zind Humbrecht
Gewürztraminer can lack acidity in hot years, but top examples like this one can be relied on to be perfectly balanced.

Hills of Vines
In typical wine-growing areas of Alsace, the vines cover the often steep slopes while the growers live close at hand in the villages below.

- Ammerschwihr, Barr, Bergheim, Guebwiller, Hunawihr, Kayserberg, Kientzheim, Mittelbergheim, Mittelwihr, Obernai, Orschwihr, Ribeauvillé, Riquewihr, Rorschwihr, Rouffach, Turckheim, Wintzenheim.
- Aromatic dry and sweet wines.
- Blanck, Deiss, J-P Dirler, Faller, Mittnacht Klack, Ostertag, Zind Humbrecht.
- Münster cheese.
- 2003, 2001, 2000, 1999.
- 5–10 years.

MUSCAT

Nancy
Strasbourg
Wide distribution
Mulhouse
Basel

ONE OF THE SURPRISES of Alsace, whose wines are often sweet, is the dryness of its Muscat—a name associated elsewhere with lusciousness. It is, however, inaccurate to refer to Muscat as if it were a single grape variety. Alsatians grow three types: Muscat à Petits Grains (both white and rosé) and Muscat Ottonel. There is little agreement over which of these makes the best wine. Despite the potentially delicious quality of Alsace Muscat, the vines are being uprooted at an alarming rate, and now cover little more land than Chasselas. It takes dedication to keep yields down and pick at the right time to ensure that the finished wine has enough acidity not to taste flabby. Fortunately, there are producers who know this, and who allow Muscat to reveal its grapey, appley, orange-and-mandarin perfume and flavor.

Meyer-Fonné Delicate, aromatic dry Muscat, like this one from Meyer-Fonné, is best drunk young while it retains all its freshness.

Wayside Shrine Religious traditions live on in these deep valleys. This cross, overlooking some vines, is situated near the picturesque town of Riquewihr.

- Barr, Bennwihr, Katzenthal, Mittelwihr, Riquewihr, Rorschwihr, Voegtlinshoffen, Wettolsheim, Wintzenheim.
- Light, grapey, dry white wine.
- Ernest Burn, Hugel, Andre Kientzler, Meyer-Fonné, René Muré-Clos St Landelin, Bruno Sorg; Schoffit, Marcel Deiss.
- Cheesecake.
- 2003, 2001, 2000, 1999.
- AC Alsace Muscat: 1–3 years. AC Alsace Grand Cru Muscat: 2–5 years.

PINOT BLANC

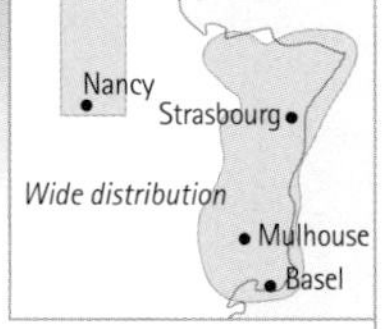

THIS COUSIN OF PINOT GRIS is nonaromatic—an exception to the Alsace rule. At its best, and when not overcropped, it can produce attractively creamy wines. Many of the Alsace growers use a clone of this variety that is known as Gros Pinot Blanc. This was at one time chiefly used in a blend with Chasselas to make wines labeled as Edelzwicker. Pinot Blanc can have so little character of its own that the *appellation contrôlée* rules permit wines to be sold as Pinot Blanc, or as the related Klevner or Clevner *(see p79)*, which are made, in whole or in part, from Pinot Gris, Pinot Auxerrois, Chardonnay, and even Pinot Noir. This laxity has given rise to a confusing range of similarly labeled wines, but it also allows some producers to make more interesting wines than pure Pinot Blanc might allow. Pinot Auxerrois, in particular, brings a welcome note of Alsatian spice.

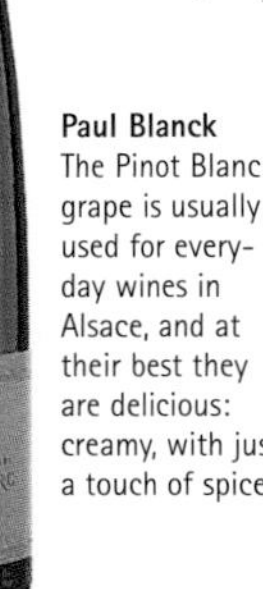

Paul Blanck The Pinot Blanc grape is usually used for every-day wines in Alsace, and at their best they are delicious: creamy, with just a touch of spice.

Grand Cru The Hengst vineyard, shown here, is one of the best in Alsace, and is entitled to the *grand cru* designation.

- Mittelbergheim, Pfaffenheim, Saint Hippolyte, Westhalten, Wintzenheim.
- Refreshing, crisp, dry white. Base for crémant sparkling wines. Component in Edelzwicker blends.
- Paul Blanck, Henri Brecht, Kuentz-Bas, Meyer-Fonné, Cave de Turckheim, Zind Humbrecht, Ostertag, Hugel, Weinbach-Faller, Marcel Deiss.
- Onion tart.
- 2002, 2001, 2000, 1999.
- White: 2–8 years.

PINOT GRIS

THE STORY OF HOW AN ALSATIAN wine came to share a name with a Hungarian wine-making area is full of mystery. According to a local legend, in 1565 Baron Lazare de Schwendi, an Alsatian general, received 4,000 vats of wine and some cuttings of Pinot Gris vines from the town of Tokay in Hungary as a reward for expelling a Turkish force. Today, Pinot Gris is not found in Hungary, but occupies four percent of Alsace's vineyards, yielding some of the region's most stylish wines. These take a middle path between the potentially acidic Riesling and the possibly oversweet Gewürztraminer. Alsatians call the grape "the Sultan" and typically drink *vendanges tardives* and *sélection de grains nobles* examples of the wine with *foie gras*. The wines may be labeled Tokay-Pinot Gris or Pinot Gris. The illegal name "Tokay d'Alsace" is also occasionally found.

Trimbach Pinot Gris Réserve
Of all the merchants in Alsace, none is finer than Trimbach, a firm whose Pinot Gris is always reliably well made.

Riquewihr
One of the most enchanting towns in Alsace (indeed, in France), Riquewihr is also home to some of the region's best merchants and growers. Some great Pinot Gris can also be found here.

- Barr, Dambach-la-Ville, Guebwiller (Kitterlé), Kayserberg, Kientzheim (Schlossberg), Mittelwihr (Mandelberg), Obernai, Riquewihr (Sporen), Thann (Rangen), Turckheim.
- Rich, dry and sweet wines.
- Ernest Burn, Bott-Geyl, Dopff & Irion, Kreydenweiss, Ostertag, Schleret, Sorg, Weinbach (Faller), Zind-Humbrecht.
- Sweet: *pâté de foie gras.*
- 2003, 1999, 1998, 1996.
- Dry: 3–8 years.

PINOT NOIR

IF ANY BLACK GRAPE WILL PRODUCE fine wine in Alsace, this variety is admittedly the one most likely to succeed, but there are plenty of examples to prove how much of a challenge it offers wine-makers. The first problem lies in producing red wine rather than pink. This has been addressed recently by introducing new clones and by the use of rotating fermenters, which extract color at the possible expense of delicacy. The Alsatian ambition to imitate red Burgundy has also led to the enthusiastic use of new oak, which is often as appropriate as a heavy gold frame around a watercolor miniature. In my opinion, it would be better if producers gave up copying Vosne-Romanée (*see p158*) and turned more attention to their often delicious cherry and raspberryish Rosé d'Alsace, a wine that is also far more fitting to the Alsace *flûte* bottle than dark, oaky red.

Albert Mann
One of the most ambitious producers of this variety, Albert Mann gives his Pinot Noir a moderate length of time in new oak casks.

The Wine is King
Signs like these are common in Alsace, where small producers and merchants take pride in their vinous heritage.

- Dambach-la-Ville, Eguisheim, Orschwiller, Ottrot, Pfaffenheim, Ribeauvillé, Rodern, St Hippolyte, Traenheim, Turckheim.
- Elegant, light, refreshing reds.
- J.B. Adam, Jean Becker, Joseph Cattin, Marcel Deiss, Caves de Eguisheim, Robert Faller, Albert Hertz, Hugel, Roger Jung, KuentzBas, Pfaffenheim, de Turckheim, Charles Wantz.
- Meat and vegetable casserole.
- 2003, 2002, 1998.
- Red: 10–15 years.

RIESLING

THIS, THE FAVORITE GRAPE of wine merchants and critics, is also the variety of which the Alsatians are most proud. Established here since at least the 15th century, when it was called Rissling or *gentil* (or *noble*) *aromatique*, Riesling has gradually supplanted Sylvaner *(see below)* to fill more than 20 percent of the vineyards, compared to 13 percent in 1969. While Alsatian Riesling has sometimes suffered from the poor image of cheaper wines from the other side of the Rhine, it has also benefited from being able to make a richer, riper style than Germany's northern regions. The character of the wine varies with the soil. The richest examples come from clay, while the ones produced on granite or limestone take longer to develop—a quality the Alsatians readily acknowledge by selling their wine 18 months after the harvest.

Domaine Weinbach, Cuvée Théo
Laurence Faller makes extra-ordinarily fine wines, including individual *cuvées* such as this one, which was named after her father.

Ribeauvillé
Once the official "capital" of Alsace, Ribeauvillé produces some of the region's finest Rieslings from its Geisberg, Kirchberg, and Osterberg *grands crus* vineyards.

- Barr, Beblenheim, Guebwiller, Kayserberg, Ribeauvillé, Riquewihr, Rouffach, Turckheim, Wintzenheim.
- Dry and sweet wines.
- Paul Blanck, Marcel Deiss, Dirler, Albert Hertz, Kientzler, Ostertag, Rolly Gassmann, Schlumberger, Roland Schmitt, Bruno Sorg, Trimbach, Weinbach, Zind-Humbrecht.
- Dry: Alsatian fish stew.
- 2002, 2001, 1998, 1996.
- *Grains nobles*: 5–15 years.

OTHERS

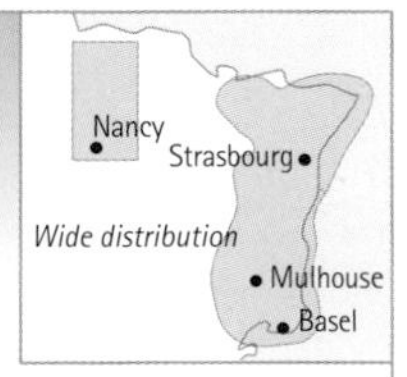

CHASSELAS IS MADE FROM A TABLE grape of the same name that covered 16 percent of the vineyard in 1969 but is now heading for extinction; most goes into Edelzwicker *(see p76)*. Crémant d'Alsace is a series of quietly successful sparkling wines made from mixed varieties, the most successful combination being Pinot Gris, Pinot Noir, and Chardonnay; the rosés are particularly recommendable. Klevener de Heiligenstein, both the wine and the grape variety, is unrelated to the Clevner (or Klevner) grape, but is the local form of Savagnin Rosé, a Jura grape. Pinot Auxerrois is like a cross between Pinots Blanc and Gris, a gently spicy variety that is officially (but wrongly) classed as Pinot Blanc; some producers ignore the legislation and label their wine as Auxerrois. The earthy Sylvaner still covers 15 percent of Alsace's vineyards (down from 27 percent in 1969) but mostly ends up in Edelzwicker. In Lorraine, the Côtes de Toul, which was recently promoted from VDQS to AC, produces tiny amounts of good light red from Pinots Noir and Meunier, and rosé from these varieties plus Gamay. The red and white Vin de Moselle VDQS from that river's banks is only worth buying when in the area.

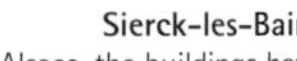

Sierck-les-Bains
Throughout Alsace, the buildings have a decidedly Germanic appearance. This can seem highly appropriate in the case of the region's restaurants, which often serve very Germanic-style dishes.

Gentil Hugel
This wine represents a welcome return to the days when grape varieties were commonly blended in Alsace.

Bordeaux

Bordeaux

In their best vintages, the red and white wines produced by the best châteaux of Bordeaux can easily outlive the men who made them.

Sweet as Honey
Growing on the north bank of the Garonne, these vines in Loupiac *(see p97)* produce luscious, sweet white wines.

One key to understanding the wines of Bordeaux, and the reasons for their confusing variation in quality, lies in the vast size of the region. At 280,000 acres (113,000 ha), it is three times the size of Burgundy *(see pp112–159)*. One consequence of this is that Bordeaux wines of one style or another are made by some 16,000 producers, of which only around 100 have achieved international fame. At least a third of Bordeaux producers bottle and label their wine under the name of their own château, which may be little bigger than a garden shed. As you might expect, the region includes a variety of soils and climates. Some areas, principally the best, including the gravelly-soiled *appellations* of the Haut-Médoc *(see p97)* and Graves *(see p96)*, favor the production of red wines in which the black-curranty Cabernet Sauvignon grape is supported by Merlot and Cabernet Franc, with an occasional dash of spicy Petit Verdot. In other *appellations*, especially St Émilion *(see p105)* and Pomerol *(see p103)*, with their heavier clay soils, it is the plummier Merlot grape that holds sway. With the exception of the great sweet wines that are produced in Sauternes *(see p110)* and Barsac *(see p92)*, the white wines of Bordeaux have been traditionally off-dry and mediocre. Recent technological advances, however, have helped to produce a new generation of good dry white wines made from the Sauvignon Blanc and Sémillon grape varieties.

Climatically, Bordeaux benefits from its proximity to the Atlantic Ocean to the west, which insulates it from extremes of temperature. Even so, the relatively northern latitude of the region means that the production of really ripe-tasting wine is possible in only around one of every three years. Confusingly, but unsurprisingly, many vintages favor only particular *appellations* or grape varieties, so that a great year for sweet white wines can be a disastrous one for reds. The guide through all this confusion used to be a classification drawn up in 1855 to rank the best châteaux in the Médoc, Graves, and Sauternes *appellations*. It is now acknowledged, however, that individual châteaux often over- or underperform, depending on factors such as the luck, skill, and equipment of the wine-maker. So Bordeaux-lovers follow the annual progress of a large number of châteaux, creating their own "running" classification.

REGIONAL OVERVIEW

- 280,000 acres (113,000 ha): 860 million bottles.
- While the entire region is influenced by the Atlantic, the climate varies greatly from one part to the next, with St Émilion and Pomerol enjoying more continental conditions.
- There is both gravel, which suits the Cabernet Sauvignon, and clay, which is better for the Merlot.
- Red: Cabernet Sauvignon, Cabernet Franc, Merlot, Malbec, Petit Verdot.
  White: Sauvignon Blanc, Sémillon, Muscadelle.

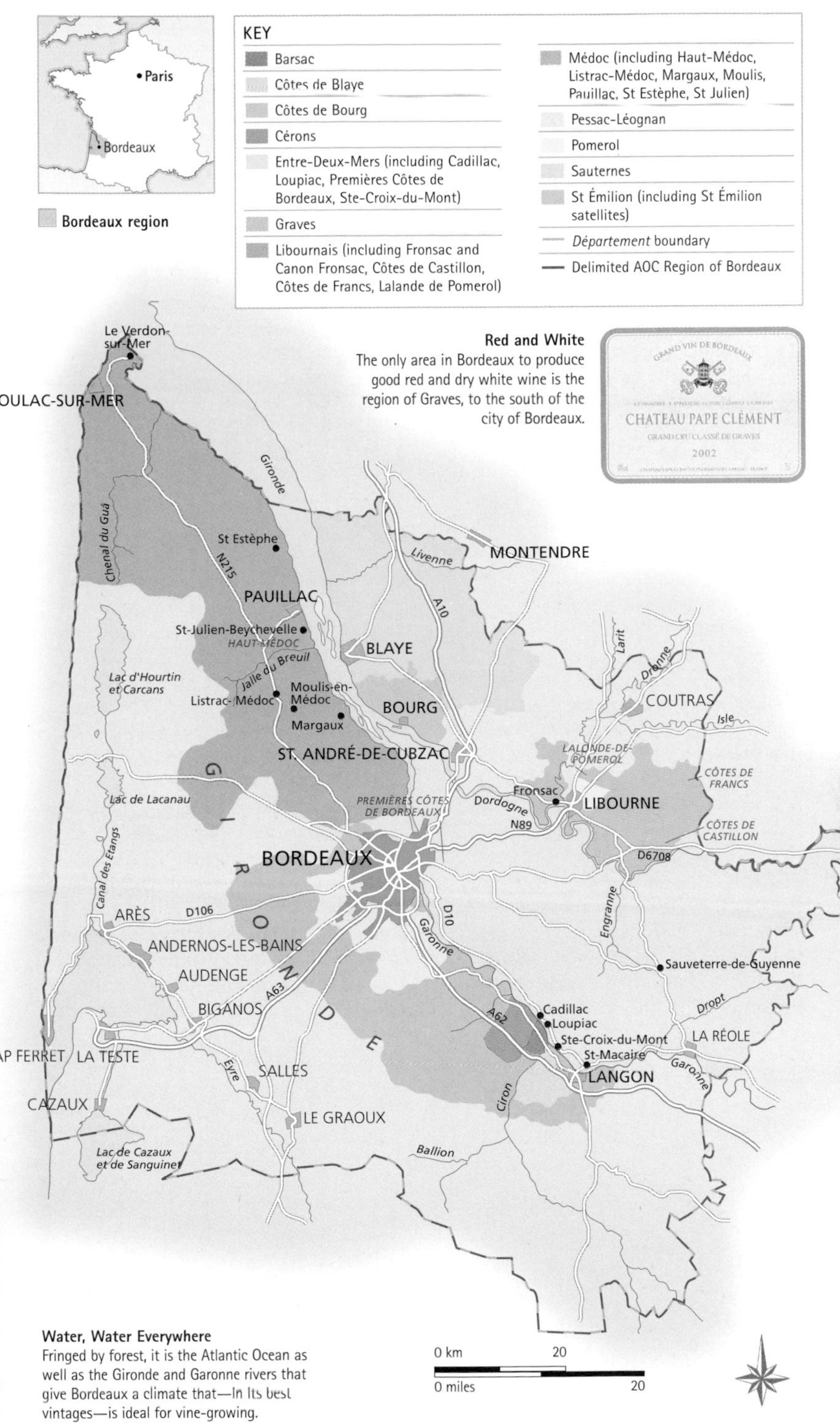

Red and White
The only area in Bordeaux to produce good red and dry white wine is the region of Graves, to the south of the city of Bordeaux.

Water, Water Everywhere
Fringed by forest, it is the Atlantic Ocean as well as the Gironde and Garonne rivers that give Bordeaux a climate that—in its best vintages—is ideal for vine-growing.

The History of Bordeaux

It was only with the 12th-century marriage between the duchess Eleanor of Aquitaine and the Norman Henry Plantagenet, heir to the throne of England, that the wine-producing history of Bordeaux really began in earnest. This alliance not only provided an instant market for the wines of Aquitaine, it also secured a crucial role for the city of Bordeaux as a port.

While the wine industry in most parts of France was developed by what the wine historian Hanneke Wirtjes describes as "patient monks," in Bordeaux, wine production was driven by merchants looking for products with which to fill the holds of their trading ships. Bordeaux was a medieval version of today's Hong Kong, and just as the clever businessmen of that island prefer to export clothes rather than cotton, the canny Bordelais soon learned to make money by exporting their wines rather than their grapes.

The Royal Seal
Norman duke Henry Plantagenet became King of England in 1154.

By the early 14th century, nearly half of all the wine passing through the port of Bordeaux was being exported to the British Isles. Much of it was made in the area known as the Haut Pays, to the east of the modern *appellation* of Bordeaux, in regions such as Bergerac *(see p270)* and Gaillac *(see p272)*. Realizing the commercial threat posed by these neighbors, the merchants and producers of Bordeaux were quick to ban the importation of their wines into the city until after November 11, St. Martin's Day, by which time the new vintage of their own wines was safely shipped. It was this same Bordelais trading mentality that helped to create the first branded wines—that is, wines sold under the name of a single château, rather than under the name of the village in which the grapes were grown. When the English diarist Samuel Pepys broke his vow to give up wine on April 10, 1663, it was with "a sort of French wine, called Ho Bryan."

Château Haut-Brion, in what is now the *appellation* of Pessac-Léognan *(see p102)*, enjoys the unusual distinction of naturally well-drained soil. Until the 16th century, however, most of the Médoc *(see p99)* was swampy woodland, unsuitable for vines. Estates on slightly higher land, such as Château Margaux and Château Lafite, began to make wine

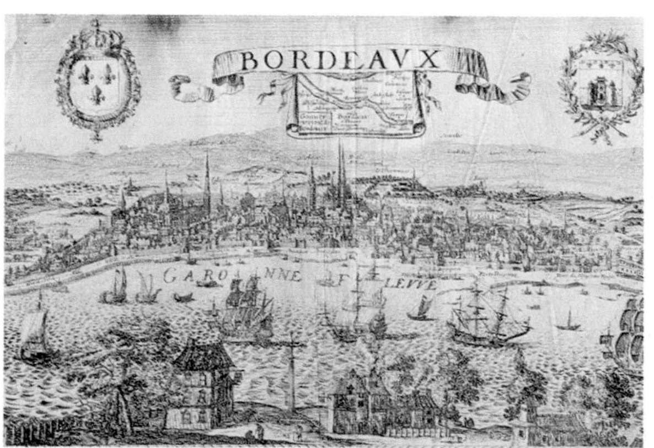

The Port of Bordeaux
As this engraving shows, by the 17th century the busy Garonne River was at the heart of the fast-developing Bordeaux wine trade.

in the late 17th century. The further development of the vineyards of the Médoc was made possible around this time by skilled Dutch engineers, who installed the drainage ditches that can still be seen today close to châteaux like Beychevelle, and paved the way for the planting of vines in rows that could be worked with an ox-drawn plow.

THE MODERN APPELLATION

By the 18th century, much of the wine from the vineyards around the port of Bordeaux was passing through the hands of an increasing number of English, Irish, Dutch, German, and Danish merchants. Between them they developed a lucrative and well-organized wine trade that survived the Revolution of 1789, and of which important elements still exist today. Perhaps the most enduring legacy of these merchants is their classification of the region's wines by price, known today simply as "The Classification." Commissioned by the Bordeaux Chamber of Commerce to help with the presentation of the wines of Bordeaux at the 1855 *Exposition Universelle* in Paris, the list includes the best estates of the Médoc and Sauternes *(see p110)*, and Château Haut-Brion in Pessac-Léognan. Though taken decreasingly seriously, the 1855 Classification is still in use today.

Since 1945, with the end of World War II, four figures in particular have shaped the *appellation* of Bordeaux as we know it today. The first is the late Philippe de Rothschild, owner of Château Mouton-Rothschild in Pauillac *(see pp100–101)*. Rothschild was one of the first wine-makers to champion the idea of bottling his own wines, rather than selling them young and leaving the task of maturing to the wine merchants. An inspired marketer, Rothschild used the name of his château to sell a mundane wine, produced from grapes grown elsewhere, which he called Mouton Cadet. The tactic proved such a success that, in spite of its mediocrity, Mouton Cadet is now as well known as any Bordeaux wine. A second instrumental figure is Professor Émile Peynaud, celebrated as the father of modern oenology. Of Peynaud's many great contributions, the most outstanding lies in spelling out the pitfalls of mishandling grapes and wine, and in the revival and popularization of the practice of separating the very best wine of the vintage from the rest, and selling the contents of the lesser vats as "second wine." Peynaud's natural successor is a consultant named Michel Rolland, who is credited with, or blamed for, the recent move toward riper and sometimes super-ripe-tasting wines, and the success of the tiny "garage" wineries that produce them. Last but not least, there is the American critic Robert Parker, whose newsletter *Wine Advocate*, launched at the end of the 1970s, used a 50–100 point scale to grade individual wines. Without Parker's enormously popular point system, many previously little-known Bordeaux estates would not enjoy the international prestige or command the high prices that they do today.

Samuel Pepys
In 1663, the famous London diarist Samuel Pepys drank a bottle of wine from Château Haut-Brion in the Médoc district of Bordeaux. This is the first reference in English to a wine made from the grapes of a single estate.

A Driving Tour of Bordeaux

Unlike Burgundy, where the wine villages are often separated only by a narrow track, the villages of Bordeaux, in general, and the Médoc, in particular, are more widely dispersed. This tour takes in all of the main appellations *of the Médoc, as well as some that are less well known.*

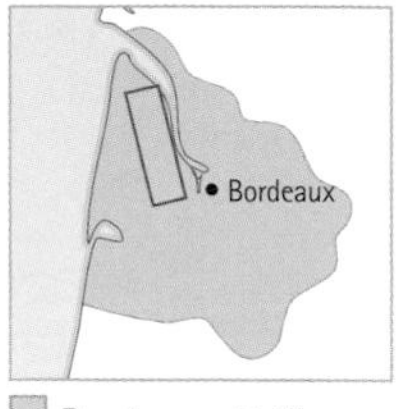

BORDEAUX

You could spend several days visiting the city of Bordeaux ①, with its art galleries, museums, and wine shops. Whatever else you do, though, make sure you go to the Maison du Vin de Bordeaux to arm yourself with informative leaflets produced by the region's various vinous associations.

Upper Class
Owned by the Champagne house of Ayala, La Lagune is one of the few classed châteaux in the Haut-Médoc.

BORDEAUX TO MARGAUX

The first stretch of the road north to the Médoc is of little vinous interest until you get to Ludon-Médoc ②, where you pass Château la Lagune, one of the few Médoc classed estates that lie outside the *appellations* of Margaux, St Julien, Pauillac, and St Estèphe. The unclassed Château Cantemerle is also here, as well as the good-value Château Maucamps. In Macau ③, turn right for a brief detour down to the banks of the Gironde, where you will find a couple of cafés and an atmosphere reminiscent of the riverside excursions portrayed by the French Impressionists.

The *appellation* of Margaux begins some distance to the south of the village from which it takes its name. As you pass through Labarde ④, you are already north of Château Giscours, one of the best-known Margaux estates. I'd recommend stopping at Château Prieuré Lichine, a little farther up the road in Cantenac ⑤. This is one of the estates most geared to welcoming visitors and offers a display of old iron firebacks and a collection of books by the man who created the estate, the Russian-American wine merchant and author Alexis Lichine. At Issan ⑥, soon after passing the towers of Château Palmer, you can make another detour to the moated, 16th-century Château Issan. Down the road is Château Rauzan Ségla, a rising star whose vineyards and wines are benefiting from heavy investment. At Margaux ⑦, at the end of an avenue of plane trees, Château Margaux stands behind impressive gates. You can stand on the spot where Thomas Jefferson must have stood around 200 years ago to admire its classical facade.

LAMARQUE AND ST JULIEN-BEYCHEVELLE

If Château Margaux reminds you of 18th-century gentlemen, the château at Lamarque ⑧ is the kind of fortress that evokes images of knights in armor. Fort Médoc, past Lamarque and not far from battlements that were built in the 17th century to ward off the English, is worth a pause. St Julien-Beychevelle ⑨ offers a wealth of grand châteaux, with Beychevelle being the first you will encounter. Also worth a look are Château Ducru Beaucaillou and the three Léoville châteaux—Barton, Poyferré and Lascases—the last of which boasts an imperious stone gateway that you pass as you leave the village.

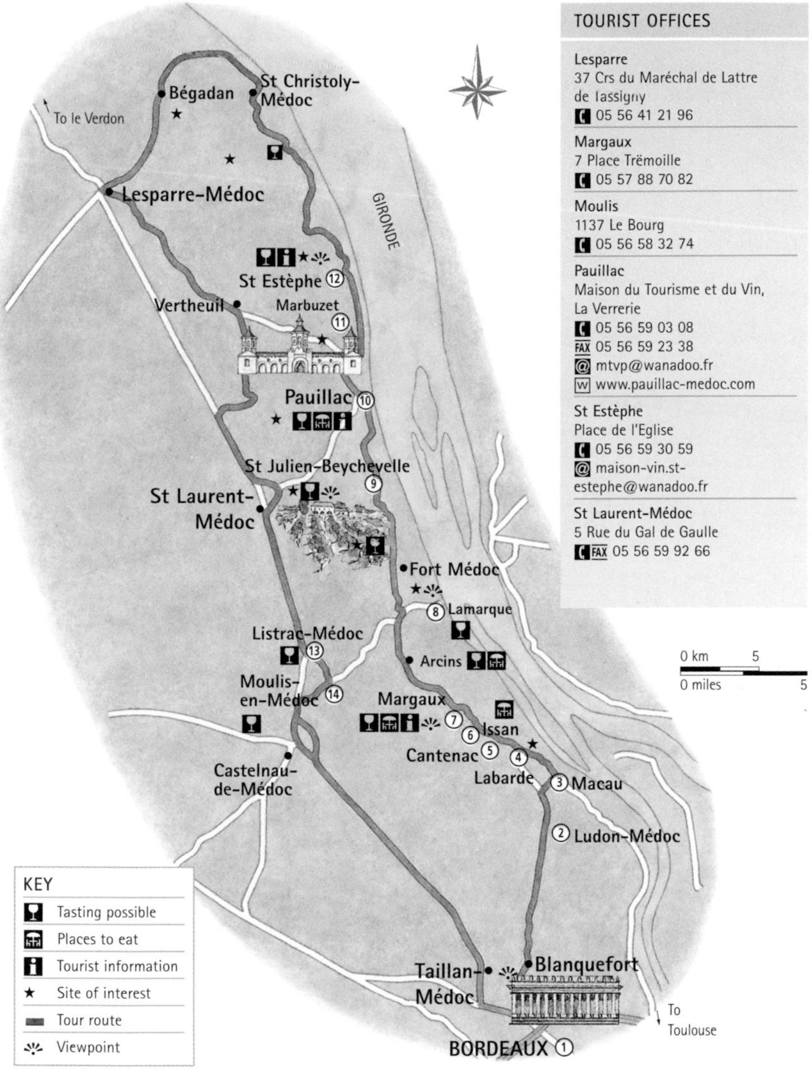

TOURIST OFFICES

Lesparre
37 Crs du Maréchal de Lattre de Tassigny
☎ 05 56 41 21 96

Margaux
7 Place Trëmoille
☎ 05 57 88 70 82

Moulis
1137 Le Bourg
☎ 05 56 58 32 74

Pauillac
Maison du Tourisme et du Vin, La Verrerie
☎ 05 56 59 03 08
FAX 05 56 59 23 38
@ mtvp@wanadoo.fr
W www.pauillac-medoc.com

St Estèphe
Place de l'Eglise
☎ 05 56 59 30 59
@ maison-vin.st-estephe@wanadoo.fr

St Laurent-Médoc
5 Rue du Gal de Gaulle
☎ FAX 05 56 59 92 66

KEY

- Tasting possible
- Places to eat
- Tourist information
- ★ Site of interest
- Tour route
- Viewpoint

PAUILLAC TO ST ESTÈPHE

On entering the *appellation* of Pauillac, you will see the rival châteaux of Pichon-Longueville Baron and Pichon-Longueville-Comtesse-de-Lalande, the former proudly showing off its modern extension. To your right is Château Latour's tower and, a little farther on to your left, before you head into the quiet town of Pauillac ⑩, lies Château Lynch-Bages. The road heads north, passing Châteaux Mouton-Rothschild and Lafite-Rothschild before leading you to the oriental facade of Château Cos d'Estournel. The road beside the château goes past Marbuzet ⑪ and on to St Estèphe ⑫.

LISTRAC-MÉDOC AND MOULIS-EN-MÉDOC

On your way back south, pause in Listrac-Médoc ⑬, where producers like Châteaux Clarke and Fonréaud are now trying to make softer reds than in the past, and in Moulis-en-Médoc ⑭, where Châteaux Poujeaux, Maucaillou, and Chasse-Spleen all offer good-value wines.

The Food of Bordeaux

This region is renowned for producing some of the world's greatest red and sweet white wines, and its name is often featured on restaurant menus in the form of the Bordelaise wine sauce that is traditionally served with entrecôte steak. However, as visitors to Bordeaux soon discover, many other dishes are also enjoyed in this region, which encompasses fields, rivers and the sea.

Mushrooms
Cèpe (cep) mushrooms are served in stews and casseroles with a variety of meats or poultry, or on their own with chopped garlic and parsley. Rich black truffles are often enjoyed with Sauternes.

I once attended a competition to find the best *sommelier* in the world, in which an entrant lost marks for failing to propose Pauillac as the ideal partner for lamb. While Mouton Rothschild has nothing to do with mutton or lamb (the "mouton" in fact refers to a small hill), there is no question that the milk-fed lambs of this part of the Médoc produce some of the most tender and tastiest meat.

It is increasingly acknowledged that beef and Bordeaux are rarely an ideal match, as the meat can make a tannic wine seem tough—but the Bordelaise sauce, made with red wine and marrow-bone, undeniably complements a steak. Even so, if I had to recommend a local dish to enjoy with a bottle of Médoc or Graves, I'd opt for grilled wood pigeon sautéed *à la bordelaise,* with artichokes, onions, and potatoes, and flambéed with fine Bordeaux brandy. Alternatively, I might choose a *confit d'oie* (preserved goose), possibly with a sorrel purée.

Pauillac Lamb à la Persillade
The finest milk-fed baby lamb comes from the region of Pauillac. It is best as a rack of lamb cooked with a thick parsley crust and served as chops.

Just as the Burgundians surprise visitors by poaching trout in red wine, chefs in Bordeaux use red wine to cook lampreys, the river fish that, like baby eels, are a delicacy fished in huge nets from the banks of the Gironde River. At one time, there was an industry for Gironde caviar, but sturgeon haven't been seen in the river for at least 10 years. Another treat, rarely associated with Bordeaux, are *cèpes,* the brown-capped, fat-stemmed wild mushrooms that are sold at the roadside and prepared *à la viande* with garlic, ham, parsley, and breadcrumbs. Local truffles are also relished in the form of a ragout stew with red wine, ham, leeks, carrots, celery, and onions. Like the truffles, now brought in from farther inland, *foie gras* is also enjoyed here as a perfect partner for a glass of Sauternes.

The wines of Bordeaux are inevitably used to make a number of desserts, such as *granité*, a sherbet made with red wine, or with a sweet white such as Sauternes or Cérons. For those who prefer simple desserts, there are *poires au St Émilion*, pears poached in red wine with orange juice and cinnamon.

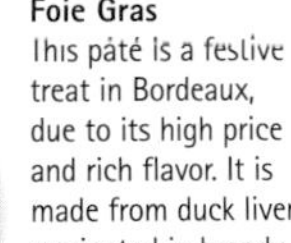

Foie Gras
This pâté is a festive treat in Bordeaux, due to its high price and rich flavor. It is made from duck liver marinated in brandy and served with Sauternes wine.

Oysters
Both wild and cultivated oysters are available in Bordeaux. They are usually eaten raw with bread and lemon juice and served with dry white Bordeaux.

REGIONAL CHEESES

Cheeses are produced throughout France, wherever there are cows, sheep or goats. The farmers of Bordeaux, however, have been too busy tending vines to develop a reputation for the quality of their cheeses. Most of the cheese you will see at the markets and in restaurants is likely to have come from the neighboring regions of the southwest. Périgord, Limousin, and Quercy continue to produce great cheeses, including the wonderful goat's milk Cabécou and Rocamadour, and Limousin's delicious Fourmes, made from ewe's milk.

Abbaye de Belloc
Actually produced in the Pays Basque, this cheese is made from the milk of red-nosed Manech ewes. It has a strong, lingering, well-cooked flavor.

Tomme de Chèvre Fermier
Variations of this salty goat's cheese can be found all over France. Often produced in the southwest, it is enjoyed by many in Bordeaux.

TRAVELING IN BORDEAUX

Despite its international fame and the numbers of tourists who visit every year, Bordeaux has been less geared up for visitors than many other wine regions. Although large numbers of new hotels, restaurants, and wine shops are now springing up with every season, many of Bordeaux's secrets still need to be sought out.

HOTELS & RESTAURANTS

The region's best establishments offer first-class food and wine, and notable places to stay.

ARCINS, NEAR MARGAUX

Le Lion d'Or, Place de la République.
05 56 58 96 79
A favorite with local producers and visiting merchants. Great rustic fare and delicious cep dishes in season. Ask nicely and M Barbier may let you bring your own, though this is a concession usually restricted to regulars.

BORDEAUX

Hôtel des Quatre Soeurs, 6 Cours du 30 Juillet.
05 57 81 19 20
This quirky, inexpensive little hotel in the city center was once popular with Wagner as a place to entertain his mistress. It has no restaurant of its own, but sits above a bustling café and close to a wide range of good eateries.

La Maison Bordeaux, 113 Rue du Docteur-Albert-Barraud.
05 56 44 00 45
A newly converted 17th-century house belonging to Brigitte Lurton, whose family owns some of the region's top estates. Cozily luxurious, it also has a restaurant offering some really fine cooking.

La Tupina, 6 Rue de la Monnaie.
05 56 91 56 37
Offers some of the best-value cuisine in Bordeaux, as well as some very well-priced wines. Roasted meats are a specialty.

BOULIAC, NEAR BORDEAUX

Le Bistroy, 3 Place Camille-Hostein.
05 57 97 06 06
Next to the luxurious St James Hotel, and under the same ownership, this bistro offers fine cooking in a casual atmosphere, at more affordable prices.

LANGON

Claude Darroze, 95 Cours du Général Leclerc
05 56 63 00 48
In a small town in Bordeaux's southwest, close to Sauternes, this is a country inn of the kind rarely found outside France. The food is of star quality and there is plenty of good-value local wine. The trompe-l'oeil decor is something of an acquired taste.

Casual Dining in Bordeaux
Even the least formal of Bordeaux's many restaurants, wine bars, and cafes offer the chance to sample good wines that are hard to find elsewhere.

PAUILLAC

Château Cordeillan Bages, Route des Châteaux.
05 56 59 24 24
Under the same ownership as nearby Château Lynch-Bages, this luxurious converted chateau makes an ideal base for exploring the northern Médoc. The ad-hoc wine school here offers tailor-made courses, and the resident sommeliers are always happy to test and expand your knowledge by serving mystery wines for you to attempt to identify.

ST ÉMILION

Hôtel au Logis des Remparts, Rue Guadet.
05 57 24 70 43
FAX 05 57 74 47 44
@ logis-des-remparts@saint-emilion.org
This is a lovely old building in the heart of St Émilion, with terraces, gardens and a swimming pool that you can retreat to after bustling through streets that are often overly full of tourists.

WINE SHOPS

While smaller chateaux are often happy to sell wine to visitors, most larger ones prefer to deal only with merchants. This makes a visit to Bordeaux's wine shops essential. Most ship overseas, but prices can be high. The following shops, in particular, are worth knowing about.

ARCACHON

Vintage International, Marché Municipal.
05 56 22 59 98
Based in the region's seaside resort, this retailer has a range of 500 Bordeaux wines dating back to 1898.

BORDEAUX
Badie, 62 Allée de Tourny.
FAX 05 56 52 23 72
Badie is over a century old and stocks more than 2,000 different wines and spirits.
l'Intendant, 2 Allées de Tourny.
05 56 48 01 29
This shop keeps its 15,000 bottles stacked around a spiral staircase.

STE FOY LA GRANDE
Cave Larégnère, 10 Boulevard Garrau.
05 57 46 31 23
FAX 05 57 46 36 42
A finalist in the competition for best wine retailer in the world, Michel Baraton has a range of 2,000 wines.

MUSEUMS

Some producers offer vineyard or winery tours. Contact tourist offices *(see below)* for details.

BORDEAUX
Musée des Vins, 41 Rue Borie.
05 57 87 50 60
FAX 05 57 87 50
Situated in a former merchant's house in the heart of the old wine-trading area, this museum illustrates the role of foreigners in the history of Bordeaux.
Musée le Vinorama, 10 Cours du Médoc.
05 56 39 39 20
FAX 05 56 39 19 51
This fascinating place traces the region's history from Roman times to the present and allows visitors to compare a wine made using Roman methods with one produced the 19th-century way.

GRADIGNAN
Ecomusée de la Vigne et du Vin, 238 Cours du Général de Gaulle.
FAX 05 56 89 00 79
A place to find over 500 old wine-maker's tools in the kind of house he would have lived in.

LANGON
Le Musée de l'Etiquette, Chateau de Mauriac.
05 56 63 39 81
Everything you ever wanted to know about labels.

ANNUAL WINE EVENTS

The city of Bordeaux hosts the biennial Vinexpo trade fair in June of odd-numbered years. This is only open to professionals, but there is a wide range of other events that will keep you amused whatever your expertise.

JANUARY
Médoc Fete of St. Vincent

APRIL
En primeur futures tastings for professionals, run by the Union des Grands Crus (union-grands-crus@vins-bordeaux.fr) and local merchants.
Bordeaux et Bordeaux Superieur "Happy Hour"
Medoc and **Lalande de Pomerol** open cellars

MAY
St Émilion and **Côtes de Bourg** open cellars
Puisseguin-St Émilion wine rally

JUNE
Satellites de St Émilion spring fair
Premier Côtes de Bordeaux and **Cadillac** open doors
Médoc Château Mouton-Rothschild Fête des Fleurs (flower festival)

JULY
Pomerol wine fair

SEPTEMBER
Castillon la Bataille, **Bordeaux** and **Bordeaux Supérieur** wine fairs
Médoc Marathon du Médoc

OCTOBER
Graves, **Fronsac/Canon Fronsac**, **St Émilion Satellites** and **Cérons** wine fairs

NOVEMBER
Loupiac wine fair

DECEMBER
Pessac-Léognan wine fair

MOULIS
Musée des Arts et Métiers de la Vigne et du Vin, Château de Maucaillou.
05 56 58 01 23
FAX 05 56 58 00 88
A complete introduction to wine-growing and making, including a piece of apparatus that lets you sample different wine aromas.

PAUILLAC
Musée Privé du Vin dans l'Art, Chateau Mouton-Rothschild.
05 56 73 21 29
The late Baron Philippe's creation, this fine international collection spans 3,000 years of wine-related art and artifacts.

WEBSITES

The official website at www.bordeaux.com is a good starting point. For more information, try www.bordeaux-news.com, or find specifics on the Bordeaux and Bordeaux Supérieur *appellations* at www.maisondesbordeaux.com. Many châteaux and merchants also have their own sites—go to www.robertjoseph-onwine.com for links. You can also find details on any town or village in the region at www.tourisme.fr.

OTHER INFORMATION

Bordeaux Maison du Vin and **Office du Tourisme**, 1 Cours du 30 Juillet.
05 56 00 22 66
www.bordeaux-tourisme.com
This main center in the city of Bordeaux is the best source of information, maps, and leaflets on wine and other activities in the entire region. There are smaller Maisons du Vin in most *appellation* towns, as well as plenty of local tourist offices.

BARSAC

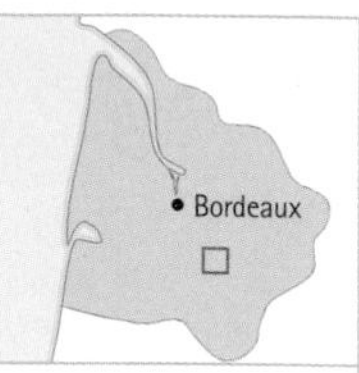

SITUATED ON THE LEFT bank of the Garonne and separated from the larger *appellation* of Sauternes *(see p110)* to the north by the little Ciron River, the *commune* of Barsac is entitled to sell its wines either as *appellation contrôlée* Barsac or as *appellation contrôlée* Sauternes *(see below)*. The Ciron is crucial to the microclimate of the area. It is the autumnal morning mists lingering over its cool water, followed by warm, sunny afternoons, that combine to create ideal conditions for the development of *Botrytis cinerea*, or noble rot, which produces the unique sweet wines of Barsac. Richer in sandstone and limestone than neighboring Sauternes, the flat land here produces wines with a natural lightness that sets them apart from all others. As a rule, wines sold as *appellation contrôlée* Barsac are more reliable than those sold as *appellation contrôlée* Sauternes.

Château Climens
Les Cypres is the "second wine" of Château Climens—almost as stylish as its big brother, the "*grand vin*" of this top estate.

Magical Mist
The famous mist, seen here around the vineyards of Château Myrat, is crucial to the development of the noble rot that makes these wines so special.

- AC Sauternes, AC Barsac.
- White: Sémillon, Sauvignon Blanc, Muscadelle.
- Elegant, lusciously sweet, white dessert wines.
- Ch Broustet, Caillou, Cantegril, Climens, Coutet, Doisy-Daëne, Doisy-Dubroca, Doisy-Védriens, Gravas, Liot, Myrat, Nairac, Piada, de Rolland, Suau.
- Warm duck's liver with grapes.
- 2003, 2002, 2001, 1999, 1997, 1996, 1995, 1990, 1989, 1988, 1983, 1976.
- 5–20 years.

BARSAC AND THE COMMUNES OF SAUTERNES

A strangely incestuous relationship exists between the neighboring *appellations* of Sauternes and Barsac, producers of the two most famous sweet wines in Bordeaux. Since the introduction of the *appellation contrôlée* system in the 1930s, producers in Barsac have been entitled to label their bottles with either the name of their own *appellation* or that of Sauternes, an indulgence denied to the Sauternais. Alternatively, the *vignerons* of Barsac can signify their double allegiance by using the increasingly popular name of Sauternes-Barsac. The heterogeneous Sauternes *appellation* itself currently covers the four *communes* of Bommes, Fargues, Preignac, and Sauternes, producing sweet wines whose quality ranges from the dire to the sublime. I suspect, however, that as more people throughout the world begin to appreciate truly great sweet wines, as well as the painstaking skill involved in their production, the wine-makers of Barsac, together with those of Bommes, Fargues and Preignac, will be eager to emphasize their own names. If sections of Minervois *(see p199)*, which received its own classification in 1985, are now allowed their own individual *appellations*, it seems a shame that the same kind of recognition should be denied to the *communes* listed above.

Natural Star
The village of Barsac may be as quiet and remote as ever, but its wines have made it famous all over the world.

BORDEAUX

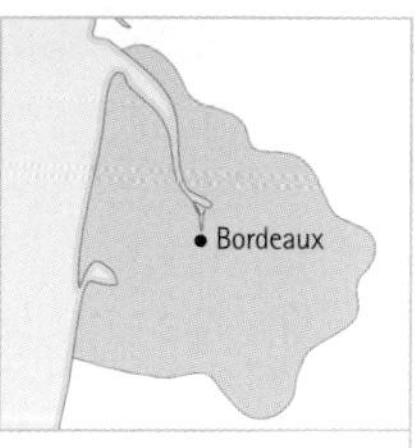

COVERING 247,000 ACRES (100,000 ha) of vineyards, the generic Bordeaux classifications listed below are used to label a quarter of all the *appellation contrôlée* wines of France. Applied to a range of wines that come from different soils and microclimates and are made with varying skills, this is one of the most successful, but unreliable, wine names in the world.

Caught by the Rules
Producer of some of the best sweet white wines in the world, Château d'Yquem *(see p110)* is forced by *appellation* rules to sell its fine dry white wines as plain *appellation contrôlée* Bordeaux.

If the marketing gurus responsible for promoting the wines of the region have got it right, the word "Bordeaux" will set you thinking of near-naked or elegantly dressed couples, and bow-ties. These, after all, are the images they have expensively splashed across the pages of glossy magazines. For most people, Bordeaux is inexorably linked to its wealth of great châteaux. The success of Mouton-Cadet, after all, owes much to the erroneous belief that it somehow offers an affordable taste of Château Mouton-Rothschild. Comparison of any vintage of these two wines, however, demonstrates the problem facing anyone trying to make and sell wines under the generic Bordeaux *appellations*. In Pauillac *(see pp100–101)*, where Mouton-Rothschild is made, grapes ripen well, thanks to the position of the vineyards. This climatic advantage is the main reason why Pauillac and its châteaux have become famous. In the less favored Bordeaux vineyards, however, the fruit often fails to ripen properly, a problem exacerbated by rules encouraging over-production, and, as the grapes on thirsty vines simply stop ripening, by more rules banning any form of irrigation.

There are, of course, in humbler parts of the region, some ambitious châteaux that consistently produce good, plain *appellation contrôlée* Bordeaux, as well as Château d'Yquem in Sauternes *(see p110)* and Château Margaux in the Médoc *(see p99)*, which are forced by quirky *appellation* rules to sell their wonderful dry white wines as plain *appellation contrôlée* Bordeaux. These, however, are exceptions to the Bordeaux rule, and the quality of most branded, merchant-bottled wines remains disappointing. One way forward for the Bordeaux region lies in the proposed strengthening of current *appellation* rules and the introduction of new, more relaxed ones that would facilitate the production of humble wines of better quality.

- AC Bordeaux, AC Bordeaux Clairet, AC Bordeaux Sec, AC Bordeaux Rosé, AC Bordeaux Supérieur, AC Bordeaux Supérieur Clairet, AC Bordeaux Supérieur Rosé, AC Crémant de Bordeaux.
- Red/rosé: Cabernet Sauvignon, Cabernet Franc, Merlot, Malbec. White: Sémillon, Sauvignon.
- Medium- to full-bodied reds. Dry whites. Dry rosés. Sparkling whites.
- Barton et Guestier, Ch Bonnet, Dourthe Frères, Maître d'Estournel, Haut Bertinerie, Landereau, Michel Lynch, Tour de Mirambeau, la Raemn, Rauzan-Despagne, Reignac, Reynon, Sirius, Thieuley.
- White: Warm potato salad with mussels, celery, onions, and black truffles.
- Red: 2004, 2003, 2002, 2000.
- 2–5 years.

Château Thieuley
Selling wines as *appellation* Bordeaux, rather than under the Entre-deux-Mers label to which it is entitled, this memorable château is owned by Francis Courselle.

CADILLAC

STRETCHED ALONG the east bank of the Garonne, and centering around its namesake town, Cadillac has long been the poor relation of its neighbors, Loupiac to the south and Sainte Croix-du-Mont to the east. Despite the *appellation* rules that demand that wines be made from botrytized (nobly rotten) grapes, there is often little evidence that this has happened. Good examples, however, can be fine, as can reds made by estates here, sold as Premières Côtes de Bordeaux.

Jean du Roy
This wine combines the apricot flavor of noble rot with Barsac-like delicacy.

- AC Cadillac.
- White: Sémillon, Sauvignon Blanc, Muscadelle.
- Sweet whites, which may be made from partially botrytized grapes.
- Carsin, Cayla, Reynon, Jean du Roy, du Juge, Manos, Thieuley.
- Light fruit tart.
- 2003, 2002, 2001, 1999.
- White: 3–8 years.

CÔTES DE BLAYE

FIRST PLANTED BY THE ROMANS, grapes were grown in Blaye and neighboring Bourg long before the Médoc, on the opposite bank of the Gironde estuary. Despite a traditionally rustic character, Blaye's red wines are improving and can offer good value. They are sold either as AC Blaye (or AC Blayais) or as the higher-alcohol, but not always superior, Premières Côtes de Blaye. Around 10 percent of the wines are white, many sold under the white-only AC Côtes de Blaye label.

Château Haut Sociando
One of the best examples of the elegant "new wave" wines from Blaye.

- AC Blaye, AC Côtes de Blaye, AC Premières Côtes de Blaye.
- Red: Merlot, Cabernet Sauvignon. White: Sauvignon Blanc.
- Medium-bodied dry reds. Dry whites.
- Haut Sociando, Tourtes.
- Grilled lamb.
- Red: 2003, 2001, 2000.
- Red: 2–6 years.

CÔTES DE BOURG

SOMETIMES CALLED THE Switzerland of the Gironde because of its hilly vineyards, this small but heavily cultivated area produces more wine than the much larger Côtes de Blaye to the north. Despite similar soils, it is Bourg that has made the better red wines, and improving winemaking techniques are leading to a higher public profile and the production of wines that offer excellent value. Good use is being made of varieties such as Malbec and Petit Verdot, which play a lesser role elsewhere.

Château Falfas
Among the best wines in the *appellation*, Château Falfas offers rich, supple flavors.

- AC Côtes de Bourg.
- Red: Merlot, Cabernet Sauvignon.
- Medium-bodied reds.
- Brûlesécaille, Falfas, Fougas, Guerry, Les Jonquières, Maldoror, Repimplet, Roc de Cambes, Rousset, Tayac.
- Chicken with mushrooms.
- 2003, 2001, 1998.
- Red: 4–8 years.

CÔTES DE CASTILLON

THIS IS THE MOST easterly *appellation* of the Libournais on the north bank of the Dordogne. Both Merlot and Cabernet Franc are grown here on a mixture of gravel, sand, and clay, producing supple, fruity wines that very often outclass those of the Côtes de Castillon's pricier neighbor, St Émilion *(see p105)*. Two-thirds of wine production has long been controlled by members of the *Coopérative de Castillon*, but investment in the area has produced a number of promising new châteaux.

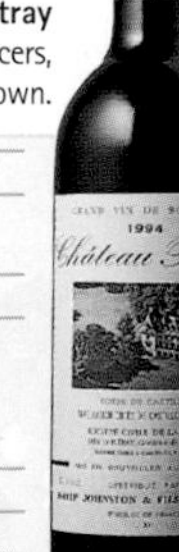

Château Pitray
One of this *appellation*'s stronger producers, whose wines are worth laying down.

- AC Côtes de Castillon.
- Red: Merlot, Cabernet Franc, Cabernet Sauvignon.
- Sturdy, dry reds.
- Belcier, Cap de Faugères, Grand Tuillac, Grande Maye, Lapeyronie, Pitray, Poupille, Robin, Vieux Château Champ de Mars.
- Duck breast.
- 2003, 2001, 2000.
- Red: 2–6 years.

CÔTES DE FRANCS

ALSO KNOWN AS Bordeaux Côtes de Francs, this revived *appellation* lies on the eastern edge of the Libournais, next to the Côtes de Castillon *(see p94)* and not far from St Émilion *(see p105)*. The soil here is similar to that of Castillon, but with more limestone and a higher altitude, which, together with the lowest rainfall and the most sunshine in the *département*, helps to produce wines of great finesse. Top producers now include the Thienponts of Château Puygueraud.

Château la Prade
This château makes a fine, black-curranty example of the *appellation*.

- AC Côtes de Francs, AC Côtes de Francs Liquoreux.
- Merlot, Cabernet Franc, Cabernet Sauvignon.
- Supple, plump, full-flavored reds.
- Charmes-Godard, de Francs, Laclaverie, la Prade, Puygueraud.
- Kidneys with cognac.
- 2003, 2001, 2000, 1998.
- Red: 3–7 years.

ENTRE-DEUX-MERS

THIS AREA PRODUCES more dry white wines than any other *appellation* in Bordeaux apart from the generic AC Bordeaux Blanc. Some reds are made and sold as AC Bordeaux or AC Bordeaux Supérieur, but the emphasis is firmly on white. Although average wine quality is now improving thanks to better equipment and better wine-making techniques in the *coopératives*, this is a far from ideal place to grow vines, and really good wines are the exception rather than the rule.

Château Bonnet
Fresh, flavorsome proof of the quality that can be produced here.

- AC Entre-Deux-Mers, AC Entre-Deux-Mers-Haut-Benauge, AC Bordeaux-Haut-Benauge.
- Sauvignon Blanc, Sémillon, Muscadelle, Ugni Blanc.
- Dry white.
- Bonnet, la Lezardière, Ste-Marie, Thieuley.
- Grilled trout.
- 2004, 2003, 2002.
- 1–3 years.

FRONSAC AND CANON-FRONSAC

Bordeaux

THROUGHOUT THE 18th and 19th centuries, the vineyards of Fronsac and Canon-Fronsac, to the west of the town of Libourne, were better known than those of nearby Pomerol *(see p103)*. They are now once again producing wines to rival those of their neighbor. The land of Canon-Fronsac, the traditional vine-growing heart of the area, is a large bluff formed by the Dordogne, which protects the vines against frost. Much of the soil in both Fronsac and Canon-Fronsac is clay-limestone over a limestone subsoil, similar to that found on the St Christophe plateau in St Émilion *(see p105)*. Merlot is the most widely planted grape, and these wines, far better made than in the past, combine Merlot's full-bodied richness with good, firm structure.

Château la Dauphine
Good Fronsac like this offers plummy, mineral flavors that are very similar to classy—and quite pricey—St Émilion.

Fronsac
The size of the church in Fronsac reveals the prosperity and importance once enjoyed by this *commune*, long before the Médoc began to gain international prestige.

- AC Fronsac, AC Canon-Fronsac.
- Red: Merlot, Cabernet Franc, Cabernet Sauvignon.
- Deep-colored reds with a powerful bouquet.
- *Fronsac:* Dalem, la Dauphine, la Fleur Cailleau, Fontenil, Moulin Haut Laroque, la Rivière, la Rouselle, la Vielle Cure Villars. *Canon-Fronsac*: Barrabaque, Canon de Brem, Canon-Moueix, Moulin-Pey-Labrie, Cassagne Haut-Canon.
- Goose breast.
- 2003, 2001, 2000, 1998.
- Red: 5–8 years.

GRAVES

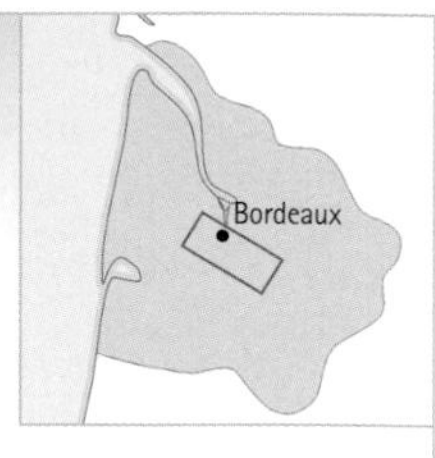

ONE OF THE GREAT WINE NAMES, and traditionally the only region in Bordeaux to make both top-quality reds and whites, Graves suffered the indignity in 1987 of losing all its best châteaux and land to the new *appellation* of Pessac-Léognan *(see p102)*. The Graves that remains is a part of Bordeaux whose wines have a style and quality of their own.

Villa Bel Air
Owner since 1990 of the Villa Bel Air estate, Jean-Michel Cazes applies the same level of care to the reds and whites here as he does to the wines of Château Lynch-Bages in Pauillac *(see pp100–101)*.

The Graves region has been shrinking for a very long time. Before the arrival of phylloxera, its vines covered some 25,000 acres (10,000 ha), compared with less than 7,500 acres (3,000 ha) today. Some of the land simply was not replanted; other land, close to the city, was lost to suburban housing and Bordeaux's Mérignac airport.

Despite this, until 1987 the Graves *appellation* extended for nearly 40 miles (60 km) southward from Bordeaux and included châteaux such as Haut-Brion.

Domaine la Grave
Although relatively little-known, this is a modern estate whose wines are remarkably reliable.

The Pessac-Léognan *appellation* took this and all the other classed growths, leaving a rump with a prestigious name but few distinguished wines.

Historically, reds have been less common than whites. As recent as 1961, the volume of white wine produced was four times that of red, but as tastes grew more sophisticated there was a switch from sweet to dry white, and from white to red. Today, for every bottle of white, there are two of red. Graves *rouge* can be an attractive, sometimes long-lived, black-curranty wine, though it often lacks the richness of flavor sought by Anglo-Saxons.

The whites are trickier. If the sweet "ladies' wines" made here in the 19th and early 20th centuries were poor, so were the dull and over-sulfured dry efforts of the 1960s and 1970s. Quality is now better, thanks to such producers as Denis Dubourdieu, who use specific yeasts that bring out the best flavors from the Sémillon and Sauvignon Blanc. The best white Graves, such as Villa Bel Air, can outclass a Pessac-Léognan.

Sweet white wine—of which 2.25 million often very ordinary bottles are produced annually—is sold, somewhat confusingly, as Graves Supérieur.

Château du Seuil
This British-owned estate produces one of the region's best dry white wines.

- AC Graves, AC Graves Supérieur.
- Red: Merlot, Cabernet Sauvignon.
  White: Sémillon, Sauvignon Blanc, Muscadelle.
- Medium- to full-bodied, supple, earthy, tobacco-scented reds. Medium- to full-bodied whites. Also sweet white Graves Supérieur.
- Ch d'Archambeau, d'Ardennes, de Cardaillan, de Chantegrive, Clos Floridène, la Grave, Landiras, Magneau, de Malle, Millet, Rahoul, Respide Médeville, Roquetaillade la Grange, St Robert, Tourteau-Chollet, Villa Bel Air.
- Medallions of veal.
- White: 2002, 2001, 2000.
  Red: 2003, 2002, 2001, 2000, 1998, 1996, 1995.
- Red: 7–20 years.
  White: 3–12 years.

HAUT-MÉDOC

THE SOUTHERN PART OF the Médoc includes Margaux *(see p98)*, Pauillac *(see pp100–101)*, and St Julien *(see p108)* whose wines are more usually sold under their own sub-*appellations*. There are also Haut-Médoc *crus classés* and *crus bourgeois*, such as Lagune, Beaumont, Cantemerle, Citran, Lanessan, Maucamps, and Sociando-Mallet, that do not have another *appellation*. Wines from vineyards closest to the Gironde have greater finesse, while those from the plateau are fuller-bodied.

Château Sociando-Mallet
This modern, fast-rising, oaky star often outclasses its far pricier neighbors.

- AC Haut-Médoc.
- Cabernet Sauvignon, Merlot, Cabernet Franc.
- Medium-bodied red.
- Ch Beaumont, Camensac, Cantemerle, Citran, la Lagune, Sociando-Mallet, Tour Carnet, Tour du Haut-Moulin.
- Rabbit casserole.
- 2003, 2002, 2001, 2000.
- 5–10 years.

LALANDE-DE-POMEROL

LYING NORTH of Pomerol *(see p103)*, this area consists of two *communes*: Néac and Lalande-de-Pomerol itself. It covers 2,250 acres (900 ha)—far more than Pomerol itself. In Lalande, the vineyards are low-lying, and situated on gravel and sand terraces. Some of those in Néac are on a high, south-facing plateau composed of very good gravel, like that of Pomerol across the Barbanne River. The best wines from this area are Merlot-dominant and compete with pricier Pomerol.

Château de Bel Air
One of the many Bel Airs, this offers Pomerol quality at an affordable price.

- AC Lalande-de-Pomerol.
- Merlot.
- Medium-bodied red.
- Ch de Bel Air, Belles-Graves, Croix-St-André, Grand Ormeau, Haut-Chatain, Siaurac, Tournefeuille, Trocard.
- Roast wild boar.
- 2003, 2001, 2000, 1998.
- 5–10 years.

LISTRAC-MÉDOC

TRADITIONALLY—but erroneously—treated as the partner of Moulis *(see p99)* to the south, Listrac covers some 1,750 acres (700 ha) of sloping, mainly clay-limestone vineyards, rising to about 1,200 ft (400 m)—among the highest in the Médoc. The wines here have tended to be tougher in style—more like St Estèphe *(see p107)* than the wines of Moulis or other *communes* of the Haut-Médoc. More recently, modern wine-making methods have helped to make for much richer flavors.

Château Fourcas Hosten
An example of the richer, more accessible moderrn wines of Listrac.

- AC Listrac-Médoc.
- Cabernet Sauvignon, Merlot, Cabernet Franc, Petit Verdot.
- Tannic, medium-bodied reds.
- Ch Clarke, Fonréaud, Fourcas-Dupré, Fourcas-Hosten.
- Roast guinea fowl.
- 2003, 2002, 2001, 2000.
- 6–10 years.

LOUPIAC

LOUPIAC LIES ON the right bank of the Garonne, opposite Barsac *(see p92)*. It is considered the best of a trio of dessert-wine-making *communes*, the other two being its neighbors Ste Croix-du-Mont *(see p109)* and Cadillac *(see p94)*. Its wines are relatively luscious, thanks to the use of botrytized grapes. While Loupiac may tend to be lighter than the best Sauternes *(see p110)* and Barsac, ambitious Loupiac producers are making wine that is better than many efforts sold under these other labels.

Domaine du Noble
An estate whose wines compete with all but the best efforts from *Sauternes.*

- AC Loupiac.
- Sémillon, Sauvignon Blanc, Muscadelle.
- Sweet whites—may be made partly from botrytized grapes.
- Clos-Jean, Ch du Cros, Loupiac-Gaudiet, Mazarin, du Noble, de Ricaud.
- *Tarte tatin* (an apple tart).
- 2003, 2002, 2001, 1999.
- Red: 5–15 years.

MARGAUX

THE ONLY *APPELLATION* IN Bordeaux to take its name from its finest estate, Margaux covers some of the most fascinatingly, and frustratingly, inconsistent wine-producing land in France. Growing in free-draining gravel soils, Cabernet Sauvignon grapes are used here to make wines that, at their best, show great finesse but, at their worst, are merely light and dull.

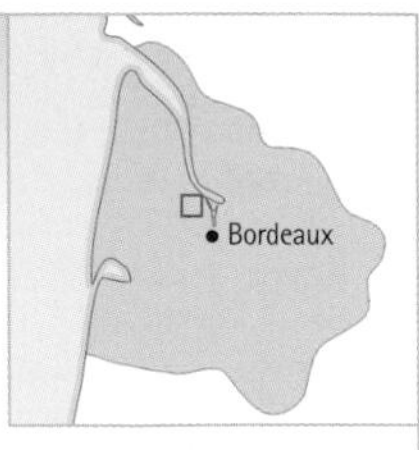

Dignified Splendor
Polished and fragrant, the red wines produced at the grand and dignified Château Margaux were appreciated by Thomas Jefferson and by Richard Nixon, who drank them at official banquets while serving guests lesser, cheaper fare.

While there is indeed a village called Margaux, whose surrounding vineyards include those of Château Margaux (the only estate in the *appellation* with the highest *premier grand cru classé* status), the *appellation* of Margaux also includes red wines made in four other villages: Soussans, Cantenac, Arsac, and Labarde. Although Bordeaux buffs like to discuss the various styles of wine produced in different parts of the *appellation*, the point of the exercise is undermined by the fact that many estates, including Margaux, make their wines from grapes grown in the vineyards of more than one *commune*.

Émile Peynaud *(see p85)*, credited with revolutionizing the quality of Bordeaux wines in general and those of Château Margaux in particular, raised a more pertinent question. How much, he wondered, of the much-vaunted lightness and delicacy for which the whole *appellation* is known is derived from the light, gravelly soil, and how much comes from the efforts of producers to make wines in a particular style? Brilliant wines made recently at Château Margaux, Château Palmer, and Château Rauzan-Ségla suggest that the answer may sometimes lie with the wine-maker and not with the soil, since these newer wines can combine perfume with an intensity of flavor more usually associated with wines from the nearby communes of Pauillac *(see pp100–101)* or St Julien *(see p108)*.

With the exceptions mentioned above, many of the wines made here leave one with the feeling of having watched a great actor on a bad day, a fact often blamed on excessive grape yields and on poor wine-making. While there is a lot of truth in this, I also suspect that, even on the best-equipped, most conscientious estates, it may be harder to consistently produce top-class wines here than in other *appellations* of the Médoc. When Jean-Michel Cazes bought Château Cantenac-Brown here, it took him far longer to achieve a marked improvement in its wines than it did at the châteaux he has acquired in other Bordeaux *appellations*.

- AC Margaux.
- Red: Cabernet Sauvignon, Merlot, Petit Verdot, Cabernet Franc.
- Medium- to full-bodied reds with a fragrant bouquet and relatively supple tannins.
- Ch d'Angludet, d'Arsac, Bel-Air-Marquis d'Aligre, Brane-Cantenac, Ch Cantenac-Brown, Dauzac, Desmirail, Durfort-Viviens, Ferrière, Giscours, la Gurgue, d'Issan, Kirwan, Labégorce, Labégorce-Zédé, Lascombes, Margaux, Marquis d'Alesme Becker, Marquis de Terme, Monbrison, Palmer, Paveil de Luze, Prieuré Lichine, Rauzan-Ségla, Siran, la Tour de Mons.
- Calves' sweetbreads.
- 2003, 2002, 2000, 1998, 1996, 1995, 1990, 1989, 1988, 1986, 1983, 1982, 1970, 1961.
- 5–25 years.

Château Palmer
Despite its lower rank in the 1855 Classification of Bordeaux, this beautiful chateau often manages to produce wines that are as fine as the best in the *appellation*.

MÉDOC

COVERING THE MOST important red wine-producing area in Bordeaux, the huge, district-wide *appellation* of Médoc stretches from Bordeaux city in the south to Soulac-sur-Mer in the north, bordered to the west by the Atlantic Ocean and to the east by the Gironde River. A separate Haut-Médoc *appellation (see p97)* for the southern half of the area, as well as six individual *commune* classifications, means that wines sold as *appellation* Médoc come mainly from the northern half of the region. A mixture of gravel, limestone, and sandy soils here makes for very varied wines, many of which have the underripe, overcropped character of wines sold as generic Bordeaux. Others, however, such as those produced at Château Potensac or Château la Tour de By, are as good as wines from much more prestigious Médoc *appellations* to the south.

Bordeaux

Château Rollan de By
Part of the important wine-producing *commune* of Bégadan, Jean Guyon makes red wines that are sturdy and satisfying.

Château la Cardonne
In the Médoc *commune* of Blaignan, this château is under the same ownership as Château Lafite-Rothschild in Pauillac.

- AC Médoc.
- Red: Cabernet Sauvignon, Merlot, Cabernet Franc, Malbec, Petit Verdot.
- Reds with firm tannins.
- Canteloup, la Cardonne, du Castéra, Greysac, Loudenne, Ormes-Sorbet, Patache d'Aux, Potensac, Rollan de By, Tour-Haut-Caussan, Tour St Bonnet.
- Entrecôte steak with a red wine and shallot sauce.
- 2003, 2002, 2000, 1998, 1996, 1995, 1990, 1989.
- 5–10 years.

MOULIS

ROLLING COUNTRYSIDE—1,235 acres (500 acres) of it—makes up the Médoc *appellation* of Moulis. One of two *appellations* situated on the Atlantic rather than the Gironde side of the district, Moulis has traditionally been considered, together with its neighbor Listrac *(see p97)*, to be a "must try harder" appellation. In fact, the velvety red wines of Moulis are quite different from the more structured wines of Listrac, with ripe fruit and a rich black-currant perfume. The soil here is clay, limestone, and gravel, which, taken together with variations in wine-making skill, makes for some very diverse wines. Many of the best come from vineyards around the village of Grand Poujeaux, where several fine estates, including Château Chasse-Spleen and Château Poujeaux, produce excellent, long-lived, oak-matured wines.

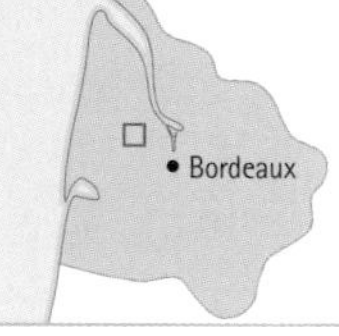

Château Poujeaux
This prestigious estate competes with Château Chasse-Spleen as the producer of the best wines of the *appellation.*

Château Chasse-Spleen
This is an ambitious estate producing superb wines that compete with those of nearby Margaux and help to create the modern reputation of Moulis.

- AC Moulis.
- Red: Cabernet Sauvignon, Merlot.
- Supple, full-bodied reds.
- Ch Bel-Air Lagrave, Biston-Brillette, Chasse-Spleen, Dutruch-Grand-Poujeaux, Gressier-Grand-Poujeaux, Maucaillou, Mauvezin, Moulin-à-Vent, Poujeaux.
- Veal brisket with chard.
- 2003, 2002, 2000, 1998, 1996, 1995, 1990, 1989, 1988, 1982.
- 8–12 years.

PAUILLAC

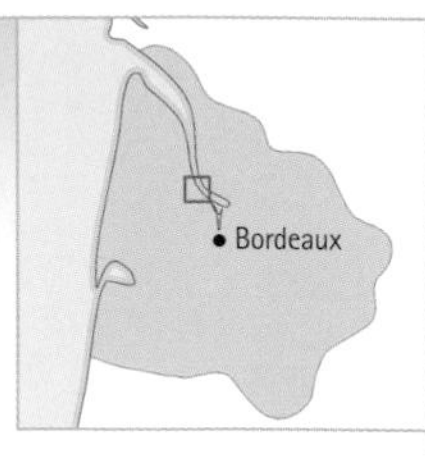

IF ONE HAD TO CHOOSE a vinous example of the Gallic expression *embarras de richesses*, it would have to be this *commune*, which boasts three of the five 1855 red *premiers crus* and nearly a third of all of the *crus classés* in the Médoc. The wines produced here are among the most immediately attractive and long-lived in the world.

Grand-Puy-Lacoste
The wine from this estate is popular with canny Bordeaux-lovers, who appreciate its elegant flavors and the fact that it is decidedly more affordable than many less impressive wines from neighboring châteaux.

The town of Pauillac has always struck me as having the atmosphere of a 19th-century vacation resort, with a river and a canal rather than the sea. There are terraced cafés, modest hotels, and even an oil refinery, now retired, but little to show that some of the world's greatest wines are produced in the vineyards nearby. Outside the town, however, on the land leading down to the river and on the road up to St Estèphe *(see p107)*, châteaux and vineyards dominate. Here are the *premiers crus* Latour, Lafite-Rothschild and Mouton-Rothschild; and a pair of rival *deuxièmes crus*, Pichon-Longueville Comtesse de Lalande and Pichon-Longueville Baron de Longueville, glaring at each other across the road. Also present are Châteaux Lynch-Bages, Pontet-Canet, Clerc Milon, Grand-Puy-Lacoste, and d'Armailhac—all of which regularly stroll into the winners' circle in competitions between wines from throughout the world.

All of this begs the question, why is Pauillac so special? What can explain the intensity of black currant and cigar-box flavors, the combination of velvet and discreetly hidden steel, or the longevity that allows the finest of these wines to taste fresh 50 years after the harvest? Conventional wisdom says that the answer lies in the combination of the Cabernet Sauvignon grape, the gravel soil, and the gentle hills on which the vines grow.

But Pauillac has good proprietors, too. While Margaux *(see p98)* has château owners who allow great vineyards to yield mediocre wines, here the Rothschild, Borie, Cazes, Tesseron, and de Lencquesaing families have all made the best of their land. Their wines have a suppleness that makes them easy to drink even in their youth. Give them the time in the cellar they deserve, however, and they will develop layers of fruit and animal flavors that—despite the efforts of pretenders across the globe—still remain unmatched anywhere else.

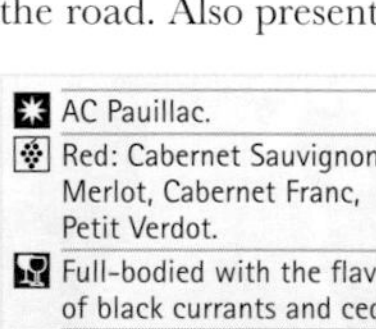

AC Pauillac.

Red: Cabernet Sauvignon, Merlot, Cabernet Franc, Petit Verdot.

Full-bodied with the flavor of black currants and cedar.

Ch d'Armailhac, Batailley, Becasse, Clerc Milon, Colombier-Monpelou, la Couronne, Duhart-Milon-Rothschild, Fonbadet, Grand-Puy-Ducasse, Grand-Puy-Lacoste, Haut-Bages-Averous, Haut-Bages-Libéral, Haut-Batailley, Lafite-Rothschild, Latour, Lynch-Bages, Mouton-Rothschild, Pedesclaux, Pibran, Pichon-Longueville Baron, Pichon-Longueville Lalande, Pontet-Canet, la Tour-Pibran.

Rack of Pauillac lamb.

2003, 2002, 2000, 1998, 1996, 1995, 1990, 1989, 1986, 1982, 1970, 1961

10–25 years.

Pichon-Longueville Comtesse de Lalande
Officially a *deuxième cru*, this château makes rich, Merlot-led wines that often stand up to the *premiers crus* wines in blind tastings.

THE GREAT WINES OF PAUILLAC

The Bordeaux classification system was drawn up in 1855, but the vineyards that produce the top wines of Pauillac were already being referred to as *premiers crus* during the 18th century.

CHÂTEAU LATOUR

Wines were being made from the vineyards of Château Latour in the 16th century—long before wine-making began in most of the rest of the Médoc. By the 18th century, these wines had already been sold in the London auction houses. At that time, Château Latour was in the same hands as Château Lafite and the château now known as Mouton-Rothschild.

Château Latour has since belonged to the owners of the *Financial Times*, the multinational drinks giant Allied-Domecq, and the owner of Chanel, to whom it was sold in the 1990s.

Latour can be a hard wine to judge in its youth, but with time, even in poor vintages, it develops wonderful sweet fruit. The "second wine," Les Forts de Latour, made from young vines and lesser vineyards, offers an affordable taste of the Latour style.

CHÂTEAU LAFITE-ROTHSCHILD

While never as powerful as Château Latour, nor as showy as Mouton-Rothschild, Château Lafite-Rothschild is, for many, the finest and most elegant of all the wines of Bordeaux. The château was founded late in the 17th century, and the quality of its output was recognized 150 years later, when the wines regularly fetched the highest prices of all Bordeaux. The château was bought by the banker Baron James de Rothschild (hence the suffix to its name) 13 years after the 1855 classification was issued. Its "second wine" is Les Carruades de Lafite.

Château Lafite-Rothschild
Though far from the showiest of wines, Château Lafite-Rothschild remains one of the most stylish. It is also one of the wines most worth laying down in a cellar for a couple of decades, to allow it to develop its unique combination of rich, complex flavors.

CHÂTEAU MOUTON-ROTHSCHILD

Until the middle of the 18th century, the estate that is now known as Château Mouton-Rothschild was part of Château Lafite, but its wines were produced and sold separately. For generations, however, it failed to attain the prestige of either Lafite or Château Latour.

This may explain the decision in 1855 to rank Mouton as a *deuxième cru*, though there are claims that anti-Semitism may have been involved, for the estate had been bought by Nathaniel de Rothschild two years earlier. Whatever the explanation, after much lobbying, in 1973, Baron Philippe de Rothschild secured its promotion to *premier cru* status. It was a major coup: no other change to the 1855 classification has ever taken place. Mouton-Rothschild's wines are bigger and more immediately seductive than those of its neighbors but, as the 1945 and 1949 vintages prove, they can age well.

Château Mouton-Rothschild
This has the distinction of being the only château to succeed in challenging the 1855 classification, achieving promotion from *deuxième* to *premier cru* status.

PESSAC-LÉOGNAN

ONE OF THE YOUNGEST *APPELLATIONS* in France, Pessac-Léognan includes some of the finest red- and dry white-producing vineyards in the world. Just outside the modern city of Bordeaux, these vineyards produced the wines that first won prestige for the entire Bordeaux region, including a famous "Ho Bryan" enjoyed by Samuel Pepys in 1663.

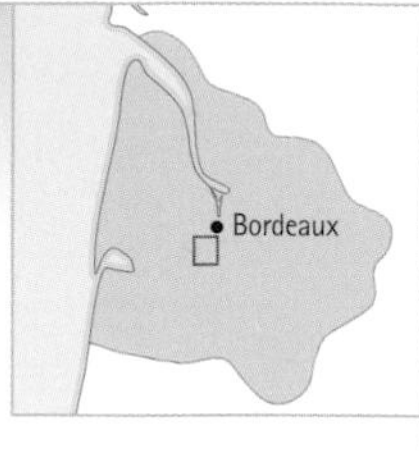

Château Carbonnieux
Techniques at this Benedictine château, long known for its reliable whites, have improved dramatically in recent years, and wines here are now better than ever.

Until the late 1980s, a cluster of illustrious estates, including Château Haut-Brion, Château Pape-Clément, Château Haut-Bailly, and Domaine de Chevalier, belonged to the *appellation* of Graves *(see p96)*, an area of gravelly vineyards extending nearly 40 miles (60 km) south from the city of Bordeaux. In 1987, however, it was decided to separate these northern vineyards from the lower-quality land farther south, classifying them under the new *appellation* of Pessac-Léognan, named after the two *communes* of Pessac and Léognan.

This is not a large *appellation*, producing a total of just over nine million bottles each year, compared to the 22 million bottles of *appellation contrôlée* Graves. It is, however, perfect grape-growing land, with hilly, well-drained gravel vineyards that suit both the Sémillon and the Sauvignon Blanc grapes used to make dry white wines, and the Cabernet Sauvignon and Merlot used in the supple reds.

Despite a more sweetly fruity, mineral edge, the red wines of Pessac-Léognan are related in style to the wines of the gravelly Haut-Médoc to the north *(see p97)*. Even the best and slowest-developing red wines, including those from Château Haut-Brion and La Mission Haut-Brion, are approachable in their youth, but take a decade to develop their complex flavors. Some estates, such as Domaine de Chevalier and Château Haut-Brion, have a long tradition of successful white wine making, using Sémillon and Sauvignon Blanc grapes. Others, such as Château Carbonnieux, have recently progressed by giant leaps, and are now making white wines that are complex and exciting.

GRAND CRU CLASSÉ DE GRAVES
2002
CHATEAV
SMITH HAVT LAFITTE
PESSAC-LÉOGNAN
MIS EN BOUTEILLE AU CHATEAU

Château Smith-Haut-Lafitte
Recent investment at this estate has resulted in a great improvement in the quality of the wines made here.

AC Pessac-Léognan.

Red: Cabernet Sauvignon, Cabernet Franc, Merlot. White: Sémillon, Sauvignon Blanc.

Supple, earthy, tobacco-scented reds. Medium- to full-bodied whites.

Ch Bouscaut, Carbonnieux, Dom de Chevalier, de Cruzeau, Ferrande, de Fieuzal, la Garde, Haut-Bailly, Haut-Brion, Haut-Gardère, Larrivet-Haut-Brion, Latour, Laville-Haut-Brion, la Louvière, Ch Malartic-Lagravière, La Mission-Haut-Brion, Pape-Clément, Smith-Haut-Lafitte, la Tour-Haut-Brion.

Red: Roast lamb.

White: 2002, 2001, 2000, 1999, 1996, 1995. Red: 2003, 2002, 1998, 1996, 1995, 1990, 1988, 1982, 1970, 1961.

Red: 6–25 years. White: 3–15 years.

Domaine de Chevalier
Both red and white wines from this *grand cru classé* estate take up to 10 years to mature.

POMEROL

FLAT AND VISUALLY UNMEMORABLE, the Libournais *appellation* of Pomerol, on the eastern bank of the Dordogne, failed to receive even a mention in the Bordeaux Classification of 1855 *(see p85)*. This has not prevented the best of the supple, velvety red wines of Pomerol from being among the most magnificent and expensive in the world.

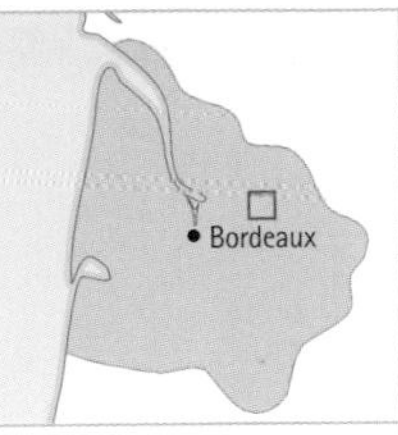

Surprised by Success
A newcomer to prosperity, the *commune* of Pomerol remains one of the sleepiest and most remote in Bordeaux. Lacking a village center, the area counts the church spire as its most important landmark.

Although the area around Pomerol was first used for vine-growing in the first century BC, it was not until the 1960s that its wines, now exclusively red, achieved international success. During the 18th century, the grapes grown in the flat, iron-rich clay vineyards of Pomerol were used to make mainly white wines. When the white grapes were eventually replaced with black, the quality of the wine they produced was not enhanced by the other food crops that were planted among the vines. For a long time, the vineyards of the area were seen as being second-best to those of St Émilion *(see p105)*, which were themselves considered decidedly second-best to those of the Médoc *(see p99)*. When George Saintsbury wrote his *Notes on a Cellar Book* in 1920, Pomerol did not even warrant a mention. The only markets for its wines were Belgium and northern France, and even there, reputations were hard to build, given the tiny annual production of most of the estates. There were, and are, no grand châteaux in Pomerol; even Château Pétrus, now the most famous estate in the appellation, producing some of the most expensive wines in the world, is no more than a modest country farmhouse making just 5,000 cases of wine each year.

The credit for changing Pomerol's fortunes in the 1950s and 1960s must go to wine merchant and producer Jean-Pierre Moueix, who took charge of Château Pétrus, Château Lagrange, Château la Fleur-Pétrus, Château Latour, Château Pomerol, and Château Trotanoy. With his son Christian, Moueix introduced the wines of the region to the British and, more importantly, to Americans, who were seduced by their rich Dundee cake flavors, the softness of their tannins, and their characteristic hint of minerals. Most of the wines of Pomerol are made primarily from Merlot grapes, but estates such as Vieux Château Certan demonstrate the essential blending role played by Cabernet Franc and Cabernet Sauvignon when they are planted on the appropriate soil.

- AC Pomerol.
- Red: Merlot, Cabernet Franc, Cabernet Sauvignon.
- Deep-colored, full-bodied reds with supple tannins.
- Ch Beauregard, Bourgneuf-Vayron, Certan-Giraud, Certan de May, Clinet, Clos de Clocher, Ch la Conseillante, la Croix, la Croix de Gay, Clos de l'Église-Clinet, Ch l'Enclos, l'Évangile, Feytit-Clinet, la Fleur-Pétrus, le Gay, Gazin, Haut-Tropchaud, Lafleur, Lafleur-Gazin, Lagrange, Lagrave, Latour à Pomerol, Nénin, le Petit-Village, Ch Pétrus, le Pin, Clos René, Ch Rouget, Trotanoy, Vieux Château Certan.
- Braised saddle of hare with cherries.
- 2003, 2001, 2000, 1998, 1996, 1995, 1990, 1989, 1985, 1983, 1982, 1970.
- 5–25 years.

Vieux Château Certan
The traditional Merlot is skillfully blended with Cabernet Franc to produce exquisite long-lived wines here.

PREMIÈRES CÔTES DE BORDEAUX

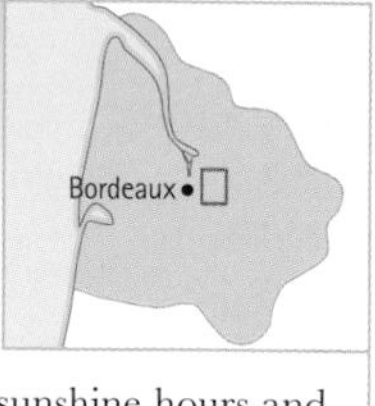

By around 1000 AD, what is now known as AC Premières Côtes de Bordeaux was already an important wine-producing area. Part of the Entre-Deux-Mers district, the Premières Côtes is a narrow limestone ridge that runs south from Bordeaux 37 miles (for 60 km) along the course of the Garonne, taking in 37 villages, each of which is entitled to add its name to the *appellation*. Many sunshine hours and a clay-and-gravel soil help to produce fruity, Merlot-dominated reds that can make great drinking at around six years old.

Both sweet and dry whites are made here, too, but dry whites must be sold under the general Bordeaux Blanc *appellation*. Intended to encourage the production of this region's generally unexceptional sweet whites, this rule gives little incentive to produce good dry white wines.

Château Carsin
This recently developed, Finnish-owned estate uses modern wine-making techniques to get the best out of the Premières Côtes.

Hillside Vines
Following a narrow limestone ridge along the north bank of the Garonne, the Premières Côtes de Bordeaux are hilly and picturesque, a marked contrast to the flatter land on the opposite bank.

- AC Premières Côtes de Bordeaux.
- Red: Merlot. White: Sémillon, Sauvignon Blanc, Muscadelle.
- Medium-weight dry reds. Sweet whites.
- Barreyre, Carignan, Carsin, Chaumont, Fayau, du Grand Plantier, Haut Rian Matherau, Pascot, Peyrat, Plasson, Reynon, Sissan, Thieuley, Vieille Tour.
- Entrecôte steak with shallots.
- Red: 2003, 2001, 2000, 1998.
- Red: 3–6 years. White: 5–10 years.

THE RISING STARS OF BORDEAUX

Red wines from estates in a number of previously underperforming Bordeaux *appellations* have scored some startling recent successes. One of these *appellations* is the Premières Côtes de Bordeaux *(see above)*, where the lead has been taken by two châteaux in particular. One is Château Reynon, where wines are produced by Professor Denis Dubourdieu of Bordeaux University. The other is the Finnish-owned Château Carsin, where wines are made by the Australian-born Mandy Jones using modern Australian-designed equipment. Surprisingly, but justifiably, the price of wines from these châteaux is often higher than that of a St Émilion Grand Cru *(see p105)*. Other rising-star *appellations* include the Côtes de Francs *(see p95)*, and the Côtes de Bourg *(see p94)*, as well as various so-called satellite *appellations* of St Émilion and Pomerol, such as St Georges-St Émilion *(see p106)* and Lalande de Pomerol *(see p97)*. The vast improvement in these wines is due mainly to the application of better vine-growing and wine-making techniques, above all the careful selection of only healthy, ripe grapes. Also crucial is the fact that people are now prepared to pay high prices for good wines from what were often considered humble *appellations*.

Château Reynon
Denis Dubourdieu, an important influence on countless Bordeaux producers, produces his own wines at Château Reynon in the Premières Côtes.

ST ÉMILION

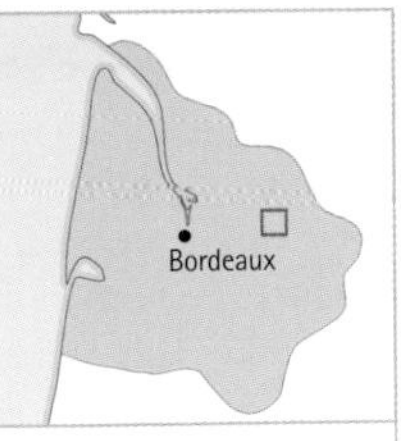

ALTHOUGH IT IS ONE OF THE MOST PRESTIGIOUS red wine *appellations* in the world, the wines of St Émilion can be some of the most difficult to buy. The most sublime of all Bordeaux wines are made in the best parts of this *appellation*, but there are also plenty of very dull wines, sold at high prices thanks to the international prestige of their name.

The Roofs of St Émilion
The small town of St Émilion nestles comfortably on its high limestone plateau, its warm terra-cotta roofs contrasting with the greens and browns of the priceless vines that surround it.

The vineyards of St Émilion have been immortalized in Roman mosaics and praised by the Roman poet Ausonius. Despite this illustrious history, the lack of bridges across the Dordogne and the Garonne left St Émilion isolated from the city of Bordeaux and its wine merchants, and as a consequence, these wines were relatively little-known outside the region until the early 20th century.

Enjoying a huge postwar revival, the glorious fruitcake richness of St Émilion's top wines now helps them to sell for some of the highest prices in Bordeaux. In 1958 the wines of St Émilion were first officially classified under a complex and rather confusing system. The very best vineyards enjoy the status of *premiers grands crus classés* A and B, and are reevaluated every decade. Next come the often quite ordinary *grands crus classés* vineyards. Finally, there is a third category, never reevaluated, that includes more than 200 *grands crus* vineyards, most of which are even more ordinary than those labeled *grand cru classé*.

Geographically and geologically, there are at least four distinct parts to the St Émilion *appellation*. Around and to the south of the town are the clay-limestone mixtures of both the St Émilion plateau and the slopes of the Côtes St Émilion, home to many of the *premiers grands crus classés* vineyards. To the west of the Côtes is the gravel and sandy soil of the Graves-St Émilion. Finally, farther west is the large area of sandy *sables anciennes*, where more ordinary St Émilion is made. In the first three areas, the Merlot grape is blended with as much as 65 percent Cabernet Franc, while on the *sables anciennes* it is Merlot that dominates.

Château l'Angélus
One of St Émilion's rising stars, this estate produces wines that have been growing ever more impressive since the 1980s.

Château Troplong-Mondot
Not the most famous, perhaps, but even in difficult years like 1994, this has been one of the most carefully made and most reliable of all St Émilion's wines.

- AC St Émilion, AC St Émilion Grand Cru, AC St Émilion Grand Cru Classé, AC St Émilion Premier Grand Cru Classé A and B.
- Red: Merlot, Cabernet Franc.
- Soft medium-bodied and deep-colored, full-bodied reds.
- Angélus, Ausone, Beauséjour, Beauséjour-Bécot, Belair, Canon, Canon la Gaffelière, Cap de Mourlin, Cheval Blanc, Dassault, la Dominique, Faugères, Fourtet, Figeac, Fombrauge, Fonplégade, Fonroque, Franc Mayn, des Jacobins, Larmande, Magdelaine, la Mondotte, de l'Oratoire, Troplong-Mondot, de Valandraud.
- Lamprey stewed in red wine.
- 2003, 2001, 2000, 1998, 1995, 1990, 1989, 1986, 1985, 1983, 1982.
- Red: 5–25 years.

ST ÉMILION SATELLITES

WITH THE ESTABLISHMENT IN 1935 of the *appellation contrôlée* system, the villages close to St Émilion were given their own *appellations*, enabling them to sell their wines under their own names rather than that of St Émilion. Little known, but carefully made, they sometimes offer far better value than many of the wines of St Émilion itself.

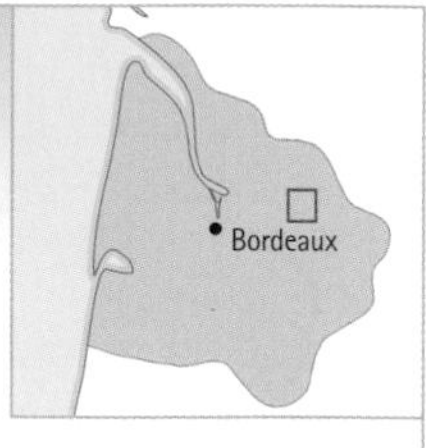

Montagne-St Émilion
Like the rest of the Libournais, this is Merlot country, producing wines that are rich and velvety with luscious plum flavors, and often comparable to pricier St Émilion.

The villages of Lussac, Montagne, Puisseguin, and St Georges are situated to the north and to the east of the town of St Émilion, giving their names to its four so-called satellite *appellations*. With a mixture of clay-limestone and gravel soil similar to that of St Émilion, all four *appellations* grow the St Émilion combination of Merlot and Cabernet Franc grapes, but with an even greater emphasis on the rich and spicy Merlot variety. "Most agreeable, early-developing claret" was the faint praise of British authority Edmund Penning-Rowsell, writing in the 1970s about the wines of the St Émilion satellites. He proposed that the wines of all four villages be classed together in a single *appellation* as St Émilion-Villages. Wine writer Hugh Johnson, on the other hand, has more recently expressed the view that "these wines make up in satisfying solidity what they lack in finesse." Far worse than this could very often be said of the wines of St Émilion itself, which sell at much higher prices.

My own opinion is that whatever the failings of the St Émilion satellite *appellations*, they are due largely to the limited wine-making ambitions of the local *coopératives* and châteaux, made worse by a tendency for growers to opt for high grape yields at the expense of quality. The exciting results of improvements in wine-making techniques can be seen in the superb wines produced recently at both Château St Georges in St Georges-St Émilion and at Château Faizeau in Montagne-St Émilion. Until more such talented wine makers come to work in this area, it is impossible to guess which of the four *appellations* has the greatest potential. At the moment, however, it is the wines of St Georges-St Émilion that age the best, and those of Puisseguin-St Émilion that are the simplest and most one-dimensional.

Rugged charm
Robust and rugged are words used to describe the wines of the St Émilion satellites. The same could be said of this Montagne-St Émilion church.

Château Corbin
Part of a rapidly growing group of innovative wine makers that are based in the region of Montagne-St Émilion, Château Corbin makes wines with more finesse than those of many of its neighbors.

- AC Puisseguin-St Émilion, AC Lussac-St Émilion, AC Montagne-St Émilion, AC St Georges-St Émilion
- Red: Merlot, Cabernet Franc.
- Soft, round, fruity reds.
- *Lussac-St Émilion*: Barbe Blanche, Bellevue, les Couzins, de la Grenière, Haut-Milon, Lyonnat, Moulin Noir, Trocard, Vieux Château Chambeau. *Montagne-St Émilion*: d'Arvouet, Beauséjour, Bonfort, Calon, Corbin, Faizeau, Fauconnerie, Vieux Château Calon. *Puisseguin-St Émilion*: Bel-Air, Branda, Haut St-Clair, Rigaud. *St Georges-St Émilion*: La Croix-St Georges, Haut St Georges, St Georges.
- Grilled lamb or pork.
- 2003, 2001, 2000, 1998, 1996, 1995.
- 5–10 years.

ST ESTÈPHE

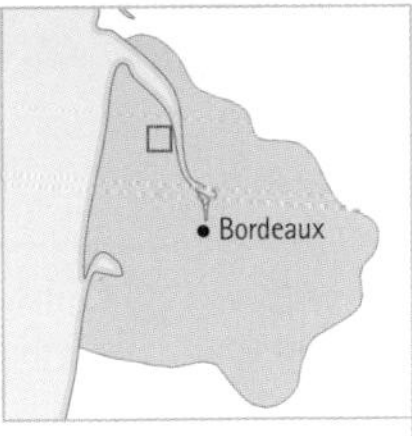

FOR TRADITIONAL CLARET DRINKERS, the tannic, slow-maturing style of St Estèphe was everything a Bordeaux ought to be. As international taste in wine has swung increasingly toward more supple reds, this northernmost *commune* in the Médoc has often seemed unfashionable. However, recent vintages have seen a move toward fruitier, more supple wines.

Château Cos d'Estournel
The carved-oak doors from the island of Zanzibar and various other non-European influences seen in the design of this unusual, custom-built winery give a strong indication of the exotic, spicy flavor of the wines within.

When the classification of the vineyards of Bordeaux took place in 1855, it was agreed that the wines of St Estèphe were not the best in the Médoc, and the *commune* was awarded only five *crus classés*, as compared to 18 in Pauillac and 21 in Margaux *(see p98)*. Forty vineyards, however, were classified as *crus bourgeois*—below a *cinquième cru*, but better than an average unclassified *cru*.

Tough and deeply colored, with a lot of tannin and acidity, the traditional St Estèphe style is the very opposite of the juicy Merlot-rich wines of nearby Pomerol *(see p103)*. More surprising is the fact that the wines of St Estèphe are also very different from those of its neighbor, Pauillac, despite the fact that both the *appellations* share a gravel soil, and both have traditionally grown mainly Cabernet Sauvignon grapes. The soil of St Estèphe, however, contains a lot of clay as well as gravel, which, in combination with the Cabernet Sauvignon, produces wines that may be a little rough if not extensively matured. The style can sometimes work well, as shown by Château Montrose and Château Cos d'Estournel, where the wines are rich, spicy, and stylish.

A wine-making revolution began in St Estèphe in the late 1980s, when a number of dynamic producers realized that, by growing more Merlot grapes, which are suited to the clay-rich soil here, and by harvesting them later, it was possible to make wines that are gentler and more supple than traditional St Estèphe. Despite this, a high proportion of wines here are still made in bulk at the local *coopérative*, proof that St Estèphe is still far from being a truly fashionable *appellation*. However, a trend is emerging, one that has proved unstoppable, for the best of these rich, berry-flavored wines to join company with some of the most sought-after in the Médoc.

Château Haut-Marbuzet
Henri Duboscq uses 50 percent Merlot grapes to make wines that are fruitier and less tannic than traditional St Estèphe.

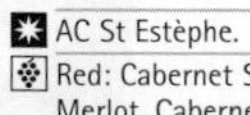

AC St Estèphe.

Red: Cabernet Sauvignon, Merlot, Cabernet Franc, Petit Verdot.

Full-bodied, deep-colored, tannic, slow-maturing reds.

Andron Blanquet, Calon-Ségur, Chambert-Marbuzet, Cos d'Estournel, Cos-Labory, Le Crock, Haut-Beauséjour, Haut-Marbuzet, Lafon-Rochet, Lavillotte, Lilian Ladouys, Marbuzet, Meyney, Montrose, les Ormes-de-Pez, Petit-Bocq, de-Pez, Phélan-Ségur, Picard, Tour de Pez, Tronquoy-Lalande.

Quails sautéed with artichoke hearts, onions, and red Bordeaux.

2003, 2001, 2000, 1998, 1996, 1995, 1990, 1989, 1986, 1982, 1970, 1961.

5–30 years.

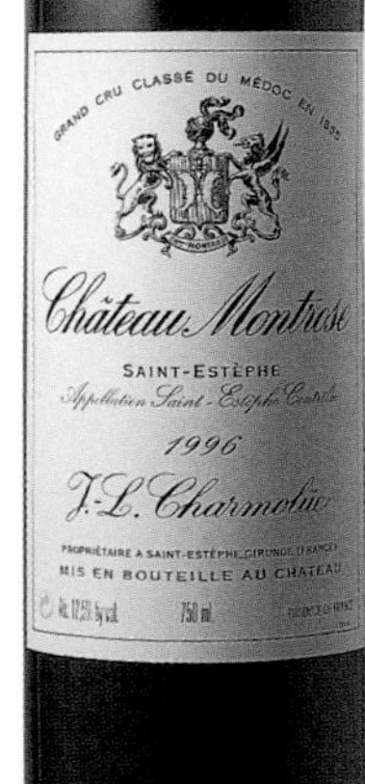

Château Montrose
One of the two *deuxième cru* estates in St Estèphe, this estate makes long-maturing wines that reveal the presence of large proportions of Cabernet Sauvignon.

ST JULIEN

OF ALL THE *APPELLATIONS* IN BORDEAUX, none offers a higher proportion of really fine red wine than St Julien. There may be no *premiers crus* châteaux here, but the combination of gravelly soil and ambitious wine-makers has resulted in the production of St Julien wines that regularly challenge some of the biggest names in the Bordeaux region.

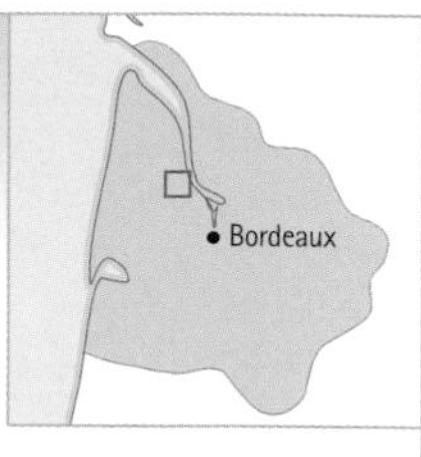

Château Lagrange
Although not everyone was happy when Japanese buyers took over this château, it has since been restored to its former glory and the wines produced here have regained their former status.

As anyone who has driven northward through the Médoc region will know, St Julien is a long way from Margaux *(see p98)*, but a very short distance from Pauillac *(see p100)*. In fact, the boundary between St Julien and Pauillac is defined only by the Juillac stream. On one side stands Château Léoville-Las Cases, and on the other its rival Château Pichon-Longueville-Comtesse-Lalande and the *premier cru* Château Latour. In blind tastings, it is often hard to predict which will be the winner, since this trio share the same gravelly soil and use a similar Cabernet-dominated blend of grapes.

The combination of cedary, cigar-box, and fresh black-currant flavors defines the character of St Julien, which is a touch less powerful than Pauillac, and less austere than St Estèphe *(see p107)*, but more structured than Margaux. Château Léoville-Las Cases' wines sell for prices close to those of the *premiers crus* of Pauillac, while its neighbor, the more affordable Château Léoville-Barton, often produces one of the best wines of the vintage. Other high-flyers among the 11 *crus classés* include Châteaux Branaire, Ducru-Beaucaillou, Lagrange, Léoville-Poyferré and Talbot, while *crus bourgeois* such as Châteaux Gloria, Moulin de la Rose and St Pierre produce wines that are better than some of the *crus classés* in other *communes*. The quality of the wine making here makes "second wines," such as Château Léoville-Las Cases' Clos du Marquis and Château Lagrange's Les Fiefs de Lagrange, well worth buying. The vineyards at the south of this *commune*, including both Beychevelle and Gruaud-Larose, produce plumper wines than those around St Julien itself.

Modern St Julien can be drunk quite young, but in good vintages it can take 10 years for the wines to take on more of the mature cigar-box flavors and lose the black-currant character of their youth.

- AC St Julien.
- Red: Cabernet Sauvignon, Merlot, Cabernet Franc, Petit Verdot.
- Rich, full-bodied, long-lived, black-curranty, cedary reds.
- Ch Beychevelle, Ch Branaire-Ducru, Ch la Bridane, Ch Ducru-Beaucaillou, Ch du Glana, Ch Gloria, Ch Gruaud-Larose, Ch Hortevie, Ch Lagrange, Ch Langoa-Barton, Ch Léoville-Barton, Ch Léoville-Las Cases, Ch Léoville-Poyferré, Ch Moulin de la Rose, Ch St Pierre, Ch Talbot.
- Sautéed fillet of lamb with chicken and parsley mousse.
- 2003, 2001, 2000, 1998, 1996, 1995, 1990, 1989, 1986, 1982, 1970, 1961.
- 8–25 years.

Château Léoville-Las Cases
Although not a *premier cru*, the wines produced by this château are unofficially ranked alongside the *premiers crus* châteaux of the nearby *appellation* Pauillac.

STE CROIX-DU-MONT

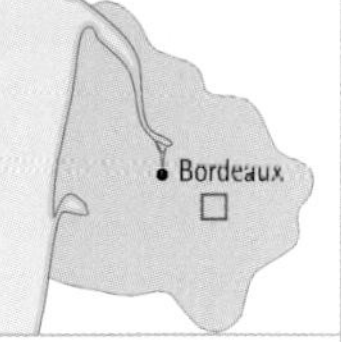

FOR THOSE WHO BELIEVE THAT VINES grow better on hills, Ste Croix-du-Mont, on the right bank of the Garonne to the south of Loupiac *(see p97)*, might seem more promising sweet wine territory than the flatlands of Sauternes *(see p110)* or Barsac *(see p92)*. The soil is good and the vineyards face south across the river, with morning mists encouraging the development of botrytis. The wines can have the full, honeyed character associated with good botrytized wines and are often better buys than those sold under more famous *appellations* like Sauternes and Barsac. Like Loupiac, however, Ste Croix-du-Mont is often lighter in color and body than top Sauternes—probably because its producers can not afford to pick nobly rotten grapes in numerous pickings, and instead do so in a single pass.

Château Loubens
One of the most reliable producers of Ste Croix-du-Mont, this château makes wines that are both luscious and subtle.

Château Croix-du-Mont
The wines of Ste Croix-du-Mont might not be as prestigious as those of Sauternes, but the region does have some truly spectacular châteaux.

- AC Ste Croix-du-Mont.
- White: Sémillon, Sauvignon Blanc, Muscadelle.
- Sweet, partly botrytized whites.
- Ch de Beaucastel, Ch Bel Air, Ch des Coulinats, Crabitan-Bellevue, Ch Croix-du-Mont, Grand Plantier, Lamarque, Lescure, Loubens, Lousteau-Vieil, Ch la Rame.
- Strawberry tart with a Ste Croix-du-Mont sauce.
- 2003, 2001, 1999, 1996, 1995, 1990, 1989, 1988, 1986, 1985, 1983, 1982.
- 5–10 years.

NOBLE ROT

The challenge facing the grape-growers of Ste Croix-du-Mont, like makers of fine sweet wine elsewhere, lies in managing the benign fungus known as *Botrytis cinerea* or noble rot. While the makers of dry wines simply wait for their grapes to ripen, dessert-wine-makers are dependent on the warm, humid weather conditions in which the botrytis develops. *Appellations* like Sauternes *(see p110)*, Barsac *(see p92)*, Loupiac *(see p97)*, and Ste Croix-du-Mont in Bordeaux, Monbazillac *(see p274)* and Jurançon *(see p272)* in the southwest, and Vouvray *(see p226)*, Bonnezeaux *(see p214)*, and Quarts-de-Chaume *(see p221)* in the Loire, all favor these conditions, with the quality of each vintage ultimately reliant on the weather from year to year. For example, the weather of 1982 was perfect for red Bordeaux, but less than great for Sauternes. Yields per vine are far smaller for botrytized wines than for dry wines, and this, coupled with the risk of poor weather destroying the crop, tends to discourage most producers from taking the risks required to harvest in successive pickings. Money has a part to play, because makers of sweet wines rarely receive the financial rewards their efforts and risks deserve. For example, in 1997, even Château Climens, one of the most famous châteaux in Sauternes and a producer of botrytized wines, charged the same price per bottle as châteaux in the Médoc that produced twice as much wine per acre.

A Strange Beauty
Grapes affected by noble rot are far from pretty, but they are essential to the production of great sweet wines.

Painstaking Harvest
Picking nobly rotten grapes is a demanding task, and a far cry from the mechanized harvesting process often used for dry wines.

SAUTERNES

NO OTHER SWEET WINE HAS EVER come close to achieving the prestige accorded to the produce of this privileged corner of Bordeaux, and indeed the quality of the best of the white wines here has improved noticeably in recent years. Despite this status, the presence of the word Sauternes on a label is no promise of any kind of quality.

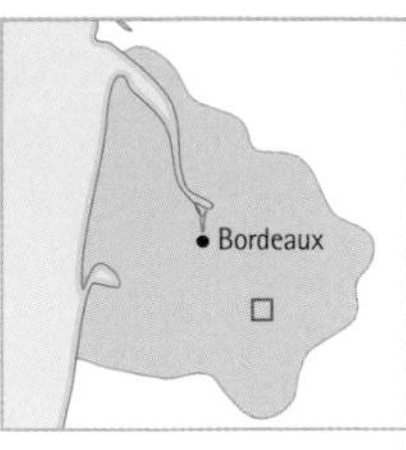

Château Rieussec
This property is one of the richest wine estates in the Sauternes region. It has an ideal situation for the production of good wines, on top of a low hill lying close to the little Ciron River.

The first wines of the Sauternes were almost certainly dry and red. Whites have been made since the 17th century, and the earliest of these were dry. They were also so light that the Dutch merchants who bought them felt the need to fortify them with brandy. In 1787, US president Thomas Jefferson bought some Château d'Yquem and was so impressed that he wrote that Sauternes provided France's best whites—that is, after Champagne *(see pp160–77)* and Hermitage *(see p258)*. No one is quite certain when the Sauternais began to make sweet wines. At Yquem it is said that a late harvest in 1859 resulted in the grapes being attacked by noble rot. Others fix the date 23 years earlier when a German grower named Focke imported a knowledge of botrytis from the Rhine. In any case, the sweet 1859 Yquem was a hit when drunk at the Russian court, and since then the top wines of Sauternes have never looked back. The best châteaux, Yquem, Rieussec, and Suduiraut, are set atop small hills close to the Ciron River, whose mists help to create the perfect conditions for botrytis. Not only does Yquem enjoy the best site, it has traditionally taken the greatest care over its wines, painstakingly harvesting in successive pickings and even declining to release a vintage when the quality is thought insufficient.

The Sauternes *appellation* is allowed to include Barsac *(see p92)*, and on average its quality has improved in recent years: excess use of sulfur dioxide is rarer than it used to be. Even so, generic Sauternes is still usually a label to be avoided, and many smaller châteaux make disappointing wines in all but the best vintages.

The explanation for this may lie in legislation that denies Sauternes producers an entitlement granted to their neighbors in Cérons *(see p111)*. The latter are allowed to "declassify" their less impressive wines and sell them as Graves *(see p96)*. The Sauternais have only two options: Sauternes and Bordeaux Blanc—the latter being the *appellation* under which they sell their (generally overpriced) dry whites.

Château d'Yquem
The high price of the wines of Château d'Yquem is justified by the extreme care taken in the vineyard and cellar.

- AC Sauternes (can also include wine from Barsac). Dry wine is sold as AC Bordeaux Blanc.
- White: Sémillon, Sauvignon Blanc, Muscadelle.
- Lusciously sweet wine.
- d'Arche, Barréjats, Bastor-Lamontagne, Clos Haut-Peyraguey, Doisy-Védrines, de Fargues, Filhot, Gilette, Guiraud, Haut-Bergeron, les Justices, Lafaurie-Peyraguey, Lamothe, Lamothe-Guignard, de Malle, Rabaud-Promis, Raymond-Lafon, Rayne Vigneau, Rieussec, Romer de Hayot, St Amand, Sigalas-Rabaud, Suau, Suduiraut, la Tour Blanche, d'Yquem.
- *Foie gras.*
- 2003, 2002, 2001, 1999, 1997, 1996, 1995, 1990, 1989, 1988, 1986, 1983, 1976.
- 5–30 years.

OTHERS

BORDEAUX IS USUALLY THOUGHT OF as a region that makes exclusively red and white wines, but it does also produce rosés and sparkling wines. Bordeaux includes several small *appellations* whose wines are rarely seen anywhere outside the region. As wine-making improves, these can be well worth seeking out for the excellent value they represent.

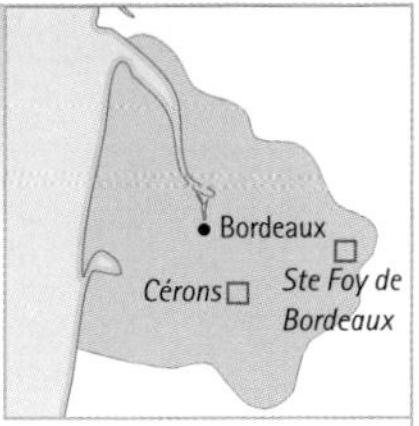

As red Bordeaux has become richer and deeper in color and flavor, a number of producers have revived rosé and *clairet* (the style that falls between red and rosé). In fact, there is a direct connection between these wines and the darker reds: in many cases they are simply the juices drawn from the vat when still only partly fermented, in order to increase the concentration of color and flavor in the remaining wine.

Created in 1990, the *appellation* of Crémant de Bordeaux is beginning to prove a source of small quantities—that is, around one million bottles per year—of good-value sparkling white and rosé wine. The principal grape used here is Sémillon, usually with the addition of Muscadelle, Sauvignon, Colombard, and some Cabernet Franc.

The little-known wines of Cérons are produced from vineyards close to Barsac *(see p92)*. Like the wines of that *appellation*, they tend to be light and delicate in style and—in the case of the Grand Enclos du Château de Cérons—first-class alternatives to other, higher-priced sweet Bordeaux. Curiously, and sensibly, Cérons producers have the option of selling their wine as Graves, unlike their neighbors in Sauternes and Barsac, who can only use their own *appellations* or Bordeaux Blanc.

Ste Foy de Bordeaux
Reds now dominate in this region because the market for sweet whites is uncertain. Producers still need to make a living, even when there is no noble rot—the fungus crucial for making fine sweet whites.

Quite unrelated to the Graves *appellation*, the reds and whites of Graves de Vayres come from a small area of gravelly soil on the left bank of the Dordogne. Their individuality was appreciated in the 19th century, when their color was mostly white. Today the best examples, such as the wines of Châteaux la Chapelle-Bellevue, Lesparre, and Canteloup, are Merlot-dominated reds.

Ste Foy de Bordeaux, to the east of Entre-Deux-Mers *(see p95)*, is another white wine region that has switched to making reds. Among the most successful wines are the ones now being produced at 18th-century châteaux such as des Chapelains, du Petit Montibeau and l'Enclos.

The wines of two *appellations,* Bordeaux-Haut-Benauge and Entre-Deux-Mers-Haut-Benauge, both come from the same nine *communes,* which lie to the west of Entre-Deux-Mers. The second of this pair makes a dry wine that can include Ugni Blanc, Colombard, and Mauzac, and is similar in style to Entre-Deux-Mers.

Bordeaux-Haut-Benauge, on the other hand, can be medium-sweet or sweet, and is produced from Sémillon, Sauvignon Blanc, and Muscadelle, which have to be used at a higher degree of ripeness. The result is more interesting than the semisweet wine of Côtes de Bordeaux-St Macaire, a lesser-known *appellation* to the south.

Château de Cérons
The grapes are the same as in Sauternes; prices, however, are lower for reasons of prestige.

Burgundy

Burgundy

This is the land of tiny estates, yielding similarly tiny quantities of what are often sublime and extraordinary red and white wines.

First, a confession. I cannot begin to be as level-headed about Burgundy as I would like. This is the region and these are the wines with which I fell most passionately in love. I lived among the vineyards in the heart of Burgundy for nearly six years and I have spent, and misspent, more money on the wines made here than on those produced anywhere else in the world. The relationship has been a tempestuous one. The greatest bottles, some of which have come from the region's most humble appellations, have been packed with wild fruit, perfume, and indescribable animal appeal. The lesser ones, far too many of which have carried prestigious labels and been undeniably expensive, have been variously dull, watery, acidic, and grubby. The problem is that, without pulling the cork, there is no way to be sure of what you are going to find.

There are several reasons for this notorious unpredictability. First, even the most southerly parts of Burgundy lie too far north to ripen grapes reliably every year. Second, while producers in Bordeaux *(see pp80–111)*, for example, have the flexibility by law to blend grape varieties to produce their best wines, in Burgundy many wines must be made from a single grape variety. In addition, an average Bordeaux château, producing 200–300,000 bottles of wine per harvest, enjoys economies of scale denied to the typically tiny Burgundy estate producing only 30,000 bottles. A final, and crucial, factor is the optimistic readiness of wine-drinkers to place their trust in the name of an *appellation*, hoping blindly that any bottle labeled Chablis *(see pp132–3)* or Beaujolais *(see pp126–7)*, Chassagne-Montrachet *(see p135)* or Pouilly-Fuissé *(see p152)*, is going to live up to their expectations.

So why persevere against all the odds? Because the tiny vineyards in each of Burgundy's five wine-producing regions, from Chablis in the north to Beaujolais in the south, can produce wines that, at their best, are unequaled anywhere else. There are, for example, many delicious Chardonnays to be found throughout the world, but none that could be mistaken for a traditional unoaked or lightly oaked Chablis. Winemakers elsewhere make good red wines from the Pinot Noir grape, but none can produce the subtle light and shade of flavors that you discover when you taste the red wines in a good Côte d'Or cellar. Likewise, the Beaujolais region

All Sliced Up
Some of the most fragmented in France, the vineyards of Burgundy form a huge patchwork with an average size of only 10 acres (four hectares). Each grower's vines are often further divided into several parcels, and the human factor contributes, inevitably, to the unpredictability of the wines.

REGIONAL OVERVIEW

- 111,000 acres (45,000 ha); 390 million bottles.
- Generally continental with cool temperatures in Chablis and substantially warmer in the Mâconnais region farther south. Temperatures in individual vineyards are also influenced by altitude.
- Varied, ranging from limestone in Chablis and the Côte d'Or, where there is also marl and flinty clay, to granite in Beaujolais.
- Red: Pinot Noir, Gamay, César.
  White: Chardonnay, Aligoté, Pinot Blanc, Pinot Gris.

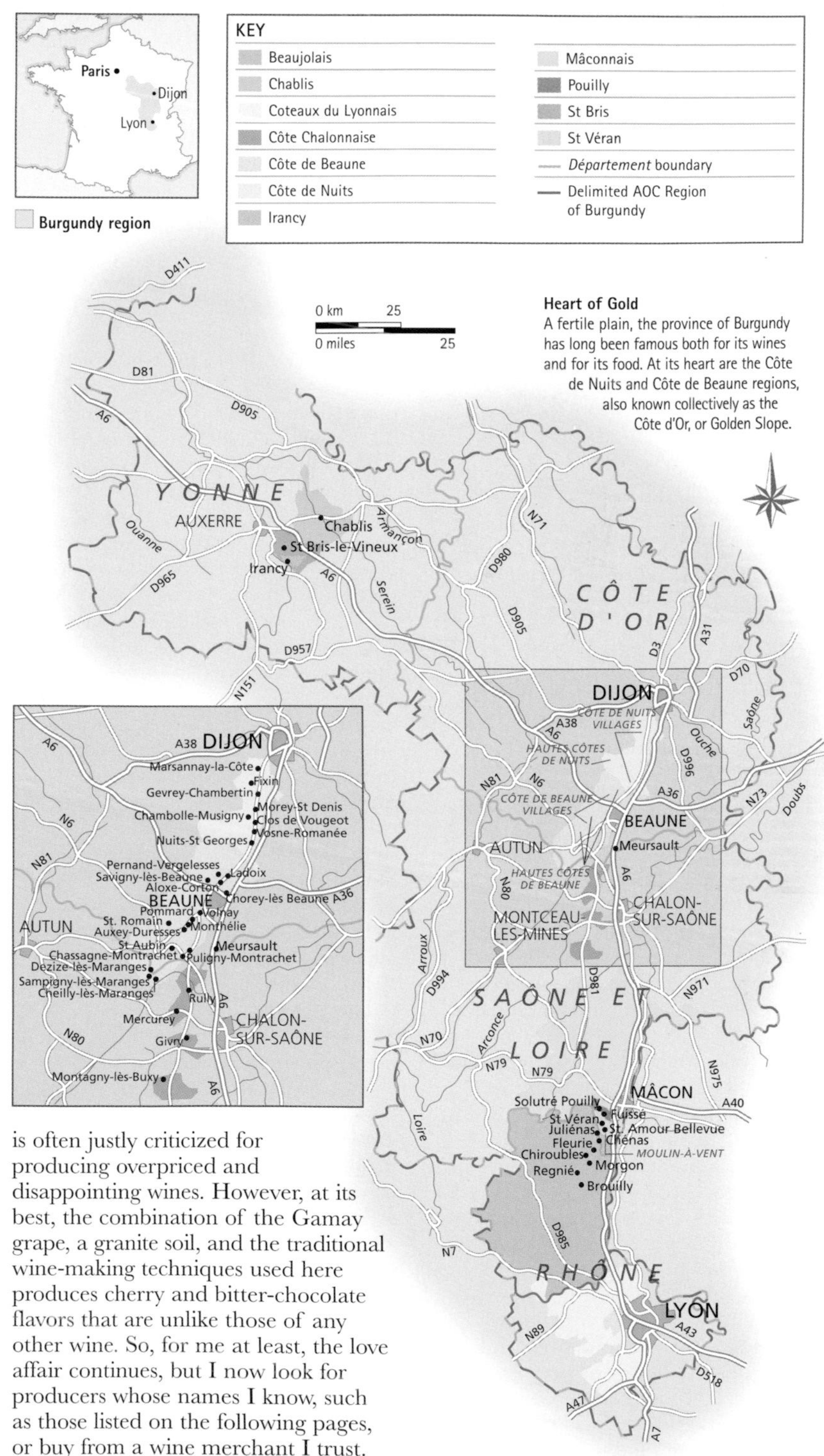

Heart of Gold
A fertile plain, the province of Burgundy has long been famous both for its wines and for its food. At its heart are the Côte de Nuits and Côte de Beaune regions, also known collectively as the Côte d'Or, or Golden Slope.

is often justly criticized for producing overpriced and disappointing wines. However, at its best, the combination of the Gamay grape, a granite soil, and the traditional wine-making techniques used here produces cherry and bitter-chocolate flavors that are unlike those of any other wine. So, for me at least, the love affair continues, but I now look for producers whose names I know, such as those listed on the following pages, or buy from a wine merchant I trust.

The History of Burgundy

The Burgundians have not forgotten the days when their Duke controlled land stretching as far north as Holland, negotiated with foreign rulers (including the sale of Joan of Arc to the English for 10,000 gold crowns), raised taxes, and oversaw the development of wealthy towns like Beaune and Dijon. Today, however, it is their wine that commands respect.

Charity Begins at the Hospital
The Hospices de Beaune was founded as a charitable hospital in the 14th century. Today, money raised from the annual auction of its wines is spent on the upkeep of a new hospital.

Burgundy's period of semi-nationhood provided the region with a strong sense of identity that still endures to this day. It also laid the foundations for a major wine industry in the area. The first evidence of wine production in Burgundy dates from Roman times. The Côte d'Or, or Golden Slope, which lies to the south of the present-day town of Dijon, was being used by wine-makers by the fourth century. In the early days, however, vine-growing there was probably not as rewarding as it is today. According to local legend, the Roman Emperor Constantine was informed in the year 312 that the inhabitants of the area were unable to pay their taxes—the vineyards were full of decrepit vines, and barely accessible by horse and cart thanks to the large number of potholes in the roads. Today, the valuable Côte d'Or vineyards produce some of the very best wines in Burgundy.

A TRADITION OF QUALITY

The proper development of these vineyards came with the Church. In 587, the King of Burgundy, Gontran, donated land to a local abbey, as did the Emperor Charlemagne some 200 years later. Specific Côte d'Or vineyards were already being isolated for their quality and, according to local legend, it was the emperor himself who ordered that vines be planted on one particular hillside, having noticed that the snows always melted earlier there. This, he said, indicated that the slope in question benefited from more sunshine. The hill was the *grand cru* Corton and the vineyard was what is now known as Corton Charlemagne. In Burgundian patois, the region's smallest plots of land, the named vineyards within every *commune*, are still known as *climats* after their quirky individual microclimates.

By the early 18th century, maps were being drawn up of the Côte d'Or indicating places such as Volnet (now Volnay), Puligny Morachet (now Puligny-Montrachet), Nuys (now Nuits-St Georges) and Chambertin (now Gevrey-Chambertin), where the best wines were made. By this time, it was known that the Pinot Noir was the ideal grape variety for this northern region's reds and that the Chardonnay was best for its whites. In fact, as early as 1395, the first edict was issued to ban the planting of the Gamay, the Pinot Noir's easier-to-grow relative.

The French Revolution of 1789 led to the breaking up of the monarchy and aristocratic and ecclesiastical estates, which were less cohesive units than their counterparts in Bordeaux. In 1790 this redistribution of land was accelerated with the introduction of the

Chevaliers du Tastevin
Burgundy's medieval image has been successfully promoted by the Confrèrie, the brotherhood of the Chevaliers du Tastevin, which literally means the "knights of the tasting cup". Founded in 1934, the group now holds banquets for members and their guests at Clos de Vougeot and at overseas "chapters".

Code Napoléon, a law that specified equal inheritance among children, regardless of age and sex.

HYPHENATED NAMES

The result of the Code Napoléon law is visible throughout Burgundy. The patchwork of vines shows the effect of carving up pieces of land between the children of deceased wine-growers. Look at the range of wines offered in any Burgundian cellar and you will see the effect of the marriages between one grower's son and his neighbor's daughter. This can also be seen in the hyphenated names of estates like Coche-Boulicault and Coche-Dury.

Exploiting and marketing tiny quantities of several different wines was difficult, especially in a region that was prone to bad weather and poor harvests. The first wine merchants were already buying, blending, and maturing wines by the early 18th century. For the next 200 years, these merchants more or less controlled the Burgundy wine market. It was not until the late 20th century that the owners of estates with an average size of only 15 acres (six ha) began handling their own wine from grape to bottle, making the most of the "small is beautiful" trend of the 1970s and 1980s. Loss of control by the merchants, combined with the introduction of *appellation contrôlée* legislation, did away with the most obvious falsifications of the Burgundy wine trade, but it also exposed the challenges of small-scale wine-making in what can be a tricky climate. The established hierarchy of *grand cru, premier cru,* village and regional wines will give you an idea of where to find the best bottles, but in reality a well-made village wine in a good year is often far better than a poorly made *grand cru* wine that sells at several times the price. So the most important words on a label are the name of the producer.

Traditional Wine Press
Old presses like this one in Burgundy changed little between the Middle Ages and the 20th century. Now, however, most are automatic and even pneumatic.

A Driving Tour of Burgundy

This tour covers most of the significant wine-producing villages of the Côte de Beaune as well as the little-known Hautes-Côtes de Beaune. Also included is the hugely ornate Château de la Rochepot, which will delight those with a taste for fairy-tale architecture as well as for wine.

BEAUNE

The medieval town of Beaune ① is home to most of Burgundy's best-known wine merchants, a well-stocked *musée du vin*, and the world-famous Hôtel Dieu, a magnificent hospital built during the 15th century and financed through the sale of wine from its vineyards.

BEAUNE TO MEURSAULT

Take the Chalon-sur-Saône road, forking right at the Cave Coopérative des Hautes-Côtes, toward Pommard ②. The Château de Pommard's cellars are worth a visit, if only because the wine made here is sold nowhere else. Volnay ③ is a slightly larger village, set high enough to allow a panoramic view of the patchwork of vineyards below. There are plenty of excellent producers here, but one of the best is Michel Lafarge. Follow the road toward Auxey-Duresses, past the village of Monthélie ④ and its château on your right. Like Monthélie, Auxey-Duresses ⑤ is a good source of underrated, and consequently affordable, red and white wines. The church here is also worth a visit for its triptych showing the Life of the Virgin. Meursault ⑥ is more of a town than a village; its main square, imposing church and well-kept wine-growers' homes and cellars reflect the success that its wines enjoy around the world. The Château de Meursault is where the wine makers Paulée hold a day-long lunch in November.

Château de Pommard
Visitors to the cellars of this château can buy fine, distinctive wines unavailable elsewhere.

PULIGNY-MONTRACHET TO CHASSAGNE-MONTRACHET

After Meursault, Puligny-Montrachet ⑦ is very quiet. Merchant Olivier Leflaive offers a good range of white wines and a restaurant where they can be tasted with local dishes. There is little of note about Gamay ⑧, except that this is where the grape of the same name was supposedly first planted in Burgundy. St Aubin ⑨ offers some fairly priced white wines from estates like the Domaine Roux. The wine-growers' track from St Aubin to Chassagne-Montrachet passes the world-famous Le Montrachet ⑩ vineyard, whose stone gateways offer a fine photo opportunity for visiting wine lovers. Sleepy but charming, Chassagne-Montrachet ⑪ is also worth a visit.

SANTENAY TO LA ROCHEPOT

Santenay ⑫ offers a spa bath, a pretty main square, a casino, and some good-value red and white wines. Nolay ⑬ has no wine, but does boast a quaint 14th-century market hall. The wooded hills here make a spectacular backdrop for the Château de la Rochepot ⑭, whose vibrantly colored roof is similar to that of the Hôtel Dieu in Beaune.

LA ROCHEPOT TO SAVIGNY-LÈS-BEAUNE

You are now in the rugged hills of the Hautes-Côtes de Beaune. Pause at the top of the cliffs at Orches ⑮, where

Hill of Corton
The vineyards of the hill of Corton produce some of the best wines in Burgundy.

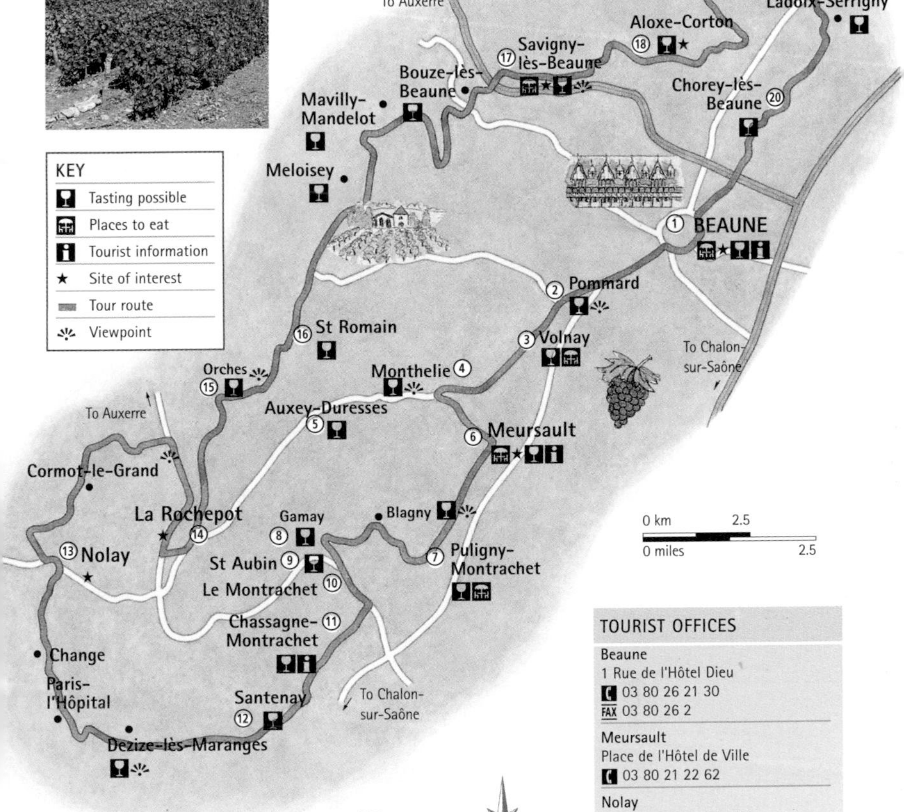

KEY

- Tasting possible
- Places to eat
- Tourist information
- ★ Site of interest
- Tour route
- Viewpoint

you may see hawks and other wild birds, before continuing on to the village of St Romain ⑯, where producer Alain Gras makes and sells some great-value white wines.

SAVIGNY-LÈS-BEAUNE TO BEAUNE

The road to Savigny-lès-Beaune ⑰ offers a good view of the Château de Savigny, home to a motorcycle museum. Drive on to Aloxe-Corton ⑱ in the shadow of the hill of Corton, site of some of the best *grands crus* vineyards in the Côte de Beaune. Some of the best wines are made in Pernand-Vergelesses ⑲. At Chorey-lès-Beaune ⑳ the Domaine Tollot-Beaut and the Château de Chorey both make stunning reds.

TOURIST OFFICES

Beaune
1 Rue de l'Hôtel Dieu
Tel 03 80 26 21 30
FAX 03 80 26 2

Meursault
Place de l'Hôtel de Ville
Tel 03 80 21 22 62

Nolay
24 Avenue de la République
Tel/FAX 03 80 21 80 73

La Rochepot
The brightly tiled roof of the medieval château rivals that of the Hôtel Dieu in Beaune *(see p129)*. It recalls the prosperous days when the Duchy of Burgundy stretched as far as Flanders.

The Food of Burgundy

The gastronomic tradition and reputation of Burgundy is almost as long-established as that of its wines: its great, classic dishes are ones that we associate with France as a whole. This is hearty, robust food of the sort that would be welcomed after a long day in the vineyard and is, naturally, the perfect accompaniment to a good bottle of Burgundy.

Burgundy is rich in terms of high-quality ingredients. The town of Bresse claims to produce some of the world's best poultry, while the famous Charolais beef cattle are prized by chefs all over the world. The Morvan, with its many rivers, produces some of the finest freshwater fish in France, and its forests are home to a variety of game. There is also an abundance of delicate mushrooms, fat, gray snails, and luscious, ripe vegetables and fruit. On top of all that are the region's wines, which not only enhance the food when drunk with it, but also play a major part in the preparation of many great local dishes.

Red wine is the basis of casseroles such as the classic *boeuf bourguignon*, and of sauces for egg and fish dishes. White Burgundy plays a similar role in chicken and rabbit dishes. The fiery *marc de Bourgogne*, a liquor distilled from the residue of grapes, is used to wash the rinds of the local cheeses.

Traditionalists used to suggest using the same wine for the dish as would be served with it. Nowadays, however, the

Charcuterie
As elsewhere in France, pork meats, including ham, pâté, sausage, and brawn, play a major role in the cuisine of Burgundy. On special occasions, the ham is often served whole.

Boeuf Bourguignon
In this classic stew, cuts of beef are marinated, then slowly cooked in Beaujolais or Burgundy wine, to which cubed bacon, onions, and mushrooms are added.

cost of a bottle of Grand Cru Chambertin, for example, is such that only a true purist, or a millionaire, would be prepared to pour half a bottle or more of this great red into the pot. Most modern chefs use a good, full-bodied red Burgundy instead.

Cream is used in many local dishes, often with ham or mushrooms. Ham, which was once the traditional Easter dish, may also be braised in wine or set in a green parsley jelly—this is known as *jambon persillé*. Other *charcuterie*, such as *sansiot* (brawn), *saucisson* (salami-like sausage), *andouillettes*, and pâtés, are made throughout Burgundy.

The town of Dijon is famous for its mustard, in which eggs are cooked in the dish *oeufs à la dijonnaise*, and also for its black currants, used as the basis of the delicious liqueur *crème de cassis*—which is used to make *kir*, a white-wine aperitif.

Burgundy is also known for a wide range of baked goods, including *pain d'épices* (spiced bread). One savory treat traditionally served at wine tastings is the addictive *gougère*, a *choux* pastry made with cheese. It is eaten cold or lukewarm and can be served plain, or garnished with mushrooms or vegetables.

Escargots à la Bourguignonne
The Romans brought their large eating snails to France, where they were quickly adopted as a classic.

Poulet de Bresse
This *appellation contrôlée* chicken is cooked in a delicious white Burgundy and cream sauce, with wild morel mushrooms.

REGIONAL CHEESES

While Burgundy is not nearly as famous for its dairy produce as it is for its wine, lush pastures and picture-book Charolais cattle make for rich, creamy cheeses that complement the region's wines perfectly. Even the smallest, most humble restaurants will usually offer a choice of perfectly ripened local cheeses. The distinction of many of the cheeses in this region, though, is the strength of the flavors, which often go far more successfully with the delicate local Pinot Noir grape variety than one might expect.

Epoisses de Bourgogne
The orange rind of this strong-smelling cheese is washed with the traditional *marc de Bourgogne* as it ripens.

Bleu de Bresse
This rich, creamy cheese, a classic of southern France, has a soft pâté that is peppered with patches of blue mold. When the cheese has ripened, a white rind forms.

TRAVELING IN BURGUNDY

Burgundy begins less than an hour and a half's drive from Paris—and finishes just short of Lyon, by which time you are well into the southern half of France, with its Roman roofs and more leisurely way of life. Unsurprisingly, this makes for a diverse range of landscapes and moods—and some of France's most rewarding places to visit.

HOTELS & RESTAURANTS

A selection of the region's best establishments, offering good local food and drink, and notable, characterful places to stay.

Cafe life in Burgundy
While it is known for its restaurants serving hearty dishes like *coq au vin*, Burgundy also boasts plenty of cafés that offer lighter fare.

BAGNOLS, NEAR LYON

Château de Bagnols.
04 74 71 40 00
FAX 04 74 71 40 09
A magical, turreted, moated castle in the heart of Beaujolais, which was impeccably and very expensively restored by its British-born owners. Quite simply one of the most beautifuil hotels in France.

BEAUNE

Au Bon Acceuil, La Montagne de Beaune.
03 80 22 08 80
FAX 03 80 22 93 12
Better known as Chez Nono, this rustic cafe-restaurant is tucked away in the hills above the town. Your fellow diners will include the owners of wine companies and their truck drivers.

L'Ecusson, Place Malmédy, Beaune.
03 80 24 03 82
This establishment offers some of Beaune's best-value fine food, and a well-priced wine list.

Le Home, 138 Route de Dijon.
03 80 22 16 43
Just outside town, this courtyard hotel is inexpensive, friendly, and comfortable. Choose between rooms in the old building or a set of motel-style ones.

CHABLIS

Bistrot des Grands Crus, 8-10 Rue Jules Rathier.
03 86 42 19 41
FAX 03 86 42 17 11
W www.hostellerie-des-clos.fr
Under the same ownership as the more luxurious Hostellerie des Clos, this casual restaurant offers similar-style cooking with subtle modern twists on local tradition.

CHAGNY

Lameloise, 36 Place des Armes.
03 85 87 65 65
FAX 03 85 87 03 57
One of the most reliable and quietly unassuming of France's luxury country hotels, Lameloise is situated between Beaune and Chalon sur Saone and offers some of the finest cuisine in the region. The wine list is great too.

CHOREY-LÈS-BEAUNE, NEAR BEAUNE

Le Château de Chorey, Rue Jacques Germain.
03 80 22 06 05
The charming rooms at this lovely old château, which is surrounded by vineyards, are just the thing if you are looking for somewhere special to stay.

MÂCON

Hôtel-Restaurant Bellevue, 416-420 Quai Lamartine.
03 85 21 04 04
FAX 03 85 21 04 02
A slightly fading hotel overlooking the river and the market. Its rooms are very comfortable and the restaurant serves good local fare and wines to match.

PULIGNY-MONTRACHET

Le Montrachet, Place des Maronniers.
03 80 21 30 06
A favorite restaurant among the locals, this is a good place to taste wines that rarely appear elsewhere.

WINE SHOPS

Many Burgundian wines are not readily available back home, so stock up while you're here.

AUXERRE

Le Cellier des Agapes, Rue de Preuilly.
03 86 52 15 22
Tucked away in Chablis country, Marc Ragaine managed to put together a sufficiently impressive range of wines to win the prize of France's best wine shop in 2003.

BEAUNE

l'Atheneúm, 5 rue de l'Hôtel-Dieu.
03 80 25 08 30
FAX 03 80 25 08 31
@ athenaeum@wanadoo.fr

Is this the best wine bookstore in the world? I can't think of a better one, and I certainly don't know of one that sells as wide a range of wine-related artifacts.

MUSEUMS

Some producers offer vineyard or winery tours. Contact tourist offices *(see below)* for details.

BEAUNE
Hôtel-Dieu, Rue de l'Hôtel-Dieu.
03 80 26 21 30
Better-known as the Hospices de Beaune, this 15th century *hospices* is famous as one of the symbols of the region, and it is a delight to visit. The Salle des Pauvres (Hall of the Poor), the kitchen, and the pharmacy are all highlights.
Le Musée du Vin de Bourgogne, Hôtel des Ducs de Bourgogne, Rue d'Enfer.
03 80 22 08 19
Tucked away behind the cathedral, this museum has everything from medieval presses to Aubusson tapestries and old drinking glasses.
CHAUMONT LE BOIS
Le Musée du Vigneron, Place St Martin.
FAX 03 80 81 95 97
This nice little place illustrates the processes of vine growing, sparkling wine production, and coopery in the past and today, with the help of old tools and archaeological relics. It was set up by Sylvain Bouhelier, a young Crémant de Bourgogne producer.
CHENOVE, NEAR DIJON
Pressoirs des Ducs de Bourgogne, 8 Rue Roger Salengro.
03 80 52 82 83
FAX 03 80 51 55 24
These 13th-century presses, one of which is still used in an annual ceremony, are worth a brief visit.
ROMANÈCHE-THORINS, NEAR MÂCON
Le Musée du Hameau en Beaujolais, La Gare.
03 85 35 22 22
The creation of local Beaujolais producer Georges Duboeuf, this is a vinous theme park, complete with 3-D films, set up in a converted train station.

ANNUAL WINE EVENTS

The annual Hospices de Beaune charity auction and the Trois Glorieuses banquets are always held on the third weekend in November, when there is also a tasting of hundreds of wines from the latest vintage. These events are open to the public, but your best chance of getting tickets is through a friendly Beaune *négociant*, or through one of his best customers. Contact the tourist office *(see below)* for the dates of other events listed here.

JANUARY
Côte d'Or (village changes every year) St Vincent festival
Chablis Region St Vincent du Grand Auxerrois festival

MARCH
Chablis Les Vinées Tonnerroises—Montée de Tonnerre wine festival

MAY
Mâcon national wine fair and competition.

JULY/AUGUST
Noyers-sur-Serein, Meursault, Chablis, Cluny, and **Gevrey-Chambertin** wine festivals
Noyers classical music and wine festival

AUGUST/SEPTEMBER
Dijon and **Beaune** international folklore competition and wine festival.

SEPTEMBER
Chenove, near Dijon Fête de la Pressée—the annual harvest festival moment when a 13th-century press is used for the first grapes of the new vintage

OCTOBER
Nuits-St-Georges wine festival
Odenas Fête du Paradis a Beaujolais festival that marks the pressing of the new vintage
Romanêche-Thorins La Fête Raclet—a Beaujolais harvest festival celebrating Benoît Raclet, the local hero who discovered the means of freeing the vines from flying pests.

NOVEMBER
Chablis wine fair
Beaujeu Les Sarmentelles—a Beaujolais festival with parades, music, and fireworks

WEBSITES

The region's official website is www.vins-bourgogne.com. For details on specific *appellations*, try www.maison-des-vins.com (Mâcon) and www.beaujolais.net (Beaujolais). Good general tourist information is available at www.terroirs-b.com or www.tourisme.fr.

OTHER INFORMATION

Office de Tourisme, Place de la Halle, Beaune.
03 80 26 21 30
The region's main tourist office can provide information on everything from wine-makers to balloon flights over the vineyards.
Maison du Tourisme du Pays Beaujolais, 96 Rue de la Sous-Préfecture, Villefranche-sur-Saône.
04 74 07 27 40
paysbeaujolais@beaujolais.net

ALOXE-CORTON

AT THE NORTHERN END of the Côte de Beaune is the *appellation* of Aloxe-Corton, home to the famous red and white *grands crus* Corton vineyards. The rest of the *appellation* produces almost exclusively red wines and has more in common with the red-wine-producing Côte de Nuits to the north than with some of its more white-oriented neighbors to the south.

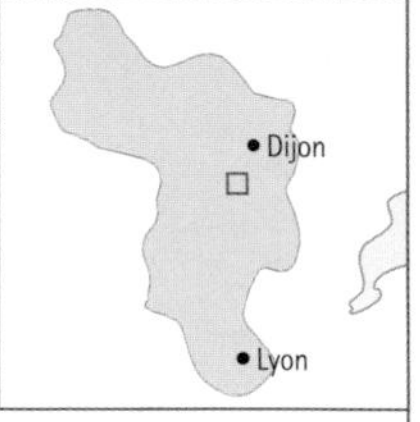

Château Corton-André
With very few small, family-owned estates, the *appellation* of Aloxe-Corton remains very much the province of big-business merchant firms such as La Reine Pédauque, owner of this spectacular château.

Local legend claims not only that comedian Charlie Chaplin considered buying a plot of vines in the *commune* of Aloxe-Corton, but also that more than a thousand years ago the wines here were a favorite of the Roman Emperor Charlemagne, who has given his name to the white wine-producing *grand cru* vineyard of Corton-Charlemagne.

Red wines make up 99 percent of the vintage in Aloxe-Corton: they are made, like almost all red Burgundy, from the powerful Pinot Noir grape. In fact, the wines produced here are among the longest-lived and slowest to develop of all the wines of Burgundy. As a result of this early impenetrability, many of the village and *premiers crus* wines of Aloxe-Corton are less popular than the softer, fruitier and more immediately appealing wines of neighboring Beaune *(see p128)* and Savigny-lès-Beaune *(see p156)*. After five to 15 years in the bottle, however, these wines develop a rich, meaty fruitiness and offer excellent value. If drunk young, the similarly austere red and white *grands crus* wines of the *commune* also tend to compare badly with top-quality wines from nearby *appellations* such as Puligny-Montrachet *(see p153)* and Chassagne-Montrachet *(see p135)* to the south. After around 10 years, however, the red wines are smooth, with deliciously gamey flavors, while the whites are richly concentrated, with sumptuous flavors of butter, cinnamon, and honey.

The attention of many wine-buyers has long been focused on Louis Latour and La Reine Pédauque, two long-established producer-merchant firms with cellars in the town of Aloxe-Corton. Neither of these, unfortunately, produces particularly exciting reds. More recently, however, welcome investment by producers and *négociants* from other parts of Burgundy, including such illustrious names as Tollot-Beaut in Chorey-lès-Beaune, Bonneau du Martray in Pernand-Vergelesses, and Antonin Guyon in Savigny-lès-Beaune, has resulted in some innovatively made wines with a much less rugged character than is traditional here.

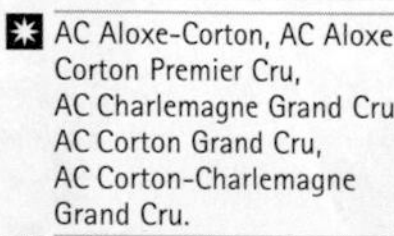

- AC Aloxe-Corton, AC Aloxe-Corton Premier Cru, AC Charlemagne Grand Cru, AC Corton Grand Cru, AC Corton-Charlemagne Grand Cru.
- Red: Pinot Noir. White: Chardonnay, Pinot Gris.
- Rich, meaty, deep-colored reds. Some full-bodied, slow-developing whites.
- Arnoux, Bouchard Père et Fils, Denis Boussey, Champy, Marc Colin et Fils, Joseph Drouhin, François Gay, Génot-Boulanger, Camille Giroud, Antonin Guyon, Louis Latour, Prince de Mérode, Antonin Rodet, Comte Sénard, Tollot-Beaut, Michel Voarick.
- Roast pheasant stuffed with thyme and lemon in a red wine sauce.
- 2003, 2002, 1999, 1998, 1997, 1996, 1995, 1993, 1990.
- Red: 5–15 years.

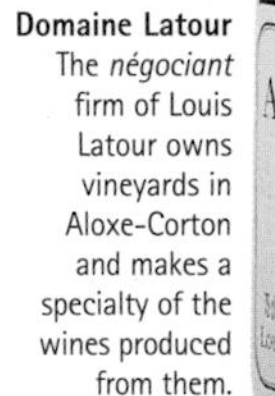

Domaine Latour
The *négociant* firm of Louis Latour owns vineyards in Aloxe-Corton and makes a specialty of the wines produced from them.

GRANDS CRUS VINEYARDS OF THE MONTAGNE DE CORTON

Covering 445 acres (180 ha) of land on the slopes of the Montagne de Corton are the vineyards of Corton Grand Cru and Corton-Charlemagne Grand Cru. Extending into the three *appellations* of Aloxe-Corton *(see p124)*, Pernand-Vergelesses *(see p150)*, and Ladoix *(see p142)*, this is the largest area of *grand cru* land in Burgundy. Chardonnay vines grown on the highest slopes are classified under the Corton-Charlemagne *appellation*, producing 300,000 bottles of white wine each year. Below them are the Pinot Noir vines that make up the red wine *appellation* of Corton Grand Cru. Half a million bottles of red wine are made from these vines each year, some labeled as Corton Grand Cru, others specifying the *climat*, or named area, in which the grapes were grown. Tiny amounts of white wine, including some well-made examples by Louis Jadot, are sold as Corton Grand Cru *blanc*. The varied regions of this *appellation* produce wines of mixed quality, so look carefully at the label before buying. Wines from the Corton-Bressandes and Corton-Clos de Roi *climats* are worth looking for, as are those from the excellent Corton-Pougets, Corton-Perrières, Corton-Grèves and Corton-Renardes. Both red and white wines are best matured for 10 years or so before drinking.

Field of Dreams
Chardonnay vines in the Corton-Charlemagne *grand cru* vineyard produce some of the greatest white Burgundies of all.

AUXEY-DURESSES

BETWEEN MONTHÉLIE *(see p146)* and Meursault *(see p145)* in the valley of the Dheune River is the beautiful village of Auxey-Duresses. Two thirds of the wine produced here is red—much of which is sold as Côte de Beaune-Villages. These early-maturing, faintly rustic wines have a tendency toward tartness in all but the warmest years. That said, in good years they are a real bargain. Generally, the white wines are better than the reds, and compare well with many humbler efforts from neighboring Meursault. Well-made examples of red and white wines from the south-facing *premiers crus* vineyards of Les Duresses and Climat du Val are worth paying more for, as are wines from the area's best producers, including Olivier Leflaive, Jean-Pierre Diconne, and Jean-François Coche-Dury.

Christophe Buisson
Well-made wines like this one from producer Christophe Buisson are full of fresh raspberry fruit flavors.

Hidden Treasure
Overshadowed by its more famous neighbors, Auxey-Duresses is the little-known source of some great-value wines, both red and white.

- AC Auxey-Duresses, AC Auxey-Duresses Premier Cru.
- Red: Pinot Noir. White: Chardonnay.
- Soft, plump, slightly rustic reds. Early-maturing oaked whites.
- Comte Armand, D'Auvenay, Bouzereau, Coche-Dury, A Creusefond, J-P Diconne, Joseph Drouhin, Louis Jadot, Jaffelin, Olivier Leflaive, J-P Prunier, P Prunier, V Prunier, Roy.
- Red: *coq au vin*.
- Red: 2003, 2002, 1999, 1998.
- Red: 3–10 years. White: 2–6 years.

BEAUJOLAIS

In an increasingly fashion-conscious world, where even wines can be seen to conform to worryingly similar styles, Beaujolais still stands apart. And so it should. At its finest, Beaujolais is a refreshing antidote to all the richest, oakiest red wines in the world and is a great companion for all kinds of food, ranging from traditional French to spicy Asian.

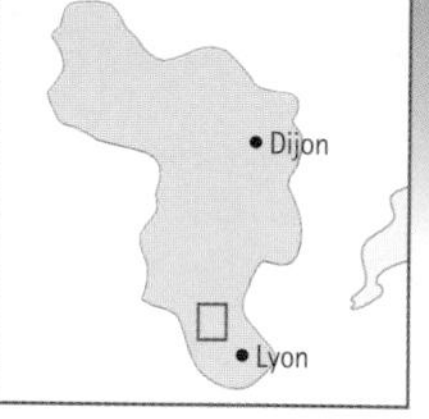

There is something deliciously androgynous about Beaujolais that somehow sets it between red and white wine, combining the color of the former with the easy drinkability of the latter. The region's unique *ménage à trois* of the Gamay grape (a variety that never performs as well elsewhere), the granite soil, and the *macération carbonique* process—a technique used by most producers here, in which berries are fermented whole *(see p26)*—produces wines with vibrant fruit flavors and almost no perceptible tannin.

For most of its history, however, this was little more than a jug wine. A century and a half after Thomas Jefferson's initials were inscribed on bottles of Château Lafite, Beaujolais was still being served in cafés directly from the cask and from pitchers, in the way of good ale. It was not until the late 1950s and 1960s that Beaujolais found its way into bottles, but all too often the wines that were sold under this name overseas had more to do with North Africa than southern Burgundy.

The man who came to the region's rescue was a young local grower named Georges Duboeuf, who in the 1960s launched a *négociant* business that sold only genuine Beaujolais and also packaged and marketed the fresh, cherryish wine in a way that was noticed throughout the world. Duboeuf's most obvious contribution was his enthusiastic promotion of Beaujolais Nouveau or Beaujolais Primeur. This helped to increase sales of the newly made wine from less than two million bottles a year in the late 1950s to a peak of some 90 million bottles a year in the 1990s and annual bedlam in wine bars and restaurants across the globe.

More recently, as tastes have switched to softer, richer wines from farther south and from the New World, the fever has calmed considerably in most countries. Even in Paris, the arrival of the new wine is greeted with more of a shrug than a cheer. For some reason, the only place where Beaujolais Nouveau still causes real excitement is Japan.

Rolling Hills
The charm of Beaujolais' landscape, with its gently rolling hills, is increased by the knowledge that every turn in the road could lead to yet another pretty village that is home to an assortment of independent wine-makers.

- AC Beaujolais, AC Beaujolais Primeur, AC Beaujolais Supérieur, AC Beaujolais (village name), AC Beaujolais-Villages.
- Red: Gamay.
- Soft, fruity reds that generally mature early.
- Aucoeur, Paul Beaudet, Berrod, Pierre-Marie Chermette, André Colonge, Joseph Drouhin, Georges Duboeuf, Henry Fessy, Ch des Jacques, Jacky Janodet, Pardon et Fils, Frédéric Pérol, Dominique Piron, Jean-Charles Pivot, Ch de Pizay, Plateau de Bel-Air, des Terres Dorés, Michel Tête, Ch Thivin, Frédéric Trichard, Maison des Vignerons.
- Chicken cooked with bamboo shoots.
- 2003, 2001, 1997.
- 1–3 years. *Crus*: 2–8 years.

Jean-Paul Brun
Today, while most Beaujolais is made light and fruity for easy drinking, Jean-Paul Brun makes more traditional wines.

Critics of the region's wines—and there are plenty—blamed the hysteria surrounding Beaujolais Nouveau for allowing producers to sell large quantities of very basic, and sometimes downright poor, wine to people who were too caught up in the moment to notice that they were drinking wine they would find unacceptable under normal circumstances. Others replied that, while rushing the wine to market within just a few weeks of the harvest inevitably led to corners being cut, the experience of drinking newly made wine was one that is as old as civilization.

Whatever the quality of the Nouveau, basic Beaujolais sold during the rest of the year is a pretty mixed bag. Good individual estates and merchants, like Duboeuf and Loron, make decent wines, but the bottles that are produced by unfamiliar estates and sold in supermarkets should be treated with suspicion. Wines labeled Beaujolais Supérieur should be made from ripe grapes, but this is an *appellation* that is only used for some 13 million bottles out of a potential total production of around 175 million. It is best to head instead for the 38 *communes* whose harvest is sold under the Beaujolais-Villages *appellation* or under the name of Beaujolais-Villages plus the name of the village (for example Beaujolais-Villages Lantignié and Beaujolais-Villages Blacé).

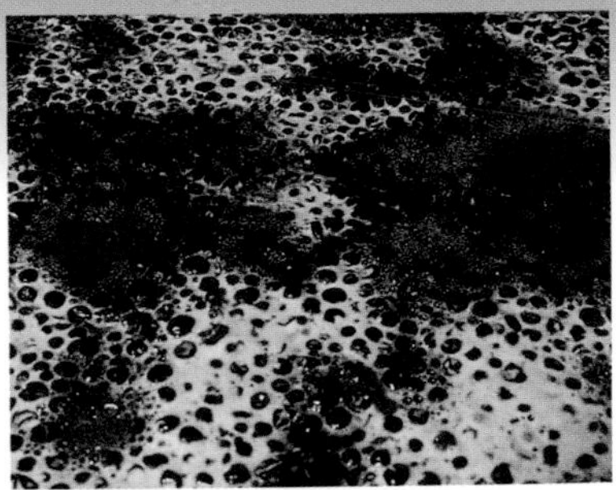

In Full Ferment
The uncrushed Gamay grapes from Beaujolais ferment to provide zingy, bright, berryish flavors that are rarely found anywhere outside this region.

Alternatively, take another step up the ladder of quality and opt for one of the 10 Beaujolais *crus*—Brouilly, Chénas, Chiroubles, Côte de Brouilly, Fleurie, Juliénas, Morgon, Moulin-à-Vent, Régnié and St Amour. Today, rosé and white Beaujolais wine is rare, with much of the white wine produced in this *appellation* now being sold as St Véran.

AGING BEAUJOLAIS

Sooner or later when visiting wine-makers in Beaujolais, if you're lucky and they like you and think that you know a thing or two about wine, one of them will no doubt pull out an obviously old bottle of Beaujolais and challenge you to guess its age. Don't worry about getting the age wrong; some of the most experienced wine tasters have missed the target by as much as a couple of decades. The point the wine-maker is striving to make is that, despite its reputation as a wine that must be drunk young, good Beaujolais can actually mature and survive in the bottle for a surprisingly long time. Good bottles of Morgon and Moulin-à-Vent *(see p148)* can develop complexity with age, but most other wines simply turn into pleasant, but rather anonymous, old red wines that could easily be mistaken for mature, but not very good, red Burgundies. More importantly, the rich flavor they develop with time is gained at the expense of the vibrant character that gives Beaujolais its unique appeal.

Worth Laying Down
Morgon, from the village of Villié Morgon, is one of the few examples of Beaujolais that can benefit from aging for five years or longer.

BEAUNE

THE UNOFFICIAL CAPITAL OF BURGUNDY and one of the greatest wine towns in the world, Beaune is home to many of the region's best wine merchants, including such famous names as Joseph Drouhin, Bouchard Père et Fils, and Louis Jadot. Often undervalued, the *appellation* of Beaune is the source of some of the most delicately appealing of red Burgundies.

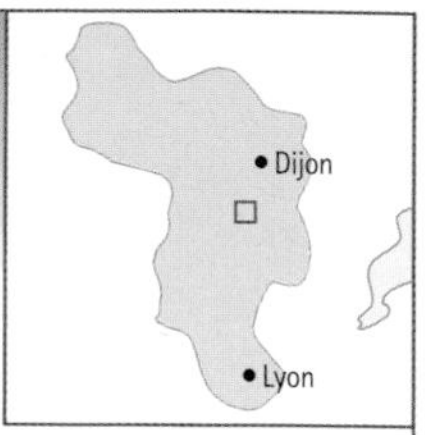

Holy Wine
This *cuvée*, which is exclusive to the firm of Bouchard Père et Fils, recalls the description made 400 years ago of Beaune that it "slipped down the throat like the little Lord Jesus dressed in velvet pantaloons".

One of the best ways to see the medieval city of Beaune is from one of the hot air balloons that float, full of tourists, above the town every day throughout the summer. From the sky, it is clear that the shape of the city has changed little in the last few hundred years, with even the road bypass that surrounds it hugging the old fortified walls. Wander through the city on a Saturday, as traders compete to sell food, clothes, and other goods, and you will see that Beaune is still the market town that it always has been. Underneath the streets, the cellars in which the city's wine merchants have traditionally stored their stock form a vast network of tunnels. Wine-selling has long been a major occupation in the city, with merchants traditionally selling wines from throughout the Côte d'Or and farther afield. Today's wine merchants do the same, but all will also offer local wines from the vineyards that surround the town on three sides. There are no *grands crus* here, but three-quarters of the vineyards in the *appellation* have been granted *premier cru* status. The best of these are Les Avaux, Les Boucherottes, Les Bressandes, Les Cents Vignes, Clos du Roi, Le Clos des Mouches, les Epenottes, Les Grèves, Les Marconnets, Les Teurons, and Les Vignes-Franches. While there are still a number of individually owned estates here, much of the best land is owned by large merchant firms such as Drouhin, Jadot, and Bouchard Père et Fils. By promoting more expensive wines from other *appellations*, the merchants of the city have, ironically, contributed to a general underestimation of the wines of Beaune. Known for their softness and their aromas of wild fruit and flowers, some of the great old wines of Beaune smell just like faded roses. As a general rule, a wine from a merchant's own Beaune vineyards will be some of his best, and some, like those from Drouhin's Clos des Mouches and Bouchard Père et Fils' Vigne de l'Enfant Jésus, can be great by any standards. White Beaune is a rarity, but can be as good as many of the wines of Chassagne-Montrachet *(see p135)*.

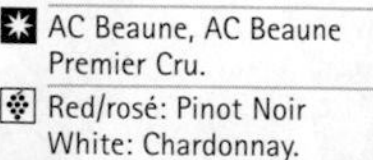

AC Beaune, AC Beaune Premier Cru.

Red/rosé: Pinot Noir
White: Chardonnay.

Succulent, delicate reds. Intense, fragrant whites.

Robert Ampeau, Arnoux Père et Fils, Bitouzet-Prieur, Bouchard Père et Fils, Pascal Bouley, Champy, Ch de la Tour, Joseph Drouhin, Dubois, Génot-Boulanger, Germain (Ch de Chorey), Camille Giroud, Louis Jadot, Michel Lafarge, Daniel Largeot, Laurent, Maillard Père et Fils, Albert Morot, Mussy, Jaques Prieur, Rapet Père et Fils, Thomas-Moillard, Tollot-Beaut.

Millefeuille of snails with cep mushrooms.

2003, 2002, 1999, 1998, 1997, 1996, 1995, 1993, 1990, 1988, 1985, 1978.

Red: 3–12 years.

Joseph Drouhin
Another great wine, delicate but with beautifully concentrated fruit flavors, this one comes from the Clos des Mouches vineyard and is made by merchant Joseph Drouhin.

HOSPICES DE BEAUNE

Colorful Glory
Now a major tourist attraction, the Hospices de Beaune functioned as a hospital until 1971.

A major date in the international wine calendar, the sale of wines from the Hospices de Beaune vineyards takes place each year on the third Sunday in November. In 1443, tax collector Nicolas Rolin, anxious to secure himself a place in heaven, built a hospital, or *hôtel-Dieu*, providing free treatment for the poor of Beaune. He also gave vineyards for the upkeep of the hospital, and these, together with subsequent gifts of land from all over the Côte d'Or, are used to make more than a quarter of a million bottles of wine each year, the proceeds of which are still used to finance a hospital and nursing home in Beaune.

ORIGINS OF THE AUCTION

In 1859 it was decided to sell the wines at an annual charity auction. Although made by a wine-maker employed by the Hospices, the young wines are sold in the cask, and are matured and bottled by the buyer. Some of the 37 *cuvées* come from individual vineyards, while others are blends from different plots within the same *appellation*. Initially, each *cuvée* bore the name of the grower who tended the vines, but this was later replaced by the name of the donor. The prices paid at auction have traditionally been thought to set the tone for the year's wines as a whole, but auction hysteria has in fact often led to the payment of inflated prices. Wine-making at the Hospices is a high-profile job, and techniques here have been the subject of controversy; indeed, revelations by one wine-maker led to a relaxation on the laws governing the way Burgundy can be acidified.

NATURE VERSUS NURTURE

Almost as important as the vineyard and the wine-making is the way in which the wine is matured. At one memorable blind tasting, experts found little resemblance between various wines that were all from the same *cuvée*, but bottled by different buyers. One thing that all the wines do have in common is an unusually high price tag, justified, naturally, by thoughts of the contribution being made to a very worthy cause.

THE CUVÉES

Reds

Auxey-Duresses Boillot
Beaune Brunet
Beaune Clos de la Roche Georges Kritter
Beaune Clos des Avaux
Beaune Cyrot-Chaudron
Beaune Dames Hospitalières
Beaune Guigone de Salins
Beaune Hugues et Louis Bétault
Beaune Maurice Drouhin
Beaune Nicolas Rolin
Beaune Rousseau-Deslandes
Clos de la Roche Cyrot-Chaudron
Corton Charlotte Dumay
Corton Docteur Peste
Mazis-Chambertin Madeleine Collignon
Monthélie Lebelin
Pernand-Vergelesses Rameau-Lamarosse
Pommard Billardet
Pommard Dames de la Charité
Pommard Raymond Cyrot
Pommard Suzanne Chaudron
Savigny-lès-Beaune Forneret
Savigny-lès-Beaune Fouquerand
Volnay Blondeau
Volnay Général Muteau
Volnay-Santenots Gauvain

Whites

Bâtard-Montrachet Dames de Flandres
Corton-Charlemagne François de Salins
Corton-Vergennes Paul Chanson
Meursault-Charmes Albert Grivault
Meursault-Charmes de Bahèzre de Lanlay
Meursault-Genevrières Baudot
Meursault-Genevrières Philippe le Bon
Meursault Goureau
Meursault Humblot
Meursault Loppin
Pouilly-Fuissé Françoise Poisard

What Am I Bid?
The annual wine auction at the Hospices de Beaune is the centerpiece of a weekend of serious tasting and partying. Visitors come from all over the world to attend.

BOURGOGNE

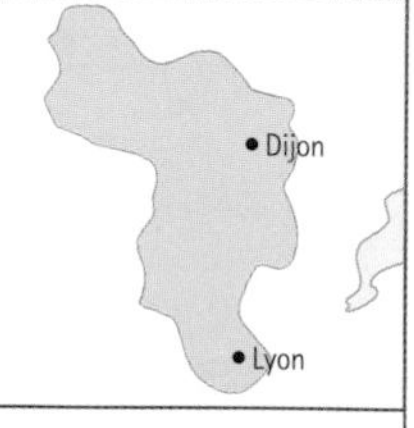

UNLIKE BOTTLES OF GENERIC BORDEAUX or Claret, which can be found on the shelves of almost every supermarket, generic Bourgogne, or Burgundy, tends to be more difficult to find. And, because of the small size of the region and the often uncertain climate that prevails here, buying good examples at inexpensive prices can be very tricky indeed.

The problem with Burgundy is that, unless you are a student of Burgundian geography and have memorized the names and addresses of the best producers, there is no way to predict the quality or style of wine in a bottle. The same word, Bourgogne or Burgundy, could appear on the label of an uninspiring wine from a merchant who has legally blended Pinot Noir from a combination of undistinguished vineyards, and on a great bottle made in tiny quantities by one of the finest grape-growers in the region. To complicate matters further, while most books quite fairly imply that red Burgundy is made exclusively from Pinot Noir grapes, you might come across a bottle bearing this label that legally has no characteristics of this grape whatsoever. In fact, you could even find that the grapes from which it was produced were not even grown on *appellation controllée* Bourgogne soil and that they are instead Gamay grapes imported from a Beaujolais *cru* village.

Plain red and white Burgundy can come from vineyards almost anywhere in the *appellation*. The least promising regions, in all but the best vintages, are the cool Hautes-Côtes de Nuits and the Hautes-Côtes de Beaune, where grapes often fail to ripen fully. Vines grown on the flatter parts of the Côte d'Or produce riper grapes, but even so, they rarely make wine of memorable quality. Some of the best basic Burgundy comes from the hillside vineyards of the Côte Chalonnaise and the Côte d'Or.

While red Burgundy made by top producers will be worth holding on to for five years or so, most examples are at their best within three or four years of production. Over time they will develop a more gamey character but this will often develop at the expense of the rich, vibrant, raspberryish flavor that makes Pinot Noir so seductive in its youth. Only the very best of white Burgundy will improve beyond three or four years.

Côte Chalonnaise
The vineyards of this somewhat unfashionable district, to the south of the better known Côte d'Or, produce some of the best of the red and white wines sold under the generic Burgundy *appellation*.

Les Vignerons d'Igé
Much of the generic Burgundy offered in supermarkets is made by *coopératives* like this one.

- AC Bourgogne.
- Red: Pinot Noir. White: Chardonnay, Pinot Gris, Pinot Blanc, Sacy.
- Light-medium reds. Dry whites that may be oaked.
- Bertrand Amboise, Bertagna, Boisset, Bouchard Père et Fils, Alain Burguet, Cave de Vignerons de Buxy, La Chablisienne, Henri Clerc, Joseph Drouhin, Camille Giroud, Les Vignerons d'Igé, Louis Jadot, Patrick Javiller, Pierre Labet, Olivier Leflaive, Cave de Lugny, Ch de Meursault, Pierre Morey, Antonin Rodet, Tollot-Beaut, Henry de Vézelay.
- Red: Snails in garlic sauce.
- White; 2003, 2002, 2001. Red: 2003, 2002, 1999, 1998, 1997, 1996, 1995.
- Red: 3–4 years. White: 2–3 years.

OTHER STYLES OF BURGUNDY

Bourgogne Ordinaire and Grand Ordinaire are all-too-honestly named wines that are generally best avoided and are, in any case, rarely found outside the region, except in a few supermarkets. The reds are mainly Gamay or low-class Pinot, while whites tend to be a dull blend of poor Chardonnay and Aligoté, and even some Melon de Bourgogne. Bourgogne Clairet and Bourgogne Clairet Grand Ordinaire are even rarer *appellations* for pale reds that are almost never seen outside the region.

Far more interesting are the regional Burgundies, such as Bourgogne Moutrecul, that are made in the Côte d'Or and the Yonne.

Of the numerous regional red Burgundies from vineyards close to Chablis, the ones to watch for are Bourgogne Irancy (soon to be known simply as Irancy), Bourgogne Epineuil's rosés, Bourgogne Côtes d'Auxerre, and Bourgogne Coulanges-la-Vineuse. In this last region, as in Bourgogne Chitry, Bourgogne Côtes d'Auxerre, Bourgogne-St Bris, and Bourgogne Vézelay, Pinot Noir is often blended with the local César, also known as "Romain" or "Gros Monsieur."

Irancy Village
Although this small commune in the north of Burgundy is not well known, it does make good, fruity, raspberryish reds.

BROUILLY AND CÔTE DE BROUILLY

Dijon
Lyon

THIS IS RARELY AMONG THE FIRST of the Beaujolais *crus* to spring to mind. While the other *crus* are all restricted to the use of the Gamay grape in the production of their wines, the wine-makers of Brouilly and the Côte de Brouilly may legally use a range of grape varieties. Brouilly's list of permitted varieties includes Aligoté, Melon de Bourgogne, and Chardonnay, while in the Côte de Brouilly, Pinot Noir and Pinot Gris are used. The Côte de Brouilly's vines are grown on the granite and schist slopes of Mont Brouilly, while Brouilly's vines have been planted on the foothills. This means that the wines of the Côte de Brouilly have more concentrated flavors and more structure, and last longer, than those of Brouilly. Even so, good Brouilly can be worth keeping for a few years.

Château Thivin
This producer makes some of the Côte de Brouilly's most complex wines.

Mont de Brouilly
Vines planted on the slopes of this hill produce the Côte de Brouilly's best wines. Brouilly is made from vines grown on much flatter land.

- AC Brouilly, AC Côte de Brouilly.
- Red: Gamay.
- Full-bodied, fruity rich reds.
- *Brouilly:* Henry Fessy, Lafond, Laurent Martray, Plateau de Bel-Air, Jean-Paul Ruet, Thorin, Ch de Tours.
  Côte de Brouilly: Jacques Depagneux, Georges Duboeuf, Ch du Grand Vernay, J C Pivot, Ch Thivin, la Voute des Crozes.
- Black pudding.
- 2003, 2001, 2000, 1997.
- 5–8 years.

CHABLIS

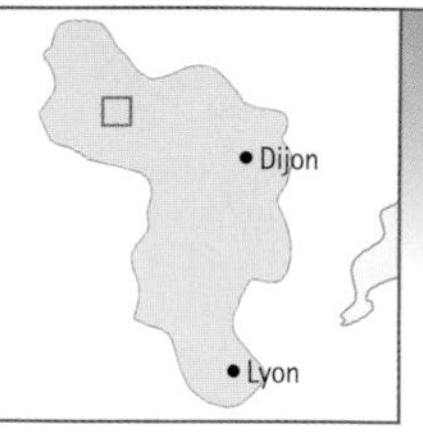

PART OF A SMALL ISLAND of vines at the northern tip of Burgundy, the Chardonnay-growing *appellation* of Chablis is known worldwide for its classic dry white wines. In these cool vineyards only 60 miles (100 km) from Paris, frost can ruin vintages. A good year, however, produces wines that are a unique combination of freshness and complexity.

Natural Selection
Now only a small *appellation* far to the north of the rest of Burgundy, Chablis was once at the center of a vast wine-making region, covering most of the *département* of Yonne.

If imitation is the sincerest form of flattery, then the wines of Chablis are surely some of the most sincerely flattered in the world. Local impostors made the most of the town's prestigious name as early as the 19th century, using it to sell wine made all over the surrounding *département* of Yonne, which was planted at the time with more than 123,550 acres (50,000 ha) of vines. More recently, wines labeled as Chablis have been produced in locations as far apart as New York State, California, and Australia's Hunter Valley. The imitation stops with the name, however; just about the only thing these wines have in common is that none of them tastes remotely like the wines made in and around the sleepy Burgundy town of Chablis.

Despite its well-deserved reputation as a source of great white wines, the 7,415-acre (3,000-ha) *appellation* of Chablis is by no means easy vine-growing land. While the area is officially part of the province of Burgundy, the cool, unpredictable viticultural conditions of Chablis have, in fact, much more in common, both geographically and climatically, with those of Champagne *(see p162)*, less than 30 miles (50 km) to the northeast, than with those of the rest of Burgundy to the south. Frost is a constant risk here and has, on occasion, been severe enough to wipe out the vineyards completely. One old grape-grower I met can remember times in his childhood when he and his friends were able to toboggan down what are now some of the top *grands crus* vineyards of the *appellation*. Today the grapes are protected by windmills, sprinkler systems, and oil burners, lined up every winter at either end of each row of vines. Even these measures, however, are not always sufficient to guarantee the vines' survival in the event of a really cold snap.

The international white Burgundy boom of the 1970s and 1980s, and the consequent pressures to increase production, led to a relaxation of the *appellation contrôlée* rules. The size of the *appellation* was increased to include a number of previously abandoned vineyards. Some land previously classified only as village Chablis was

- AC Petit Chablis, AC Chablis, AC Chablis Premier Cru, AC Chablis Grand Cru.
- White: Chardonnay.
- Crisp, sometimes oaked..
- Christian Adine, Barat, Billaud-Simon, Pascal Bouchard, Jean-Marc Brocard, La Chablisienne, Jean Collet, Jean Dauvissat, René et Vincent Dauvissat, Defaix, J-P Droin, Joseph Drouhin, Duplessis, Jean Durup, Corinne et Jean-Pierre Grossot, Laroche, Long-Depaquit, de la Maladière, des Maronniers, Louis Michel, Sylvain Mosnier, Gilbert Picq, Pinson, Raveneau, Simmonet-Fèbvre, Verget, Vocoret.
- Salmon grilled with lemon juice, parsley, and fennel.
- 2003, 2002, 2000, 1998, 1997, 1996, 1995, 1990.
- Village wines: 2–5 years. *Premiers crus* wines: 4–8 years. *Grands crus* wines: 6–12 years.

Domaine François Raveneau
Probably the most famous estate in Chablis, the wines produced here are some of the finest and most long-lived of the *appellation*.

Quiet Life
A tributary of the larger Yonne, the appropriately named Serein River flows slowly through the sleepily serene town of Chablis.

promoted to *premier cru* status, and the "*petit*" traditionally used to identify the poorer vineyards of the *appellation* was removed from a large chunk of the area previously known as Petit Chablis. This expansion has led to some vigorous argument in the quiet town of Chablis, with traditionalists claiming that the soil of the newer vineyards does not produce the flinty, mineral flavors for which the best wines are famous. These purists believe that the special character of Chablis is a result of a very particular type of chalk, known as Kimmeridgian, found beneath the best vineyards of the *appellation*. In contrast, much of the surrounding land is made up of Portlandian chalk, which is geologically similar, but not identical, to the Kimmeridgian variety. In the past, the *appellation* laws have supported this view, either entirely excluding the Portlandian vineyards from the *appellation*, or classifying them as Petit Chablis.

Plenty of dull white Burgundy is now sold under the Chablis *appellation*, a trend that changes to the *appellation* rules have only exacerbated. Equally significant is commercial pressure to produce big, buttery wines, qualities that have little to do with the traditional, steely wines of Chablis. My advice is to step very carefully when buying wines here. Some of the best buys are the intensely flavored wines from the seven south- and west-facing *grands crus* vineyards, and the stylish but somewhat more variable wines from the more numerous *premiers crus* vineyards. A good producer is essential, and some of the best in the area are listed in the box *(see p132)*. Each of the *grands crus* vineyards of Chablis produces wines with their own particular character, but all need several years in the bottle to achieve the rich, dry combination of butter, nuts, and minerals that sets the wines of Chablis apart from all of the other Chardonnay wines in the world.

In addition to the argument over where the grapes should be grown, there is another controversy raging in the bars of Chablis. Should the wines be fermented and matured in new oak? A number of producers say yes, arguing that many of today's wine-drinkers expect and enjoy at least a hint of oaky vanilla in their Burgundy. Others, however, disagree. Putting the wine in oak barrels, they believe, robs it of its unique, steely purity, reducing it to nothing more than an alternative to the wines of Meursault *(see p145)*. Drinking an unoaked wine from a good producer such as Laroche, and comparing it with overoaked lesser wines that are almost unrecognizable as Chablis, I sympathize with the unoaked school of producers. Then someone will hand me a glass of delicious, buttery, oak barrel-fermented *grand cru* Chablis from producer Jean-Paul Droin, and my reservations about the oak will fly straight out the window.

William Fèvre
Under the same ownership as Bouchard Père et Fils, this has become one of the most reliable estates in Chablis, offering a wide range of long-lived *premiers* and *grands crus*.

The Vaudevey Vineyard
Together with six other plots, the Vaudevey, or Vau de Vey, vineyard was promoted to *premier cru* status in 1986, part of a recent relaxation of the *appellation contrôlée* rules here.

CHAMBOLLE-MUSIGNY

TOGETHER WITH ITS NEIGHBOR, VOUGEOT, Chambolle-Musigny was one of the first parts of the Côte de Nuits to be planted with vines. The wines produced here are famous for their delicacy—often described as "feminine"—and their luscious depth of flavor, a fabulous combination of qualities that has made this one of the richest villages in Burgundy.

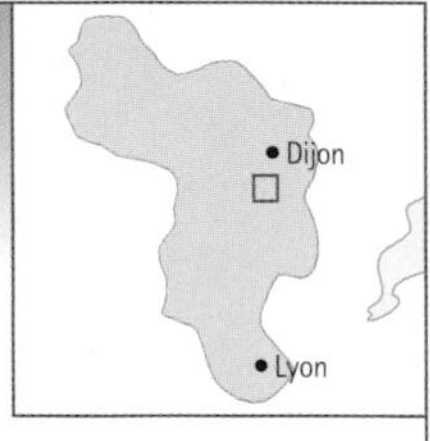

Château de Chambolle-Musigny
Jacques-Frédéric Mugnier makes aromatic wines from the Grand Cru Musigny vineyard.

The wines of the *commune* of Chambolle-Musigny, which includes the two *grands crus* vineyards of Musigny and Bonnes Mares, as well as the *appellations* of Chambolle-Musigny and Chambolle-Musigny Premier Cru, have long been seen as quite distinct from those made in the surrounding villages of the Côte de Nuits. For one 19th-century observer, a Dr. Lavalle, these were the "most delicate wines in the Côte de Nuits." One possible explanation for the delicacy of Chambolle's wines lies in the high proportion of limestone in the soil. Another theory credits the traditional use of both Pinot Blanc, used elsewhere for white wine, and the more famous Pinot Noir in the red wines made here.

Rural Calm
Tucked away behind the *route nationale*, the village of Chambolle-Musigny is one of the quietest and most charming in the Côte d'Or.

The practice of combining grapes continues today, though the permitted white variety is now Pinot Gris rather than Pinot Blanc, still used in combination with Pinot Noir. Paradoxically, despite the presence of Pinot Gris in the vineyards, the only white wine that can now legally be made in Chambolle-Musigny uses Chardonnay grapes grown on Musigny Grand Cru land. Only tiny quantities of the highly-prized Musigny *blanc* are produced each year, all at Domaine Comte Georges de Vogüé.

There has, in the past, been an unfortunate tendency for the producers of Chambolle-Musigny to treat the terms "delicate" and "dilute" as though they were synonymous. Proof, however, that an entire *appellation* can improve the quality of its wines came in the early 1990s, when the growers of Chambolle-Musigny decided to tighten the criteria required for a bottle to carry the village name. The result is consistently fine wines that are delicate but full of substance, with lingering perfumed flavors. As well as the Musigny and Bonnes Mares *grands crus*, there are also some extremely good *premiers crus* vineyards. A number of these, most notably Les Amoureuses, often produce wines of a quality to match those of *grand cru* status.

- AC Chambolle-Musigny, AC Chambolle-Musigny Premier Cru, AC Bonnes Mares Grand Cru, AC Musigny Grand Cru.
- Red: Pinot Noir. White: Chardonnay.
- Silky, refined, long-lived reds.
- Barthod-Noëllat, Bertagna, Ch de Chambolle-Musigny, Bruno Clair, Confuron-Cotetidot, Joseph Drouhin, Faiveley, Geantet-Pansiot, Robert Groffier, Anne et François Gros, Hudelot-Noëllat, Louis Jadot, Dominique Laurent, Philippe Lecheneault, Leroy, Hubert Lignier, Denis Mortet, Mugneret-Gibourg, Henri Perrot-Minot, Georges Roumier, Bernard Serveau, de Vogüé.
- Suckling wild boar.
- 2003, 2002, 2001, 1999, 1998, 1996, 1995, 1993, 1990, 1988, 1985.
- Red: 5–20 years.

AC Chambolle-Musigny
Although simpler in style and without the aging potential of Musigny Grand Cru wines, many village wines, such as this one from the Château de Chambolle-Musigny, are still magnificent examples of red Burgundy.

CHASSAGNE-MONTRACHET

CHASSAGNE-MONTRACHET PRODUCES some of the world's finest white wines. Traditionally, however, the wines produced here have been red. As recently as 1985, despite the international reputation of white Chassagne, well over half of the vintage was red. By 1997, thanks to the worldwide popularity of the Chardonnay grape, 60 percent of the year's wines were white.

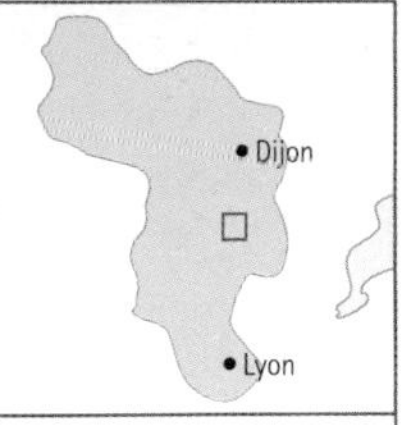

Fruitful estates
The growers of Chassagne-Montrachet, many of whom have built their homes among the vines, have no difficulty selling the Chardonnay grapes from their sometimes tiny plots.

The traditional (red wine) grapes used in the *commune* of Chassagne-Montrachet were Gamay for the poorer land and Pinot Noir in areas with richer soil. The Montrachet Grand Cru vineyard, however, shared with the neighboring commune of Puligny-Montrachet *(see p133)*, is one of the few vineyards in Chassagne-Montrachet that has traditionally been used to grow white grapes. Alongside the neighboring *grands crus* vineyards of Bâtard-Montrachet (also shared with Puligny) and Criots-Bâtard-Montrachet, it is now considered by many people to produce some of the finest dry white wine in the world. The best *premiers crus* vineyards include Morgeot, Chenevottes, Ruchottes, En Maltroye, and En Cailleret. Wines from Chassagne are generally fuller-bodied and with a slightly more mineral character than those from neighboring Puligny, often developing especially interesting flavors after a decade or so stored in the cellar.

Despite the recent huge popularity of Chassagne's white wines, there will always be red wine made here. This is simply because much of the soil, similar to the limestone marl of the Côte de Nuits, is better suited to the Pinot Noir grape than to the Chardonnay that is fast replacing it. Unfortunately, however, while a few producers do make fine red Chassagne, most of Chassagne's red wine has more in common with the simple, fresh wines of Santenay to the southwest *(see p156)* than with the delicate wines of Volnay *(see p157)* or Beaune *(see p128)*. Selling their reds is rarely a problem for the wine-growers here, however. The technique seems to be simply to force it on customers who come in search of the world-famous white.

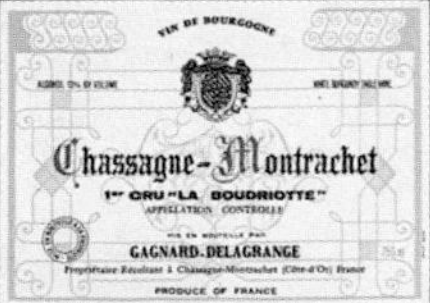

Gagnard–Delagrange
In producing their sublime wines, the wine-makers here use grapes grown in one of the least-known of Chassagne's *premiers crus* vineyards.

Domaine Ramonet
With grapes from *premiers crus* and *grands crus* vineyards, André Ramonet remains one of the very best white wine producers in the world.

- AC Chassagne-Montrachet, AC Chassagne-Montrachet Premier Cru, AC Grands Crus: Criots-Bâtard, Montrachet, Bâtard-Montrachet.
- Red: Pinot Noir. White: Chardonnay.
- Full-bodied fruity reds. Spicy, full-flavored whites.
- Guy Amiot, Marc Colin, Michel Colin-Deléger, Delagrange-Bachelet, Joseph Drouhin (de Laguiche), Henri Germain, Louis Jadot, Louis Latour, Olivier Leflaive, Maltroye, Michel Niellon, Ch de Puligny Montrachet, Ramonet, Rodet, Roux, Verget.
- Grilled trout.
- White: 2003, 2002, 2001, 1996, 1995, 1992, 1989. Red: 2003, 2002, 2001, 1999, 1998, 1997, 1996, 1995, 1990, 1989, 1988.
- Red: 3–10 years. White: 3–20 years.

CHÉNAS

THE SMALLEST OF THE Beaujolais *crus*, the flat, silty soils of Chénas have kept it way behind the better-known *cru* villages such as St Amour *(see p154)*, Morgon *(see p148)*, and Fleurie *(see p139)*. When the *appellation* boundaries were drawn up, Chénas was shortchanged. Steep granite slopes in the west of the *appellation* produce the best Chénas wines, which are medium-bodied with a hint of oak. The Château de Chénas *coopérative* produces 45 percent of the wine, and its medieval cellars are worth a visit.

Château de Chénas
Producer of almost half the wine in Chénas, this is a first-class *coopérative*.

- AC Chénas.
- Red: Gamay.
- Medium-weight, soft, fruity reds.
- Louis Champagnon, Château de Chénas, Georges Duboeuf, Hubert Lapierre, Bernard Santé.
- Chicken stewed with truffles.
- 2003, 2001, 1997.
- Red: 3–5 years.

CHIROUBLES

THIS IS THE *COMMUNE* that is said to make the most fragrant wines of the Beaujolais *crus*. It is also the highest above sea level, forming a natural amphitheater 1,300 ft (400 m) above the Beaujolais plain. The soil is a light, thin, granite-sand that gives these wines a delicate, violet-perfumed character, which, for many, represents the very essence of Beaujolais. Refreshing and fruity, these reds are delicious drunk young, accompanied by a wide variety of *charcuterie*, ranging from *andouillettes* to *saucisson*.

Château de Raousset
Light, fragrant Chiroubles is delicious when drunk young, but can improve with age.

- AC Chiroubles.
- Gamay.
- Elegant, light, refreshing red.
- Émile Cheysson, Georges Duboeuf, Hubert Lapierre, Alain Passot, Ch de Raousset.
- *Andouillettes* with mustard.
- 2003, 2001.
- 2–4 years.

CHOREY-LÈS-BEAUNE

Dijon
Lyon

THE VILLAGE OF Chorey-lès-Beaune lies on the flat plain to the north of the city of Beaune, its vineyards extending over both sides of the N74, bordering Savigny-lès-Beaune *(see p156)* to the west, and Aloxe-Corton *(see p124)* to the north. Chorey's best wines have more in common with the fruity, raspberry-jam reds of Beaune *(see p128)* and Savigny-lès-Beaune than with the tough, tannic reds of Aloxe-Corton. Fruity and soft, these wines are best drunk within three years of the harvest. In the past, much of the wine produced in Chorey-lès-Beaune has been sold as generic *appellation contrôlée* Côte de Beaune-Villages, but the recent success of local producers such as Tollot-Beaut has encouraged both growers and *négociants* to print the name of the *commune* proudly on the label.

Tollot-Beaut
Rich and oaky, many wines made at the Tollot-Beaut estate are as fine as more expensive wines from nearby Beaune.

Château de Chorey
Sister château to the Château de Savigny, the Château de Chorey offers good wine, as well as a place to stay for visitors to the region.

- AC Chorey-lès-Beaune, AC Côte de Beaune-Villages.
- Red: Pinot Noir.
- Soft, plump, fruity reds for early drinking.
- Charles Allexant, Arnoux Père et Fils, Ch de Chorey (François Germain), Doudet-Naudin, Joseph Drouhin, Drouhin Laroze, François Gay, Guyon, Daniel Largeot, Maillard Père et Fils, Tollot-Beaut.
- Terrine of ham with parsley.
- 2003, 2002, 1999, 1998.
- Red: 2–5 years.

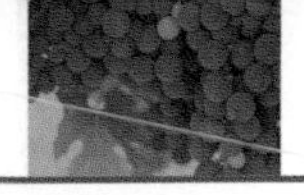

CLOS DE VOUGEOT AND VOUGEOT

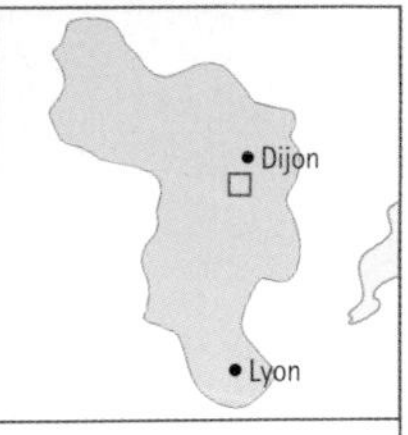

BEGUN AS A PLOT OF JUST A FEW VINES in the 12th century, the Clos de Vougeot is now the largest, and arguably the most famous, *grand cru* in Burgundy. This walled vineyard is also a wonderful, living illustration of the origins of the region's wine industry and of the many changes that took place as a result of the French Revolution.

Château du Clos de Vougeot
Set like a ship in an ocean of vines, this château-monastery is now one of Burgundy's most famous tourist attractions. Inside are medieval wine presses and a grand banqueting hall.

It was a group of Cistercian monks from the nearby monastery that first planted vines here during the 12th century. By the early 14th century, donations of land had swollen the estate to its current size of 125 acres (50 ha), and stone walls, the *clos*, had been constructed around it. More than 200 years later, following the Revolution of 1789, the vineyard was bought as individual holdings by six merchants. Each holding has been further split over the years, and the vineyard is now shared among more than 80 individuals.

There are several problems caused by the parceling-out of the vineyard. First, there is the question of unequal land quality. The plots at the top of the *clos* are unquestionably finer than those in the middle, which in turn are better than the frequently waterlogged clay soils at the bottom. The monks solved this problem by bottling the wines from each section separately. Today, however, every bottle of Clos de Vougeot is eligible for the same *grand cru* status. Even more significant, however, is the tiny scale of the plots and the constraints this places on their owners. Average production per owner is just 200 cases, with a third of the *vignerons* producing fewer than 75 cases of wine each year. In the absence of specialized micro-vinification equipment, it is very difficult to crush, ferment, and press such a trifling quantity of grapes. Both these points are worth bearing in mind if you encounter a disappointing wine. The château is the headquarters of the *Confrérie des Chevaliers du Tastevin,* a fraternity of wine-makers and setting for banquets and an annual wine-tasting.

Beyond the walled vineyard, there are 30 acres (12 ha) of vines, producing 70,000 bottles of red and 10,000 bottles of white Vougeot and Vougeot Premier Cru. These rarities often offer better value than Clos de Vougeot.

Jaffelin
Like many of Burgundy's best *négociants*, or wine merchants, the firm of Jaffelin owns Clos de Vougeot vineyards.

Georges Mugneret
Several members of the Mugneret family make good examples of Clos de Vougeot. Georges Mugneret refers to the *appellation* as Clos-Vougeot.

- AC Clos de Vougeot Grand Cru, AC Vougeot Premier Cru, AC Vougeot.
- Red: Pinot Noir.
- Plump, full-bodied, spicy red with flavors of red summer fruits, chocolate, and licorice.
- Amiot-Servelle, Robert Arnoux, Bertagna, Bouchard Père et Fils, Champy, Chanson Père et Fils, Jean-Jacques Confuron, Joseph Drouhin-Laroze, René Engel, Faiveley, Genot-Boulanger, Anne et François Gros, Jean Grivot, Louis Jadot, Jaffelin, Méo-Camuzet, Leroy, Denis Mortet, Mugneret-Gibourg, Jacques Prieur, Prieuré Roch, Raphet, Henri Rebourseau, Daniel Rion, Ch de la Tour.
- Oxtail stewed in red wine.
- 2003, 2002, 2001, 1999, 1998, 1996, 1995, 1993, 1990, 1988, 1985.
- 10–15 years.

CÔTE DE BEAUNE AND CÔTE DE BEAUNE-VILLAGES

THESE TWO SIMILARLY named *appellations* are in fact quite separate, with the Côte de Beaune label covering a tiny area close to the town of Beaune itself. More confusion is caused by the fact that the Côte de Beaune-Villages *appellation* is often thought to be the southern counterpart of Côte de Nuits-Villages *(see below)*, when in fact the two *appellations* operate quite differently. The latter applies to a very limited area, while most of the red wines produced in those parts of the Côte de Beaune entitled to their own *appellation* may also be sold as Côte de Beaune-Villages. The *appellations* of St Romain *(see p155)*, Chorey-lès-Beaune *(see p136)*, Pernand-Vergelesses *(see p150)*, and Auxey-Duresses *(see p125)* all often sell many of their less successful red wines as Côte de Beaune-Villages.

Bouchard Père et Fils
This established merchant specializes in making Côte de Beaune-Villages wines.

St Romain
The hillside town of St Romain sells often very attrractive wine under its own name as well as under the *appellation* of Côte de Beaune-Villages.

- AC Côte de Beaune, AC Côte de Beaune-Villages.
- Red: Pinot Noir.
- Light, soft, fruity reds.
- *Côte de Beaune:*Jean Allexant, Cauvard, Joseph Drouhin. *Côte de Beaune-Villages:* Bernard Bachelet, Bouchard Père et Fils, Maurice Chenu, Coron Père et Fils, Edouard Delaunay, Jaffelin, Lequin-Roussot, Naigeon-Chauveau.
- Snails served with garlic and parsley butter.
- 2003, 2002, 1999, 1998, 1997, 1996.
- 2–5 years.

CÔTE DE NUITS-VILLAGES

BURGUNDIANS HAVE ALWAYS associated quarries with good vine-growing land. Any wine from a vineyard called "Perrière" will have been grown on the site of a former quarry. The villages of Prissey, Comblanchien, and Corgoloin, whose limestone workings produced the coffee-colored marble used at Orly Airport, are therefore, in theory at least, well-placed to make good wine. They are, however, too small to warrant a single *appellation* and instead label their wines as Côte de Nuits-Villages. The same designation is also used for some wines from Fixin *(see p139)* and Brochon, at the northern end of the Côte de Nuits-Villages. Although it would be legal to blend the wines of the two extremes of the Côte de Nuits-Villages, in practice this is rare. Similarly, while the *appellation* permits white wine, very little is made.

Jayer-Giles
This estate is one of the few to take the Côte de Nuits-Villages label seriously and to produce long-lived wines under it.

Wood from the Trees
Côte de Nuits-Village wines are aged in barrels. However, they are seldom rich and complex enough to warrant as much new oak as they are sometimes given.

- AC Côte de Nuits-Villages.
- Red: Pinot Noir. White: Chardonnay (very little is produced).
- Medium- to full-bodied, simple, fruity reds.
- De l'Arlot, Daniel Chopin-Groffier, Jean-Jacques Confuron, Maison Joseph Drouhin, Michel Esmonin, Fougeray de Beauclair, Louis Jadot, Jayer-Giles, Henri Naudin-Ferrand, de la Paulette, Quillardet.
- Duck roasted with bay leaves and cherries.
- Red: 2003, 1999.
- Red: 3–6 years.

FIXIN

AT FIRST GLANCE the vineyards that form a square around the village of Fixin, with the best *premiers crus* located at the end closest to Gevrey-Chambertin *(see p140)*, look as though they might be a northern continuation of Gevrey-Chambertin. However, the microclimate here is quite different and the grapes ripen over a week later. Fixin's soil is different, too, with more clay in the flatter land on which the village wines are made. These conditions make for rustic, tannic wines that take years to evolve into rustic, softer ones. It is not surprising, therefore, that much of the wine has been sold as Côte de Nuits-Villages *(see p138)*. Recently, better wine-making has resulted in more approachable wines and more reason to print the village name on the label. White Fixin is rare, but Bruno Clair's is good.

Domaine André Geoffrey
The wines of Fixin can be tough and fruitless, but those produced on this estate are stylish and drinkable.

The Hard Edge
The cool microclimate and the clay soil of the small village of Fixin have led to wines that traditionally tended to be quite tannic and unripe.

- AC Fixin, AC Fixin Premier Cru.
- Red: Pinot Noir.
- Medium-bodied reds that tend to be rustic.
- Vincent Berthaut, Bruno Clair, Michel Defrance, Derey Frères, Doudet-Naudin, Fougeray de Beauclair, Pierre Gelin, André Geoffrey, Jean-Pierre Guyard, Philippe Joilet, Armell et Jean-Michel Molin, Denis Philibert, Charles Vienot.
- Hare cooked in an earthenware pot.
- 2003, 1999, 1998, 1995,
- 5–12 years.

FLEURIE

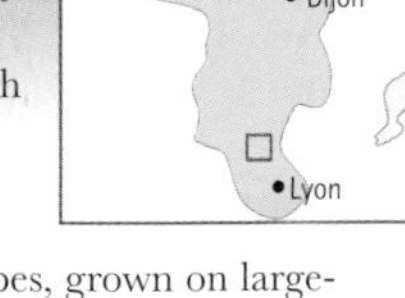

IF THIS BEAUJOLAIS *CRU*, located between Moulin à Vent and Chiroubles, were called something completely different, its wines would probably still be associated with fields of spring flowers, because that is exactly what good examples smell like. This, the third largest and often the priciest of the Beaujolais *crus*, should be the very essence of classic Beaujolais, with its Gamay grapes, grown on large-crystal granite, being made into fresh, light red wines packed with summery flavors. For a panoramic view over this varied *commune*, climb to the top of the La Madonne chapel. The best, longest-lived wines might well come from the La Madonne and the Point du Jour vineyards, but there are other plots that could stake a reasonable  claim to *premier cru* status if it were ever introduced for Beaujolais.

Domaine Berrod
The wines produced by Domaine Berrod have the floral character with which Fleurie is associated.

Madonna and Vines
The sloping vineyard of La Madonne produces some of the finest, longest-lived wines in Fleurie.

- AC Fleurie.
- Red: Gamay.
- Medium-bodied, floral, fragrant reds.
- Paul Beaudet, Berrod, Michel Chignard, Guy Depardon (du Point du Jour), Jean-Marc Deprés, Joseph Drouhin, Georges Duboeuf (des Quatre Vents, Ch des Deduits), Pierre Ferraud, Yves Métras, André Métrat (la Roilette), Albert Morel, Tête, Thorin, de la Treille.
- *Andouillettes.*
- 2003, 2001, 1997, 1995.
- 2–8 years.

GEVREY-CHAMBERTIN

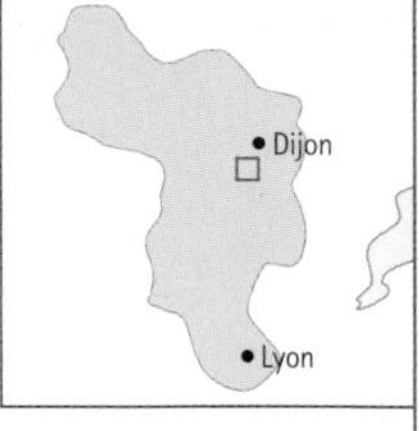

APPRECIATED BY EMPEROR NAPOLÉON BONAPARTE in the 19th century, the red wines produced around Gevrey-Chambertin have continued to enjoy great popularity to this day, making it one of the richest villages in the region. The *appellation* is the largest in the Côtes de Nuits, producing wines that range, predictably, from the truly sublime to the very average.

Limestone Exposure
This unusually situated vineyard offers a rare chance to see the limestone rock that underlies the *appellation* of Gevrey-Chambertin. Normally, of course, the chalk is well hidden beneath the topsoil and the vines.

Monks from the Abbaye de Bèze planted vines here in the seventh century, quickly followed by an astute peasant named Bertin. Today, both the monks' walled Clos de Bèze and Bertin's field, or Champ Bertin, produce some of the finest red wines in Burgundy. At the northern end of the Côte de Nuits, the *appellation* of Gevrey-Chambertin includes nine *grands crus* and 27 *premiers crus* vineyards. The very best of the *grands crus* are the neighboring Clos de Bèze and Chambertin vineyards at the center of a slope of *grands crus* vineyards to the south of the village. Now divided among 25 owners, the best wines made from these grapes are sublime and long-lived, combining the flavors of plums and cherries with a hint of spice. Of the remaining *grands crus*, the best are Griottes-Chambertin, Latricières-Chambertin, Ruchottes-Chambertin, and Mazis-Chambertin. More variable are Chapelle-Chambertin and Charmes-Chambertin, often producing wines that are less impressive than those from the best *premiers crus* vineyards, such as Clos St Jacques and Les Cazetiers. Village wines are of variable quality, too, made from vines extending right down the hillside onto the flat land on the other side of the main road. That said, however, this is an *appellation* where the skill of the producer is more crucial than the position of the vineyard, and where well-made village wines outclass poorly made wines from supposedly superior land.

Clos St Jacques
Although only a *premier cru*, the Clos St Jacques vineyard is capable of producing wines that—from the right producers—are as good as *grand crus*.

Denis Mortet
Making rich, concentrated wines, Denis Mortet is a young producer with huge potential.

- AC Gevrey-Chambertin, AC Gevrey-Chambertin Premier Cru, AC Chambertin Grand Cru, AC Clos de Bèze Grand Cru, AC Chapelle-Chambertin Grand Cru, AC Charmes-Chambertin Grand Cru, AC Griottes-Chambertin Grand Cru, AC Latricières-Chambertin Grand Cru, AC Mazis-Chambertin Grand Cru, AC Mazoyères-Chambertin Grand Cru, AC Ruchottes-Chambertin Grand Cru.
- Red: Pinot Noir.
- Full-bodied, cherrylike reds.
- Denis Bachelet, Bourrée (Vallet), A. Burguet, Champy, Bruno Clair, Pierre Damoy, Joseph Drouhin, Dugat-Py, Faiveley, Leroy, Denis Mortet, Armand Rousseau.
- Eggs poached in red wine.
- 2003, 2002, 2001, 1999, 1998, 1996, 1995, 1993, 1990, 1988, 1985.
- 5–25 years.

GIVRY

THE SMALLEST AND FOR many years the least distinguished of the *appellations* of the Côte Chalonnaise, Givry has experienced something of a renaissance in recent years as a result of careful replanting and better vineyard management. Growing 90 percent Pinot Noir vines, both Givry and Givry Premier Cru are largely red wine *appellations*, with the best vineyards, such as the *premier cru* Clos Salomon, facing south and producing medium-bodied, silky wines full of the flavors of cherries and red currants. Chardonnay grapes are used to make small amounts of clean, crisp white wine with a spicy finish. Dynamic growers such as Jean-Marc Joblot and François Lumpp are rapidly gaining a reputation for their wines, many of which are as good as more expensive wines from other parts of the region.

Domaine Joblot
This unusually well-made wine from the Clos de la Servoisine vineyard shows the potential of the *appellation*.

Clos Salomon
The walled *premier cru* vineyard of Clos Salomon is one of the very best in Givry, producing wines that are deliciously smooth and fruity.

- AC Givry, AC Givry Premier Cru.
- Red: Pinot Noir. White: Chardonnay.
- Soft, earthy reds. Floral whites.
- René Bourgeon, Cave des Vignerons de Buxy, Michel Derain, Jean-Marc Joblot, François Lumpp, Gérard et Laurent Parize, Ragot, Clos Salomon, Thénard, Emile Voarick.
- Red: Wood pigeon simmered with onions and red wine.
- Red: 2003, 2002, 1999, 1996.
- Red: 4–8 years. White: 2–4 years.

HAUTES-CÔTES DE BEAUNE AND DE NUITS

RISING TO 1,310 FT (400 m) above the western edge of the Côte de Nuits *(see p138)* and the Côte de Beaune *(see p138)* are the two mainly red *appellations* of the Hautes-Côtes de Nuits and the Hautes-Côtes de Beaune. Woodland and pasture among the vines make this some of the most beautiful landscape in Burgundy, but vineyards here are cool and exposed, giving the wines an unripe character in all but warm years. In the 1960s, only 1,235 acres (500 ha) were under vine here, but thanks to dedicated producers, the rapidly improving wines of the area are enjoying a revival. Vineyards have been carefully replanted, and many growers are now embracing a more traditional approach to vineyard management. At their best, these light wines are supple and fruity, and offer good value for money.

Domaine du Bois Guillaume
Fresh and bone-dry, this white wine is only produced in small amounts in the cool vineyards of the Hautes-Côtes de Beaune.

Sun Worshipers
Many growers train their vines high in the exposed, high-altitude vineyards of the Hautes-Côtes, allowing the grapes to catch every ray of the sunshine they need for proper ripening.

- AC Bourgogne Hautes-Côtes de Nuits, AC Bourgogne Hautes-Côtes de Beaune.
- Red: Pinot Noir. White: Chardonnay.
- Light reds. Dry whites.
- *Hautes-Côtes de Beaune:* Philippe Germain, Lucien Rateau. *Hautes-Côtes de Nuits:* Chopin-Groffier, Gerbet, Michel Gros, Cave des Hautes-Côtes, Lechenaut.
- Red: Spicy tripe sausages.
- Red: 2003, 2002, 1999.
- Red: 2–6 years.

JULIÉNAS

THE LAND AROUND JULIÉNAS, one of the most northerly of the 10 Beaujolais *cru* villages, was allegedly some of the first in Beaujolais to be planted with vines. Today, the *appellation* includes four *communes*, with well-drained granite soils to the west, and ancient alluvial soils, laid down by the Saône River, to the east. When young, the wines of Juliénas are often underrated, passed over in favor of wines from better-known *cru appellations* such as Fleurie *(see p139)* and Moulin-à-Vent *(see p148)*. At their best, however, these are lively wines with powerful, fruity aromas, often developing unusual complexity after a few years in the bottle. One ceremony not to be missed is held here every November, when an artist or writer deemed best taster of the new vintage is awarded his or her weight in wine!

Pascal Granger
Wines from this talented producer often offer a delightful mouthful of fresh cherry and rich chocolate flavors.

Frosty Vines
Midwinter temperatures can be surprisingly low in hilly Juliénas, despite its southerly location a few miles beyond the town of Mâcon.

- AC Juliénas.
- Red: Gamay.
- Medium-bodied, spicy reds.
- Ernest Aujas, Jean Benon, Bernard Broyer, François Condemine, Gérard Descombes, Thierry Descombes, Georges Duboeuf, Pierre Ferraud, Pascal Granger, Ch de Juliénas, Henri Lespinasse, René Monnet, Bernard Santé, Michel Tête, Raymond Trichard.
- Pike and veal quenelles.
- 2003, 2001, 1997, 1995.
- 2–5 years.

LADOIX

THE MOST NORTHERLY *appellation* in the Côte de Beaune and one of the least well known, Ladoix ends, confusingly, halfway through its namesake village of Ladoix-Serrigny. Despite some promising whites, this is mainly a red wine *appellation,* producing an unusually wide range of wines. Rugged village wines from the flatter and less well-exposed vineyards are sold mainly as Côte de Beaune-Villages *(see p138),* while richer, smoother wines are made from grapes grown in the two *grands crus* and seven *premiers crus* vineyards to the north of the village. Four of the *premiers crus* vineyards of the *appellation* lie on the slopes of the Montagne de Corton, as do the famous *grands crus* vineyards of Corton and Corton-Charlemagne, which are shared with neighboring *appellations* Aloxe-Corton *(see p124)* and Pernand-Vergelesses *(see p150)*.

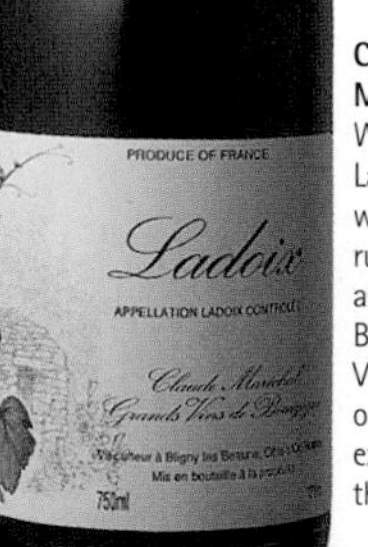

Claude Maréchal
While many Ladoix village wines are fairly rustic, and sold as Côte de Beaune-Villages, this one is an exception to the rule.

Sitting Pretty
The village of Ladoix-Serrigny is seen at its best from the hillside vineyards to the west, rather than from the busy *route nationale* that runs through its center.

- AC Ladoix, AC Aloxe-Corton Premier Cru, AC Corton Grand Cru, AC Corton-Charlemagne Grand Cru.
- Red: Pinot Noir. White: Chardonnay.
- Rustic reds. and dry whites.
- Chevalier, Edmond Cornu, François Gay, Claude Maréchal, A & J-R Nudant, Michel Tête.
- Lamb with red wine and thyme.
- Red: 2003, 2002, 1999,
- Red: 4–6 years. White: 2–3 years.

MÂCON AND MÂCON-VILLAGES

DESPITE THE GREATER PRESTIGE enjoyed by the white-wine-producing villages of the Côte d'Or and Chablis, the Mâconnais is the true engine-room of white wine production in Burgundy. Varying in quality from everyday to excellent, a huge quantity of Chardonnay wine, sold as *appellations contrôlées* Mâcon and Mâcon-Villages, is made here every year.

Mâcon-Lugny
From the village of Lugny, this wine is sold by the prominent *négociant* firm of Louis Latour.

Somewhere in the ancient wine-producing district of the Mâconnais is the meeting point of northern and southern France. Suddenly, both the climate and the attitude of the people have more to do with the Mediterranean than with the English Channel. The grape harvest here takes place two weeks before that of the more northerly Côte d'Or, and produces wines with richer, riper flavors. Despite a long tradition of red wine production, the Mâconnais today makes three times as much white wine as the rest of Burgundy put together. Light and dry, these fairly affordable wines vary from pleasant, undemanding bottles for drinking young to château-bottled wines that are as good as those from Côte de Beaune *appellations* such as Meursault *(see p145)*. In theory, only wines made from grapes grown in the district's best vineyards can be sold as *appellation contrôlée* Mâcon-Villages. In practice, however, the label is used to sell more than 90 percent of the white wines made here. Better wines come from the vineyards surrounding 42 named villages, each of which is entitled to add its name to the Mâcon-Villages classification. The best include Charmes, Prissé, and Pierreclos. Best of all are the wines made by individual producers, including Dominique Lafon and Jean Thevenet in the new *appellation* of Clessé, who prove that top-quality wines can be made here, despite the more limited ambitions of the *coopératives* responsible for most of Mâconnais wine production.

Chardonnay Country
Chardonnay is the grape of this region, flourishing in its limestone soils and ripening well in the southern sunshine.

Light, fruity, and rather unmemorable, only a quarter of the district's wines are red. Made from either Pinot Noir or Gamay grapes, these are sold under the generic *appellation contrôlée* Bourgogne *(see p130)*, or as *appellations contrôlées* Mâcon or Mâcon Supérieur.

AC Mâcon, AC Mâcon Supérieur, AC Mâcon-Villages or AC Mâcon-village name (white only), AC Mâcon-village name (red only).

Red: Gamay, Pinot Noir. White: Chardonnay.

Light, fruity reds. Light, dry whites.

D & M Barraud, Paul Beaudet, Berceau du Chardonnay, de la Bongran, André Bonhomme, Cave des Vignerons de Buxy, Cordier, Deux Roches, Georges Duboeuf, Feuillarde, Fichet, Guffens-Heynen, Cave de Lugny, Lafon, Roger Luquet, Mommessin, de Ruère, Saumaize-Michelin, Roger Thevenet, Valette, Cave de Viré.

White: Deep-fried whitebait.

White: 2003, 2002, 2001, 1997.

White: 2–4 years. Red: 2–5 years.

Domaine de la Bongran
Talented and innovative producer Jean Thevenet makes delicious but controversial late-harvest wines.

MARANGES

THIS LITTLE-KNOWN and often overlooked *appellation*, to the southwest of Santenay, is the result of the amalgamation in 1989 of the even less well-known *appellations* of Cheilly-lès-Maranges, Dezize-lès-Maranges and Sampigny-lès-Maranges. Wines from these *appellations* were sold mainly as Côte de Beaune-Villages. Talented producers such as Vincent Girardin are making a name for Maranges, and their wines offer good value. In less skilled hands, Maranges is still pretty rustic.

Vincent Girardin
A name to look for, Girardin is one of several good Maranges producers.

- AC Maranges, AC Maranges Premier Cru.
- Red: Pinot Noir.
- Medium to full-bodied earthy, rustic reds.
- Bernard Bachelet, Pierre Bresson, Fernand Chevrot, Vincent Girardin, Claude Nouveau.
- Eggs poached in red wine.
- 2003, 2002, 1999, 1998.
- Red: 4–6 years.

MARSANNAY

AT THE NORTHERNMOST END of the Côte de Nuits, Marsannay is one of the few *appellations* in Burgundy to produce excellent, raspberryish rosé. This is some of the best rosé in France, and very little is exported. Marsannay is also developing a reputation for its reds, which are fruity but fairly tannic, offering good value when well made. The tiny quantities of white produced in Marsannay often represent the best buy of all, with buttery, mineral flavors similar to those of Meursault *(see p145)*.

Bruno Clair
Marsannay's *appellation* status owes much to wines made by Bruno Clair.

- AC Marsannay, AC Marsannay Rosé.
- Red and rosé: Pinot Noir. White: Chardonnay.
- Light to medium-bodied red. Medium-bodied dry rosé. Light, dry white.
- Bruno Clair, Charlopin, Fougeray de Beauclair.
- Ham and parsley terrine.
- Red: 2003, 2002, 1999.
- Rosé: 1–3 years.

MERCUREY

THE BIGGEST *APPELLATION* in the Côte Chalonnaise, the region around the village of Mercurey is named after a local Gallo-Roman temple to Mercury, the messenger of the gods. While local *négociants* have long appreciated Mercurey's affordable red, and more recently white, wines, the harvest from such a large *appellation* is inevitably of varying quality. Wines from less well-situated vineyards have a tendency to be thin, while in a good year, wines from the top *premiers crus* vineyards are similar to the best wines of Pommard *(see p151)*. The number of *premiers crus* here has increased dramatically in the last decade, from five covering 40 acres (15 ha), to 30 with a total area of over 250 acres (100 ha). As a result, you need to proceed carefully when buying wine here.

Dijon
Lyon

Michel Juillot
A talented producer of top-class Mercurey, Michel Juillot is also one of Burgundy's most avid vinous experimenters.

Gentle slopes
Like the rest of the Côte Chalonnaise region, the *commune* of Mercurey is made up of a series of small hills, with vineyards planted on many of the region's gentler slopes.

- AC Mercurey Premier Cru, AC Mercurey.
- Red: Pinot Noir. White: Chardonnay.
- Medium to full-bodied reds. Medium-bodied whites.
- Brintet, de Chamirey, Faiveley, Genot-Boulanger, Emile Juillot, Michel Juillot, Meix-Foulot, Jean Raquillet, Antonin Rodet, de Suremain, Emile Voarick.
- St Florentin cheese.
- Red: 2003, 2002, 1999, 1996.
- Red: 5–10 years. White: 4–6 years.

MEURSAULT

FOR HUNDREDS OF YEARS CHARDONNAY has been the primary grape of Meursault, where it flourishes in the poor, rocky soil. While the crown for the finest white Burgundy goes to Corton-Charlemagne or the *grands crus* of Chassagne-Montrachet, the wines of Meursault are deliciously dry and rich, full of the flavors of butter, nuts, and spices.

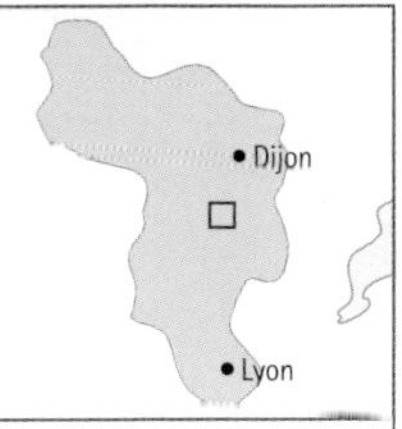

Hidden Blagny
Tucked away in the hills behind Meursault, the tiny hamlet of Blagny produces long-lived white wines, sold either as AC Meursault-Blagny or as AC Meursault Premier Cru.

As much as one-third of all the white wine from the Côte d'Or (the *département* covering both the Côte de Nuits and the Côte de Beaune) comes from the *commune* of Meursault. In contrast to many white-wine-producing Burgundy *communes*—such as Chassagne-Montrachet *(see p135)*, where white wines are a fairly recent phenomenon—Meursault has long been linked to the white Chardonnay grape. During the 18th century, former United States president Thomas Jefferson visited the region and noted that "at Meursault only white wines are made, because there is too much stone for the red."

J-F Coche-Dury
Wines from the Perrières vineyard tend to be long-lived. This one is made by Jean-François Coche-Dury, one of the best wine-makers in Meursault.

Considerably cheaper than the white wines of Corton-Charlemagne and Chassagne-Montrachet, the hazelnut and melted butter flavors of white Meursault are popular all over the world and are eagerly copied by California wine-makers. The wines of Meursault fall into a number of categories. First, there are the plain AC Meursault wines, which can be very plain indeed. Next come wines from good, named but non-*premiers crus* vineyards such as Les Clos de la Barre. Finally, there are many impressive *premiers crus* vineyards, of which Les Perrières produces some of the finest wines, long-lived though somewhat slow to develop. More easily accessible are wines from the well-named vineyard Les Charmes. The best of these come from Les Charmes-Dessus. Also an excellent choice are wines from Les Genevrières and Les Gouttes d'Or. From La Pièce-sous-le-Bois in the nearby village of Blagny come fine whites, some sold as AC Meursault-Blagny and others as AC Meursault Premier Cru.

Red wines from Blagny are sold under their own *appellation,* the tiny AC Blagny Premier Cru. Reds from Meursault are made in small quantities each year and are light and fruity, and best drunk young.

Domaine des Comtes Lafon
In the hands of Dominique Lafon of the Domaine des Comtes Lafon, the Clos de la Barre vineyard produces fabulous wines of almost *premier cru* quality.

- AC Meursault, AC Meursault Premier Cru, AC Meursault-Blagny Premier Cru, AC Meursault Côte de Beaune, AC Meursault-Santenots.
- White: Chardonnay. Red: Pinot Noir.
- Broad, buttery whites with mineral overtones.
- Robert Ampeau, d'Auvenay, Bitouzet-Prieur, Bouzereau, Coche-Debord, Coche-Dury, Jean-Pierre Diconne, Jean-Philippe Fichet, Genot-Boulanger, Henri Germain, Albert Grivault, Patrick Javillier, François Jobard, Rémi Jobard, des Comtes Lafon, Latour-Guiraud, Olivier Leflaive, Matrot, de Meu, de Meursault, Michelot, Pierre Morey, Jacques Prieur, Prieur-Brunet, de Puligny-Montrachet, Roult, Roux, Verget.
- Crayfish.
- White: 2003, 2002, 2001, 1996, 1995, 1992, 1989.
- White: 3–20 years.

MONTAGNY

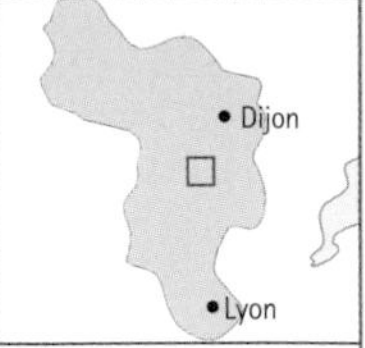

LYING AT THE SOUTHERN TIP of the Côte Chalonnaise, Montagny is one of the many strange anomalies in the *appellation* system. For no explicable reason, *premier cru* status is given to all the wines produced here, as long as their natural alcohol content is at least 11.5 percent. Even odder, another rule states that wines made in Montagny-lès-Buxy, Buxy, St Vallerin, and Jully-lès-Buxy can be labeled as *appellation contrôlée* Montagny, but only wines from the *commune* of Montagny-lès-Buxy itself may have a vineyard name printed on the label. When well made, the rich white wines of Montagny are full of hazelnut and gun-flint flavors. In warm years, however, they tend to flabbiness. Some of the best wines are produced by the Cave de Buxy *coopérative*, which makes some excellent examples, both oaked and unoaked.

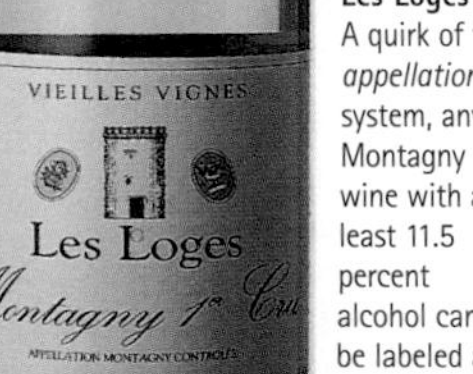

Les Loges
A quirk of the *appellation* system, any Montagny wine with at least 11.5 percent alcohol can be labeled as *premier cru.*

Roofs of Montagny
Only wines made from grapes grown in the quiet *commune* of Montagny-lès-Buxy itself may have a vineyard named on the label.

- AC Montagny, AC Montagny Premier Cru.
- White: Chardonnay.
- Medium- to full-bodied dry whites, now often aged in oak.
- Maurice Bertrand et François Juillot, Coopérative des Caves de Buxy, Ch de Davenay, Joseph Faiveley, Louis Latour, Bernard Michel, Moillard, Antonin Rodet, Ch de la Saule, Jean Vachet.
- Choux pastry puffs with Gruyère or Franche-Comté cheese.
- 2003, 2002, 2000.
- 4–7 years.

MONTHÉLIE

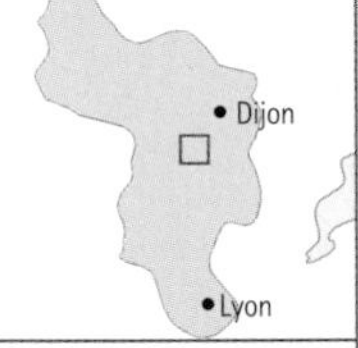

DRIVING THROUGH THE small village of Monthélie toward St Romain gives you a panoramic view of the vineyards, some of which face due south, while others face northeast. Most of the 11 *premiers crus* vineyards of the *appellation* are situated on the same limestone hillside as those of neighboring Volnay *(see p157)*, producing red wines that, when well made, are rich and ripe with a firm structure and a lingering, silky finish. Although generally considered less good than those of Volnay, wines from top Monthélie producers, such as Monthélie-Douhairet, often disprove this theory. Village wines, however, are made from grapes grown on the flatter land below, and can be dilute and rustic. Fine white wines from the *premier cru* Les Champs-Fuillot are made by Paul Garaudet and Denis Boussey.

Jean-Philippe Fichet
Based in nearby Meursault, Jean-Philippe Fichet makes firmly structured village Monthélie that can offer excellent value.

Monthélie Vineyards
The best of the Monthélie vineyards lie on the hillside to the east of the village. Flatter vineyards like these produce more ordinary wines.

- AC Monthélie, AC Monthélie Premier Cru.
- Red/rosé: Pinot Noir. White: Chardonnay
- Medium-weight, elegant, fruity reds. Medium-weight whites.
- Denis Boussey, Coche-Dury, Comtes Lafon, M Deschamps, Dupont-Fahn, J-P Fichet, Paul Garaudet, Jehan Changarnier, Ch de Monthélie, Monthélie-Douhairet, Pierre Morey.
- Eggs poached in red wine.
- 2003, 2002, 1999.
- Red: 3–7 years.

MOREY-ST DENIS

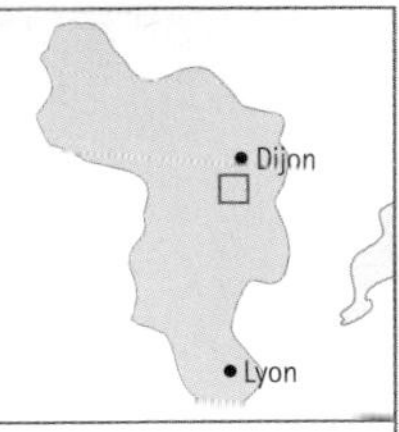

OFTEN OVERSHADOWED BY the flair of nearby Vosne-Romanée *(see p158)* and the opulence of neighboring Gevrey-Chambertin *(see p140)* and Chambolle-Musigny *(see p134)*, the Côte de Nuits village of Morey-St Denis boasts a range of brilliant vineyards and some excellent producers who make some of the most reliable red wines in Burgundy.

The wine-making history of Morey-St Denis is every bit as impressive as that of its illustrious neighbors, Gevrey-Chambertin, Chambolle-Musigny, and Vosne-Romanée. Walled vineyards were planted here by monks, and were well-regarded as early as the 12th century. Despite this, and despite the presence of several excellent *grand cru* vineyards, the wines of Morey-St Denis have occasionally missed being included among the very best in Burgundy. Until 1927, when the *commune* of Morey took the name of one of its two best vineyards, the wines made here were often sold under the names of Gevrey-Chambertin and Chambolle-Musigny.

Despite the descision to adopt the name of the Clos St Denis, probably the finest of the *grands crus* vineyards in this commune is the large, 42-acre (17-ha) Clos de la Roche. The other *grands crus* vineyards of the *appellation* are Clos de Tart, owned exclusively by the merchant firm of Mommessin; Clos des Lambrays, newly promoted to *grand cru* status, and a tiny 4.5-acre (1.84-ha) slice of the Bonnes-Mares vineyard lying mainly in Chambolle-Musigny. The best *premiers crus* vineyards are Clos Sorbé, Les Sorbés, Aux Charmes, Clos des Ormes, La Bussière, and Les Fremières. Outstanding village wines are made by producers including Ponsot, Dujac, Lignier, and Groffier, and all are as good as less well-made *grands crus* wines elsewhere.

Wine writers have always struggled to find the right words to describe the difference between the wines of Morey-St Denis and its neighbors, often falling back on words like "feminine" and "elegant." For my part, I prefer to describe them as fine late-developers. Much of the unique character of these wines is due to the shallow soil here, which forces the vines to push their roots deep into the limestone beneath.

White wines are, as elswehere in this part of the Côte d'Or, a true rarity in Morey-St Denis, but those made from grapes grown in the stony soil of the *grand cru* Monts Luisants vineyard have unusual, wonderfully mineral flavors and are well worth buying when you see them.

Clos des Lambrays Vineyard
This vineyard was recently elevated from *premier* to *grand cru* status, and the quality of the wines produced in recent vintages certainly justifies its promotion.

- AC Morey-St Denis, AC Morey-St Denis Premier Cru, AC Clos St Denis Grand Cru, AC Clos de la Roche Grand Cru, AC Bonnes Mares Grand Cru, AC Clos des Lambrays Grand Cru, AC Clos de Tart Grand Cru.
- Red: Pinot Noir.
- Earthy reds, tending to rusticity.
- Pierre Amiot, Bertagna, Bryczek et Fils, Champy, Dujac, Alain Hudelot-Noëllat, des Lambrays, Philippe et Vincent Lecheneaut, Hubert Lignier, Henri Perrot-Minot, Jean-Marie Ponsot, Georges Roumier, Armand Rousseau, Clos de Tart, Ch de la Tour, Tortochot.
- Entrecôte with mushrooms.
- 2003, 2002, 2001, 1999, 1998, 1996, 1995, 1993, 1990, 1988, 1985.
- Red: 5–20 years.

Champy Père et Cie
Bottled by the well respected and long-established *négociant* firm of Champy, this wine comes from the *premier cru* Clos des Ormes vineyard.

MORGON

THE VINEYARDS OF MORGON, one of the largest and best-known of the 10 Beaujolais *crus* *(see pp126–7)*, cover an area centered on the village of Villié-Morgon. Dominating the area is the Mont du Py, which rises to 985 ft (300 m) above the village and is the source of the *appellation*'s finest wines. Made up of thin layers of easily-split rock rich in manganese, ferric oxide, and pyrites, or fool's gold, the unique soils of the slopes are known locally as *terre pourrie,* or rotting earth, because of the rapid disintegration of the rock. The grapes grown here produce tightly structured wines with a bouquet of cherries and apricots that often mature perfectly for up to two decades. The flatter vineyards of the *appellation* produce more typical Beaujolais, which, though good, lacks the structure and longevity of wines from the Mont du Py.

Marcel Lapierre
With vineyards on the slopes of the Mont du Py, Marcel Lapierre makes wines that are delightfully sturdy and long-lived.

Château de Foncronne
This modern stained-glass window in the Château de Foncronne shows the wine-growing history of the area.

- AC Morgon.
- Red: Gamay.
- Full-bodied, long-lived reds.
- Aucoeur, Gerard Brisson, François Calot, de la Chanaise, Louis-Claude Desvignes, Georges Duboeuf (Jean Descombes), Henri Fessy, Jean Foillard, Gauthier, Dominique Jambon, Marcel Lapierre, Piron, Ch de Raousset, Pierre Savoye, Jacques Trichard.
- Veal with Dijon mustard.
- 2003, 2001, 1997, 1995,1991.
- 4–20 years.

MOULIN-À-VENT

THE *APPELLATION* OF MOULIN-À-VENT is known as the "King of Beaujolais," thanks to the combination of its age, its size, and the concentrated flavors and longevity of its wines. Granted *cru* status as early as 1936, Moulin-à-Vent covers more than 1,660 acres (670 ha) of acidic, manganese-rich land in the northern part of the Beaujolais district. The manganese in the soil is often credited with giving the wines their rich flavors and deep color, as well as a powerful aroma of flowers and ripe fruits and an unusual capacity for development in the cellar—up to 20 years for the best wines. With a long history of wine-making in the area, local rituals are still in evidence, especially after the grape harvest, when the new wine is blessed in the church of Romanèche-Thorins and carried around the town.

Château du Moulin-à-Vent
Classically dark and long-lived wines are produced by the Bloud family at the imposing Château du Moulin-à-Vent.

Moulin-à-Vent
The disused windmill from which this *appellation* takes its name, is one of the most famous landmarks of the region.

- AC Moulin-à-Vent.
- Gamay.
- Concentrated, rich reds.
- Berrod, Jean Briday, Michel Brugne, Georges Duboeuf, Gay-Coperet, Guérin, Ch des Jacques, Paul Janin, Hubert Lapierre, du Matinal, Ch du Moulin-à-Vent, des Perelles, de la Pierre, Benoît Trichard.
- Charcoal-grilled woodcock with a raspberry and black-currant sauce.
- 2003, 2001, 1995, 1994, 1991.
- 4–8 years.

NUITS-ST GEORGES

TOUGH AND TANNIC WHEN first made, the magnificent red wines of Nuits-St Georges are some of the most misunderstood in Burgundy. More austere when young than the wines of neighboring *appellations* such as Vosne-Romanée *(see p158)*, the sumptuous black-currant and game flavors of these wines often take as long as 20 years to reach their peak.

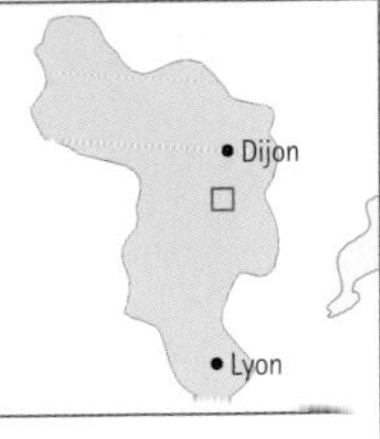

Château Gris
Overlooking its namesake vineyard, one of the best in Nuits-St Georges, Château Gris can be clearly seen from the *autoroute* running below and is a well-known landmark of the *appellation*.

The site of a Gallo-Roman villa and home during the Middle Ages to a monastic winery, the attractive town of Nuits-St Georges lies toward the southern tip of the Côte de Nuits. Sandwiched between Beaune and Dijon, sleepy Nuits-St Georges feels very much like a place that is driven around and not through. Despite this, several of the region's most successful *négociants*, including Boisset, Faiveley, and Labouré-Roi, have their headquarters here.

As in Beaune *(see pp128–9)*, there are, surprisingly, no *grands crus* vineyards in Nuits-St Georges. The *appellation* does, however, boast more than 30 excellent *premiers crus* vineyards, many of which produce exciting wines that regularly outclass those from *grands crus* vineyards nearby. Reflecting the various different soil types of the *appellation*, the character of a *premier cru* wine from Nuits-St Georges depends very much on the location of its vineyard. The stony soils to the south of the town are home to *premiers crus* vineyards including Les Cailles, Les St Georges, and Les Vaucrains, all of which produce classic, full-bodied wines with lots of tannin. To the south around the village of Prémeaux-Prissey are the vineyards of Clos de la Maréchale and Clos Arlot, whose perfectly made wines are the richest in Nuits-St Georges. Softer and more seductive are wines from *premiers crus* vineyards to the north of the *appellation*, such as Aux Boudots and Aux Murgers on the boundary with Vosne-Romanée *(see p158)*.

While arguing over their favorite vineyards, devotees agree that the best wines here share a tight structure and deep, gamey, black-currant flavors. Although softening beautifully after a few years in the cellar, these wines can—and indeed, if typical, should—be quite austere in their youth.

Hospices de Nuits
The charitable Hospices de Nuits raises money by auctioning the wines from its estate. These wines are sold young and can be aged by the buyer.

Domaine de l'Arlot
Recently created, this estate in the south of the *appellation* produces wines that are rich, modern, and impeccably made.

- AC Nuits-St Georges, AC Nuits-St Georges Premier Cru.
- Red: Pinot Noir. White: Chardonnay.
- Full-bodied, even chunky reds.
- De l'Arlot, Robert Arnoux, Bertagna, Lucien Boillot, Robert Chevillon, Georges Chicotot, A Chopin, Jean-Jacques Confuron, R Dubois, Faiveley, Forey, Henri Gouges, Jean Grivot, Jayer-Gilles, Laurent, Philippe et Vincent Lecheneaut, Machard de Gramont, Alain Michelot, Mugneret-Gibourg, Leroy, des Perdrix, Pernin Rossin, Prieuré Roch, Henri et Gilles Remoriquet, Daniel Rion, Thomas-Moillard, Fabrice Vigot.
- Hare with red wine.
- 2003, 2002, 2001, 1999, 1998, 1996, 1995, 1993, 1990, 1988, 1985.
- Red: 5–20 years.

PERNAND-VERGELESSES

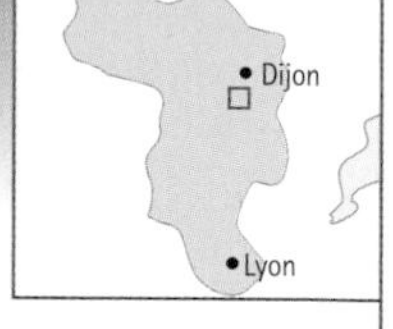

What's in a name? If the *grand cru* vineyard of Corton-Charlemagne, shared between the *appellations* of Aloxe-Corton *(see p124)*, Ladoix-Serrigny *(see p142)* and Pernand-Vergelesses, were called Pernand-Charlemagne, I suspect the other wines of this picturesque hillside *commune* might be better known and more expensive. How many of the wines would justify their higher prices is less certain. The reds are pleasant and softly jammy, but often short of finesse and complexity. The whites, despite a tendency to thinness in cooler years, are better than the reds, with crisp, well-defined fruit and delicate flavors. Wines from the *premiers crus* vineyards of Les Vergelesses, Île des Vergelesses, and Les Fichots are a good buy, and worth cellaring for five years or so before drinking.

Rollin Père et Fils
This village white from the reliable producer Rollin Père et Fils is likely to offer very good value.

Île des Vergelesses
Although relatively little-known, this *premier cru* vineyard has given its name to both the village and the *appellation*.

- AC Pernand-Vergelesses, AC Pernand-Vergelesses 1er Cru.
- Red: Pinot Noir. White: Chardonnay.
- Medium-weight, elegant reds. Crisp, appley, herbal whites.
- Arnoux, Bonneau de Martray, Champy, Chandon de Briailles, Delarche, Drouhin, Dubreuil-Fontaine, Germain, Antonin Guyon, Laleure-Piot, Louis Latour, Pavelot, Rapet, Rollin.
- Smoked goose fillets.
- White: 2004, 2003, 2002, 2001.
- Red: 4–8 years. White: 2–5 years.

THE HYPHENATED NAMES OF THE CÔTE D'OR

Many of the villages of the Côte de Beaune and the Côte de Nuits carry names that are hyphenated. The fashion for hyphenated names swept the area during the 1860s, when canny producers realized that, while wines from named vineyards such as Le Corton, Le Chambertin, Le Musigny, and Le Montrachet were famous and therefore easy to sell, those from neighboring vineyards were much less marketable. As a result, many villages, including Gevrey, Aloxe, Chambolle, Puligny, Pernand, and Chassagne, simply adopted the names of their best-known vineyards, giving them names such as Gevrey-Chambertin, Aloxe-Corton, and Chambolle-Musigny. Some already-famous *communes*, including Beaune, Volnay, Pommard, and Meursault, needed no such help, while others, such as Fixin and Monthélie, had no famous vineyard to call on. The *communes* of Chorey and Savigny rather cleverly appended the words "lès Beaune" (near Beaune) to their names. The name game has worked well for most, but not all. The village of Ladoix *(see p142)*, for example, has arguably gained little by adding the Serrigny vineyard to its name; its toughish wines are still often hard to sell.

Like their villages, the producers of the Côte d'Or often sport hyphenated names, such as Coche-Dury, Coche-Débord, and Millaut-Battault. These are a result of the laws of equal inheritance that became part of French law in the early 19th century. If, for example, Jean Dupont and his sister Marie were to marry their neighbors Hélène and Jacques Durand, their newly combined estates would be called Domaine Dupont-Durand and Domaine Durand-Dupont. Inevitably, given the size of the villages and the frequency of marriages between wine-making families, confusingly similar names are common.

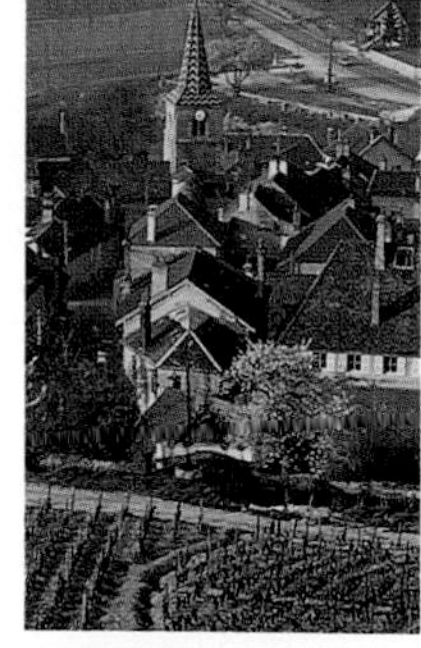

Pernand-Vergelesses
The successful marketing ploy of joining a prestigious vineyard to the original village name is a popular Côte d'Or phenomenon.

POMMARD

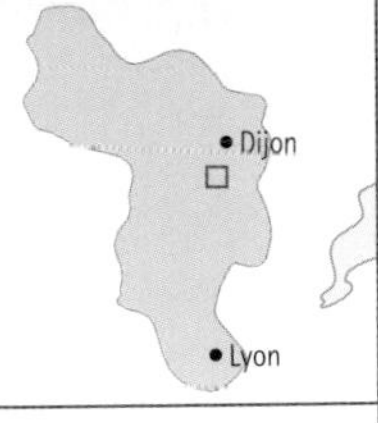

DESPITE POMMARD'S POSITION, between Beaune (see p128) and Volnay (see p157), its wines bear little resemblance to the light, delicate wines of either of those two *appellations*. Instead, these powerful red offerings are among the richest and most tannic in Burgundy. Although inaccessible in their youth, they are definitely worth waiting for.

Domaine Mussy
Typical of Pommard, the powerful *premiers crus* wines of Domaine Mussy need at least five years to soften in the bottle before drinking.

A few miles to the south of Beaune, the small village of Pommard has a long history of prosperity and international fame, and has been selling its wines on both sides of the Atlantic Ocean since the 18th century. In recent years, a combination of fame and easy pronunciation has helped to make the wines of Pommard some of the most saleable in the Côte d'Or, especially in the United States. Perhaps inevitably, laziness and greed have taken their toll here, too, often prompting growers and merchants to collude in turning a blind eye to poor wine making and fraud of all sorts. One of the most notorious malpractices has been the regular use of grapes grown in humble *appellation contrôlée* Bourgogne vineyards to make wines sold as *appellation contrôlée* Pommard. A partial explanation for the frequent adulteration here lies in the character of the wines themselves. As Lalou Bize-Leroy, possessor of one of the sharpest palates in Burgundy, once famously said, the wines of Pommard are rather like its church: solid, square, and, on first impression, less than inviting. Like the wines of nearby Aloxe-Corton (see p124), these are wines with significant amounts of tannin, and definitely need cellaring. Adding so-called inferior grapes to the mixture has often made Pommard much easier to sell young.

Recent years have seen great improvements here, and good Pommard, although still not as drinkable in its youth as the wines of Volnay or Beaune, is as good when mature as the best of both those *communes*. Without doubt, the top vineyard here is Les Rugiens, but look also for fine wines from Les Fremiers, Les Arvelets, En Largillière, Les Epenots and Les Chanlins.

Tending the Vines
The early spring task of pruning is taking place here in the vineyards of the attractive Château de Pommard, a 50-acre (20-ha) walled estate on flat land to the southeast of the village.

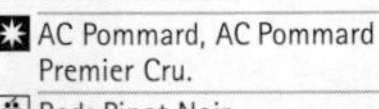

- AC Pommard, AC Pommard Premier Cru.
- Red: Pinot Noir
- Full-bodied, broad wines with prominent black cherry flavors.
- Albert-Grivault, Ampeau, Comte Armand, J-M Boillot, Pascal Bouley, Champy, Coste-Caumartin, de Courcel, Paul Garaudet, Michel Gaunoux, Germain Père et Fils, Vincent Girardin, Bernard & Louis Glantenay, Raymond Launay, Olivier Leflaive, Lejeune, Leroy, Aleth Leroyer-Girardin, de Montille, Pierre Morey, Mussy, Parent, Ch de Pommard, Pothier-Rieusset, Pousse d'Or, Rebourgeon Mure, Virely-Rougeot.
- Boar with red wine and cherries.
- 2003, 2002, 1999, 1998, 1997, 1996, 1995, 1993, 1990, 1989, 1988, 1985, 1978.
- 5–15 years.

Comte Armand
Fine village and *premiers crus* wines are made on this renowned estate.

POUILLY-FUISSÉ AND ITS SATELLITES

PART OF THE HUGE white wine-producing district of the Mâconnais, the *appellation* of Pouilly-Fuissé produces six million bottles of white wine every year. Made entirely with the Chardonnay grape and varying in quality from the basic to the sublime, the wines of Pouilly-Fuissé are undoubtedly some of the most famous white Burgundies in the world.

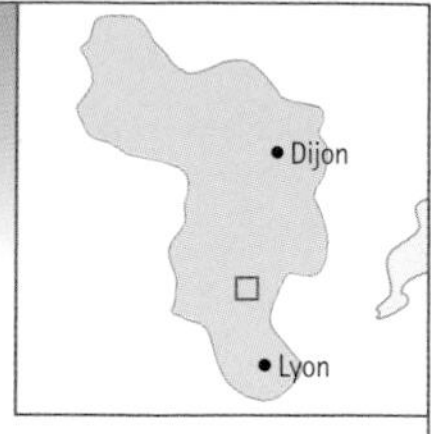

Surrounded by Chardonnay vines, at the base of the ancient Rock of Solutré, is the hamlet of Pouilly, which, together with the village of Fuissé to the east, gives its name to the *appellation* of Pouilly-Fuissé. A large *appellation* extending over four *communes,* the wines sold as Pouilly-Fuissé fall into two camps. First, there is the fresh, light, but frankly dull Pouilly-Fuissé available in supermarkets and liquor stores around the world, which is practically indistinguishable from the far less expensive Mâcon-Villages *(see p143)* produced to the north of Pouilly-Fuissé. Second, and much more important, there is the gloriously complex and long-lived Pouilly-Fuissé made by talented producers such as Vincent et Fils of Château Fuissé, Guffens-Heynen, Verget, and Domaine Cordier, as well as a growing number of younger producers, which regularly puts to shame many a wine from other more illustrious Burgundy *appellations,* such as Meursault *(see p145)* and Puligny-Montrachet *(see p153).*

Differing soils obviously have a part to play in the variable quality of the wines of Pouilly-Fuissé, with the fullest-flavored wines coming from the vineyards around the villages of Vergisson to the northwest and Fuissé to the southeast, in contrast to more complex wines made from grapes grown in the area around Pouilly in the center of the *appellation.* Much more significant than variations in the soil, however, is the care and skill of the wine-growers, and that of the producers at the large wine-making *coopératives* that make a high proportion of the wine here. For this reason, it is essential to buy your Pouilly-Fuissé from a good producer or *négociant.* Failing this, it is not worth buying at all.

The *commune* of Pouilly adds its name and some of its prestige to two small satellite *appellations* to the east of Pouilly-Fuissé: Pouilly-Vinzelles and Pouilly-Loché. The wines produced here are said to be lighter and simpler than those of Pouilly-Fuissé, though considering the featherweight character of many poorer examples of Pouilly-Fuissé, this would occasionally be something of an achievement. Besides, there are some excellent wine-makers here who are proving just how good the wines can be. Producers worth looking for are the Cave des Grands Crus Blanc in Vinzelles and the Bret Brothers at La Soufrandière.

Prehistoric Hunting Ground
Land around the base of the Rock of Solutré, which towers over the tiny hamlet of Pouilly, is littered with the bones of prehistoric animals.

- AC Pouilly-Fuissé, AC Mâcon-Chaintre, AC Mâcon-Fuissé, AC Mâcon-Solutré, AC Mâcon-Vergisson, AC Pouilly-Vinzelles, AC Pouilly-Loché.
- White: Chardonnay.
- Medium- to full-bodied dry whites, some of which are aged in oak barrels.
- Auvigue, Daniel et Martine Barraud, Cordier, Corsin, Michel Delorme, Joseph Drouhin, Georges Duboeuf, Dupond d'Halluin, Ferret, Ch de Fuissé, des Gerbeaux, René Guérin, Guffens-Heynen, Louis Jadot, Roger Lassarat, Noblet, Robert-Denogent, Jacques et Nathalie Saumaize, Saumaize-Michelin, Simonin, La Soufrandise, Valette, Verget.
- Skate wings baked in the oven with cheese, lemon juice, and breadcrumbs.
- 2003, 2002, 2001, 1996.
- White: 3–6 years.

Château-Fuissé
Owner of one of the best estates in Pouilly-Fuissé, Monsieur J-J Vincent produces some of the very best of the area's wines. His *vieilles vignes cuvée* is as good as many of the greatest white wines in Burgundy.

PULIGNY-MONTRACHET

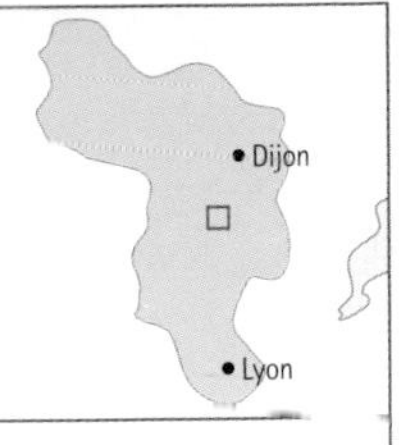

OF ALL THE WHITE WINES in Burgundy, none are more eagerly sought after than those of Puligny-Montrachet in the Côte de Beaune. Flourishing in the pebbly limestone soils of Puligny-Montrachet, the Chardonnay vine is king here, and this small *appellation* of gently sloping vineyards is home to four of the greatest dry white *grands crus* in the world.

Valuable Vines
The Chardonnay vineyards of Puligny-Montrachet are some of the most valuable in the world. Often, the entire vintage is sold in advance, even before the grapes are harvested.

Despite the fact that this was one of the first parts of Burgundy to be planted with vines, the potential of Puligny-Montrachet's finest *terroir* was not recognized until relatively recently. Records show that, early in the 17th century, part of Le Montrachet, now considered the very best of Puligny's *grands crus* vineyards, was sold for an unusually low price, since at this time the wines of Le Montrachet enjoyed only a lowly reputation. Confusion often arises over the differences between the wines of Puligny-Montrachet and those of its neighbor, Chassagne-Montrachet *(see p135)* to the south. Even though the two *appellations* share some of their best *grand cru* land, many of the wines they produce are, in fact, quite different. The primary difference is that only a tiny proportion of the wine produced in Puligny-Montrachet is red, as compared to nearly half of that from Chassagne-Montrachet. Both the white village wines and the white *premiers crus* wines of Puligny-Montrachet are considered, at their best, to be finer than the white wines of Chassagne-Montrachet, with the best parts of the shared *grands crus* vineyards of Bâtard-Montrachet and Le Montrachet falling in Puligny.

A number of top *négociants* and producers own both vines and cellars in Puligny-Montrachet, including Domaine Leflaive and Louis Jadot at the Domaine du Duc de Magenta. In spite of this, enormous international demand has encouraged the sale of substandard and overpriced wine by others. Wines from the four *grands crus* vineyards, however, are generally a good buy, especially when made by a top producer, as are wines from many of the *premiers crus* vineyards, including Le Cailleret, Champ Canet, Les Pucelles, and Les Chalumeaux.

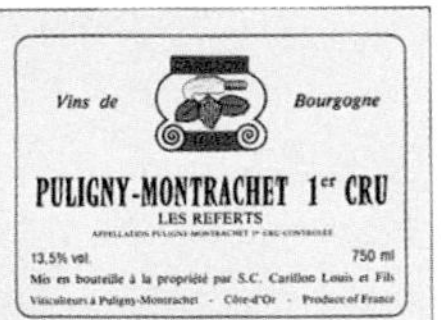

Louis Carillon
Making good, but not too excessive, use of new oak barrels, Louis Carillon is one of the rising talents of Puligny-Montrachet.

AC Puligny-Montrachet, AC Puligny-Montrachet Côte de Beaune, AC Puligny-Montrachet Premier Cru, AC Bâtard-Montrachet Grand Cru, AC Bienvenues-Bâtard-Montrachet Grand Cru, AC Chevalier-Montrachet Grand Cru, AC Montrachet Grand Cru.

White: Chardonnay.

Elegant, steely whites.

Guy Amiot, D'Auvenay, J-M Boillot, Louis Carillon, Chartron et Trébuchet, Henri Clerc, Coche-Dury, Joseph Drouhin, Louis Jadot, Louis Latour, Leflaive, Olivier Leflaive, Duc de Magenta, Maraslovac-Leger, Matrot, Marc Morey, Pascal, Jacques Prieur, Ch de Puligny-Montrachet, Sauzet.

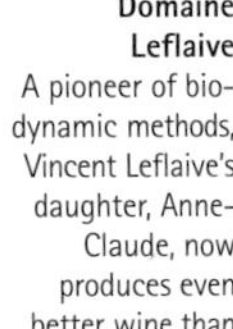

Pan-fried salmon steaks.

2003, 2002, 2001, 1996, 1995, 1992, 1989, 1985.

White: 4–14 years

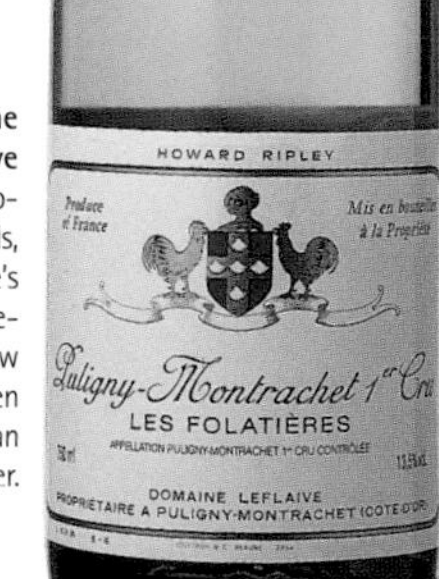

Domaine Leflaive
A pioneer of bio-dynamic methods, Vincent Leflaive's daughter, Anne-Claude, now produces even better wine than her famous father.

RÉGNIÉ

THE *COMMUNE* OF RÉGNIÉ-DURETTE became the 10th Beaujolais *cru* in 1988. There are two styles of wine made here, one light and fragrant, the other full-bodied and well-structured. Most common, though, are wines for early drinking with vibrant, well-defined fruit flavors. After a shaky start, when questions were asked about how deserving it was of promotion, this *appellation* is now building a good reputation for itself, thanks to the efforts of a number of committed producers.

Domaine Aucoeur
Noël Aucoeur makes Régnié wines that are supple and richly flavored.

- AC Régnié.
- Red: Gamay.
- Light- to medium-weight, fruity reds.
- Noël Aucoeur, René Desplace, Dominique Piron, de Ponchon, Joël Rochette, Georges et Gilles Roux.
- Honey-roast ham.
- 2003, 2001.
- 2–4 years.

RULLY

THE RED WINES OF RULLY, most northerly of the Côte Chalonnaise *appellations*, often remind me of those from Côte de Beaune *appellations* such as Volnay *(see p157)*. Sparkling white wines are sold under the Crémant de Bourgogne *appellation*, and can be some of the best in Burgundy. Still white wines are fresh and appley, while reds are medium-bodied, with wild raspberry and violet aromas. Twenty five *premiers crus* produce red and white wines with greater complexity and aging potential than the village wines.

Jacques Dury
This producer makes classic Burgundy that competes with Côte d'Or wines.

- AC Rully, AC Rully Premier Cru.
- Red: Pinot Noir. White: Chardonnay.
- Elegant, well-structured reds. Oak-aged dry whites.
- Delorme, Joseph Drouhin, Dureuil-Janthial, Dury.
- Red: Eggs poached in wine.
- Red: 1997, 1996, 1995.
- Red: 3–5 years. White: 2–5 years.

ST AMOUR

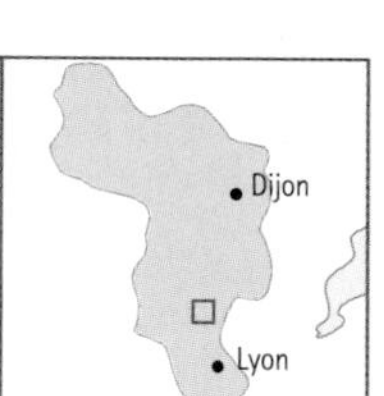

DESPITE THE ROMANCE OF ITS NAME, the "*amour*" in question is in fact St Amator, a martyred Roman soldier turned Christian, whose statue stands in the village of St Amour-Bellevue. The most northerly of the Beaujolais *crus*, St Amour is an area of geological transition, straddling the granite of Beaujolais to the south and the limestone of the Mâconnais to the north. As a result of the mixed limestone and granite-based gravel soils, the wines of St Amour include some of the lightest and most supple reds of the region, many of them more in the style of the Mâconnais *(see p143)* than the rest of Beaujolais. For a taste of the landscape as well as the wines, the hillside hamlet of Plâtre-Durand, with a tasting room in the Caveau du Cru St Amour, is worth a visit.

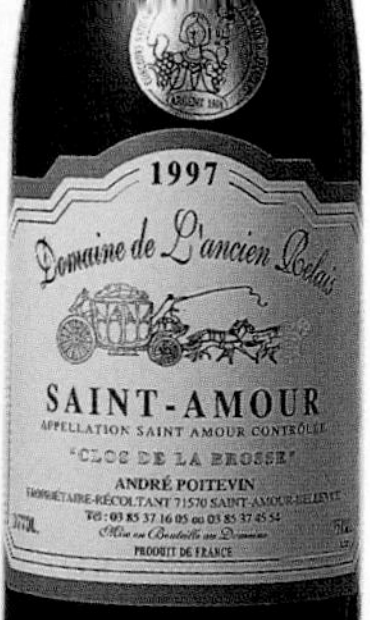

André Poitevin
A fine, juicy example with the perfumed, yet far from lightweight, character typical of the best of St Amour's wines.

Lovely Spot
The unique combination of subsoils here is responsible for the delicate style of the *commune*'s best wines.

- AC St Amour.
- Red: Gamay.
- Soft, plump, fruity reds, usually best for early drinking.
- Des Billards, Georges Duboeuf, Jean-Paul Ducoté, des Ducs, Henry Fessy, Janin, Patissier, du Plateau de Bel-Air, André Poitevin, Revillon, Michel Tête, Georges Trichard.
- Traditionally made coarse-cut pork sausage stewed with Beaujolais, garlic, onions, shallots, and wild mushrooms.
- 2003, 2001, 1997, 1995.
- Red: 2–6 years.

ST AUBIN

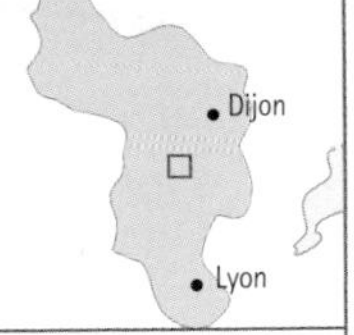

NORTH OF THE RED AND WHITE wine producing *appellation* of Chassagne-Montrachet *(see p135)*, and east of the world-famous white wine vineyards of Puligny-Montrachet *(see p153)*, is the Côte de Beaune *commune* of St Aubin. There are 570 acres (230 ha) of vineyards here, just over half of which are planted with Chardonnay and Pinot Blanc vines. Many of the 29 *premiers crus* vineyards of the *appellation* also produce whites, with the best including Les Murgers des Dents de Chien and En Remilly. At their best, these hazelnut-tinged wines easily outclass many of the wines of Puligny-Montrachet. With ripe, wild strawberry fruit and more complexity than the village wines, *premier cru* red wines can offer good value here, but, unlike the whites, they rarely shake off their essentially rustic character.

Roux Père et Fils
This is a rich, buttery, nutty wine that is every bit as good as many pricier ones from nearby Puligny-Montrachet.

Hidden Treasure
Tucked away in the hills, St Aubin is often unjustly overlooked by visitors and wine-drinkers drawn by the fame of the nearby villages of Puligny-Montrachet and Meursault.

- AC St Aubin, AC St Aubin Premier Cru.
- Red: Pinot Noir. White: Chardonnay, Pinot Blanc.
- Supple reds. Crisp medium-weight whites.
- J-C Bachelet, Champy, Marc Colin, Hubert Lamy-Monnot, Olivier Leflaive, Henri Prudhon, Ch de Puligny-Montrachet, Roux Père et Fils, Thomas.
- White: Flaky pastry filled with snails, garlic, and ceps.
- White: 2003, 2002, 2001, 1996.
- White: 3–8 years.

ST BRIS

ONE OF THE ENDURING MYSTERIES of French wine is why these characterful white wines from the north of Burgundy were for so long entitled to no more than a *VDQS* classification. Today, the crisp, dry wines with herbaceous, smoky flavors similar to those of Sancerre, a further 60 miles (100 km) to the southwest, are sold under the new Saint Bris *appellation*, but confusingly, labels are no longer allowed to mention that, unlike other white Burgundies, this is pure Sauvignon Blanc.

Jean-Marc Brocard
J-M Brocard's wines are very often compared to those of Sancerre.

- AC St Bris.
- Sauvignon Blanc.
- Light, crisp, fruity dry whites.
- Jean-Marc Brocard, la Chablisienne, Joel et David Griffe, St Prix, Sorin-Defrance.
- Crayfish.
- 1998, 1997, 1996.
- 1–3 years.

ST ROMAIN

AT AN ALTITUDE of 1,150 ft (350 m), St Romain is almost Hautes-Côtes de Beaune territory *(see p141)*, with cool conditions that are often unfavorable for ripening grapes. Red wines here are pleasant but rustic, while whites are fresh, minerally, and unoaked—perfect for those who wish to avoid the modern oaky style of *appellations* such as Puligny-Montrachet *(see p153)*. Thanks to the legendary cooper Jean François, St Romain is best known as the exporter of some of the world's best oak barrels.

Christophe Buisson
This is a refreshing, minerally wine with a hazelnut richness.

- AC St Romain.
- Red: Pinot Noir. White: Chardonnay.
- Light, soft, fruity reds. Crisp, racy whites.
- Christophe Buisson, Chassorney, Germain et Fils, Alain Gras, Thevenin-Monthélie.
- White: Frogs' legs.
- White: 2003, 2002, 2001.
- White: 3–5 years.

ST VÉRAN

CREATED IN 1971, this *appellation* lies in both Beaujolais and the Mâconnais, covering white wines from the seven villages of Davayé and Prissé to the north of Pouilly-Fuissé *(see p152)*, and Chanès, Chasselas, Leynes, St Amour, and St Vérand to the south. The combination of limestone and Chardonnay produces wines that combine richness with a slight mineral edge. A number of talented and ambitious producers also help St Véran to offer some of the best value in the region.

Jacques Saumaize
Rich, buttery wine with a fresh appley note and a mineral backbone.

- AC St Véran.
- White: Chardonnay.
- Light, dry whites.
- D et M Barraud, Corsin des Deux Roches, Georges Duboeuf, Ch Fuissé, Producteurs de Fuissé, Roger Luquet, J Saumaize.
- Chicken baked with Dijon mustard and *crème fraîche*.
- 2003, 2002, 2001.
- 2–4 years.

SANTENAY

FAMOUS SINCE ROMAN times for its lithium-rich spa waters, Santenay is one of the most southerly wine villages in the Côte de Beaune. White Santenay is worth buying, but all but two percent of the wines made here are red, falling into two basic styles. Santenay from vineyards around and to the south of the village is full-bodied and earthy, while that from the 14 *premiers crus* vineyards at the northern end of the *appellation* is light and elegant, similar in style to the wines of Beaune *(see pp128–9)*.

Adrien Belland
The grapes used here come from some of the finest vineyards in Santenay.

- AC Santenay, AC Santenay Premier Cru.
- Red: Pinot Noir.
- Earthy, rustic reds.
- Adrien Belland, Fernand Chevrot, Marc Colin, Vincent Girardin, Olivier Leflaive, Nouveau, Pousse d'Or, Prieur-Brunet.
- Shoulder of Lamb.
- Red: 1996, 1995, 1993.
- Red: 3–12 years.

SAVIGNY-LÈS-BEAUNE

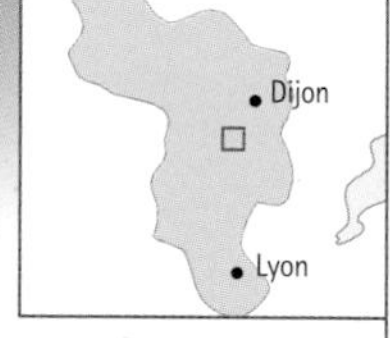

TUCKED AWAY IN THE VALLEY of the tiny Rhoin River, the *appellation* of Savigny-lès-Beaune includes 950 acres (385 hectares) of vines, centered around the village of Savigny-lès-Beaune. From the east of the *appellation* come wines that are well structured but slightly rustic, while wines from vineyards to the north, closer to Pernand-Vergelesses *(see p150)*, are softer, with creamy fruit flavors. Hillside vineyards in this area make up the *appellation*'s 22 *premiers crus*, while Savigny-lès-Beaune wines come from the flatter land in between. Around 90 percent of the wine produced here is red, but some white is also made—often, unusually in the Chardonnay-loving Côte de Beaune, using a proportion of the Pinot Blanc grape with its easily recognizable flavors of cream and Brazil nuts.

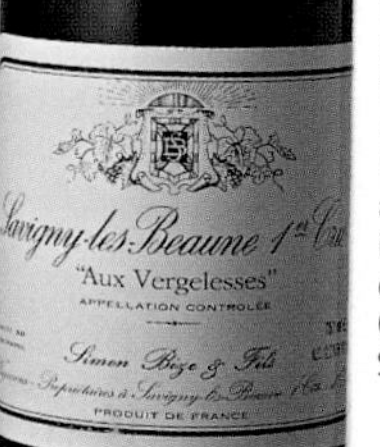

Simon Bize
This estate produces wines that are unusually long-lived, aging them in its cellars opposite the Château de Savigny.

Varied vineyards
The vineyards of Savigny-lès-Beaune are among the most varied in the region. The best, which include Aux Vergelesses and Les Lavières, are as good as many *premiers crus* in neighboring Beaune.

- AC Savigny-lès-Beaune, AC Savigny-lès-Beaune Premier Cru.
- Red: Pinot Noir. White: Pinot Blanc, Chardonnay.
- Elegant, medium-weight reds. Light, spicy whites.
- Arnoux, Bize, Champy, Chandon de Briailles, Bruno Clair, Girard-Voillot, Drouhin, Dubreuil-Fontaine, Maurice Ecard, Pavelot, Tollot-Beaut.
- Fillet of duck
- Red: 1998, 1996, 1995, 1993.
- Red: 6 years. White: 2–3 years.

VOLNAY

EVERY LOVER OF THE WINES of Burgundy has a favorite red wine from the region. Many would probably choose one of the prestigious names of the Côte de Nuits, but my own *appellation* of choice is Volnay, whose uniquely-perfumed blend of violets, raspberries, and ripe plums has always struck me as both ethereal and utterly seductive.

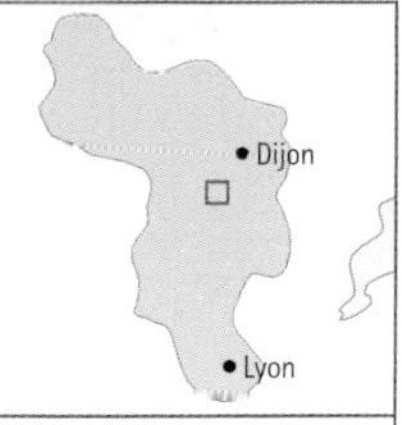

Marquis d'Angerville
This wine was produced by the Marquis d'Angerville, whose father helped to found the *appellation contrôlée* system.

Situated between Pommard and Meursault, the prosperous hillside village of Volnay was famous as early as the 17th century for a pale and delicate red wine known as *vin paillé* or "strawed wine." The wine was made from grapes pressed between straw lattices and fermented with very little maceration (contact between the fermenting juice and the grape skins). According to the cleric-author of *La Situation de la Bourgogne*, writing in 1728, "the grapes of this *terroir* can be left only a short time in the fermenting vat. If they are left there a moment longer than necessary, the wine will lose its delicacy...".

Sleepy streets
Tucked away high in the hills above the *route nationale* and looking down over *premiers crus* vineyards, the picturesque village of Volnay has a quiet but distinctly prosperous air.

During the early part of the 20th century, the Volnay name was regularly used by unscrupulous merchants to sell wines made from grapes grown as far away as southern France and Algeria. One Volnay estate owner, the Marquis d'Angerville, responded by helping to lay the foundations of the *appellation contrôlée* system, leading, in 1932, to the establishment of the *Institut National des Appellations d'Origine*.

Appropriately, the talents of a number of excellent producers, including the recently deceased son of the Marquis d'Angerville mentioned above, have now helped to make Volnay one of the most reliable *appellations* in the region. Other factors contributing to the reliability of Volnay's wines, as well as their smoothness and fragrance, include the shallow, chalky soil and the southeastern exposure of the vineyards. Although there are no *grands crus* here, more than half of the vineyards are *premiers crus*, the most impressive of which include Taille Pieds, Les Caillerets, Clos des Ducs, Clos des Chênes, and Bousse d'Or. Volnay is predominantly a red wine *appellation*, and the tiny amount of white wine produced here is sold as AC Meursault *(see p145)*.

- AC Volnay, AC Volnay Premier Cru.
- Red: Pinot Noir.
- Elegant, velvet-textured wines with red berry flavors.
- Marquis d'Angerville, Roger Bellend, Boigelot, J-M Boillot, Lucien Boillot, Bouchard Père et Fils, Pascal Bouley, Caillot, Camille Giroud, Champy, Coche-Dury, Joseph Drouhin, Génot-Boulanger, Vincent Girardin, Jaffelin, Michel Lafarge, Comtes Lafon, Olivier Leflaive, Leroy, de Montille, Fernand et Laurent Pillot, Prieur-Brunet, Pousse d'Or, Rebourgeon Mure, Régis Rossignol-Changarnier, Vaudoisey, Voillot.
- Roast saddle of hare.
- 1998, 1997, 1996, 1995, 1993, 1990, 1988, 1985.
- Red: 3–18 years.

Michel Lafarge
A superb Volnay producer, Michel Lafarge makes wines that manage to combine richness, perfume, and purity.

VOSNE-ROMANÉE

THE ENTIRE CÔTE D'OR REGION can be compared to a golden crown full of precious jewels, but if one village is to be chosen as the most exotic of all its gems, then it has to be Vosne-Romanée. The most southerly of the Côte de Nuits villages, Vosne-Romanée is home to some of the most prestigious vineyards in Burgundy and produces stylish red wines.

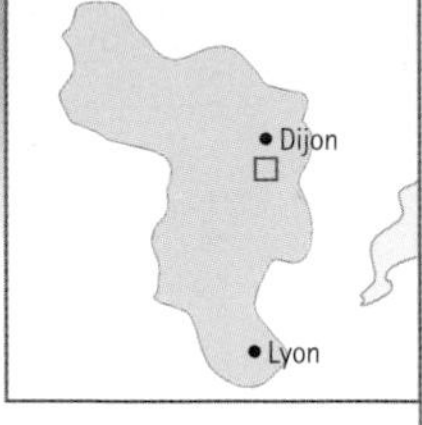

Clos des Réas
The *premier cru* Clos des Réas vineyard is owned by a branch of the famous wine-making Gros family, producing rich, complex, perfumed wines.

One 18th-century source states that Vosne-Romanée produced "*pas de vin commun*," or "no wine of ordinary quality." Today, this village is still unusual in producing red wines of almost uniformly high quality, and there are fewer disappointments among even the most basic wines of Vosne-Romanée than in nearby *appellations* such as Gevrey-Chambertin *(see p140)* or Nuits-St Georges *(see p149)*.

The *appellation* of Vosne-Romanée boasts some brilliant *premiers crus* and *grands crus* vineyards. The finest, or at least the most expensive, of the *grands crus* is the 4.4-acre (1.8-ha) La Romanée-Conti. Taking its name from Roman remains unearthed here and from its 18th-century owner, the Prince de Conti, La Romanée-Conti is now part of the world-famous Domaine de la Romanée-Conti (known to initiates as the DRC), which also includes the neighboring La Tâche vineyard. The wines produced here are extraordinarily rich, stuffed with plums and with more than a hint of spice. Other great *grands crus* vineyards here include La Romanée, owned by the *négociant*-producer firm Bouchard Père et Fils, Romanée-St Vivant, Richebourg and the recently promoted but so far disappointing La Grande Rue.

Among the best of the 17 *premiers crus* vineyards of the *appellation* are Les Beaux Monts, Les Brûlées, Les Chaumes, Aux Malconsorts, Les Suchots, Clos des Réas, and Cros-Parantoux. In an area blessed with a plethora of excellent producers, Domaine de la Romanée-Conti competes with great wine-makers including Lalou Bize-Leroy of Domaine Leroy and René Engel, Anne Gros, and Jean-Nicolas Méo of Domaine Méo-Camuzet.

Just beyond the *appellation*'s northern boundary are the *grands crus* of Echézeaux and Les Grands Echézeaux. Belonging to the nearby village of Flagey-Echézeaux, the wines here are similar to some of the best examples of Vosne-Romanée, though rarely quite as rich and complex.

Divine Intervention
This much-visited crucifix stands close to the tiny *grand cru* vineyard of La Romanée-Conti, the source of some of the best, and most expensive, red wines in Burgundy.

- AC Vosne-Romanée, AC Vosne-Romanée Premier Cru, AC Grands Crus: Richebourg; La Romanée; La Tâche; Romanée-St Vivant; Romanée-Conti; La Grande Rue.
- Red: Pinot Noir.
- Elegant, velvety reds.
- Arnoux, Bouchard Père et Fils, Cacheux, Confuron-Cotédiot, Joseph Drouhin, Engel, Faiveley, Forey, François Gerbet, Jean Grivot, Anne Gros, Jayer-Gilles, Leroy, Méo-Camuzet, Mongeard-Mugneret, Mugneret-Gibourg, des Perdrix, Pernin-Rossin, Jaques Prieur, Prieuré-Roch, Rion, Romanée-Conti, Romaneé-St Vivant, Rouget, Jean Tardy, Thomas-Moillard.
- *Coq au vin.*
- 2003, 20021, 2001, 1999, 1998.1996, 1995, 1993, 1990, 1988, 1985.
- Red: 5–20 years.

Lalou Bize-Leroy
Once a partner in the Domaine de la Romanée-Conti, Lalou Bize-Leroy now makes impeccable wines from her own organic vineyards nearby.

OTHERS

ALONGSIDE THE CLASSIC PINOT NOIRS and Chardonnays of Burgundy, a surprisingly wide range of lesser-known wines is also produced. Rarely seen outside their area of origin, many of these wines deserve to be much better known. One such is the distinctive Bourgogne Aligoté Bouzeron, made around the Côte Chalonnaise village of Bouzeron.

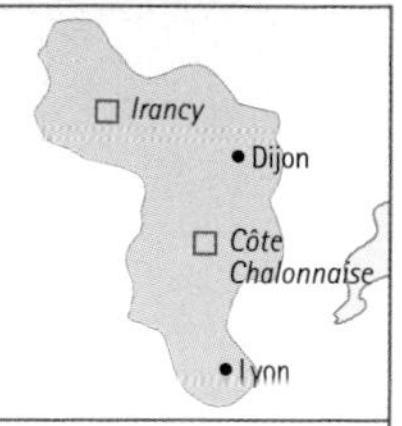

Living History
Vineyards around the Yonne village of St Bris-le-Vineux are used to grow both Sauvignon Blanc and the local César grape—both varieties that are no longer popular in more southern parts of Burgundy.

Mention the Aligoté grape variety to a wine enthusiast and he or she will probably think of Kir, the blend of white wine and black-currant liqueur that was invented by Canon Kir, one-time mayor of Dijon. Taste most Aligoté wines in their unadulterated form and you will have no difficulty in understanding why the good cleric decided to sweeten his. Although attractively fresh and appley at their best, these wines are very often savagely acidic. However, notable exceptions to the tooth-stripping Aligoté rule are the wines made from grapes grown around the village of Bouzeron in the Côte Chalonnaise. Here the grape performs well enough to have been awarded its own *appellation,* Bourgogne Aligoté Bouzeron, soon to be renamed more simply as *appellation contrôlée* Bouzeron.

Passetoutgrains was once the name of the most popular everyday red wine in Burgundy—made, as the name suggests, from a mixture of any grape varieties that were to hand. Its successor, the Bourgogne Passetoutgrains *appellation,* has now evolved into a traditional blend of Gamay and Pinot Noir grapes. The officially sanctioned grape ratio is two parts Gamay to one part Pinot Noir, though many producers quietly admit that they prefer to use rather more of the Pinot Noir. Small quantities of good Bourgogne Passetoutgrains are produced at a surprising number of top estates and, full of interesting cherry and raspberry flavors, can be drunk as alternatives to *cru* Beaujolais *(see pp126–7).*

Crémant de Bourgogne is Burgundy's generic white and rosé sparkling wine *appellation.* An increase in permitted grape varieties to include Pinot Noir, Chardonnay and Pinot Blanc, as well as the more traditional Aligoté and Gamay, has resulted in a dramatic improvement of these wines in recent years. Today, examples made from Chardonnay occasionally make a good alternative to less-than-top-class *blanc de blancs* Champagne, while Crémant de Bourgogne *blanc de noirs* offers attractively pure Pinot Noir flavors.

One almost-extinct red wine worth looking for is made from the traditional César grape, grown in the Irancy area, close to Chablis. The legality of naming César on bottles produced in the various *appellations* of the area is not clear, but these wines have a fascinating flavor that falls somewhere between that of red Burgundy *(see p130)* made from the Pinot Noir grape and that of red Anjou wines *(see p214)* made from Cabernet Franc.

Jean-François Coche-Dury
The Aligoté grape variety tends to produce meanly acidic flavors, but may also be made into rich and unusual whites like this example.

CHAMPAGNE

Champagne

Much more than just a wine, Champagne is now synonymous throughout the globe with the notions of quality, luxury, and celebration.

Dom Pérignon
Credited with inventing Champagne, the famous abbot's greatest legacy lies in the art of blending.

Uncork a great Champagne and you might find yourself drinking something that seems to be much more than a wine. At its best, Champagne can be the most extraordinary drink: dry, yet with some honeyed sweetness; rich, yet fresh; delicate, yet mouth-filling; easy to drink, yet offering layers of different flavors ranging from fruits to nuts and even dark chocolate. Some or all of this is what I hope to find when I hear the pop of the cork. Experience, however, has taught me that, despite the fortune that this region has spent on protecting its name, the mere presence of the word "Champagne" on the label of a wine bottle gives me no reason to expect anything very special at all. So why are some Champagnes so sublime, while others can taste sourly acidic, sugary, or simply dull? The answer lies largely in the geography of this region. Champagne may have had the historic advantage of its close proximity to Paris and the wine-drinkers of neighboring countries to the east, but it has always been a cold, northerly region. In these temperatures, grapes find it impossible to ripen sufficiently to produce still red and white wines that are good enough to compete with the wines of vineyards farther south. Not that this handicap deterred the 16th-century Champenois, who dyed their wine with elderberry juice in an attempt to mimic the richer color of red Burgundy.

Champagne owes its success to a series of human interventions. Dom Pérignon, the 17th-century abbot of Hautvillers, is the man erroneously credited with putting the bubbles into what had previously been still wines. In fact, fizziness was something that he initially sought to avoid, because of the tendency at this time for many bottles of his wine to explode. His greatest contribution to wine-making was in fact the care he took in developing the art of blending wines from various parts of the region, rather than following the example of the Burgundians in keeping them separate.

Watery Safeguard
Water is sprayed over the vines to protect them against frost, which can be a major hazard in this northern region.

The combination of better wine, which still tended to fizz, and newly developed, stronger, nonexploding bottles was a great success, first in London, then in Paris. Ever since, most Champagne has been blended—a blend of grapes, of vineyards, and of vintages. And, as Dom Pérignon understood, the quality of the wines that go into that blend is far more important than the bubbles that have given Champagne its worldwide fame.

REGIONAL OVERVIEW

- 74,000 acres (30,000 ha): 270 million bottles.
- Marginal and highly variable, this region is subject to the effects of the northern latitude and the Atlantic Ocean. Summers can be very cool, and vines are often threatened by frost in the spring.
- Chalk is the main distinguishing component of this region, extending down as much as 1,000 ft (300 m). The topsoil includes chalk rubble, clay, sand, lignite, marl, and loam.
- White/rosé: Chardonnay, Pinot Noir, Pinot Meunier.

Palate Pleaser
Unlike other regions, where wines are produced in individual villages, Champagne tends to offer a blend of grapes that have been grown in various parts of the *appellation*.

Into the Wine
These vineyards near Cramant are planted exclusively with Chardonnay grapes, which produce fine *blanc de blanc* wines.

The History of Champagne

A glass of a fine Champagne, such as Krug or Dom Pérignon, would be as recognizable to a Champagne enthusiast as a Chanel dress or a Guerlain eau de toilette *would be to someone interested in clothes or scent. It is no coincidence that so many Champagne companies now come under the same ownership as* couturiers *and* perfumiers.

Champagne flies wonderfully in the face of the philosophy of most French wines. Elsewhere, the notion that lies at the very core of the *appellation contrôlée* system is that wine should express the character of the specific vineyard in which its grapes were grown. Even the finest Champagne, however, is mostly a blend of wines from different sites. While there are individual vineyard wines, the most illustrious Champagnes, such as Dom Pérignon and Roederer Cristal *(see p175)*, are blends whose success lies in the way they embody the individual house style of their producers. Richard Geoffroy, the man responsible for making the wine named after Dom Pérignon, says that his focus is on "style, style, style."

Within those house styles, Champagne comes in a number of different colors and flavors. Its color ranges from white to shades of rosé, which can be made either by blending red and white wine or by allowing the skins of the black grapes to tint the juice rather than removing them before they do so. Next, there is sweetness, the scale of which extends from aggressively bone-dry Brut Sauvage, Ultra Brut, or Brut Zéro to lusciously sweet Doux. In fact, the wines at the far ends of the scale are rarely made these days. The driest Champagne you are likely to come across is Brut, which contains up to 15 g of sugar per liter of wine. For the sweeter-toothed, there is the oddly named Extra Sec or Extra Dry, which has 12–20 g, the even more misleading Sec or Dry, which has 17–35 g of sugar, and finally Demi Sec or Rich, with 35–50 g per liter. Sugar hides acidity very effectively, so slightly sweeter Champagnes go down more easily than the cheap dry examples offered in supermarkets.

Château Chandon
The modern Champagne industry was a 19th-century success story, and the producers soon adopted lifestyles to match. Moet & Chandon is now part of a luxury goods group that also produces perfume and fashion accessories.

A MATTER OF STYLE

The style of any wine is determined by the grape variety that it is made from. Most Champagnes, including rosés, are blends of Pinot Noir, Pinot Meunier, and Chardonnay, but there are also pure Chardonnays (*blancs de blancs*) and wines made with no white grapes at all (*blancs de noirs*). There are vintage Champagnes, made from the fruit of a single harvest and judged by the

Drink of Princes... and Princesses
The major Champagne houses have traditionally used imagery associated with the royal families of Europe.

producer not to require improvement by the addition of older wines, and finally the far more numerous nonvintage blends. To complicate matters even further, there are oddities like "recently disgorged" vintage Champagnes that develop fresh, yet rich, characters of their own through having been left on their yeast for several years longer than usual. And, subject to no rules at all, there are the so-called *prestige cuvées* that command the highest prices. Any Champagne producer can come up with a fancy name, bottle, and price for one of his vintage or nonvintage wines, but there is no guarantee that the stuff that goes into that bottle is as special as its attractive, upmarket packaging.

Any or all of these styles may be produced by Champagne's individual estates, *coopératives* and merchants. Historically, it was merchants such as Moët & Chandon *(see p174)*, Krug *(see p173)*, Roederer, and Bollinger who did the job best. The money they made from their sales across the world gave them numerous advantages. They had the greatest access to good grapes, both from their own vines and from their choice of *grands crus* vineyards. They had the financial means to keep "reserve" wine from previous years to use in their nonvintage wine, and they had the best wine-making equipment and blending skills.

Coopératives, by contrast, were thought to have the disadvantage of having to rely on grapes grown by their members in the vicinity of the winery. In other words, they had a far smaller palette to blend from. Also, the fact that most of their wines were sold cheaply under various customers' names did little to encourage them to focus on quality. Small estates, with only limited funds and their own grapes to work with, were believed to suffer from an even greater handicap. More recently, however, the picture has changed as critics have acknowledged the poor quality of some big-name Champagnes. Mumm's efforts were, at one time, unfavorably compared with the same company's Californian wines. *Coopératives* have launched own brands that sometimes compete on level terms with those of the merchants, and a growing number of sophisticated, well-sited, top-quality independent estates have proven that they can defy expectations by making some of the best Champagne of all. In the 21st century, the well-known names face a growing number of challenges. There are new markets opening up around the world and new competitors appearing both in Champagne itself and in other regions. With luck, the winners will be the Champagne-drinkers, who will get an even better wine at a fairer price.

Veuve Clicquot Fan
The widow Clicquot, who invented the process of disgorging wine, had a strong promotional style—as this fan shows.

A Driving Tour of Champagne

Despite the international fame of wines made by large producers from a mixture of grapes grown in various parts of the region, Champagne comprises many individual towns and villages. This tour, beginning and ending in the historic city of Reims, takes in a range of the most interesting of these.

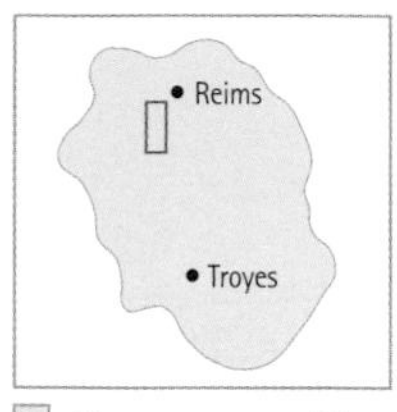

Champagne ☐ Tour

Montagne de Reims
The lower slopes of the "Mountain of Reims" are famed for their Pinot Noir grapes.

REIMS TO BOUZY

In Reims ①, the unofficial capital of this region, take advantage of the guided cellar tours offered by houses such as Louis Roederer, Pommery, Taittinger, Ruinart, Lanson and Charles Heidsieck, whose cellars have been carved out of the chalk beneath the city. Make sure, too, that you take a break from wine to visit the magnificent cathedral, where Joan of Arc watched the coronation of Charles VII in 1429. After Sillery ②, you drive past the so-called Montagne de Reims, a low hill covered by top-class Pinot Noir vines. A century or so ago, Sillery's wines were sold under the name of this hill. In Mailly-Champagne ③, you could pause to stock up on a few bottles from the *coopérative*, one of the region's best. The villages of Verzenay ④, Verzy ⑤, Ambonnay ⑥ and Bouzy ⑦ are all sources of good Pinot Noir, in the form of both Champagne and Bouzy Rouge Coteaux Champenois. For a fine example, visit Paul Bara in Bouzy or Egly-Ouriet in Ambonnay.

LOUVOIS TO AY

Louvois ⑧ has a château whose garden is said to have been modeled on that of Versailles, while Mareuil-sur-Ay ⑨ is home to Billecart-Salmon, one of the region's top firms. In Ay ⑩, you can visit Ayala, Bollinger, Deutz, and Gosset, as well as the Musée Champenois, which displays old wine-making implements.

ÉPERNAY TO VERTUS

Épernay ⑪ is best known for its Avenue de Champagne, where houses such as Mercier and Moët & Chandon are based. Other firms here include Pol Roger, de Castellane, and Perrier Jouët. In Chavot ⑫, stop to photograph the landscape from the church atop Mont Félix, before heading southeast to Avize ⑬, where you can visit the cellars of Jacques Sélosse, one of the region's best producers, and the Union-Champagne *coopérative*. In Le Mesnil-sur-Oger ⑭, a village in the heart of Chardonnay country, Krug makes single-vineyard *blanc de blancs*. Not far from here is Vertus ⑮, a medieval town with streams, the perfect spot for a picnic.

MONTMORT TO CHÂTILLON-SUR-MARNE

From Montmort ⑯, with its 16th-century château, head northwest via the pretty village of Mareuil-en-Brie ⑰ to Orbais l'Abbaye ⑱, whose name refers to its Benedictine abbey. Stop off in Dormans ⑲ to visit the 13th-century château and park, and to experience a taste of turn-of-the-20th-century riverside vacations. In Châtillon-sur-Marne ⑳, take a look at the statue of pope Urban II, on a hill overlooking the town.

HAUTVILLERS TO REIMS

Go through the wine villages of Venteuil and Damery to Hautvillers ㉑ abbey, where Dom Pérignon carried out his first blending experiments. The abbey is a "must-see" for many, and the village of Hautvillers is also worth exploring. From here, head east to the Royal Champagne in Bellevue, one of France's top country hotels. The final part of the tour takes you through the villages of Chamery ㉒, Sacy ㉓ and Pargny-lès-Reims ㉔, all of which offer opportunities to taste Champagnes made by growers, as opposed to those produced by the bigger companies in the towns.

KEY

- Tasting possible
- Places to eat
- Tourist information
- ★ Site of interest
- Tour route
- Viewpoint

TOURIST OFFICES

Chatillon sur Marne
4 Rue de l'Eglise
03 26 58 32 86
FAX 03 26 51 87 85
otchatillon51@aol.com
www.otchatillon51.com

Epernay
7 Avenue de Champagne
03 26 53 33 00
FAX 03 26 51 95 22

Hautvillers
Place de la République
03 26 57 06 35
FAX 03 26 51 72 66
ot@ccgvm.com
www.ccgvm.com

Reims
12 Boulevard Général Leclerc
03 26 77 45 00
FAX 03 26 77 45 19

A Touch of Class
The Champagne houses were among the first producers to open their doors to the public. As can be seen on this vat from Pommery, the attention to detail was very important and reflected the status of a house.

The Food of Champagne

The region that has given us the world's most famous sparkling wine can claim surprisingly few traditional dishes that are specifically its own. The inhabitants of this cool, fertile farming region have been blessed with fine raw materials and have always eaten well, but, borrowing extensively from neighboring regions, they have not proved to be particularly inventive cooks.

One unusual feature of the cuisine of the Champagne region is its limited use of beef; this is not a part of France with a rich history of cattle farming. Where beef is used, it is usually as part of a mixture of meats, most memorably in a local version of the Burgundian *pot au feu*, known here as *potée champenoise* or as *potée des vendangeurs* (grape-pickers' stew). This hearty dish is made from five meats and five vegetables, often salt pork, shin of beef, silverside of beef, chicken, and spicy sausage, together with carrots, leeks, turnips, savoy cabbage, and onions. Another mixed-meat dish is *épaule d'agneau farcie à la Champenoise*, in which a shoulder of lamb is stuffed with chopped pork and tomatoes flavored with juniper and Champagne.

Pork is a staple meat in this region, and pigs, traditionally fattened on acorns, appear in dishes ranging from smoked Ardennes ham and pork chops grilled with sage leaves to spicy tripe-filled

Land of Plenty
A great variety of fruit and vegetables, including peas, onions, tomatoes, asparagus, plums, and cabbages, is grown in the rich farmland of Champagne and sold in shops and markets throughout the region.

Truite Ardennaise
Delicate brown trout are common in the many rivers that run through the entire Champagne region. In this simple but delicious dish, the fish is sautéed in butter before being finished off with a sauce of *crème fraîche* and Ardennes ham.

sausages and *pieds de porc à la Ste-Menehould*, pigs' trotters simmered slowly in a rich stock.

A variety of meats and fish are cooked with the sparkling or still white wines of the region, including pike, eels, ham, chicken, guinea fowl, pheasant, and *sanglier* (wild boar) from the extensive forests of the Ardennes. The local red wines are also used in cooking, and many restaurants offer *poulet sauté au Bouzy*, a variation on the Burgundian *coq au vin*. *Ouyettes* (goose pies) are a specialty here, as are tiny song thrushes, often stewed with juniper berries, *à l'Ardennaise*. Popular river fish dishes include trout fried in butter with a ham and *crème fraîche* sauce, and pike with bacon and gherkins. Accompaniments include potatoes fried with onions and garlic or a salad of dandelion leaves and crisply fried bacon.

To finish the meal there might be a Genoese sponge cake filled with praline cream, or almond meringues, also filled with thick cream. A personal favorite is *fraises Eugénie*, fresh strawberries served with warm *sabayon*.

Jambon des Ardennes
Hilly and densely forested, the Ardennes region is famous for its cold-smoked hams, eaten as an appetizer with pickles, and in many traditional local dishes.

Pâté en Croûte
Pâtés of all kinds, including pork, goose, wild boar, goose liver, and more, are made in Champagne, often wrapped in a rich pastry shell and baked in the oven.

REGIONAL CHEESES

In the year 1217, the Comtesse de Champagne sent 200 Brie de Meaux cheeses as a gift to the King of France. One of the oldest and finest of French cheeses, Brie from the village of Meaux was popular with the Emperor Charlemagne as early as the ninth century. Today, Brie is made in huge quantities on farms and in factories all over the Champagne region, and varies from the simple to the sublime. Langres à la Coupe and Chaource are two other regional specialties. Produced in smaller volumes, they are of far more consistent quality.

Langres à la Coupe
This cylindrical cheese has a well in the middle into which Champagne or *marc* is poured. The rind is rubbed with brine and annatto for color.

Chaource
This mild cow's-milk cheese does not take long to mature. It quickly forms a tasty, edible white rind and develops a soft, oozingly creamy center.

TRAVELING IN CHAMPAGNE

One way of looking at Champagne as a region to visit is to think of it as an iceberg. Above the waterline are the big-name producers, Reims Cathedral, and the award-winning Restaurant des Crayères, but just as worthwhile are the host of small villages, individual estates, and charming little bistros that are also to be found here.

HOTELS & RESTAURANTS

A selection of the region's best establishments, offering good local food and drink, and notable places to stay.

AMBONNAY

Auberge St-Vincent, 1 Rue St-Vincent.
03 26 57 01 98
FAX 03 26 57 81 48
If you don't like snails, or can't imagine a meal without meat, the Auberge St Vincent is not for you. This small country inn specializes in *escargots* and vegetables, pastas, and salads—and it does so with great skill. The rooms are comfortable, too.

EPERNAY

Le Théatre, 8 Place Mendès-France.
03 26 58 88 19
FAX 03 26 58 88 38
As the name suggests, this was once a place of entertainment. Today, it's still a hot ticket, with fairly high prices, but the cooking deserves the applause it gets.

ETOGES

Château d'Etoges, 4 Rue Richebourg.
03 26 59 30 08
A moated 17th-century château with romantic towers, the perfect place in which to spirit a fine bottle up to your bedroom after a meal of classic local cuisine.

MOUSSY, NEAR ÉPERNAY

L'Auberge Champenoise, Le Village.
03 26 54 03 48
A welcoming inn offering good, simple, fairly priced traditional dishes.

OEUILLY NEAR ÉPERNAY

Micheline et Jean-Mary Tarlant, 21 Rue Principale.
03 26 58 30 60
A small family wine estate that offers cozy rooms in converted cottages among the vines.

REIMS

Boyer "les Crayères", 64 Boulevard Vasnier.
03 26 82 80 80
A gastronomic mecca. The food is sublime and the Champagne list is predictably impressive, too, with plenty of older vintages.

Flo, 96 Place Drouet d'Erlon.
03 26 91 40 50
FAX 03 26 91 40 54
Worth visiting for the vastness of its wine and Champagne list alone, this restaurant also offers a great terrace and skillfully cooked local dishes.

WINE SHOPS

Many of the wines from smaller local producers are hard to find back home, so it's a good idea to stock up before you leave.

EPERNAY

Pérardel, 9 Rue Jean Chandon Moët.
03 26 56 97 30
A local outlet of the best wine retailer in France, with an extraordinarily wide and well-chosen range of wines.

REIMS

Marché aux Vins Pérardel, 3 Place Léon Bourgeois.
03 26 40 12 12
This is the Reims branch of the same shop.

La Cave d'Erlon, 40 Place d'Erlon.
03 26 47 44 44
FAX 03 26 47 55 12
In the heart of the town, Fabrice Parisot offers wines from all the main Champagne houses as well as examples from 30 individual estates.

VISITING PRODUCERS

Many of the bigger Champagne houses offer tours, for an entry fee that includes tastings. Some require reservations.

EPERNAY

de Castellane, 57 Rue de Verdun.
03 26 51 19 11
Besides the customary visit to underground cellars, de Castellane also offers the chance to climb an ornate tower, from which you can enjoy the view over the town and surrounding vineyards. One of the better places to learn about the minutiae of making Champagne.

Alfred Gratien, 30 Rue Maurice-Cerveaux.
03 26 54 38 20
A small traditional firm that still ferments its wine in barrels, Gratien also offers individual tours by appointment. The wines are some of the region's best.

Mercier, 68-70 Avenue de Champagne.
03 26 51 22 22
A huge seller in French super-markets, Mercier also offers one of the most professional tours. No reservation is needed and

Secret Champagne
Champagne's restaurants offer wines that are rarely found elsewhere.

the entry fee includes a video presentation and a 12-mile train trip around the cellars. Mercier also boasts the world's biggest barrel. Too bad the wine is so poor.
Perrier-Jouët, 28 Avenue de Champagne.
03 26 53 38 00
As you might expect from the Belle Epoque bottle, you can combine a (free) cellar visit with a tour of a fine collection of late 19th and early 20th century glass. Reservations are essential.

LE MESNIL SUR OGER
Launois Père & Fils, 2 Avenue Eugène Guillaume.
03 26 57 50 15
Rivaling the bigger houses, this small family firm based in one of the best Chardonnay villages adds a fine museum to the tour and tasting. Great value, but reservations are essential.

MAILLY
Grand Cru Mailly, 28 Rue de la Libération.
03 26 49 41 10
A *cooperative* making top-class Champagne, including pure Pinot Noir *blanc de noirs*. Booking is not necessary and the entry charge is often waived for evidently knowledgeable and/or enthusiastic visitors.

REIMS
Piper-Heidsieck, 51 Boulevard Henry Vasnier.
03 26 84 43 44
Not the most traditional of houses (quirks include a bottle "dressed" by Jean-Paul Gaultier), Piper offers visitors the chance to taste in the ambience of a nightclub. The wines and the tour are both good.
Pommery, 5 Place Du Général Gouraud.
03 26 61 62 63
Descend the 101-step staircase into some 13 miles of cellars cut between over 100 Roman chalkpits and take in the tunnels named after cities that were big customers a century or so ago. There is also a collection of bas-reliefs. No appointment is necessary.

ANNUAL WINE EVENTS

There are various fairs and festivals in the Champagne region during the spring and summer, but one that is particularly worth going out of your way to visit is the Fête de Mailly-Champagne, which takes place in May. Contact tourist offices *(see below)* for further details.

JANUARY
Venues change annually
St Vincent fair—a program of concerts, exhibitions, parades, and wine tastings

MAY
Mailly Fête de Mailly-Champagne

JULY/AUGUST
Reims music in the open air—150 classical and jazz concerts in venues in and around Reims

AUGUST
Route du Champagne
villages along the route offer tastings, concerts, and art exhibitions during August

SEPTEMBER
Bar-sur-Aube wine fair

Ruinart, 4 Rue des Crayères.
03 26 77 51 51
One of the region's very oldest houses, with great cellars. Ruinart charges admission, but it's worth every penny. By appointment.
Veuve Clicquot-Ponsardin 1 place des Droits-de-l'Homme.
03 26 89 54 41
Free tour and tasting leads you through one of Champagne's biggest cellars. Call ahead.

MUSEUMS

An individual cellar tour is great for getting to know a particular Champagne house, but these offer a more general overview of wine making in the region.

OGER
Le Musée de l'Amour et des Traditions au XIXième Siècle, Champagne Henry de Vaugency, 1 Rue d'Avize.
03 26 57 50 89
FAX 03 26 51 57
Two award-winning museums about domestic life in the 19th and early 20th centuries, with a great collection of labels.

REUIL
Le Musée du Vignoble en Miniature du Domaine Bacchus, 4 Rue Bacchus, L'Echelle.
03 26 58 66 60
FAX 03 26 57 65 30
A real curiosity: 90 square yards of meticulously miniaturized scenes in which 150 tiny figures bring to life the traditions of village grape-growing, harvesting, and wine-making in Champagne.

VERZENAY
Le Musée de la Vigne et du Champagne, Le Phare de Verzenay.
03 26 07 87 87
FAX 03 26 07 87 88
This wooden building overlooking the vineyards offers a chance to discover every aspect of the Champagne process, using a variety of exhibits and videos.

WEBSITES

Three useful websites are www.champagne.fr, www.champagne-multimedia.com, and www.umc.fr. Alternatively, go to the tourist site www.tourisme.fr, and type in the name of any town or village for specific information.

OTHER INFORMATION

Office du Tourisme, 7 Avenue de Champagne, Épernay.
03 26 53 33 00
Offers a broad range of information, from producer addresses to maps and festival dates.

BILLECART-SALMON

NO CHAMPAGNE has given me such consistent pleasure as the wine from this small family firm. The style is generally lighter and more delicate than most, and this is as apparent in the nonvintage as in the individual *cuvées*: Elisabeth Salmon Rosé, Nicolas-François Billecart, Blanc de Blancs and Grande Cuvée. Billecart-Salmon also arguably produces the finest, most reliable rosé in all of Champagne—a style that nowadays accounts for almost 20 percent of its annual sales.

Cuvée Elisabeth Salmon
The very epitome of pink Champagne, this fine *cuvée* has lovely raspberry flavors.

- Pinot Noir, Chardonnay, Pinot Meunier.
- Stylish, ultra-reliable Champagnes of all styles, with especially good rosé.
- Cuvée Nicolas-François Billecart, Cuvée Elisabeth Salmon Rosé, Blanc de Blancs, Grande Cuvée.
- None.
- 1997, 1995, 1990, 1989, 1988, 1985, 1982.

BOLLINGER

THE CHAMPAGNE OF James Bond—in the movies, at least (in the novels, he favors another brand)—is also a favorite with wine-makers. The key to this firm's success lies in owning over 350 acres (140 ha) of top-quality vineyards and in pursuing a style that repays aging and serving with meals. Others offer "recently disgorged" wines *(see p31)*, but Bollinger's RD is the classic. Its Vieilles Vignes Françaises ("old French vines") is a rarity: made from vines that aren't grafted onto American rootstock.

Bollinger 1990
Vintage Bollinger provides the quintessence of this house's rich style.

- Pinot Noir, Chardonnay, Pinot Meunier.
- Rich, complex, full-flavored, mouth-fillingly yeasty wines across the board.
- Grande Année, RD (Récemment Dégorgé), Vieilles Vignes Françaises.
- None.
- 1996, 1990, 1989, 1988, 1985, 1982.

GOSSET

FOUNDED IN 1584, this is one of the oldest wine companies in the world. Indeed, it remained in the hands of the same family for over four centuries until it was bought by Beatrice Cointreau. The Gosset style is decidedly traditional thanks to (old) barrel fermentation and a high proportion of black grapes. All the wines are of high quality, ranging from the nonvintage Grande Excellence to the top wine, the vintage Célébris. The nonvintage Grande Réserve is a wine to drink with food.

Célébris
A prestige *cuvée* with a Chardonnay character, and well worth cellaring.

- Pinot Noir, Chardonnay, Pinot Meunier.
- Slow-developing Champagne with more biscuity flavor than is often fashionable nowadays.
- Grande Excellence, Grand Rosé, Grande Millésime, Célébris.
- None.
- 1995,1990,1989,1988.

ALFRED GRATIEN

UNDER THE SAME OWNERSHIP as the Loire sparkling-wine producer Gratien & Meyer, this is another traditional house. Wines are fermented in (old) barrels and given unusually lengthy periods of contact with the yeast used to kick off the second fermentation. There is no malolactic fermentation *(see p24)*. This method provides the richness and freshness associated with "recently disgorged" *(see p31)* wines. Mature when sold, they improve with keeping and go particularly well with food.

Cuvée Paradis
This *cuvée* represents the quintessence of the rich, yeasty Gratien style.

- Pinot Noir, Chardonnay, Pinot Meunier.
- One of the most distinctive, richly old-fashioned, full-flavored, biscuity Champagnes.
- Cuvée Paradis, Vintage Brut.
- Gratien & Meyer (Saumur).
- 1996, 1990, 1989, 1988, 1987, 1985, 1983.

CHARLES HEIDSIECK

THIS FIRM DEMONSTRATES the importance of a skilled wine maker, as well as commitment to quality and investment. In the 1970s, wines from Charles Heidsieck were sold in supermarkets and made to the standards that this implies. Under the late Daniel Thibault, quality was transformed and nonvintage wines launched whose labels revealed the year when the *cuvée* was blended. These regularly beat vintage efforts in the International Wine Challenge.

Brut Réserve Mise en Cave 1992
This is a nonvintage wine with the quality of a vintage Champagne.

- Pinot Noir, Chardonnay, Pinot Meunier.
- Recently much improved, impeccably-made wines that are richly flavored enough to drink with food.
- Mis en Cave Non-vintage, Cuvée des Millénaires.
- Piper Heidsieck.
- 1995, 1990, 1989, 1985.

HENRIOT

REVERSING THE TREND that has been prevalent elsewhere in the Champagne region, Henriot recently went back from corporate ownership—under the same umbrella as Veuve Clicquot *(see p176)*—to belonging to the original family (which also bought and revolutionized the quality of Bouchard Père et Fils in Burgundy). The wines here are marked by Chardonnay—both in the vintage Brut Souverain and in the rich but elegant vintage Blanc de Blancs.

Blanc de Blancs
This is one of the best examples of pure Chardonnay produced in all Champagne.

- Pinot Noir, Chardonnay, Pinot Meunier.
- Much improved producer with rich, toasty Champagnes and particularly good Blanc de Blancs.
- Souverain Brut, Blanc de Blancs, Enchantelleurs.
- Bouchard Père et Fils.
- 1995, 1990, 1989, 1988, 1985.

JACQUESSON

THIS FAMILY FIRM PROUDLY claims Napoléon as one of its most distinguished customers and presents its Champagnes with gorgeous, instantly recognizable labels. The contents of the bottles are creamy yet dry, ranging from the nonvintage (modestly called "Perfection") to the vintage Blanc de Blancs and the vintage Brut. The "late-disgorged" style (known as *dégorgement tardif*) is Jacquesson's convincing answer to Bollinger's RD *(see left)*: a gloriously mature, yet fresh wine.

Perfection
This small family firm's Champagnes are among the richest on the market.

- Pinot Noir, Chardonnay, Pinot Meunier.
- Rich, complex and stylish wines that—especially the Blancs de Blancs—deserve to be far better known.
- Signature Brut, Blanc de Blancs, Dégorgement Tardif.
- None.
- 1995, 1990, 1989, 1988, 1985, 1983.

KRUG

THE ROLLS-ROYCE OF CHAMPAGNE, and now, like Moët & Chandon and Veuve Clicquot, part of the LVMH group, Krug makes unusually winelike Champagne. This is a Champagne to drink at dinner, but not for refreshment. There is also a long-lived vintage wine and a single-vineyard *blanc de blancs* called Clos de Mesnil, but none of the wines can top Krug's nonvintage and nonvintage rosé, both of which contain an unusually high proportion of mature wine.

Grande Cuvée
This could well be the greatest of all nonvintage Champagnes.

- Pinot Noir, Chardonnay, Pinot Meunier.
- Rich, mouth-filling wines, including dazzling nonvintage.
- Grande Cuvée, Rosé, Vintage, Clos du Mesnil.
- Pommery, Moët & Chandon, Krug, Dom Ruinart, Veuve Clicquot, Mercier.
- 1990, 1989, 1988, 1985.

LANSON

LANSON'S NAME, BUT NOT its vineyards, was bought in 1991 by Marne et Champagne, the region's second-biggest producer, which sells under its own and its customers' labels (and has recently changed its name to Lanson). The non-vintage Lanson remains one of the region's reliable rather than best examples, but the vintage can be a long-lived wine that is well worth buying. Lanson's top wine, the Noble Cuvée, is emphatically recommendable, as is the recently revived Demi-Sec.

Lanson
The gold label denotes a vintage Champagne; Lanson's are unusually long-lived.

- Pinot Noir, Chardonnay, Pinot Meunier.
- Full-flavored wines that repay patience.
- Noble Cuvée, Blanc de Blancs.
- Massé, Marne et Champagne brands including Besserat de Bellefon and Alfred Rothschild.
- 1996, 1993, 1990, 1988.

LAURENT-PERRIER

A LARGE AND AMBITIOUS family-owned firm, Laurent-Perrier owns a number of other Champagne houses, including Salon and de Castellane and half of the previously unconnected Joseph Perrier. Despite the volumes produced, the quality of the richly flavored, heavily Pinot Noir-influenced non-vintage is very consistent. Also produced is a set of more ambitious non-vintage Champagnes called Grand Siècle, including a *blanc de blancs*, a rosé, and the particularly excellent La Cuvée.

Grand Siècle
This highly unusual blend is made up of three different vintages.

- Pinot Noir, Chardonnay, Pinot Meunier.
- Very elegant dry (including ultra-dry) white Champagne, plus serious rosé and rich "La Cuvée" blends.
- Grand Siècle (especially Cuvée Alexandre).
- de Castellane, Delamotte, Joseph Perrier, Salon
- 1996, 1990, 1988, 1985.

MOËT & CHANDON

THIS IS THE ONE CHAMPAGNE that everyone has heard of, which is hardly surprising when you consider that over 20 million bottles are sold every year and the contents of large bottles are regularly sprayed around by winners at sports events. While the non-vintage is reliable, the vintage Brut and vintage Rosé are among the best in the region. The brilliant *prestige cuvée* Dom Pérignon, which is also produced in surprising volumes, is worth leaving in the cellar for a decade or so.

1993 Brut Impérial
Often overshadowed by non-vintage wines, this is great, nutty-toasty wine.

- Pinot Noir, Chardonnay, Pinot Meunier.
- Lovely toasty wines that—including the non-vintage—improve with keeping.
- Vintage Brut Impérial, Dom Pérignon (white and rosé).
- Mercier, Pommery, Veuve Clicquot, Krug, Ruinart, Canard Duchêne.
- 1996, 1992, 1990, 1989, 1988.

POL ROGER

THE WINES MADE BY this family-owned firm are highly popular with those who like delicate, finely structured, non-vintage and vintage Champagne. Unusually, Pol Roger likes to use the region's three grapes equally. The strongest overseas link is with the UK, where Pol Roger's first exports were sent, and where Sir Winston Churchill was one of its greatest fans. The wartime leader is commemorated by the black border around the label of the Cuvée Sir Winston Churchill.

Extra Dry
This is one of the finest, most delicate Champagnes; the opposite of the rich Bollinger style.

- Pinot Noir, Chardonnay, Pinot Meunier.
- Stylish, mostly Pinot Noir-influenced wines that last very well.
- Brut Chardonnay, Cuvée PR Réserve Spéciale, Cuvée Sir Winston Churchill.
- None
- 1996, 1990, 1989, 1988, 1985.

POMMERY

POMMERY BOASTS CELLARS named after the cities to which the biggest shipments were sent in the 19th century, as well as no fewer than 450 acres (300 ha) of great vineyards. Since joining the LVMH group along with Moët & Chandon, Ruinart, and Veuve Clicquot, Pommery has kept its light, delicate style. The Cuvée Spéciale Louise Pommery, named after the daughter of the founder, is among the best of all the *prestige cuvée* wines. The POP quarter bottles are less impressive.

Louise
A lovely, rich and classily complex wine, Louise will certainly improve with time.

- Pinot Noir, Chardonnay, Pinot Meunier.
- Fast improving, subtle non-vintage wines, Chardonnay-influenced Royal Apanage, rich Cuvée Louise.
- Louise, Royal Apanage.
- Krug, Mercier, Moët & Chandon, Ruinart, Veuve Clicquot.
- 1996, 1991, 1990, 1989, 1988.

ROEDERER

ONE OF THE BIG family-owned Champagne houses, Roederer is also quietly one of the most dynamic, having taken over Deutz Champagne and made investments in vintage port, the Rhône Valley, and Bordeaux, not to mention a winery producing top-class sparkling wine in California. Roederer's flagship is Cristal, whose reputation—and clear glass bottle—date back to the days when the Czar of Russia was a customer. The excellent Brut Premier is worth leaving in a cellar for 5–10 years.

Cristal Brut
An ultra-rich, Pinot Noir-influenced wine. The rare Cristal Rosé is great, too.

- Pinot Noir, Chardonnay, Pinot Meunier.
- Richly approachable when young, this house's non-vintage wines develop great complexity with time. Also a frequent success in unfashionable vintages.
- Blanc de Blancs, Cristal.
- Deutz, Roederer Estate/Quartet (California).
- 1996, 1991, 1990, 1989, 1988.

RUINART

THE OLDEST CHAMPAGNE house, Ruinart was founded in 1729 by a priest called Dom Ruinart. It has grown enormously since it was bought in the 1960s by Moët & Chandon but continues to enjoy great independence. The style of the wines is full-flavored and old-fashioned, and the emphasis is on Chardonnay, much of which comes from Ruinart's vineyards. The *blanc de blancs* (grown on the Montagne de Reims as well as the Côte des Blancs) is especially recommendable.

Brut
This is a first-class Champagne with rich, nutty, appley flavor, revealing the influence of the Chardonnay.

- Pinot Noir, Chardonnay, Pinot Meunier.
- Full-bodied but stylish Champagnes.
- Blanc de Blancs, R de Ruinart, Dom Ruinart Rosé.
- Moët & Chandon, Mercier, Pommery, Veuve Clicquot, Canard Duchene, Krug.
- 1996, 1993, 1992, 1990, 1988.

SALON

THE ADJECTIVE "UNIQUE" is far too easily used these days, but it genuinely does apply to this subsidiary of Laurent-Perrier that sells only one wine: a vintage *cuvée* made only in the finest years. Less unusually, Salon normally chooses not to allow its wine to go through malolactic fermentation *(see p27)*. The resulting leanness leads to the wine being released long after other houses' wines of the same vintages have sold out. Buy Salon's wines when you see them: they are among the best Champagne of all.

Blanc de Blancs
Leaner than most, the flavor of this Champagne lingers fascinatingly on the palate.

- Chardonnay.
- Unusually austere, slow-evolving wine that is not usually sold until ready to drink.
- The vintage *cuvée* is the only wine produced.
- De Castellane, Delamotte, Lemoine, Laurent-Perrier, Joseph Perrier.
- 1995, 1990, 1988, 1985, 1983.

TAITTINGER

WITH MORE THAN 620 acres (250 ha) of top-class vines, Taittinger is one of the biggest producers of Champagne. The light, creamy style of the wines can be explained by the firm's preference for Chardonnay, of which it has a fine selection of vineyards in the Côte des Blancs. The vintage wine is beautifully biscuity, but the star is without doubt the Comtes de Champagne *prestige cuvée* that, for some wine tasters, is the best *blanc de blancs* Champagne of them all.

Comtes de Champagne
This is a rare example of a 100 percent Chardonnay *prestige cuvée.*

- Chardonnay, Pinot Noir, Pinot Meunier.
- Chardonnay-influenced wines. The vintage wines and deluxe *cuvée* are more worth buying than nonvintage efforts.
- Comtes de Champagne, white and rosé.
- None.
- 1995, 1991, 1990, 1988.

VEUVE CLICQUOT

THE INSTANTLY RECOGNIZABLE yellow label and the connection with Nicole-Barbe Clicquot-Ponsardin, the woman who helped to elaborate the way in which Champagne is disgorged, have both helped to make this an internationally renowned fizz. This is not a Champagne that wins top marks from lovers of more delicate wines like Pol Roger, but anyone who loves Champagne will appreciate the richness and consistency of Veuve Clicquot's top wine, La Grande Dame.

La Grande Dame
This rich Champagne is thought by many to be one of the best *prestiges cuvées.*

- Chardonnay, Pinot Noir, Pinot Meunier.
- Immediately recognizable, full-flavored, reliable wines.
- La Grande Dame, white and rosé. Rich Reserve semisweet.
- Krug, Mercier, Moët & Chandon, Ruinart.
- 1996, 1990, 1989, 1988.

THE STILL WINES OF CHAMPAGNE

For most people, apart from those who like to use a swizzle stick to remove the bubbles from their Champagne, this region's wines will always be sparkling whites or rosés. Bubble-free red, rosé, and white wine is, however, what this region used to produce, and is still the style of wine obstinately being made by some small estates and bigger companies under the labels of Bouzy Rouge, Rosé des Riceys, and Coteaux Champenois. The two things these wines have in common are their generally high prices and the fact that they are only worth buying in warmer vintages. Bouzy Rouge from a cool year, for example, tastes like the most aggressively unripe red Burgundy, while Coteaux Champenois made in cool conditions is more like extra-green Chablis. Unfortunately, a good vintage rarely occurs in the same village more than once in 10 years. Those who are curious to taste these wines should seek out a white wine from Lilbert-Fils and Egly-Ouriet, who also make an excellent red, and Alexandre Bonnet's Rosé des Riceys. An interesting trend, championed by producers like Maurice Vesselle and Herbert Beaufort, is still *blanc de noirs*, a still white wine that is made in a way similar to Champagne, from black grapes.

Seeing Red
The village of Bouzy provides Pinot Noir grapes for top-quality Champagne, and for still red wine.

OTHERS

WHILE A SMALL NUMBER of "big name," or *grande marque*, Champagne houses generally tend to hog the limelight, the Champagne region boasts a plethora of other producers, ranging from big *coopératives* to tiny family estates. The quality of their wines varies enormously, ranging from acidic and dull examples to subtle and sublime ones.

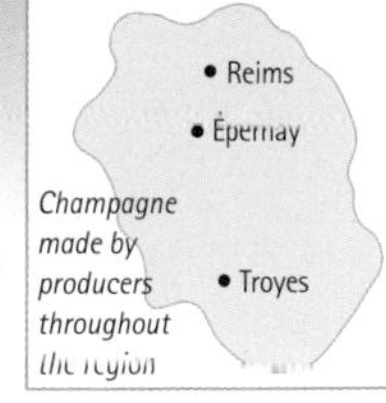

Making History
Champagne Demoiselle, the firm whose wines are stored in this cellar, is a relatively recent creation. Its wines, however, are already competing with some of the big names of the past.

Eagle-eyed readers scanning the alphabetically organized entries of the previous pages will have noticed the absence of a number of well-known Champagne houses. Where, they might wonder, are Mumm and Mercier and Perrier-Jouet, to name but three brands whose names are widely seen in glossy advertisements prior to New Year's Eve? I make no apology for consigning these, and several other big names, to the "Others" category for the simple reason that, in my and many other critics' opinions, their Champagnes—though, in the cases of Mumm and Perrier-Jouet, recently much improved—are just not as good as those of the producers I have covered in individual detail. Nor, significantly, are they better than some of the *coopératives* and smaller producers that I felt it was appropriate to include in this section.

Among the firms worth mentioning here is Groupe Lanson International, a company that is often left out of wine books because its Champagne is sold under hundreds of different labels. Not only does Groupe Lanson International own Lanson and the generally decent Besserat de Bellefon, it also sells Champagne under the Alfred Rothschild label, which is rarely seen outside France. Another firm that has swallowed other Champagne houses is Vranken, which now produces wines under its own name and others', including Heidsieck Monopole and Demoiselle. Bruno Paillard is an up-and-coming merchant worth watching, both for its own wines and for those made by its subsidiaries Delbeck and Boizel. Ayala (recently bought by Bollinger) and de Cazanove are older firms that have improved the quality of their wines recently, as have De Venoge and Canard Duchêne, which is a subsidiary of Veuve Clicquot. De Castellane and Deutz belong respectively to Laurent-Perrier and Roederer and make reliable, good-value wines, as do some of the smaller firms such as Charles Ellner, Delamotte, Duval-Leroy, Drappier, Forget-Brimont, Hamm, Harlin, Joseph Perrier, Alexandre, and Bonnet. *Coopératives* that I'd recommend include the *cuvée* Orpale wines from the Union Champagne and wines sold under their own names by Beaumont de Crayères, Jacquart, Mailly Grand Cru, Pannier, Palmer, and Nicolas Feuillatte. Of the smaller estates, I'd choose Paul Bara, Jacques Beaufort, Chartogne-Taillet, Egly-Ouriet, Gimonnet, Margaine, Pierre Moncuit, Jacques Selosse, Jean Vesselle, and Vilmart.

Duval-Leroy
The Champagne made by this company is often sold under the labels of its customers—which range from supermarkets to luxury hotels.

Jura and Savoie

Jura and Savoie

Two of the most overlooked wine regions in France, Jura and Savoie offer unique flavors and styles that are not to be found anywhere else on earth.

Arbois deserves a place in the history of wine. It was here, in the late 19th century, that Louis Pasteur carried out his experiments on why grape juice turned into wine and, more specifically, why that wine so often turned into vinegar. Pasteur, who grew up here, must have been influenced by the way in which the yeast that formed on the surface of Jura and Savoie's *vins jaunes* had the same effect on them as it does on *fino* sherry. These "yellow wines" take their name from the color they develop after they have been purposefully oxidized under a yeast *flor*.

Château Chalon
The sunny, sloping vineyards of Savagnin grapes in the commune of Château Chalon produce the finest, most famous, and longest-lived of all *vins jaunes*.

Today, while the Juraciens still tend to claim that *vin jaune* is their finest wine, I'd vote for the equally unusual *vin de paille*, a sweet white wine named after the ancient method of drying the grapes out on straw mats before fermenting their juice. Today, this wine is made in the same way as the Amarone of the Veneto region in Italy—the bunches of grapes being either hung from the rafters of huts or laid out on racks.

The Jura now focuses on producing far greater quantities of red wine, from Pinot Noir and the local Trousseau and Poulsard varieties, and dry white wine, from Savagnin and Chardonnay. However, the Jura vineyards now occupy a fraction of the 50,000 acres (20,000 ha) they covered before the arrival of phylloxera. As recently as the 1960s, this region, whose wines were praised over 2,000 years ago by Pliny, seemed in danger of giving up wine-making altogether. Rescue came in the form of a clever marketer named Henri Maire, whose firm now owns the vineyard where Pasteur conducted his experiments.

If it weren't for the readiness of vacationers in nearby ski resorts such as Val d'Isère to be overcharged for the wines of Savoie, it is quite possible that they might also have disappeared. These light, berryish reds and rosés, made from Mondeuse, and fresh whites, which are largely produced from a variety confusingly known both as Roussette and as Altesse, are ideal après-ski fare and go perfectly with the local cheeses. They are generally quite short-lived, however, and outside Savoie they have a hard time competing with fuller-flavored wines from other French wine regions.

Unlike in most places in France, there is little variation in the quality produced in Savoie from one vintage to the next. Your best bet is to buy the most recent vintage, rather than one that has been stored for too long and allowed to lose its fruit flavor.

REGIONAL OVERVIEW

8,600 acres (3,500 ha): 35 million bottles.

Jura and Savoie experience a continental climate, with hot summers and cold winters. Their close proximity to mountain ranges can provoke sudden changes in the weather.

Clay and limestone.

Red Jura: Pinot Noir, Poulsard, Trousseau.
White Jura: Chardonnay, Savagnin.
Red Savoie: Gamay, Pinot Noir, Mondeuse.
White Savoie: Jacquère, Chasselas, Chardonnay.

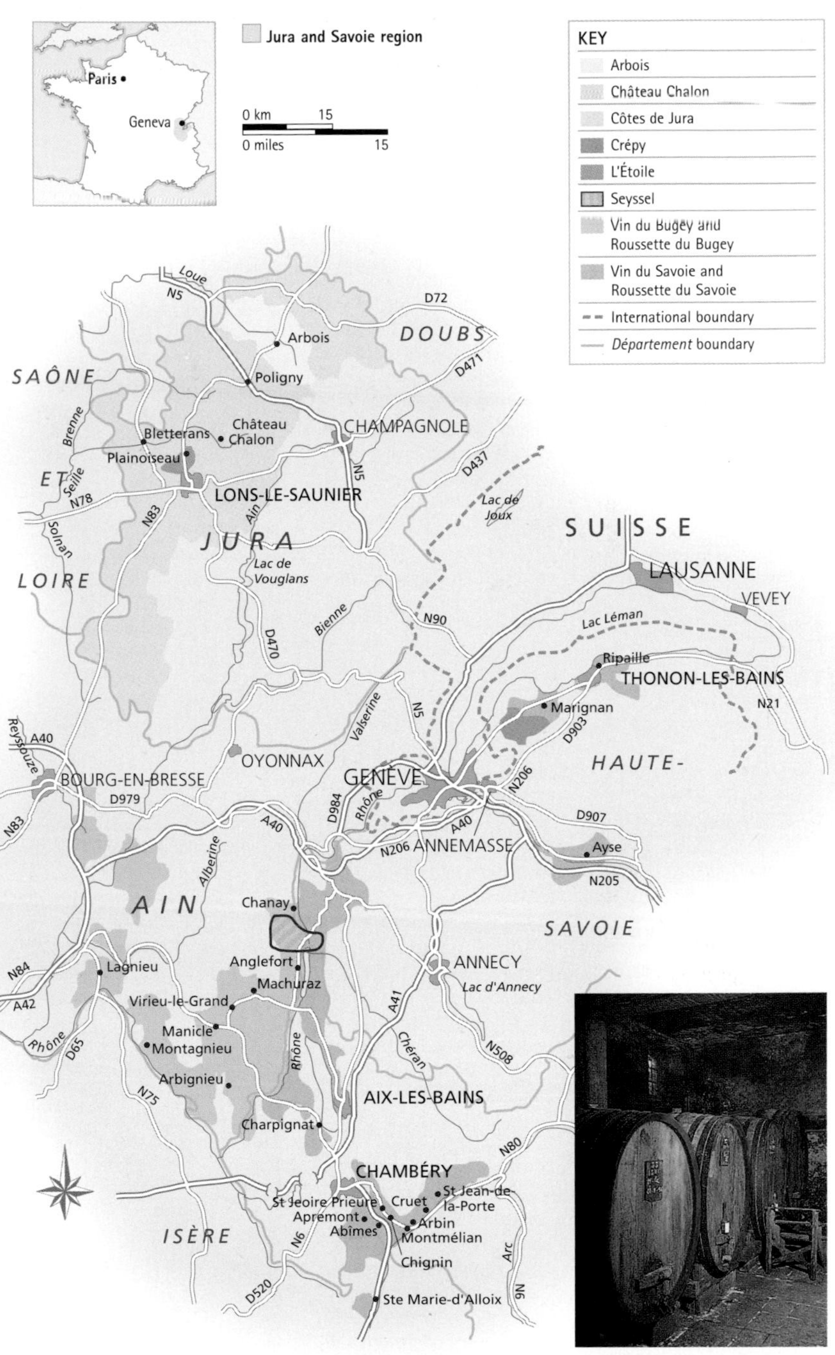

Mountains of Grapes
Located close to the ski slopes of the French Alps, the vineyards of Jura and Savoie are situated on the lower slopes of the Jura mountains. The climate here is continental, with warm summers and cold winters.

Château d'Arlay
This estate in Arbois produces some of the best *vins de paille* to be found in Jura and Savoie. These very sweet "straw wines" are made from grapes that were traditionally dried on straw mats.

TRAVELING IN JURA AND SAVOIE

Although Savoie is familiar enough to skiers, its wines and vineyards remain largely undiscovered. Jura is, if anything, even less well known. Indeed, it often feels like a hidden region tucked away between the well-trodden paths of Burgundy and Alsace. But for those adventurous enough to take the detour here, there are delights aplenty.

HOTELS & RESTAURANTS

A selection of the region's best establishments, combining good local food and wine with notable, characterful places to stay.

JURA

ARBOIS

Hotel des Messageries, 2 Rue de Courcelles.
Tel 03 84 66 13 43
FAX 03 84 37 41 09
@ hotel.lesmessageries@wanadoo.fr
A modestly comfortable, friendly old post house in the heart of this charming town. There is no restaurant, but there is a pleasant terrace on which to enjoy an aperitif before walking to La Balance-Mets et Vins (see below)

La Balance–Mets et Vins, 47 Rue de Courcelles.
Tel 03 84 37 45 00
As the name suggests, this is a great place to explore the way local Jura wines go with a wide range of dishes—and the role they can play in the kitchen. Try one of the *menus dégustations.*

Jean-Paul Jeunet, Le Paris, 9 Rue de l'Hotel de Ville.
Tel 03 84 66 05 67
Competes with Château de Germigney *(see below)* for the prize of top restaurant in this region. Terrific local cooking is served alongside a very impressive range of wines.

PORT-LESNEY

Château de Germigney, Rue Edgar Faure.
Tel 03 84 73 85 85
FAX 03 84 73 88 88
@ germigney@relaischateaux.com
An 18th-century manor house surrounded by lakes and woodland (watch out for falling chestnuts in the fall), this lovely country hotel is decorated in a way that is at once traditional and modern. The restaurant similarly boasts both lighter modern dishes and traditional examples prepared with the local *vin jaune.*

SAVOIE

ANNECY

Hôtel du Palais de l'Isle, 13 Rue Perrière.
Tel 04 50 45 86 87
FAX 04 50 51 87 15
A handsome 18th-century private house on the Thiou River and close to the Palace. The best rooms are furnished with furniture by Philippe Starck.

CHAMBÉRY

Hôtel de la Banche, Place de l'Hôtel de Ville.
Tel 04 79 33 15 62
Located on a pedestrianized square close to the old town, this friendly, inexpensive hotel serves as an ideal base for visitors to the Savoie region. The restaurant is good, too, especially if you like frog legs.

Le Bourget-du-Lac

Ombremont, Le Bourget-du-Lac.
Tel 04 79 25 00 23
FAX 04 79 25 25 77
@ ombremont@relaischateaux.com
As its name suggests, this cozy 1900's villa overlooks the Lac du Bourget, and is close to both Chambéry and Aix-les-Bains. There are only 12 rooms, so booking is definitely advisable if you're planning to stay. The highlights of the restaurant menu are the fish dishes, which offer perfect accompaniments to a wide range of local wines.

WINE SHOPS

Many of the wines you will taste while in the Jura and Savoie region are difficult to find at home, so it's a good idea to stock up on your favorites while you're here.

JURA

ARBOIS

Les Jardins de St-Vincent, 49 Grande Rue.
Tel 03 84 66 21 75
This retailer has an impressive range of wines from across the Jura region, to suit all tastes and budgets.

VILLARD DE LANS

Le Tonneau. 18 Rue du Camp-d'Ambel.
Tel 04 76 95 19 05
Le Tonneau is well-stocked shop with over 200 wines, including a good range of Savoies.

MUSEUMS

Some producers in this region offer vineyard or winery tours. Local tourist offices *(see below)* can provide details of these.

The secret delights of the Jura
Arbois is the perfect place to sample *vin jaune* with food.

JURA

ARBOIS

Maison de Louis Pasteur, 83 Rue de Courcelles.
03 84 66 11 72
FAX 03 84 66 12
Louis Pasteur, the inventor of the pasteurization process, was as important to the history of wine production as he was to the history of the dairy industry. In this house, in which he lived until his death in 1895, you can visit the laboratory where he carried out many of his experiments.

Musée de la Vigne et du Vin, Château Pécauld.
03 84 66 40 45
FAX 03 84 66 40
Vin jaune and *vin de paille* are unlike any other wines made anywhere in France. In this museum, you can learn about their history and about the way they are made today.

Lons-le-Saunier–Musée d'Archéologie, 25 rue Richebourg.
03 84 47 12 13
FAX 03 84 24 30 34
A collection of 300,000 exhibits, including France's oldest dinosaur, whose 210-million-year-old remains were found nearby.

SAVOIE

MONTMÉLIAN

Musée Régional de la Vigne et du Vin, 46 Rue du Docteur Veyrat, Montmélian.
04 79 84 42 23
FAX 04 79 84 08 20
Situated in the heart of the region, this museum is a good place to learn about the Savoie region's traditional grape varieties and vinous history.

ANNUAL WINE EVENTS

Of all France's regions, Jura and Savoie are indisputably among the most worth visiting for the simple reason that their wines are very hard to find elsewhere in France, let alone overseas. One particularity of Arbois is the opportunity to sample wines that have been left to mature in the cellars of their producers.

FEBRUARY

Poligny La Percée du Vin Jaune—annual tasting of the latest release (after six years in the barrel) of *vins jaunes* made by some 75 producers in 50 cellars

JULY

Arbois Les Festi'caves—an annual festival, held in Arbois, celebrating food and music

Arbois Les Petites Fetes de Dyonisos—a gastronomic and literary fair held in Arbois, focusing on mythology

Culoz wine festival

Pupillin Le Poulsard en Fete—a wine festival held in a beautiful old village, focusing on one of the traditional grape varieties of the region

SEPTEMBER

Arbois, **Pupillin** and **Vadans** Fete du Biou—a series of picturesque fairs held in the wine-producing communes; the highlight of the colorful parades is a huge bunch of grapes called the "biou"

Arbois Vendanges à l'Ancienne—a harvest festival set around the Château Pécauld

Montmélian Qu'ara Bara—a 700-year-old festival of farming, local crafts, gastronomy, and wine

OCTOBER

Belley Entretiens de Belley—another harvest festival

WEBSITES

The website of the local wine producers' association of Jura is at www.jura-vins.com. There is also a very comprehensive site representing a *cooperative* close to Château-Chalon— www.fruitiere-vinicole-voiteur.fr—although this does provide much more information in French than in English. The local tourist association also has a very well-laid-out and informative website at www.arbois.com.

For information about the wine producers of the Savoie region, the best place to start is www.chez.com/vinsavoie/institutions.htm. For general tourist information, there are also two excellent local websites provided by Savoie's tourist offices: www.france-rhonealps-tourism.com and www.haute savoie-tourism.com.

Alternatively, you can log on to the tourist website for the whole of France at www.tourisme.fr and type in the name of any town or village in Jura or Savoie about which you would like to learn more.

OTHER INFORMATION

JURA

Comité Interprofessionnel des Vins du Jura, Château Pécauld, BP 41, 39600 Arbois.
03 84 66 26 14
FAX 03 84 66 10 29
@ CIVJ@jura-vins.com

Office de Tourisme Val de la Cuisance, 10 Rue de l'Hôtel de Ville, Arbois.
03 84 66 55 50
FAX 03 84 66 25 50
@ otsi@arbois.com

SAVOIE

Comité Régional du Tourisme Rhône-Alpes, 104 Route de Paris, Charbonnières-les-Bains.
04 72 59 21 59
FAX 04 72 59 21 60

Syndicat Régional des Vins de Savoie, 3 Rue du Château, Chambéry.

ARBOIS

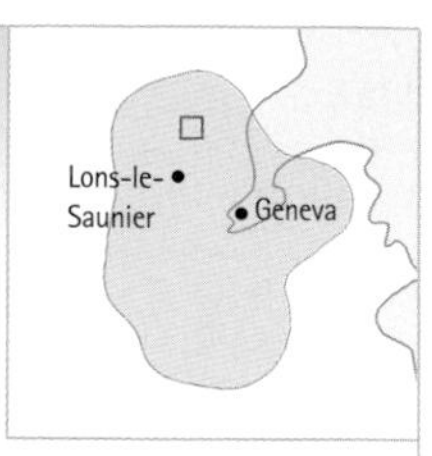

ONE OF THE BEST-KEPT SECRETS of the wine world, Arbois is a picturesque medieval market town that has hardly changed at all since Louis Pasteur lived here more than a century ago. Even compared to the other French regions that are still producing traditional wines, the white wines of Arbois seem to have been caught in a time warp all of their own.

A Hidden Treasure
Tucked away in the hills, the small town of Arbois is surrounded by sloping vineyards. Grape varieties are grown here that are found almost nowhere else in France.

This once-important wine-making region enjoys a climate of its own that is less sheltered than that of Alsace and more continental than that of nearby Burgundy, the region to which it was once attached. Winter is bitterly cold here, and although summer and fall can be warm, grapes often have a tough time ripening. Wine-making is also often much poorer than it ought to be, with heaviness and staleness being all too easy to find. While it is generally believed that the best wines of the region are to be found within the *appellations* of Château Chalon *(see p185)* and L'Étoile *(see p186)*, similar wines made by good estates in Arbois can be of a very similar quality. The red and rosé wines that are made from the Pinot Noir grape variety compete with red Burgundy *(see pp130–131)*, while those made from the local Poulsard and Trousseau grapes can, when allowed to maintain their freshness, be quite berryish and spicy. White wines made from Savagnin, a local grape variety that is both unrelated to and quite unlike Sauvignon Blanc, come in three styles: the very sherrylike, intentionally oxidized *vin jaune*, the somewhat sherrylike, unintentionally oxidized white Arbois, and the Recioto-like, raisiny *vin de paille* that is made from grapes that have been dried to concentrate their juice, before being aged for up to four years in wood. Wines from the village of Pupillin fall under Arbois' own supposedly, though often unconvincingly, superior villages *appellation*. Good producers of Arbois, such as the Fruitière Vinicole d'Arbois and the Domaines Rolet and Puffeney, are leading a trend toward fresher-tasting reds and whites. However, there are plenty of bottles, including the large number offered by the dynamic merchant Henri Maire, credited with rescuing this region from near extinction, which, unfortunately, show no such spark.

- AC Arbois, AC Arbois Mousseux, AC Arbois Pupillin.
- Red/rosé: Poulsard, Pinot Noir, Trousseau. White: Chardonnay, Savagnin. *Vin jaune:* Savagnin.
- Light, quite floral reds. Light, dry whites. Dry rosés. Characterful, nutty *vins jaunes.*
- Lucien Aviet, Ch Béthanie, Maurice Chassot, Désiré Petit et Fils, Jacques Foret, Fruitière Vinicole d'Arbois, Pierre Overnoy, Jacques Puffeney, Rolet, du Sorbief, André et Mireille Tissot, Jacques Tissot.
- *Vin jaune: Ragoût* of goose with apples.
- 1996, 1995, 1990.
- Red: 3–5 years. White/rosé: 2–4 years. *Vin jaune:* 10–20 years.

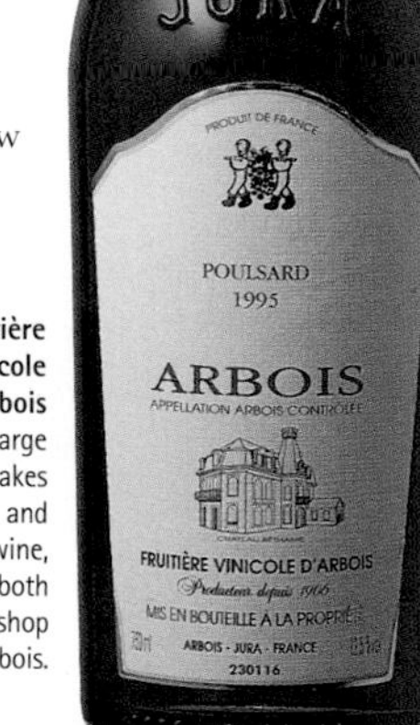

Fruitière Vinicole d'Arbois
This large producer makes good red and white wine, and sells both in its shop in Arbois.

BUGEY

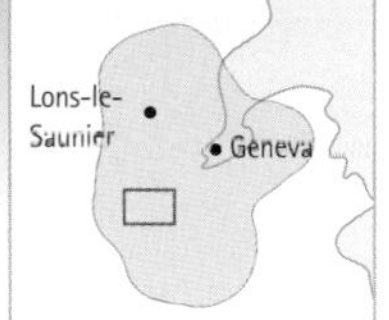

THE VINEYARDS OF BUGEY are scattered from Bourg-en-Bresse to Ambérieu, and along the eastern bank of the Rhône River from Seyssel to Lagnieu. The vines are planted on limestone soil, with red, white, and rosé wines being made under the Vin du Bugey *VDQS* or, in the case of Virieu-le-Grand, Manicle, Montagnieu, Machuraz, and Cerdon, with the name of the village. Of the varietal wines, the Gamay produces vibrant, easy-going reds, while Pinot Noir yields a pale imitation of Burgundy. The most interesting Bugey wines are the deeply colored, slightly bitter reds made from the Mondeuse. The rosés, made mainly from the Gamay or Pinot Noir, are light and fresh, while the whites are light, fresh, and off-dry. The *VDQS* can also be used for sparkling wines.

Christian Beaulieu
The red wines of Bugey are often light and feeble, but this example shows that rich, fruity wines can be produced here.

Underrated vineyards
The region of Bugey produces attractive, light *VDQS* wines that can be better than *appellation contrôlée* wines from elsewhere.

- *VDQS* Vins du Bugey (village names may be added).
- Red/rosé: Poulsard, Gamay, Mondeuse, Pinot Noir.
  White: Roussette, Jacquère, Chardonnay, Pinot Gris, Aligoté.
- Light reds. Light, dry whites. Dry rosés.
- Christian Beaulieu, Caveau Bugiste, Caveau du Mont July, Cellier de Bel-Air, Eugène Monin.
- Partridge cooked with bacon and cheese and served with noodles.
- Red/rosé: 1997, 1996.
- Red/rosé: 1–3 years.

CHÂTEAU CHALON

NAMED AFTER THE HILLTOP village rather than an estate, Château Chalon's *vins jaunes* are produced from Savagnin grapes grown on limestone and marl soil. Wines bearing the Château Chalon label must be aged for at least 75 months in sealed, partially filled casks, during which time they develop their yeasty flavor and a sherrylike character. The special 62-cl "clavelin" bottle used for all Château Chalon supposedly represents the amount of *vin jaune* produced from one liter of base wine.

Jean Bourdy
This producer is one of the most reliable sources of dry, salty Château Chalon.

- AC Château Chalon.
- *Vin jaune:* Savagnin.
- Nutty-flavored *vins jaunes* that are golden in color.
- Berthet-Bondet, Jean Bourdy, Courbet, Durand-Perron, Jean Macle.
- Chicken breast cooked in *vin jaune.*
- 1990, 1989, 1985.
- 20 years.

CÔTES DU JURA

THIS ISOLATED REGION has retained traditional grape varieties and methods of wine-making in its use of Poulsard, Trousseau, and Pinot Noir for red wines and Savagnin and Chardonnay for its whites. Styles include lightly fruity reds and rosés, nutty dry whites, sparkling wines, and sherrylike *vins jaunes.* The most interesting wines are probably the sweet *vins de paille* that are made from grapes dried to concentrate their juice, before being aged for up to four years in wooden casks.

Jean Bourdy
This pale red wine is made from the plummy Poulsard grape.

- AC Côtes du Jura.
- Red/rosé: Poulsard.
  White: Chardonnay, Savagnin.
  Vin jaune: Savagnin.
- Light, pale reds. Light, dry whites. Dry rosés. Strong, nutty *vins jaunes.*
- Ch d'Arly, Jean Bourdy.
- *Vin jaune:* Cream cheese.
- Red: 1996, 1995, 1990.
- *Vin jaune:* 10–15 years.

CRÉPY

Like many of the wines produced in neighboring Switzerland, the wines of Crépy are made from Chasselas Roux and Vert. They are light, floral, and slightly spritzy. Liked by skiers, they carry price tags to match. There is much debate as to whether these wines should be allowed to go through malolactic fermentation *(see p27)*. Those that don't are dry, crisp, and fruity, with a slight spritz. Those that do are fuller-bodied and almondy, and can be kept for a year or two.

Grande Cave de Crépy
This is a crisp, dry wine with a touch of fizz and a slightly almondy note.

- AC Crépy.
- White: Chasselas.
- Crisp, light, dry white wines.
- Fichard, Grande Cave de Crépy, Mercier, Georges Roussiaude.
- Vegetable soup with Emmental or Beaufort cheese.
- 2003, 2002.
- 1–3 years.

L'ÉTOILE

This tiny *appellation* lies in the centre of the Jura, just north of Lons-le-Saunier and beside a little village called Le Pin—which, given the success of the Bordeaux château of that name, ought to help sales. Most of the wine from the *appellation's* 175 acres (70 ha) is made by the local *coopérative*. There is potentially good *vin jaune*, light, herbal whites made from Chardonnay, Savagnin, or Poulsard, and a Côtes du Jura *méthode traditionelle* made from the same three grape varieties.

Château l'Étoile
This is a light, dry white whose aromas reveal notes of herbs and bracken.

- AC L'Étoile, AC L'Étoile Vin Jaune.
- White: Savagnin.
- Still dry whites. Nutty *vins jaunes*.
- Ch l'Étoile, Michel Geneletti, Montbo.
- *Vin jaune*: Emmental.
- 2002, 1999, 1996, 1995, 1990.
- *Vin jaune:* 10–40 years. White: 2–4 years.

VIN DE SAVOIE

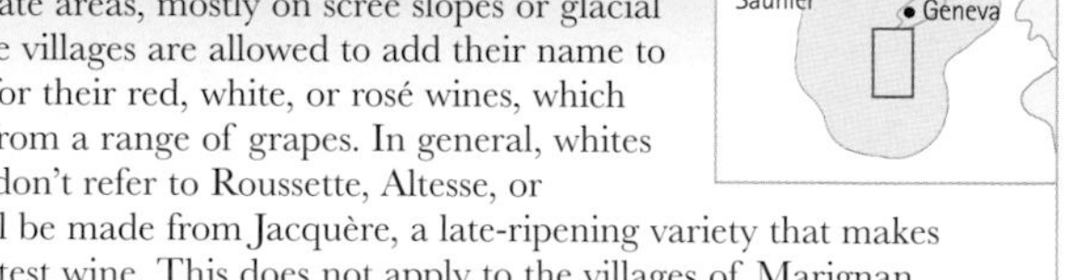

The vin de Savoie *appellation* is made up of a diverse series of separate areas, mostly on scree slopes or glacial moraine. Some villages are allowed to add their name to the *appellation* for their red, white, or rosé wines, which can be made from a range of grapes. In general, whites whose labels don't refer to Roussette, Altesse, or Bergeron will be made from Jacquère, a late-ripening variety that makes Savoie's lightest wine. This does not apply to the villages of Marignan, Marin, and Ripaille, where the Chasselas is used. Altesse is also known as Roussette and used for its own *appellation*, Roussette de Savoie. The Mondeuse grape is used for reds in the *communes* of Chautagne, Cruet, Jongieux, and St Jean de la Porte. The Vin de Savoie *appellation* can also be applied to a number of sparkling wines.

Louis Magnin
This Chignin Bergeron, made from the Jacquère grape, is one of the most refreshing light white wines in France.

Mountain Fresh
The light white wines produced in this vineyard next to the Lac St André are ideal après-ski fare.

- AC Vin de Savoie, AC Vin de Savoie Mousseux, AC Vin de Savoie Pétillant, AC Roussette de Savoie.
- Red: Gamay, Mondeuse, Pinot Noir. White: Chardonnay, Roussette, Jacquère, Chasselas.
- Light reds. Crisp, dry whites.
- Dominique Allion, Louis Magnin, Claude Marendon, Michel Menetrey, Raymond Quénard, Trosset, Varicon et Clerc.
- White: Chicken with salt pork.
- White: 1998, 1997, 1996.
- White: 1–3 years.

SEYSSEL

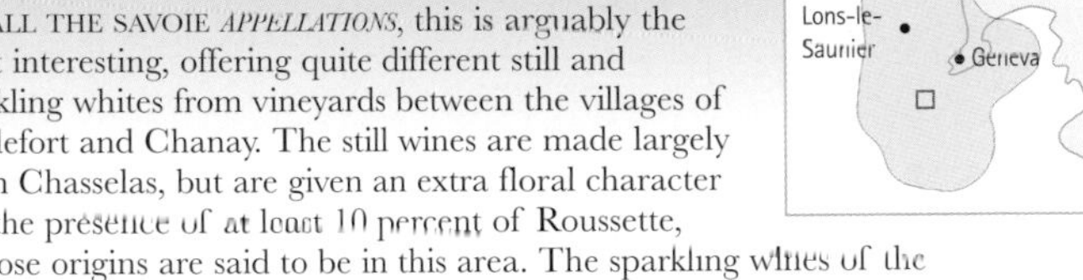

Lons-le-Saunier
Geneva

OF ALL THE SAVOIE *APPELLATIONS*, this is arguably the most interesting, offering quite different still and sparkling whites from vineyards between the villages of Anglefort and Chanay. The still wines are made largely from Chasselas, but are given an extra floral character by the presence of at least 10 percent of Roussette, whose origins are said to be in this area. The sparkling wines of the *appellation*, in which Chasselas and Roussette are used as supporting actors to the local Molette variety, are far better known than the still wines. Examples include the vintage Royal Seyssel Cuvée Privée, which is at once elegant and biscuity—like fine Champagne, but with more flowers and less fruit. Both the sparkling and the still styles of Seyssel make excellent accompaniments to the local specialty, *raclette*.

Maison Mollex
A fresh example of the Roussette grape from one of the most reliable producers in the region.

Source of Bubbles
Many of the best grapes from these vineyards will probably be used for sparkling wine.

- AC Seyssel, AC Seyssel Mousseux.
- Still white: Chasselas, Roussette. Sparkling white: Molette, Chasselas, Roussette.
- Light, dry whites.
- Mollex, Clos de la Péclette, Royal Seyssel, Varichon & Clerc.
- Still: Salad of fresh crayfish served with crusty bread and a sauce of melted butter flavored with shallots, white wine vinegar, and parsley.
- Still: 2002, 2001.
- 1–3 years.

OTHERS

Lons-le-Saunier
Geneva

Crémant du Jura and Macvin de Jura made throughout region

THE CRÉMANT DU JURA SPARKLING WINE, made from a mixture of Savagnin, Pinot Blanc, and Chardonnay, is potentially delicious and good value if you pick a producer such as Grand Frères. The most distinctive "other" wine of the region has to be the Macvin de Jura, which stands firmly apart from all of France's red and white wines as a historic curiosity. Like Muscat de Beaumes-de-Venise, Banyuls, and Rasteau, it counts as a *vin doux naturel*—but it lacks the rich, fruity appeal of those wines, and offers instead a taste (an acquired taste, one might say) of the distant past. Its production process involves the cooking of the juice of Savagnin grapes until half or more of the liquid has evaporated. The boiled and unfermented juice is then fortified with local brandy and flavored with herbs and spices. The result, which is technically questionable as "wine" because of the lack of fermentation, is left to mature in a cask for six years and tastes a little like vermouth. This truly original method is believed to have been devised by the nuns of the abbey of Château Chalon in the 9th century. The Domaine Bourdy, which makes the best examples of Macvin, uses a recipe from 1579.

Domaine Grand Frères
Rich, sparkling Crémant du Jura like this is rarely seen outside the region, but is worth buying.

Château Chalon
It was at the abbey here that the curious technique for producing the vermouthlike Macvin originated over a thousand years ago.

LANGUEDOC-ROUSSILLON

Languedoc-Roussillon

Until recently the sleeping giant of the wine world, this region—the largest area of vineyards on the planet—is now producing some really great wines.

The first thing to mention about this region is its size. The vineyards cover over 740,300 acres (300,000 ha), three times as as much as those of Bordeaux. This is the source of one in 10 bottles of the world's wine, and one in three bottles of French wine.

Until recently, however, Languedoc-Roussillon was rarely mentioned in wine books. The explanation is simple: very little of the wine produced here carried the essential words *appellation contrôlée* on its labels. In fact, much of the annual harvest was either sold in returnable bottles or dispatched direct to the subsidized European wine lake.

French and Euro-bureaucrats would gladly have seen most of the non-*appellation* vineyards being converted into orchards, but a few dynamic individuals had other plans. Men like Robert Skalli of Fortant de France and an Englishman called James Herrick, who had made his fortune in wine in Australia, realized that Languedoc-Roussillon had a good climate and plentiful land. What it lacked were internationally popular grape varieties and the skills required to turn them into commercial wines. So thousands of hectares of Chardonnay, Merlot, Sauvignon Blanc, Viognier, Syrah, and Cabernet Sauvignon were planted, while overseas buyers sent wine-makers into the *coopératives* to oversee the harvest and fermentation processes. The effect was superficially dramatic. Within a few years, the shelves were filled with varietal *vins de pays* that competed directly with their counterparts from the New World.

Unfortunately, while the best of these wines were good, far too many were unimpressive, lacking both the fruity intensity of the New World and the complexity traditionally associated with France. The biggest handicap here probably lies in the limited aspirations of the region's wine-growers—even some of the most important ones. While the outsider Aimé Guibert of Mas de Daumas Gassac had the temerity to try to make a *Vin de Pays de l'Hérault* that would sell for the price of a good Bordeaux, many of his neighbors still fail to make the most of either their vines or their grapes.

Among the *appellations*, matters are just as confused. Some areas, like Banyuls *(see p194)*, Collioure *(see p194)*, Maury *(see p198)*, Faugères *(see p197)*, St Chinian *(see p201)*, and Pic-St Loup in the Coteaux du Languedoc *(see p196)*, have proven that they can make wines of great quality. Elsewhere,

Fruit and Nuts
These Côtes du Roussillon vines are grown alongside almond trees and illustrate the tradition here of varied agriculture.

REGIONAL OVERVIEW

- 815,000 acres (330,000 ha): 290 million bottles.
- The entire region is highly influenced by the proximity of the Mediterranean, but some areas, such as the hills of the Minervois and Limoux, are cooler, thanks to their slightly higher altitudes.
- Very varied, with limestone in the hills and fertile alluvial soil on the plains.
- Red: Grenache, Cabernet Sauvignon, Merlot, Cinsault, Carignan, Syrah, Mourvèdre.
  White: Clairette, Chardonnay, Ugni Blanc, Grenache Blanc, Muscat, Sauvignon, Viognier.

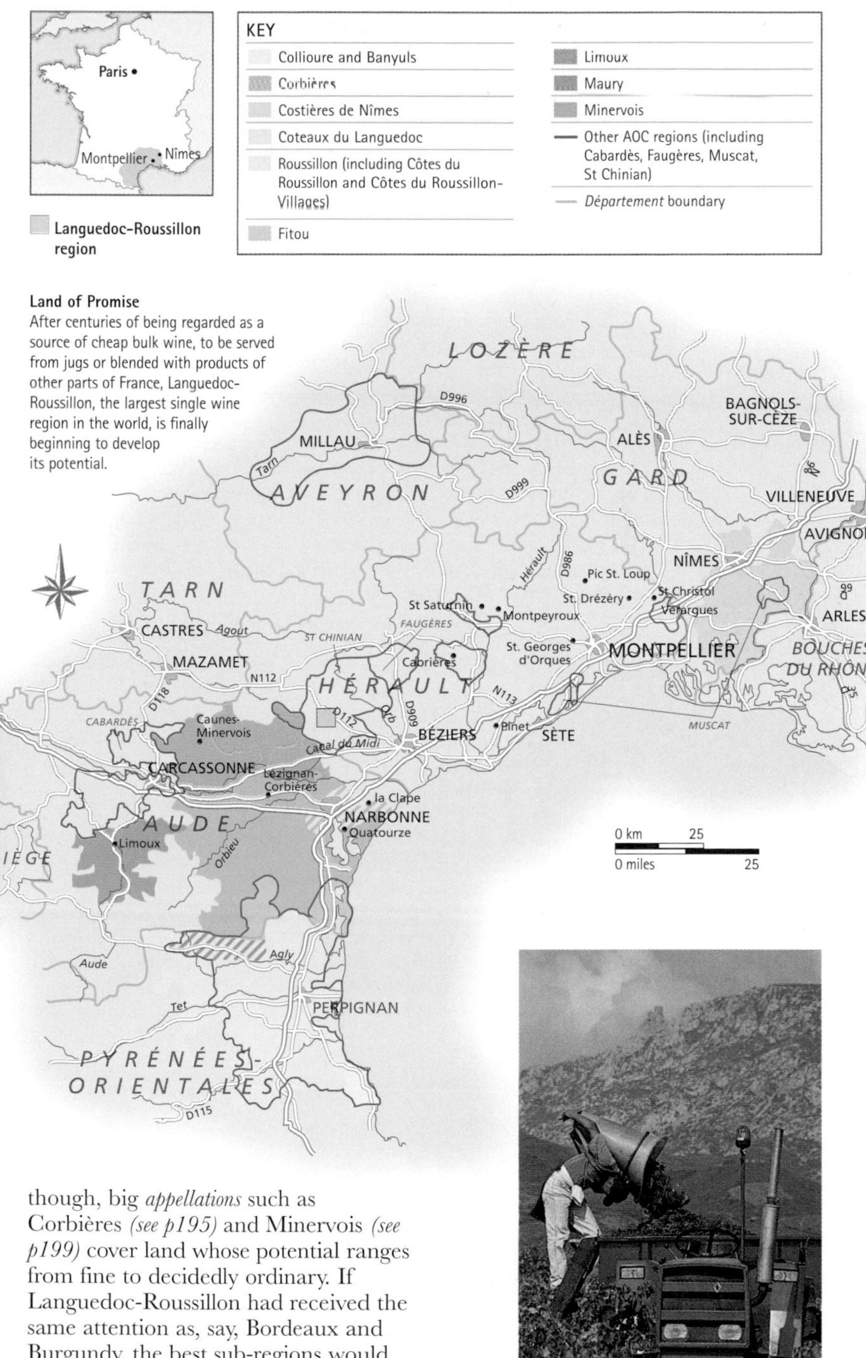

Land of Promise
After centuries of being regarded as a source of cheap bulk wine, to be served from jugs or blended with products of other parts of France, Languedoc-Roussillon, the largest single wine region in the world, is finally beginning to develop its potential.

though, big *appellations* such as Corbières *(see p195)* and Minervois *(see p199)* cover land whose potential ranges from fine to decidedly ordinary. If Languedoc-Roussillon had received the same attention as, say, Bordeaux and Burgundy, the best sub-regions would have been far more clearly identified a long time ago. As it is, you are far better off buying a *vin de pays* from a good producer than trusting an *appellation*.

Heading to Port
Mas Amiel's rich, darkly luscious Maury is one of France's most impressive fortified wines, and one that easily stands up to comparisons with many vintage ports.

TRAVELING IN LANGUEDOC-ROUSSILLON

Well known as a perfect destination for those who appreciate the combination of sun, sea, and savage landscapes, this vast southern region is also a great place to go wine exploring, for the simple reason that it is packed full of unexpected and exciting wines—both traditional and novel—just waiting to be discovered.

HOTELS & RESTAURANTS

A selection of the region's best establishments, offering good local food and wine, and notable, characterful places to stay.

AGDE

Le Numero Vin,
2 Place de la Marine.
04 67 00 20 20
As the name suggests, wine is the focus at this restaurant close to one of the Languedoc's leading seaside resorts, and its list is among the best in the area. But the food is definitely up to snuff, too, with plenty of imaginatively prepared dishes using local seafood and herbs.

AIGUES-MORTES

les Arcades,.
23 Boulevard Gambetta.
04 66 53 81 13
FAX 04 66 53 75 46
www.les-arcades.com
Within the city walls, but on a quieter (everything is relative in tourist season here) street, this is a very chic hotel whose decor makes great use of Provençal colors. The food is some of the best—and most innovative—in town (try the zucchini flowers stuffed with seafood) and the rooftop pool and terrace offer a welcome haven from the camera-toting masses.

BANYULS-DELS-ASPRES

Domaine de Nidolières.
04 68 05 81 47
FAX 04 68 05 85 80
A very well-kept secret among the wine fraternity, this is an unprepossessing country inn tucked away in the vineyards, serving absurdly generous portions of authentic local food. Plan to take a very long walk after your meal.

BIZE-MINERVOIS

La Bastide de Cabezac,
18 Hameau Cabezac.
04 68 46 66 10
FAX 04 68 46 66 29
www.labastidecabezac.com
A tastefully modernized 18th-century coaching inn with a very tranquil feel and a restaurant whose chef makes inventive use of the local seafood and herbs. This is a good place to explore new-wave Minervois wines.

Affordable Delights
Often far less extravagantly priced than their counterparts in Provence, the restaurants of Languedoc-Roussillon are often every bit as fine.

CARCASSONNE

Hotel du Donjon–les Remparts, 2 Rue du Comte-Roger.
04 68 71 08 80
FAX 04 68 25 06 60
www.hotel-donjon.fr
An impeccably converted medieval building, right in the heart of this walled city that looks precisely like the set of a Hollywood movie. The restaurant is recommendable, too. A place to enjoy out of season.

COLLIOURE

Hostellerie des Templiers, Quai de l'Amirauté.
04 68 82 98 31
FAX 04 68 98 01 24
www.hotel-templiers.com
Part hotel, part art gallery, the Hostellerie boasts an extraordinary collection of over 2,000 works of art by the likes of Dufy, Picasso, Dali, and Matisse, who all paid their bills in kind. The decor is comfortable rather than luxurious, and prices are very affordable—especially when you consider that you may be spending the night with a masterpiece. Enjoy the seafood on the terrace overlooking the pretty little port.

CUCUGNAN

l'Auberge de Cucugnan,
2 Place de la Fontaine.
04 68 45 40 84
FAX 04 68 45 01 52
An old inn in a village surrounded by Cathar *(see below)* castles. Comfortable rooms and hearty local cooking.

MONTPELLIER – LES BEAUX-ARTS

Le Jardin des Sens,
11 Avenue St Lazare.
04 99 58 38 38
www.jardindessens.com

One of the most famous gastronomic meccas in the region. Reserve early, especially if you want to stay in one of the dozen rooms. The food is impeccably and imaginatively cooked in ways that introduce North African and Asian influences far more successfully than is often the case in "fusion" cuisine.

MONTSÉGUR

Hotel-Restaurant Costes, 52 Rue Principale.
05 61 01 10 24
montsegur.com/costes.ht
If you liked *The Da Vinci Code*, pack a copy of Sophy Burnham's *The Treasure of Montségur* when you come here. It's a great novel about a treasure that was said—by the Cathars, a medieval religious sect who died for this kind of belief—to prove that Christ did not die on the cross but traveled with Magdelen, his wife (and mother of his child), to Languedoc. The hotel is a friendly, modest country inn, offering basic accommodation and simple food at fair prices.

SÈTE

Le Grand Hotel, 17 Quai de Tassigny.
04 67 74 71 77
FAX 04 67 74 29 27
www.sete-hotel.com.
With views of the main canal in this too-often overlooked town, this attractive old building is less of a "Grand Hotel" than it sounds. But it is a great base to use when touring the region. Eat in local seafood restaurants, but enjoy breakfast in the covered courtyard.

ANNUAL WINE EVENTS

As this region's wines gain in prestige and visitors discover the previously often-overlooked appeal of its villages and towns, Languedoc-Roussillon has developed a growing number of fairs and festivals. Recent additions as these are, most of them happily retain their local character.

JANUARY
Uzès truffle festival—a great opportunity to sample and buy black truffles and to enjoy them with some of the region's fuller-bodied red wines

SEPTEMBER
Nimes wine festival—a busy fair in this lovely old town, including plentiful food and music, as well as a spot of bull running to remind you of the proximity of Spain

OCTOBER
Banyuls harvest festival—improbably, perhaps, the annual celebration of this rich, sweet wine includes a giant barbecue on the beach; the alcoholic strength of the Banyuls may prove welcome if the weather is chilly

WINE SHOPS

Many of the wines from this region are hard to find at home, so stock up while you're here.

BÉZIERS

Clos St-Gabriel, Avenue Joseph Lazare.
04 67 62 54 12
Philippe Catusse is an enthusiast for the wines of this region—and most other parts of France.

MONTPELLIER

La Cave des Arceaux, 7 Rue Marioge.
04 67 92 44 84
Frédéric Jeanjean's recently launched shop offers over 400 wines from this region and some well-chosen examples from other parts of southern France.

Les Caves Notre Dame, 41 Rue de l'Aiguillerie.
04 67 60 56 76
A chain of three shops in Montpellier (the others are at 961 Rue de la Croix de Lavit and 1348 Avenue de la Mer) that offer a good range of local wines.

MUSEUMS

Some producers offer vineyard or winery tours. Contact tourist offices *(see below)* for details.

LÉZIGNAN-CORBIÈRES

Le Musée de la Vigne et du Vin, 3 rue de Turgot.
04 68 27 07 57
In the heart of Corbières, this 30-year-old museum offers an insight into the way wine used to be made in this region, and the often very different way it is produced today.

NARBONNE

Musée de la Vigne et du Vin à Narbonne, Domaine de l'Hospitalet, Route Narbonne Plage.
04 68 45 34 47.
FAX 04 68 45 23 49
An impressive exhibition in a cellar carved into the rock. The focus here is on the "golden age" of Languedoc wine-making that ended in 1907 with riots by the region's producers. The old photographs are fascinating.

WEBSITES

There are lots of useful websites relating to wine production in this region. Some of the best are www.languedoc-wines.com, www.coteaux-languedoc.com, www.limoux-aoc.com, www.aoc-cabardes.com, www.cru-fitou.com, www.vins-du-roussillon.com, and www.vins-languedoc-roussillon.fr. For tourist-oriented information, try www.sunfrance.com or go to www.tourisme.fr and type in the name of any town or village.

OTHER INFORMATION

The Comité Régional du Tourisme Languedoc Roussillon–"La Septimanie"–Le Millénaire II, 417 Rue Samuel Morse, Montpelier.
04 67 22 81 00
FAX 04 67 64 47 48

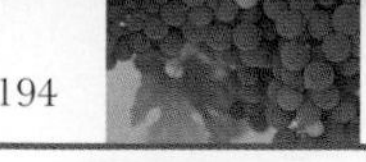

BANYULS

IF PATRIOTIC FRENCHMEN drink *vin jaune* as a Gallic alternative to sherry, they can also enjoy Banyuls' wine instead of tawny port. The four *communes* of Banyuls-sur-Mer, Cerbère, Collioure, and Port Vendres form Banyuls, France's most southern *appellation*. The grape that grows best on the thin, acidic soil here is Grenache, which must make up at least 75 percent of all Banyuls Grand Cru. Banyuls' red, white, rosé, and tawny wines are all *vins doux naturels*, with the reds being the most famous. Aged in oak for 30 months, red Banyuls smells of raisins, coffee, stewed fruit, and almonds and can last for 40 years. While some Banyuls wines take on an oxidized, *rancio* character, others, protected from the air to preserve their fruitiness, are known as *rimages*.

Domaine du Mas Blanc
Domaine du Mas Blanc's Cuvée de la St Martin is one of the finest examples of Banyuls' famous fortified wines.

Sunbathing in Banyuls
Like many of the world's best fortified wines, Banyuls wine benefits from being warmed by the sun during production.

- AC Banyuls, AC Banyuls Grand Cru.
- Red/white/rosé: Grenache Noir, Grenache Gris, Grenache Blanc, Macabéo, Malvoisie.
- Rich, red *vins doux naturels*. White, rosé *vins doux naturels*.
- De la Casa Blanca, Cave de l'Abbé Rous, du Mas Amiel, du Mas Blanc, L'Etoile, Clos des Paulilles, Cellier des Templiers, La Tour Vieille, Vial Magnères.
- Red: Roquefort cheese.
- Red: 2003, 2002, 2001, 1998, 1997.
- Red: 2–25 years.

CABARDÈS

EVERY YEAR, MILLIONS of vacationers pass this recently recognized *appellation* as they drive along the freeway north of Carcassonne. There are plenty of ambitious producers, but defining the style of Cabardès is tricky, because this is a schizophrenic *appellation*. Some wines are Bordeaux-like and based on Cabernet Sauvignon and Merlot (and sometimes labeled "Vent d'Ouest"), while others (possibly labeled Vent d'Est) lean more toward the Rhône. Try before you buy.

Château Constance
The quality of this wine is higher than that of many others found in Cabardès.

- AC Cabardès.
- Red/rosé: Grenache, Syrah, Cinsault, Cabernet Sauvignon, Cabernet Franc, Merlot, Malbec, Fer.
- Light, fruity reds. Peppery rosés.
- De Cabrol, Ch Constance, de Pennautier, Ventenac.
- Red: Assorted pork meats.
- Red: 2003, 2002, 2001.
- Red: 2–5 years.

COLLIOURE

COLLIOURE IS UNFORTIFIED Banyuls, or vice versa. These two *appellations* share the same steep, narrow terraces around the pretty seaside town and artists' colony of Collioure and the villages of Port-Vendres, Banyuls-sur-Mer, and Cerbère. Most Collioure is full-bodied red, made from Grenache Noir and Mourvèdre, blended with Carignan, Cinsault, and Syrah. As the Carignan is phased out and less well-situated vineyards are replaced with orchards, the quality of Collioure is improving.

Domaine la Tour Vieille
The Cuvée Puig Oriol from this estate is a powerful, long-lived red wine.

- AC Collioure.
- Red/rosé: Grenache Noir, Mourvèdre.
- Heady, full-bodied reds. Flavorsome, dry rosés.
- Du Mas Blanc, de Jau, Clos de Paulilles, de la Rectorie, des Templiers, la Tour Vieille, Vial Magnères.
- Red: Meat and bean stew.
- Red: 2003, 2002, 2001.
- Red: 4–6 years.

CORBIÈRES

THIS *APPELLATION* WAS ONE OF THE biggest beneficiaries of the international wine boom of the 1970s and 1980s, with its red wines offering good value for money before the emergence of East European and New World wines. Today, Corbières has plenty of competition from these areas and nearby Minervois *(see p199)* and the Coteaux du Languedoc *(see p196)*.

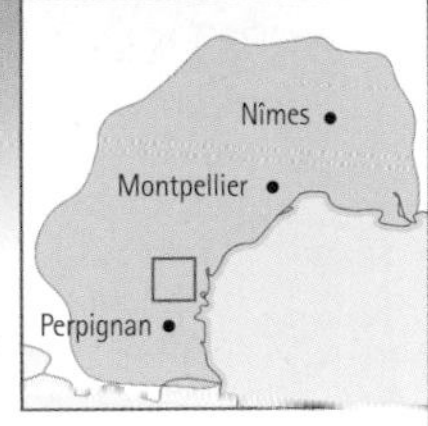

A Taste of the Sea
Parts of the Corbières *appellation*, like this area near Periac de Mer, are very close to the Mediterranean, which has a direct influence on the flavor of the wines that are produced here.

Corbières is a huge and enormously varied region to the southeast of Carcassonne. Due to its size and the diversity of its soils, altitudes, microclimates, and grape varieties, it is very difficult to generalize about the quality or style of the wines produced here. The *appellation* is as likely to be found on a cheap, basic, effort in a supermarket as an impressively ambitious one from a smaller estate. In an attempt to make some sense of the region, 11 separate unofficial vineyard zones have been identified. Following the success of the La Livinière subregion in Minervois, it is likely that some of these will be officially recognized. Unfortunately, even within these zones there can be huge variations in both altitude and climate. To date, some of the region's best wines have been produced in Lézignan and Alaric in the north of the region, in Boutenac in the center, and on the hills of Termenes in the southwest. Sigean, located on the Mediterranean coast, also produces good wines, although this hilly area is probably the most varied of all the 11 zones.

Skilled producers, who focus on using the grapes from the Syrah and old Carignan vines planted on limestone soil (especially in Boutenac), make wines with rich, ripe, fruity flavors and enough structure to make them worth keeping for a few years. It has, however, been too easy to sell dull examples of Corbières to those who have not yet tasted the better Vins de Pays d'Oc *(see p279)* from the same region. Today, over 90 percent of Corbières is red, but some of its better-made dry whites, made from grapes including Muscat, Vermentino, Marsanne and Roussanne, are worth trying.

Château d'Aguilhar
The rugged countryside that surrounds Château d'Aguilhar has changed little over the years.

- AC Corbières.
- Red/rosé: Carignan, Syrah, Mourvèdre, Grenache. White: Bourboulenc, Maccabeo, Grenache Blanc, Picpoul, Terret.
- Spicy, full-bodied, dry reds. Medium-bodied, dry rosés. Rare but refreshing, light, aromatic, dry whites.
- Ch d'Aguilhar, Aiguilloux, Caraguilhes, des Chandelles, Etang des Colombes, Grand Caumont, Grand Moulin, Héléne, de Lastours, Vignerons de la Méditerranée, Meunier St Louis, d'Ornaisons, les Palais, Pech-Latt, Producteurs de Mont Tauch, du Révérend, St Auriol, St Estève, Celliers St Martin, Salvagnac, du Vieux Parc, Villemajou, la Voulte Gasparets.
- Red: Game stew.
- Red: 2003, 2002, 2001, 1998.
- Red: 3–8 years.

Château de Lastours
This brilliant estate is also a home for developmentally diasabled residents, who help to produce the château's wines.

COSTIÈRES DE NÎMES

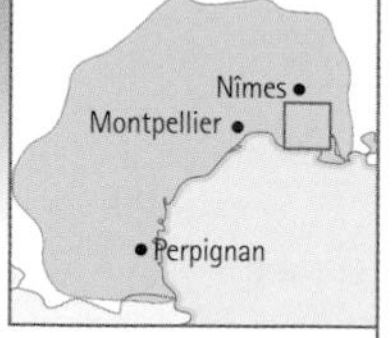

WINES FROM THE PEBBLY VINEYARDS OF Costières de Nîmes, located between the Rhône and Languedoc regions, have had a good reputation since Roman times. In the last century, most of the area's predominantly Carignan grapes were used to make basic red wines. Then, in the 1980s, ambitious estate owners fought to attain promotion from *VDQS* to *appellation* status, and changed the name of the *appellation* from Costières du Gard to Costières de Nîmes. Today, Costières de Nîmes covers 24 *communes* from Beaucaire to Vauvert along the Rhône, and, although a token amount of white wine is made, most of the wines made here are red or rosé. Carignan still contributes up to 40 percent of the blend, but the Grenache and Syrah, which form at least 25 percent of the blend, are increasingly prevalent.

Mas des Bressades
Rich Costières de Nîmes wine like this is a good alternative to the pricier wines of the Rhône's Crozes-Hermitage and St Joseph.

Ready for the Harvest
Rain is fortunately not often a problem in this southern region of France, but it pays to be prepared.

- AC Costières de Nîmes.
- Red: Grenache, Carignan, Syrah. White: Clairette, Bourboulenc Grenache Blanc. Rosé: Carignan, Cinsault, Mourvèdre, Syrah.
- Medium- to full-bodied reds. Soft whites. Dry rosés.
- Ch de l'Amarine, Ch de Campuget, Mas de Bressades, Ch Mourgues du Grès, de Nages, Tuilerie de Pazac, Valcombe.
- Sausage, meat and bean stew.
- 2003, 2001, 1998, 1996.
- Red: 2–6 years. White/rosé: 1–3 years.

COTEAUX DU LANGUEDOC

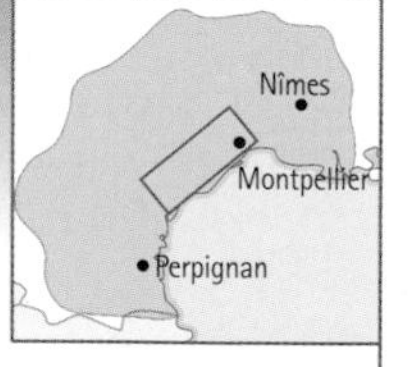

THESE VINEYARDS ON THE HILLS and the great plain of the Languedoc had already been established by the Greeks by the time Julius Caesar conquered Gaul. In fact, wine-makers back in Rome were so impressed by the wines of this area that they unsuccessfully attempted to curtail competition from them. In the 18th century, Languedoc's wines flourished once again, before being struck by phylloxera in the 1880s. Today, Languedoc is seen as one of the most exciting wine-making areas in France, with its whites and rosés, which rely on technical wine-making, often providing better value than wines from Provence. One *commune* which is showing great potential is Pic St Loup, where wine-makers like l'Hortus are making wines that outclass many a Châteauneuf-du-Pape *(see p251)*.

Prieuré de St Jean-de-Bébian
From an estate owned by the former editors of two French wine magazines, this is an impeccably made, richly flavored red.

Abbaye de Valmagne
As is the case in many other parts of France, a church has provided the ideal setting in which to mature red wine.

- AC Coteaux du Languedoc.
- Red/rosé: Carignan, Cinsault, Grenache, Syrah, Mourvèdre. White: Grenache, Bourboulenc, Clairette.
- Full-bodied reds. Light, dry rosés. Light, dry whites.
- D'Aupilhac, de l'Hortus, Mas Bruguière, Mas Julien, Peyre-Rose, Prieuré de St Jean-de-Bébian.
- Red: Steak grilled with herbs.
- 2004, 2002, 2001, 1998, 1997.
- Red: 3–8 years. White/rosé: 1–3 years.

FAUGÈRES

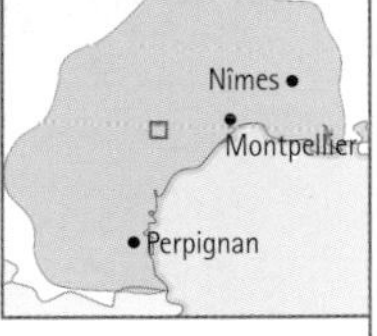

UNTIL ABOUT 20 YEARS AGO, despite being one of the areas of southern France with the greatest potential for making great red wine, Faugères was surprisingly sidelined into producing Muscats and *eaux-de-vie*. Today, the steeply sloping foothills of the Cévennes, a mountainous corner of the Herault between St Chinian and Cabrières, are planted with Carignan, Cinsault, Grenache, Lladoner Pelut, Mourvèdre and Syrah vines. Apart from a small amount of dry rosé, almost all of the wine produced here is red. The best examples, like those of the well-established Domaine Alquier and the relative newcomer Michel Louison's Château des Estanilles, are rich, full-bodied and spicy, with enough structure to reward several years of bottle aging. For those on a tighter budget, Cave Coopérative de Laurens produces good, inexpensive wines.

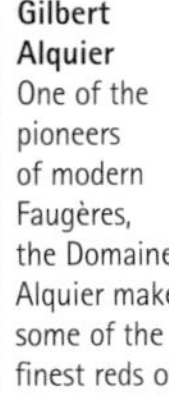

Gilbert Alquier
One of the pioneers of modern Faugères, the Domaine Alquier makes some of the finest reds of the *appellation*.

Well-Sited Vineyards
Faugères' sloping vineyards offer the perfect location for grapes to ripen and develop rich, deep flavors.

- AC Faugères.
- Red: Carignan, Syrah, Grenache, Mourvèdre.
- Full-bodied, spicy, often rustic reds.
- Ch des Adouzes, Gilbert Alquier, Ch Chenaie, Ch des Estanilles, Ch Grézan, Cave Coopérative de Laurens, la Liquière, de Météore, Moulin Couderc, des Peyregran, du Rouge Gorge, St Antonin.
- Game pâté.
- 2003, 2002, 2001, 1998.
- 2–4 years.

FITOU

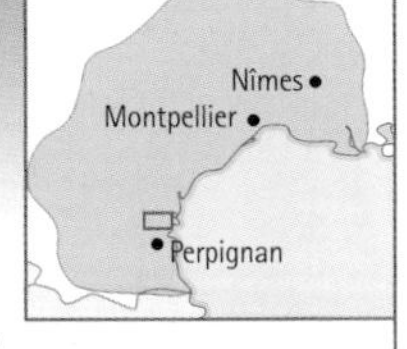

THE OLDEST *APPELLATION* IN Languedoc-Roussillon, Fitou is divided into two zones that both border Corbières *(see p195)*. The smaller zone lies around the coastal town of Fitou, while the larger's vineyards dominate the land between Villeneuve-les-Corbières and Tuchan. Although the *communes* here can produce Rivesaltes *vins doux naturels*, most of the wines are reds, made mainly from Carignan blended with Grenache, Lladoner Pelut, and Syrah. However, Carignan tends to produce dull wines unless the vines are old and yields are modest. Recently, wine production has been a problem here, with many producers coasting along on the success they enjoyed in the 1980s. These wines should be herb-flavored, taking on a wild, spicy character after four or five years, but Fitou that is worth aging is a rare find now.

Château L'Espigne
This Fitou has an unusually rich flavor and a level of complexity that is seldom found in this *appellation*.

Mediterranean Vines
Many of Fitou's vineyards are near the sea, but the best wines are made from grapes grown on slopes farther inland

- AC Fitou.
- Red: Carignan, Grenache, Mourvèdre, Syrah.
- Medium- to full-bodied reds.
- Ch l'Espigne, Lepaumier, Lerys, Ch de Nouvelles, Maîtres Vignerons de Cascastel, Cave Pilote de Villeneuve-les-Corbières, Mont Tauch, de la Rochelierre, de Rolland, Val d'Orbieu (Vignerons de la Méditerranée).
- Pigeon simmered with onions.
- 2003, 2002, 2001, 1998.
- 3–4 years.

LIMOUX

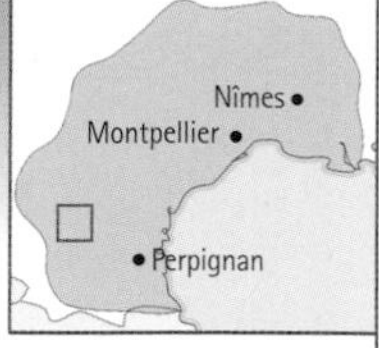

ACCORDING TO THE LIMOUXINS, Limoux has been producing sparkling wine since 1531, long before Dom Pérignon in Champagne. Today, three styles are produced: Blanquette Méthode Ancestrale is made from the dull Mauzac grape, while Blanquette de Limoux and Crémant de Limoux are both blends of Mauzac and Chardonnay or Chenin Blanc, with more Mauzac being used for the Blanquette. Recently, Limoux has also earned a reputation—and an *appellation*—for its still Chardonnay, especially the Tocques et Clochers range from the Sieur d'Arques *coopérative*, and fast-improving modern reds, including Baron d'Arques, a joint venture between this winery and Château Mouton-Rothschild.

St Laurent
This *méthode traditionelle* sparkling wine benefits from the use of a wide range of grape varieties.

Limoux Cellar
The combination of chalky soil, coolish climate, and fermentation in barrels like these gives Limoux Chardonnay a character similar to white Burgundy. Indeed, it is often alleged that Limoux wine has been illegally used by Burgundians for blending.

- AC Limoux, AC Blanquette Méthode Ancestrale, AC Blanquette de Limoux, AC Crémant de Limoux.
- White: Mauzac, Chardonnay, Chenin Blanc. Red: Cabernets Sauvignon & Franc, Malbec, Merlot, Syrah, Grenache.
- Dry, sparkling whites. Barrel-fermented still whites. Bordeaux and Rhone-like reds.
- De l'Aigle, G&R Antech, Collin, de Flassian, Denois, de Fourn, Guinot, Sieur d'Arques.
- White: Mussels in garlic.
- 2002, 1998, 1996, 1994.
- Sparkling: 5–6 years. Still: 3–4 years.

MAURY

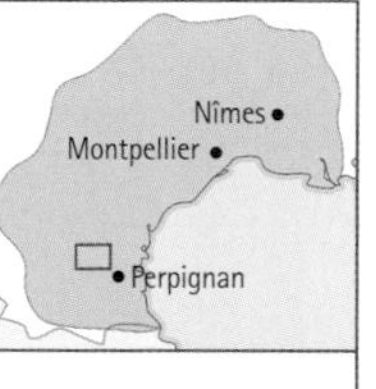

UNLIKE BANYULS *(see p194)*, which appears on most French wine lists, the wines of Maury, to the south of Corbières *(see p195)*, remain fairly unknown. This is somewhat surprising given the prestige this town's wines enjoyed in the second century BC and the potential quality of its climate and soil. Perhaps one of the reasons for Maury's recent fall from grace is the reliance the *appellation* traditionally placed on the Macabéo and Carignan grapes, which tend to produce dull wines. However, this began to change in 2000, as regulations raised the proportion of the more flavorsome Grenache to 75 percent. Like Banyuls, Maury can be fresh and light or in the form of tangy *rancio*, and as an aperitif or with dessert. For a taste of fine Maury, try a mature bottle from Mas Amiel.

Mas Amiel
Mas Amiel leads the way in quality Maury, producing a range of rich, concentrated, plummy wines.

A Perfect Situation
Maury's hot climate and schistous soil provide the ideal conditions for the Grenache grape to ripen, and subsequently be used in the production of unique, fortified wines.

- AC Maury.
- Red: Grenache Noir, Grenache Gris, Grenache Blanc.
- Rich, fortified reds which compete with vintage and tawny port.
- Mas Amiel, Jean-Louis Lafage, les Vignerons de Maury, Maurydoré, la Pléiade, Robert Ponderoux.
- Cheddar and/or parmesan cheese served with fresh grapes.
- Mainly non vintage.
- 5–25 years.

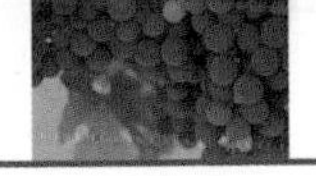

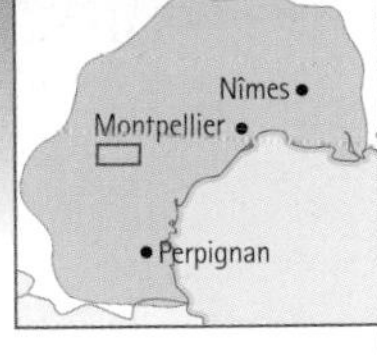

MINERVOIS

ALTHOUGH OFTEN SEEN AS CORBIÈRES' SIBLING, this region, stretching across the south-facing limestone hills between St Chinian *(see p201)* and Carcassonne, has a character of its own. Like Corbières *(see p195)*, Minervois has a range of environments. In the cool, rainy western area, Syrah and Grenache grow well, while in the arid heartland it is Mourvèdre that excels. The best Minervois is made in Minervois la Livinière, to the north, but elsewhere, too, quality tends to be higher than in Corbières. This is thanks to the lower proportion of Carignan, and the skill of producers such as Domaine Piccinini. Although 95 percent of Minervois is red, whites are made from Rhône and Mediterranean grape varieties.

Domaine Piccinini
This estate has been one of the pioneers of the "La Livinière" region.

Gorge de la Cesse
The landscape in this large region, ranging from hot, limestone slopes in the heartland to rugged mountains in the west, is among the most varied in southern France.

- AC Minervois.
- Red: Carignan, Grenache, Syrah, Mourvèdre. White/rosé: Grenache Blanc, Bourboulenc, Macabéo.
- Full-bodied, dry reds. Dry whites. Dry, fruity rosés.
- Ch Domergue, Fabas, Ch de Gourgazaud, Ch de Lastours, Ch Maris, Ch les Ollieux, d'Oupia, Ch les Palais, Paraza, Piccinini, Ste Eulalie, la Tour-Boisée, Ch Villerambert-Julien.
- *Ragout* of veal.
- 2002, 1998, 1996, 1995, 1994.
- Red: 3–5 years. White/rosé: 1 year.

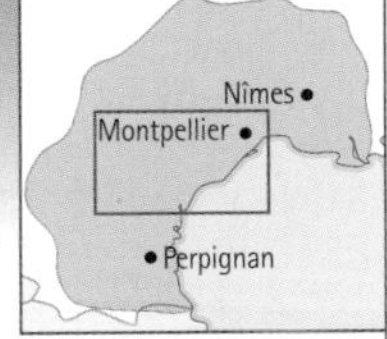

MUSCAT APPELLATIONS

WHILE FRANCE'S BEST-KNOWN fortified Muscat is from Beaumes-de-Venise, nine out of 10 bottles of *vin doux naturel* come from Languedoc-Roussillon's five Muscat *appellations*. Of Frontignan and Mireval, coastal neighbors near Sète, Frontignan has the greater fame, thanks partly to legends citing Hercules and Thomas Jefferson as enjoying its *vins doux naturels* and *vins de liqueurs*. The wines of Mireval, however, made from Muscat Blanc à Petits Grains, are often more elegant, as are the rare Muscats de Lunel. More run-of-the-mill, Muscat de Rivesaltes, made from Muscat Blanc à Petits Grains or Muscat d'Alexandrie, differs greatly from the blended wines of Rivesaltes. Also look for the appealing, apricoty Muscat de St Jean-de-Minervois.

Muscat
Fortified Muscat, like this Muscat de Rivesaltes, should taste like a mixture of fresh grapes and marmalade.

Château de la Peyrade
Most of France's fortified Muscats are made by *coopératives*, but some estates, like Château de la Peyrade, also produce top-class Muscat.

- AC Muscat de Frontignan, AC Muscat de St Jean-de-Minervois, AC Muscat de Lunel, AC Muscat de Mireval, AC Muscat de Rivesaltes.
- White: Muscats Blanc & Rosé à Petits Grains, Muscat Doré de Frontignan, Muscat d'Alexandrie
- White vins doux naturels.
- Cazes, de Corneilla, Deltour-Grousset, Força Real, de Jau, Lacoste, Mas Liaro, Nouvelles, Ch de la Peyrade, Sarda-Malet.
- Lemon and raisin cheesecake.
- Mainly non vintage.
- 1–3 years.

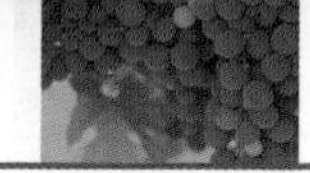

ROUSSILLON

BEST-KNOWN AS HALF OF Languedoc-Roussillon, this large area has yet to create an independent identity for itself—despite the proven potential of some of its vineyards. However, new grape varieties are being introduced, wine-making is improving dramatically, and the quality of some individual *communes* is steadily being established.

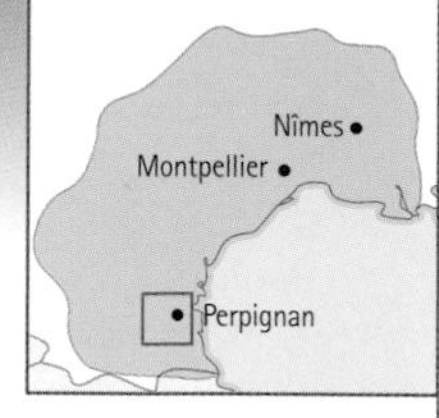

Côtes du Roussillon
Sheltered by high mountain ranges on three sides, the vineyards of Côtes du Roussillon are planted in the sunniest region in France. This hilly landscape is home to a wide range of grape varieties.

Wine-making in Roussillon probably dates back to the 7th century BC, when vines were imported by Greeks who were attracted to the area by the minerals to be found on the Catalan coast. The vines continued to thrive during the Middle Ages, when the sweet wine they produced was known as "Vin d'Espagne." The mountain ranges on three sides of the vineyards form a natural amphitheater that shelters the vines. To the north there are Les Corbières, and to the west Le Canigou and Les Albères, which form the frontier with Spain. With more than 2,550 hours of sunshine a year, this is France's sunniest region, and the ripening of grapes is not the problem it is elsewhere. Vintages of Roussillon rarely vary, since the climate is generally fairly consistent.

Although Roussillon has a longer history of vine growing than neighboring Languedoc, it still somehow seems to be striving for its own regional identity. The area's two main *appellations* for still, dry wines are the Côtes du Roussillon and the Côtes du Roussillon-Villages. The Côtes du Roussillon covers an area of about 12,350 acres (5,000 ha) for red, white, and rosé wines, while the Côtes du Roussillon-Villages is limited to red wines from 25 villages located along the Agly River (of which Caramany and Latour-de-France are allowed to add their names to the wine's label). While Carignan is still the dominant grape, quality has improved in the area as the percentage of the Syrah and Mourvèdre varieties has been increased. Either of these grapes must now comprise 20 percent of the final blend. As for Carignan, this often performs best when producers use the *macération carbonique* process to extract as much fruitiness as possible from this potentially dull grape. White wines are still forced by regulations to use a high percentage of the Maccabéo and Malvoisie varieties, while no more than 50 percent of the more flavorsome Grenache Blanc, Roussanne, Marsanne, or Vermentino grapes may be used. Luckily for the consumer, wine-makers sometimes find that their hands slip while they are preparing the blends.

- AC Côtes du Roussillon, AC Côtes du Roussillon-Villages, AC Grand Roussillon.
- Red/rosé: Carignan, Syrah, Grenache, Mourvèdre, Maccabéo.
  White: Maccabéo, Malvoisie.
- Varied, but potentially spicy reds. Floral whites. Dry rosés.
- Caves de Baixas, Brial, de la Casenove, de Castelnou, Cazes, des Chênes, Mas Crémat, Fontanel, Força Réal, Gardiés, Gauby, Ch de Jau, Laporte, Lequerde, Maîtres Vignerons de Tauteval, de Rombeau, Mas Rous, St François, Sarda-Malet, des Schistes, Cellier de Trouillas, les Vignerons Catalans, Vignerons de Pézilla.
- Roasted veal fillet with Madeira sauce.
- Red: 2003, 2001, 2000, 1998.
- Red: 2–6 years.
  White: 1–4 years.

Domaine Gauby
Domaine Gauby is an excellent estate whose wines prove that subtle, elegant wines can be produced in this region.

ST CHINIAN

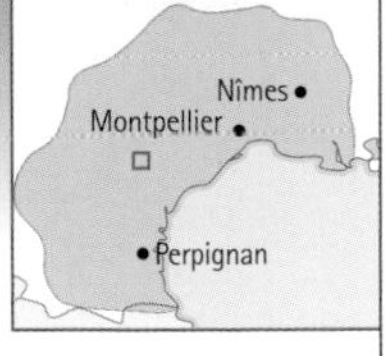

ST CHINIAN GAINED ITS *appellation* status in 1982, although its potential to produce great red wine was recognized as early as 1300. Located in the Hérault, north of Narbonne and northwest of Béziers, St Chinian encompasses 20 villages. The high altitude here and the schistous and gravelly, chalky soil help to make wines that are lighter and more elegant, but often less interesting than those of neighboring Faugères *(see p197)*. However, producers like Domaine Canet-Valette, the Châteaux Cazal-Viel, and Coujan and the *coopérative* at Roquebrun are making interesting cherryish wines while preserving the *appellation*'s natural finesse. Both the reds and the rosés are made primarily from Syrah, Carignan, Grenache, Cinsault, and Mourvèdre.

Clos Bagatelle
This estate produces spicy wines that develop well after four or five years in the cellar.

Autumn Gold
One of the best times to visit St Chinian is in the few weeks following the harvest, when the vines' leaves have turned to shades of copper and gold.

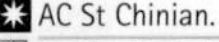

- AC St Chinian.
- Red/rosé: Carignan, Syrah, Grenache, Mourvèdre, Cinsault.
- Full-bodied, dry reds. Dry rosés.
- Ch des Albières, de Astide Rousse, Clos Bagatelle, Canet-Valette, Ch Cazal-Viel, Coujan, Coopérative de Roquebrun, Deslines, Ch Milhau-Lacugue, des Pradels, Soulie des Joncs, Ch des Villespassans, Viranel.
- Potatoes cooked with onions, Bayonne ham, garlic, and parsley.
- Red: 2003, 2001, 1998, 1996.
- Red: 2–5 years.

OTHERS

OF THE OTHER *APPELLATIONS* OF Languedoc-Roussillon, two that deserve to be left on the shelf are Clairette de Bellegarde and Clairette du Languedoc. Made, as their name suggests, from the Clairette grape, the best that can be said for these wines is that they offer a taste of the past. Unfortunately, the past was a time when people enjoyed drinking white wines that had little flavor in their youth and a tremendous propensity for oxidation. Although it is only the existence of *appellations* like these that prevents the Clairette grape from becoming an endangered species, I can see no good reason why anyone would actually choose to use it in the production of classic, dry white wines like Clairette de Bellegarde. The sweet, dry, fortified, and unfortified Clairette du Languedoc *rancio* wines are much more interesting alternatives.

Typically, while the dull white Clairettes have *appellation* status, the light but pleasantly flavored reds of the Côtes de la Malepère and the Côtes de Millau all still have only *VDQS* status. Of these, the former taste like a cross between Côtes du Rhône *(see pp254–5)* and basic Bordeaux *(see p93)*, while the latter are more like a blend of Côtes du Rhône and Beaujolais *(see pp126–7)*.

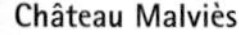

Château Malviès
This château is one of the leaders in a move to produce more fruity Côtes de la Malepère wines.

Clairette de Bellegarde
Coopératives such as this one are happy to promote and sell their wines on-site.

The Loire Valley

The Loire Valley

Of all the wine regions in France, none offers a wider variety of dry, sweet, and sparkling wines to enjoy on a warm summer day than the Loire.

When it comes to marketing wine, a river can be very useful. Every year, thousands of tourists follow the Loire River as it stretches across France. As they stop for a meal and choose a local wine, though, unless they have a helpful *sommelier* to hand, they could find the choice a little confusing.

At the western, maritime end of the river, there are the dry, nonaromatic white wines of Muscadet *(see p219)*. When well made, these crisply refreshing wines are the perfect partners to all kinds of seafood. Nowadays, however, wine drinkers tend to demand more flavor than the grapes used to make Muscadet are able to deliver.

Historic Quality
The majestic Château de Chinon overlooks both the Loire River and the vineyards of Cabernet Franc grapes that give the wines of this *appellation* their berryish flavors.

REGIONAL OVERVIEW

- 87,150 acres (35,000 ha): 390 million bottles.
- Atlantic to Continental. Muscadet, on the coast, is quite damp and frost is a problem, as it is elsewhere in this region. Heading east, the summers get warmer and the winters harsher.
- Varied, with granite in Muscadet, schist in Layon, sandy gravel in Chinon, tufa chalk in Vouvray, and gravelly limestone in Sancerre.
- Red: Cabernet Franc, Malbec, Gamay.
White: Chenin Blanc, Sauvignon Blanc, Melon Blanc.

Move eastward along the river and you will reach Anjou *(see p214)* and Saumur *(see p223)*—the first of which is usually associated with sugary rosé; the second, with inexpensive sparkling wine. But take a moment to look at the wine lists in

restaurants here and you will see that both these *appellations* produce a number of much more interesting, bubble-free styles. A little farther to the east, Haut-Poitou *(see p217)* and Touraine *(see p225)* offer the chance to taste a range of wines made from Sauvignon Blanc, the variety with which the Loire Valley is most often associated. At their best, these wines have the fresh, light appeal of gooseberries, black currants, and crunchy raw vegetables. Too many of them, however, taste green and unripe. An excess of green flavors can also be a feature of the red wines of Chinon *(see p216)*, Bourgueil, and St Nicolas de Bourgueil *(see p215)*. However, in ripe

Loire Valley region

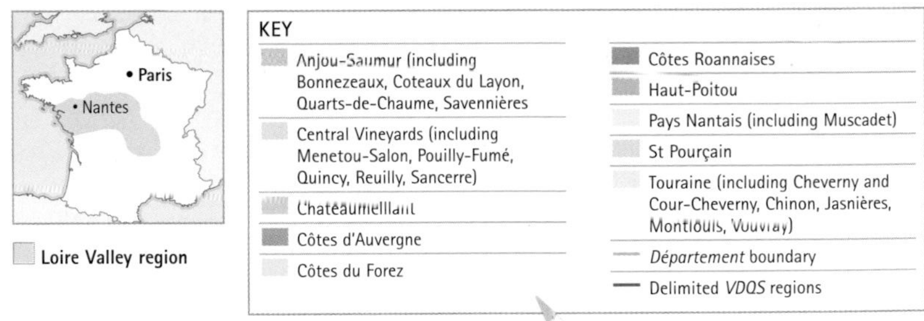

vintages and in the hands of skilled wine-makers, these can offer a great counterpoint to red Bordeaux.

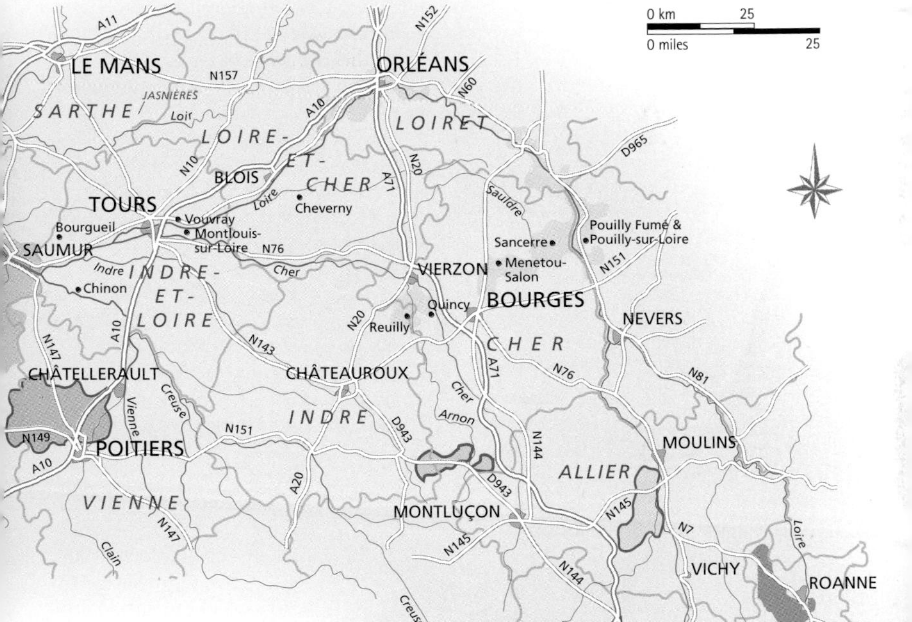

Unfortunately, Vouvray *(see p226)*, which showcases the versatility and longevity of Chenin Blanc, is suffering from the current lack of interest in this grape variety. Hopefully, the growing interest in sweet Chenins will bring it back into the spotlight.

At the end of our journey, we hit true Sauvignon country in the shape of Sancerre *(see p222)*, Pouilly Fumé *(see p220)*, Quincy *(see p221)*, and Menetou-Salon *(see p218)*. But even here, the Loire Valley holds surprises—like the red and rosé wines of Sancerre, made from Pinot Noir.

Watching the River Flow
As the Loire and its offshoots flow westward to the Atlantic, they pass through vineyards that produce an enormously varied range of dry, sweet, still, and sparkling wines.

The History of the Loire Valley

Built between the 13th and 16th centuries, the many magnificent châteaux of the Loire Valley served as fortresses, and later as luxurious palaces, for the kings of France. With royal patronage and easy access to the foreign markets of England and the Netherlands, the region, and particularly towns such as Angers, grew rich on the profitable wine trade.

Château de Chinon
Henry II, first of a long line of Anglo-Norman kings, died here at the now spectacularly ruined Château de Chinon in the early part of the 13th century.

No one knows for sure how wine-making first began in the Loire Valley, but it seems very likely that grape vines were brought here from the areas now known as Bordeaux to the south and Burgundy to the east. The Romans occupied the area for the first four centuries AD, leaving their mark in the form of place names such as Pouilly-sur-Loire *(see p220)*, derived from the words *Paulica villa*, or the villa of Paulus. Likewise, the red wine *appellation* of Saumur-Champigny *(see p223)* may take its name from the Latin *campus ignis*, or the fiery field, while the Porte César in Sancerre *(see p222)* is named after the Roman emperor Julius Caesar. Evidence that the Romans brought their wine-making technology here exists in the form of excavated kilns (used for firing terra-cotta wine amphorae) dating from the first century. By 591 AD, wine making was sufficiently established here for Bishop Gregory of Tours, in his book *The History of the Franks*, to describe a successful harvest and to complain that the marauding Bretons were occupying vineyards in the region we now know as Muscadet *(see p219)*. By the 12th century, the red wine of Anjou was being shipped to England by the merchants of Angers, while large quantities of red and white wines were also exported from various parts of the region to the prosperous independent principality of Flanders. A vigorous Loire Valley wine trade continued until the middle of the 20th century, boosted by the region's proximity to Paris, as well as to the Atlantic coast and overseas markets.

Illuminated Grape Harvest
This page, from the 15th-century illuminated manuscript *Les Très Riches Heures du Duc de Berry*, shows the grape harvest at the Château de Saumur.

GRAPE VARIETIES

Cabernet Franc and Sauvignon Blanc vines arrived in the Loire Valley from Bordeaux between 1000 and 1500. Sauvignon Blanc, however, was not widely planted here until the 16th century, when it was introduced to what are now the *appellations* of Pouilly-sur-Loire, Sancerre, Quincy *(see p221)*, and Reuilly *(see p221)*. Despite its apparently invincible position in these *appellations* today, Sauvignon Blanc was, until the 18th century, less favored to the now almost-forgotten Chasselas grape, which was popular with growers because of its higher yields. It was only after the vineyards were replanted following their 19th-century

Tufa Wine Cellars
A soft chalk boiled by volcanic action, tufa underlies many parts of the Loire Valley and for centuries has been excavated to make both homes and wine cellars.

devastation by phylloxera that Sauvignon Blanc was established as the major grape of these *communes*.

Also popular in the region is Melon de Bourgogne, sometimes known as Muscadet, which arrived in Anjou during the Middle Ages. By the 17th century, although banned in Burgundy, it was planted as a hardy white grape to replace existing black vines in what now corresponds to the *appellation* of Muscadet. With the exception of California, Melon de Bourgogne is now grown nowhere else.

Just as closely linked with the Loire Valley is Chenin Blanc. This grape is little-known elsewhere in Europe, and no one is sure of its origins, though one theory, supported by Jancis Robinson in her book *Grapes, Vines and Wines*, suggests that Chenin Blanc is native to the Loire Valley region. Whether this is true or not, it has been used to make wine here since the 15th century, and probably far longer.

INTO THE 21ST CENTURY

Until quite recently, the Loire was one of the few places in the world where fresh white wines could be produced with any reliability. Since then, however, the invention of equipment to control temperature during transportation and the planting of superior grape varieties in regions enjoying more favorable climates have dealt the region a hefty body blow. Although the best wines of the Loire are improving in quality, far too many are poorly made and come from over-cropped, underripe grapes. It makes little sense to buy a watery, acidic Loire Sauvignon Blanc when similarly priced, more flavorsome wines are made from the same grape in southern France, elsewhere in Europe, and in the New World. Those who have studied the recent history of the Loire Valley know that its wine regions are liable to shrink as well as grow. The vines of the once-famous wine-producing Côtes d'Auvergne district, for example, now cover only one-fiftieth of the 148,260 acres (60,000 ha) they occupied before the arrival of phylloxera.

Renaissance Glory
Straddling the Cher River to the east of Tours, the Château de Chenonceaux was built as a medieval fortress and reconstructed in 1512 in the modern Renaissance style.

A Driving Tour of the Loire Valley

Beginning at the city of Tours, this route takes you along various tributaries of the middle reaches of the Loire, through Vouvray, famous for its rich Chenin Blanc wines, down to Azay-le-Rideau with its elegant château and through the Cabernet Franc red wine vineyards of Chinon and Bourgueil.

Riverside Charm
Built on the bank of the Vienne River, the quiet town of Chinon makes an ideal place to stay overnight.

TOURS

No wine lover's visit to the Loire Valley is complete without a visit to the Musée des Vins de Touraine beneath the Église de St Julien in Tours ①. Take the time, too, to explore the cathedral and to stroll around the narrow streets of the city center, which is full of well-preserved Renaissance buildings.

VOUVRAY TO CHINON

Home of the Chenin Blanc grape, Vouvray ② is, for many people, the quintessential town of Touraine. Here you can see many comfortable homes and well-equipped wine cellars dug by their troglodytic inhabitants from the chalk hills. Among many great producers here, I particularly recommend Philippe Foreau, Domaine Huët, and Domaine des Aubuisières. Take a break from wine to visit the extravagantly beautiful Renaissance château of Chenonceaux. Here you can imagine chivalrous interludes on the three-story bridge that straddles the Cher River, a tributary of the Loire, and ponder the unashamed acres of cellulite in the Rubens' paintings that hang inside. Rejoin the Loire at the richly historical town of Amboise ③, home to, among other things, the 18th-century Pagode de Chanteloup and a chapel said to be the final resting place of Leonardo da Vinci. Heading westward along the bank of the Loire, you will come to Montlouis-sur-Loire ④. For a taste of the dry, sweet, still and sparkling wines made here, visit Jacky Blot's Domaine de la Taille aux Loups in nearby Husseau. My choice for lunch or an overnight stay is the sleepy town of Chinon, which you can reach by following the road to Esvres, Saché ⑤ and Azay-le-Rideau ⑥, with its island château. From here the D757 leads to Chinon ⑦. The Domaine Couly-Dutheil is one of the largest estates in the region and its cellars here offer the chance to try wines from a variety of vineyards.

BOURGUEIL AND ST NICOLAS-DE-BOURGUEIL

The D749 will take you out of Chinon, across the Loire, and up to the villages that give their names to the red wine appellations of Bourgueil ⑧ and St Nicolas-de-Bourgueil ⑨. Following a narrow road northward out of Bourgueil to the village of Chevrette, you will find a wine museum and tasting room at the Cave Touristique de la Dive Bouteille. Producer Max Cognard, who also has cellars in Chevrette, makes wines labeled variously as *appellation contrôlée* St

Nicolas-de-Bourgueil or as *appellation contrôlée* Bourgueil, and will gladly explain the sometimes subtle differences between the two.

LANGEAIS TO LUYNES

From Bourgueil, head east to Langeais ⑩, where there is an unspoiled 15th-century château. Then take the D57 out of the village for half a mile or so to take advantage of a panoramic view over the river and vineyards of Bourgueil. In Cinq-Mars-la-Pile ⑪ is a ruined château and, at Luynes ⑫, the château that was once home to 17th-century churchman Cardinal Richelieu.

Historic Amboise
The Pagode de Chanteloup in the town of Amboise is all that remains of an 18th-century château. An earlier château still stands in the town, complete with the hooks used to hang political prisoners.

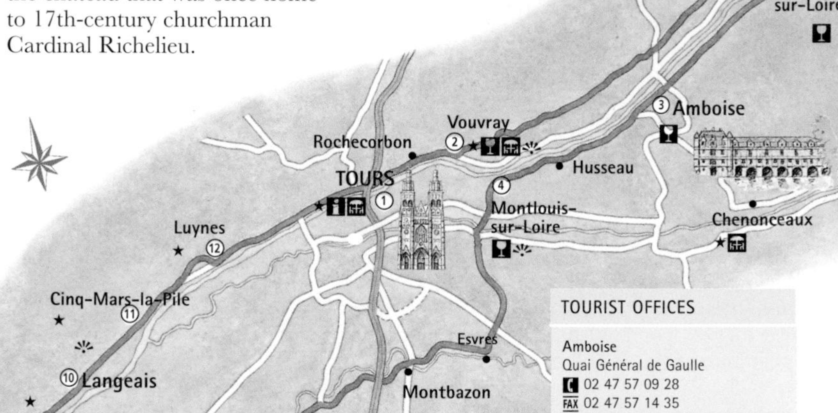

KEY
- Tasting possible
- Places to eat
- Tourist information
- ★ Site of interest
- Tour route
- Viewpoint

Dig for Victory
Like many buildings in Vouvray, this wine cellar is dug from the town's chalky rock.

TOURIST OFFICES

Amboise
Quai Général de Gaulle
02 47 57 09 28
FAX 02 47 57 14 35
@ tourisme.amboise@wanadoo.fr
W www.amboise-valdeloire.com

Azay-le-Rideau
4 Rue du Château
02 47 45 44 40
FAX 02 47 45 31 46
@ tourisme@ot-paysazaylerideau.fr
W www.ot-paysazaylerideau.com

Chinon
Place d'Hofheim
02 47 93 17 85
FAX 02 47 93 93 05
@ tourisme@chinon.com
W www.chinon.com.

Chenonceaux
1 Rue Bretonneau
02 47 23 94 45
FAX 02 47 23 82 41

Tours
78-82 Rue Bernard Palissy
02 47 70 37 37
FAX 02 47 61 14 22
@ info@ligeris.com
W www.ligeris.com

Vouvray
12 Route Rabelais
02 47 52 68 73
FAX 02 47 52 67 76/02 47 52 70 88
@ commune.vouvray@wanadoo.fr
W www.vouvray.org

The Food of the Loire Valley

Mention the Loire to any Frenchman and there is a strong chance that he will describe it as "la Douce France," the part of his country where life is sweet. This is the place where you will find fish from the river and the sea as well as game, pork, and every kind of dairy food, not to mention the wide range of fruit and vegetables that grow in abundance here.

The foods that you will come across vary as you follow the Loire River toward the sea. At the eastern end of the river you will find pike stuffed with pork, and the goat's cheese that has been produced near Sancerre since the Moors brought goats here in the eighth century.

In Touraine, as elsewhere in France, meat and fish are traditionally combined in ways that might surprise modern diners. The *vol au vent d'Amboise*, for example, has little in common with the small mouthfuls bearing this name that are passed around at cocktail parties. This one measures 10 in (25 cm) across and is made with pike, scallops, veal sweetbread, morel mushrooms, truffles, cream, and eggs. Sweetbreads, a local specialty, also feature in *la beauchelle*, a pie whose ingredients also include white wine and mushrooms. Veal is often mixed with cream and mushrooms to make stuffed artichokes.

Game is also popular: partridge, pheasant, duck, and quail appear on most menus. One of the tastiest game dishes, *magrets à la Clavelière*, is a fillet of duck cooked with shallots, grapes,

Fish in Abundance
Salmon, trout, carp, and pike are all caught fresh from the Loire River. In addition, the Atlantic Ocean provides local residents with a range of other fish.

Fruits de Mer
The Atlantic Ocean and the Loire River are perfect sources for a wide range of fresh shellfish. One of the best ways to serve them is simply piled high on a large platter with a slice of lemon and a glass of chilled Muscadet.

Armagnac, and Muscadet. *Lièvre à la royale*, an even richer dish, unites hare with *foie gras*, red wine, and four cloves of garlic and four shallots per person.

Among the fish dishes that you might encounter in the Loire are bass grilled in a salt crust, shad cooked with sorrel, salmon in a *beurre blanc*, or *beurre nantais* (butter, shallots and wine) sauce, and carp stuffed with mushrooms. There could also be monkfish, sole meunière, whitebait (known here as *petite friture*, or *buisson de goujon*), and *chaudrée*, a soup that combines fish and garlic. Often treated as delicacies elsewhere, lobster, mussels, and oysters are featured on the menus of some quite humble restaurants in and around Nantes. The wine, parsley, and mussels all go into the same pot for *moules marinières*, while oysters are sometimes served hot with cream and leeks.

To accompany one of the Loire's sweet wines, try *tarte tatin*, a caramelized, upside-down apple tart, *tarte aux poires* (pear tart), *gâteau nantais*, made with almonds and rum, or *méli-mélo de fruits rouges*, a dessert of strawberries, raspberries, blackberries, black currants, red currants, Muscadet, and sugar.

Saumon au Beurre Blanc
Salmon is delicious served with a traditional, delicate butter sauce made with vinegar, dry white wine, preferably Muscadet, and shallots.

Moules Marinières
This light, fresh-tasting mussel dish is popular everywhere. The mussels are cooked in a sauce of white wine, shallots, herbs, and, for added richness, cream.

REGIONAL CHEESES

Historically, most of the cheese to be found in this region, especially around Anjou, was made from cow's milk. However, goat's cheeses such as the Crottin de Chavignol are found close to the border with Burgundy and can be traced back as far as 1573. During the maturing and ripening process, as different molds form and flavors strengthen, the surfaces of many of these cheeses become pungent rinds. Even today, cheese is sent to the market wrapped in hay or rolled in ash, as was the tradition 300 years ago.

Crottin de Chavignol
When fresh, this goat's cheese has a white surface that hardens and blackens with age. When fully ripe, it is strong and has a meaty texture.

Tomme de Chèvre
Varieties of this cheese can be found throughout France. In the Loire, it is rubbed during the ripening process with a cloth that has been soaked in Muscadet.

TRAVELING IN THE LOIRE VALLEY

A long region that offers varied landscapes and human habitations ranging from the caves cut into the chalk hills of Vouvray to the spectacular châteaux that line the Loire River and its tributaries. Take your time and follow the river, or focus on exploring one of the major appellations *in the west, center, or east.*

HOTELS & RESTAURANTS

A selection of the region's best establishments, offering good local food and wine, and some characterful places to stay.

ANGERS

Auberge d'Eventard, Route de Paris.
02 41 43 74 25
One of the best places to sample traditional dishes made from local fish and accompanied by the best of the region's wines.

CHENONCEAUX

Hôtel du Bon Laboureur et du Château, 6 Rue du Dr Bretonneau.
02 47 23 90 04
An affordable, but simple, place to stay after visiting the nearby chateau. Good traditional food.

CHINON

Hostellerie Gargantua, 73 Rue Voltaire.
02 47 93 04 71
In the heart of beautiful Chinon, with great views of the river, this quaint, turreted hotel is an ideal base from which to explore.

Au Plaisir Gourmand, 2 Rue Parmentier.
02 47 93 20 48
A lovely country restaurant in the center of Chinon, offering a long list of wines from this *appellation.*

ROCHECORBON

Domaine des Hautes Roches, 86 Quai de la Loire.
02 47 52 88 88
Great food and wine in an unforgettable setting. Rooms carved into the chalk give you a taste of the "troglodyte" existence still enjoyed by many in this region.

ROMORANTIN-LANTHENAY

Le Lion d'Or, 69 Rue Georges Clemenceau.
02 54 94 15 15
A very luxurious Renaissance mansion serving great food. Prices are appropriately high.

SANCERRE

Auberge de la Pomme d'Or, 1 Rue Panneterie.
02 48 54 13 30
FAX 02 48 54 19 22
Wander through the old town to this inn, one of the Loire's most welcoming. The chef offers modern twists on local dishes, and the cellar is full of the *appellation*'s best wines.

TOURS

Hotel de l'Univers, 5 Boulevard Heurteloup.
02 47 05 37 12
A magnificent Belle Époque hotel with furniture to match. Ask for the room used by Winston Churchill.

Ancient and Modern
Restaurants in the Loire offer new vintages and very venerable ones.

WINE SHOPS

Many Loire wines are difficult to find back home, so it's a good idea to visit a wine shop here.

ORLÉANS

Cave Marc & Sébastien, 7 Place du Chatelet.
02 38 62 94 11
A truly recommendable shop whose owners are passionate about a wide range of wines, and eager to share their enthusiasm.

MUSEUMS

Some producers offer vineyard or winery tours. Contact tourist offices *(see below)* for details.

CHINON

Musée Animé du Vin et de la Tonnellerie, 4 Impasse du Docteur Gendron.
02 47 93 25 63
FAX 02 47 93 01 34
An inventive museum covering wine making and coopery.

LE PALLET

Le Musée du Vignoble Nantais, 82 Rue Abelard.
02 40 80 90 13
FAX 02 40 80 49 81
In the heart of Muscadet country, this museum boasts 1,000 wine-making tools, including some used nearly 500 years ago.

ST LAMBERT DU LATTAY

Le Musée de la Vigne et du Vin D'Anjou, Les Celliers de la Coudraye, Place des Vignerons.
02 41 78 42 75
The daily life of wine-makers over the years—and an exhibit called "l'Imaginaire du Vin," which uses smells and poetry.

SAUMUR

Le Musée Maxime Mabileau, Route de Montsoreau.
02 41 83 13 32
FAX 02 41 83 13 49
@ phc@gratienmeyer.com
A museum devoted to sparkling wine producer Gratien et Mayer, and Maxime Mabileau, who rose from the humblest ranks at the age of 13 to run the firm.

TOURS

Le Musée des Vins de Touraine, Cellier St-Julien, 16 Rue Nationale.
02 47 01 07 93
FAX 02 47 21 68 90
In the cellars of the 13th century Abbey of St-Julien, this is one of the most interesting and most wide-ranging wine museums in France. It is especially useful in revealing the historic importance of wine to this region—and vice versa.

OTHER LOCAL WINE MUSEUMS

Ecomusée du Pays de Vouvray, 30 Rue Victor Hérault, Vouvray.
02 47 52 60 61

Musée de la Vigne et du Vin, Lhomme.
02 43 44 43 62
FAX 02 43 44 67 66

Musée de la Vigne, 3 Rue Gustave Marc, Onzain.
02 54 20 78 52
W www.ville-onzain.fr

Musée de la Vigne et du Viticulteur, Château de Moncontour, Vouvray.
02 47 52 60 77
FAX 02 47 52 65 50
W www.moncontour.com
@ info@moncontour.com

WEBSITES

A few canny Loire Valley wine producers have registered their own private websites under generic-sounding *appellation* names. There is a(n excellent) site, for example, at www.vouvray.com, but it belongs to (and promotes) Château Moncontour. The following sites are also good, and independent: www.vins-valdeloire.com, www.sancerre.net, www.producteurs-de-saumur-champigny.fr, www.visaloire.com, www.saumurbrut.com, www.paysdelaloire.fr. If you are looking for more general tourist information, log on to www.tourisme.fr and type in the name of any town or village about which you would like to learn more.

ANNUAL WINE EVENTS

Every *appellation* in the Loire Valley has an annual fair at which it shows off its wines. The Foire de la Loire in Angers, held every year during the first week of February, offers the chance to taste wines from the entire region. For more information and dates of events, contact local tourist offices (see below).

JANUARY/FEBRUARY
Angers, **Azay-le-Rideau** and **Vouvray** wine fairs

FEBRUARY
Chalonnes wine fair

MARCH
Thouars, **Loudun**, **St-Nicolas-de-Bourgueil**, **Thouars**, and **Vihiers** wine fairs

MARCH/APRIL
Bourgueil and **Chinon** wine fairs

APRIL
Montlouis, **Reuilly**, and **Châteaumeillant** wine fairs

MAY
Saumur wine and book fair
Panzoult wine fair

JUNE
Sancerre and **Blois** wine fairs
Amboise wine fair in the Parc des Mini-Chateaux—tastings in a park full of miniature châteaux

JULY
Puy-Notre-Dame wine and food festival
St-Aubin-de-Luigne festival of wine and eels
Pouilly-sur-Loire, **St Nicolas-de-Bourgueil** and **Verdigny** wine fairs
Sancerre wine and jazz
St Lambert du Lattay wine and andouillette fair
St Lambert du Lattay promenade in the Coteaux du Layon

AUGUST
Quincy sea and wine fair
Menetou-Salon open doors
Saumur wine fair
Vouvray festival
Thouarcé Touraine-Amboise festival
Aubigne-sur-Layon festival of art, wine, and music
Bué en Sancerre sorcerer's fair (folklore galore)
Sancerre French wine festival
St-Pourçain-sur-Sioule wine fair

SEPTEMBER
Saumur, **Chacé**, and **Varrains** Fete du Champigny

OCTOBER
Chateau de Martigne-Briand Belle Epoque harvest festival
Romorantin Journeés Gastronomiques—food days

NOVEMBER
Montrichard Saumur-Champigny wine fair

NOVEMBER/DECEMBER
Coteaux du Giennois Foué Avaloue du St Père wine fair

OTHER INFORMATION

Office de Tourisme, 78 Rue Bernard-Palissy, Tours.
02 47 70 37 37
The region's main tourist office can help with a range of local information, whether you want wine tastings or a place to stay.

Comité Interprofessionel de Touraine, 19 Square Prosper-Mérimée, Tours.
02 47 05 40 01
Maisons du Vin across the region offer local guidance, but this is the place to come for wine information on the area as a whole.

ANJOU

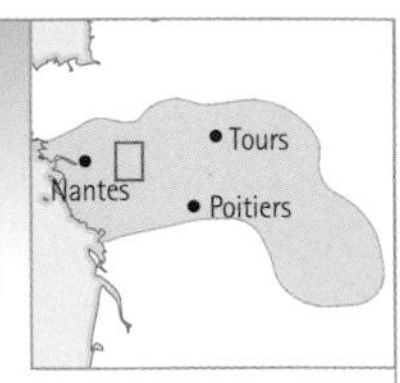

ROSÉ D'ANJOU, THE COMMERCIAL WINE sold cheaply in supermarkets throughout the world, may represent nearly half of the wine produced in Anjou, but it is not the wine by which the *appellation* should be judged. For fine examples of rosé wines, try the Cabernet d'Anjou, arguably the longest-lived rosé in the world, or the Rosé de Loire. Anjou's white wines are traditionally made from Chenin Blanc, to which Chardonnay or Sauvignon Blanc may now be added. This blending, plus a little aging in new oak, has brought some welcome roundness to what, in cool years, can be green wines. Anjou Coteaux de la Loire can provide an affordable taste of late-harvest Chenin Blanc, with Anjou-Gamay being a generally feeble alternative to Beaujolais *(see pp126–7)*. For superior reds, try Anjou Villages, whose reds offer rich, black-curranty flavors.

Château de la Genaiserie
Yves Soulez, the producer of this wine, is one of the best wine-makers in the Loire.

A Touch of Ceremony
The wine-makers in this part of the Loire Valley still make the most of every opportunity to celebrate their traditions.

- AC Anjou, AC Anjou Coteaux de la Loire, AC Anjou Gamay, AC Anjou Mousseux, AC Anjou Pétillant, AC Cabernet D'Anjou.
- Red/rosé: Cabernet Franc, Cabernet Sauvignon, Grolleau. White: Chenin Blanc, Chardonnay, Sauvignon Blanc.
- Medium-bodied reds. Crisp, dry whites. Medium-sweet rosés.
- Arnault et Fils, de Fesles, J-Y Lebreton. Gaudard, Genaiserie.
- Pike in butter and shallot sauce.
- Red: 2003, 2002, 1997, 1995.
- Red: 3–8 years.

BONNEZEAUX

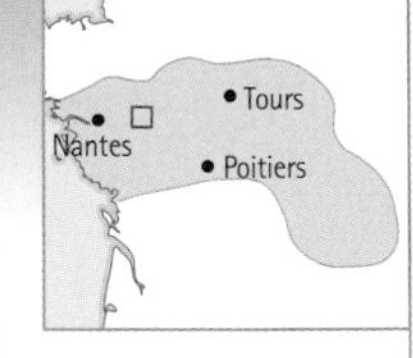

THE VINEYARDS OF THIS Coteaux du Layon *grand cru* face south on La Montagne, Beauregard, and des Fesles, three steep schist slopes bordering the Layon River. The only grape variety grown here is Chenin Blanc, which is often harvested in numerous pickings when botrytized. Yields here are low, with the minimum required ripeness for the grapes at harvest being higher than that of Sauternes *(see p110)*. In fact, grape-growers here have been known to pick absurdly ripe grapes with sugars equivalent to an alcoholic strength of up to 40 percent. At its best, Bonnezeaux is intensely sweet, with flavors of pineapple and licorice when young and a honeyed-vanilla complexity that develops with age. In recent years, many vines that were once abandoned have been replanted, expanding the *appellation* from 94 acres (38 ha) in 1979 to 198 acres (80 ha).

Mark Angeli
Not only is this one of the richest, sweetest, and most luscious wines of the Loire, it is also one of the world's best white wines.

Thouarcé
This fine windmill, overlooking the vines of Thouarcé, is the most recognized landmark in this region of France.

- AC Bonnezeaux Grand Cru.
- White: Chenin Blanc.
- Lusciously sweet, long-lived, ideally botrytized.
- Mark Angeli, Ch de Fesles, Gilardeau, Godineau, Grandes Vignes, la Petite Croix, Petits Parts, du Petit Val, René Renou, L&C Robin, de Trompe-Tonneau, la Varière.
- Grilled *foie gras* with truffles.
- 2003, 2002, 2001, 997, 1995, 1990, 1989, 1986, 1985, 1979.
- 5–15 years.

BOURGUEIL AND ST NICOLAS-DE-BOURGUEIL

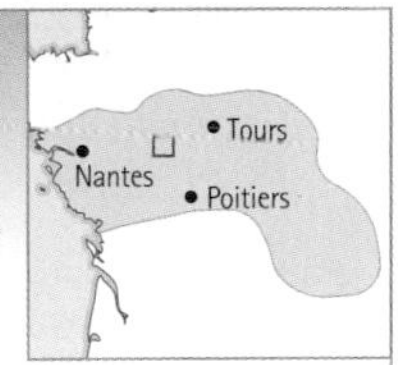

THE *APPELLATIONS* OF BOURGUEIL and St Nicolas-de-Bourgueil, located between Tours and Saumur, both claim that their wines have individual qualities. Renowned as some of the finest Cabernet Franc–based reds in the Loire, the difference between the two can be hard to discern. Bourgueil's vines are grown on either a sand and gravel plateau or on clay and tufa slopes, and its wines have a fruity character. On the higher slopes, the grapes ripen up to 10 days earlier than on the plateau, resulting in more complex wines. St Nicolas-de-Bourgueil's soil is sandier than that of Bourgueil and although its wines are lighter, they are just as good. A *coopérative* controls one third of the *communes* here, but methods vary, with some producers placing greater reliance than others on aging in wood.

Pierre-Jacques Druet
Pierre-Jacques Druet produces some of the best traditional wines of Bourgueil.

Ingrandes de Touraine
As is the case almost everywhere in the Loire Valley, Bourgueil has a wealth of prosperous châteaux and farms.

- AC Bourgueil, AC St Nicolas-de-Bourgueil.
- Red/rosé: Cabernet Franc, Cabernet Sauvignon.
- Fragrant, light reds; dry rosés.
- *Bourgueil*: Y. Amirault, Max Cognard, Delauney Druet. *St Nicolas-de-Bourgueil:* Y. Amirault, Max Cognard, Delauney Druet, F. Mabileau.
- Stuffed cabbage.
- Red: 2003, 2002, 2000, 1997, 1995, 1990, 1989.
- *Bourgueil:* 3–10 years. *St Nicolas-de-B.* 2–5 years.

CHÂTEAUMEILLANT

THIS AREA COVERS about 247 acres (100 ha) in the middle of France, around the town of Châteaumeillant and between St Pourçain and Touraine. The volcanic soil explains why, as in Beaujolais *(see pp126–7)*, Gamay is the most widely planted vine and why white wine is no longer made here. Other grapes used for red and rosé wines are Pinot Noir and Pinot Gris. The reds, though tannic, are fresh and best drunk young, but it is the light, fresh rosés that stand out.

Cave des Vins de Châteaumeillant
This rosé is light, fresh and berryish with a tannic backbone.

- VDQS Châteaumeillant.
- Red/rosé: Gamay, Pinot Noir, Pinot Gris.
- Dry, light, but firm reds. Dry, light rosés.
- Du Chaillot, Cave des Vins de Châteaumeillant, Cellier du Chêne-Combeau.
- Rosé: Cheese omelette.
- Red: 2003, 2002, 2000.
- Red: 2–5 years.

CHEVERNY AND COUR-CHEVERNY

THESE ARE TWO OF the first *appellations* heading west from Orléans to Blois. Cour-Cheverny's whites are made from Romorantin, which produces light, dry wines with a delicate, floral aroma. Cheverny's white wines, on the other hand, are made from Sauvignon, and have lively fruit and good balance. Both these and the region's red wines, made mainly from Gamay, are best drunk young.

François Cazin
This wine offers the chance to taste the flavor of the floral Romorantin variety.

- AC Cheverny, AC Cour-Cheverny.
- Red/rosé: Gamay. White: Sauvignon Blanc, Romorantin.
- Light reds. Crisp, dry whites. Dry rosés.
- Les Caves Bellier, François Cazin, de la Gaudronnière.
- Cour-Cheverny: Pike.
- White: 2002, 2001
- White: 1–3 years.

CHINON

THE TOWN AND FORTIFIED CASTLE of Chinon and its vineyards lie within a triangle formed at the merging of the Loire and Vienne rivers. Although the wine produced here was once quite often green and edgy with a rustic character, this *appellation* now produces some of the world's best examples of Cabernet Franc. Better wine-making skills have improved the average quality of Chinon's wines significantly, as has the gradual phasing out of the hard-to-ripen Cabernet Sauvignon grape variety. Most producers here age their wines in small barrels, although when over-oaked, the black-currant flavour, for which they are best known, can be lost. The rosés, rarely found outside Chinon, are also worth trying, as are the similarly rare Chenin Blanc dry whites.

Olga Raffault
There are several members of the Raffault family living in Chinon. The two names to look for are Olga and Jean-Maurice.

Clos de l'Echo
This vineyard, situated next door to the ruins of the Château de Chinon, produces some of the best wine in the *appellation.*

- AC Chinon.
- Red/rosé: Cabernet Franc. White: Chenin Blanc.
- Fragrant, medium-bodied reds. Dry, aromatic whites. Dry, light-bodied, fruity rosés.
- Philippe Alliet, Bernard Baudry, Couly-Dutheil, Delaunay, Ch de la Grille, Charles Joguet, Logis de la Bouchardière, du Raffault, Olga Raffault.
- Red: Veal casserole
- Red: 2003, 2002, 2000, 1997, 1995, 1990, 1989.
- Red: 5–10 years. White: 3–7 years.

COTEAUX DU LAYON

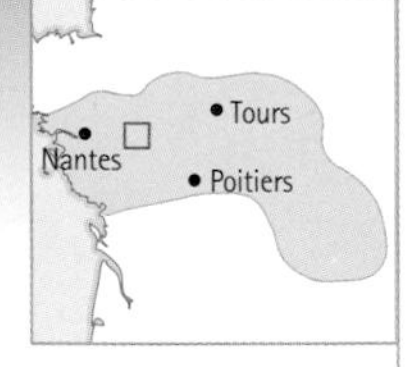

THE COTEAUX DU LAYON borders the Layon River from Neuil to Chalonnes and has been famous for its sweet white wines since the fourth century. While the Coteaux du Layon *appellation* covers whites made in 25 *communes* that overlap Anjou Coteaux de la Loire *(see p214)* and Saumur *(see p223)*, the area's best wines are made to tight regulations in Beaulieu, Faye, Lambert, Rablay, Rochefort, St Aubin, and St Lambert, seven villages that make up the *appellation* of Coteaux du Layon-Villages. These *communes* each have characters of their own, with Beaulieu making more delicate wines than Rablay. All Coteaux du Layon wines are produced from ultra-ripe grapes, harvested in numerous pickings. The best are produced by the one-village *appellation* of Coteaux du Layon-Chaume.

Domaine des Forges
Claude Branchereau, the owner of this estate, is one of the most quality-conscious producers in the Coteaux du Layon.

Château la Genaiserie
With its numerous chateâux and grand hotels, the Coteaux du Layon is a beautiful region of France to visit.

- AC Coteaux du Layon, AC Coteaux du Layon-Chaume, AC Coteaux du Layon-Villages.
- White: Chenin Blanc.
- Medium and sweet whites.
- P. Aguilas, P. Baudoin, des Baumard, du Breuil, Cady, Delesvaux, Forges, Godineau, Ogereau, Pierre Bise, Pithon, Ch la Plaisance, des Rochettes, de la Roulerie, des Sablonnettes, Soucherie, la Varière.
- Sweet: Apple tart.
- 2003, 2002, 2001, 1997, 1995, 1990, 1989, 1985, 1976.
- Sweet: 10–20 years.

HAUT-POITOU

IF THE *COOPÉRATIVE* AT NEUVILLE had not successfully promoted Diane de Poitiers, a *méthode traditionelle* wine, this *VDQS* might be almost unknown. Haut-Poitou covers about 1,730 acres (700 ha) of vineyards scattered across a wide, flat plain stretching south of Saumur *(see p223)*, down to Poitiers itself. In this dry, hot *appellation*, vines grow on limestone and marl soil and produce wines that in warm years are often characterized by their fruity flavors. Among the white wines produced here, Sauvignon Blanc was the first to attract attention. Today, its wines continue to be produced in the original floral style, with a light, crisp acidity. Haut-Poitou also makes reds and rosés from Pinot Noir, Gamay, Merlot, Malbec, and Cabernet Sauvignon.

Cave de Haut-Poitou
One of the most dynamic *coopératives* in France, this winery single-handedly created Haut-Poitou's good reputation.

Modern Times
The traditional vineyards here have been adapted to allow the use of modern equipment to harvest the grapes.

- VDQS Haut-Poitou.
- Red/rosé: Pinot Noir, Gamay, Merlot, Malbec, Cabernet Franc, Cabernet Sauvignon. White: Sauvignon Blanc, Chenin Blanc, Chardonnay.
- Light reds. Light, crisp still whites. Dry sparkling whites.
- R. Champalou (Ch de Brizlay), G. Descoux, Cave Haut-Poitou, J. Morgreau, de la Rôtisserie.
- White: *Port Salut* (cheese).
- White: 2002, 2001, 1998, 1997, 1995.
- Red: 1–4 years. White: 1–3 years.

JASNIÈRES

LIKE SAVENNIÈRES *(see p224)* and Vouvray *(see p226)*, this small, 119-acre (48-ha) *appellation* that lies within the Coteaux du Loire provides the perfect example of how the Chenin Blanc grape can be affected by the marginal climate of the Loire. In cooler years, its dry white wines are acidic enough to threaten to remove the enamel from your teeth. However, when the climate allows, the flavor of Jasnières' dry white wine can be a combination of flowers, nuts, honey, and apples, but with a steely, acidic backbone. Since the early 1990s, the wine-makers here have been making sweet, and even dry, botrytized wines in good years. These botrytized wines have a more instant appeal than more traditional Jasnières and have helped to maintain interest in this *appellation*.

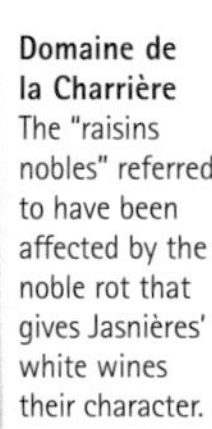

Domaine de la Charrière
The "raisins nobles" referred to have been affected by the noble rot that gives Jasnières' white wines their character.

Prime Position
As in other areas of France, Jasnières' vines are planted on slopes, while a variety of other crops are grown on the flatter land.

- AC Jasnières.
- White: Chenin Blanc.
- Steely, dry whites. Dry or sweet botrytized whites.
- Claude Cartereau, de Cezin, de la Charrière, Joël Gigou, Jean-Jacques Maillet, Renard-Potaire, Bénédicte de Rycke, des Vaux du Loire.
- Braised foreloin of pork with prunes.
- Sweet: 2002, 2001, 2000, 1997, 1996, 1995, 1994, 1993, 1990, 1989, 1985.
- Dry: 5–10 years. Sweet: 7–20 years.

MENETOU-SALON

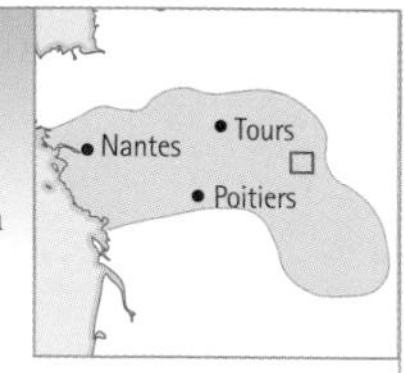

THE VINEYARDS OF Menetou-Salon lie between the city of Bourges and the vineyards of Sancerre *(see p222)* to the east. In just 40 years, the grape-growers of Menetou-Salon have expanded their vineyards from 50 acres (20 ha) in 1959 to 500 acres (200 ha) today. Menetou-Salon's wines (especially those from vineyards around Morogues) are often good alternatives to the average and lesser-quality wines of neighboring Sancerre. Most Menetou-Salon red wines are light, fruity, and best drunk young. Some of the best, however, are matured in oak barrels and age well. Menetou-Salon's white wines, on the other hand, are typical of Sauvignon Blanc, but tend to lose their initial floral appeal quite quickly, replacing it with an earthiness that makes fine, delicate whites a rare find.

Domaine Jean Teiller
Good Menetou-Salon like this competes directly with wines from the better-known regions of Sancerre and Pouilly Fumé.

Limestone Soil
The Sauvignon Blanc and Pinot Noir grapes grown in Menetou-Salon, near Morogues, owe their flavor to the limestone soil that is found here.

- AC Menetou-Salon.
- Red/rosé: Pinot Noir. White: Sauvignon Blanc.
- Light reds. Refreshing, crisp, dry whites. Dry rosés.
- De Beaurepaire, R Champault, Charet et Fils, de Chatenoy, P Clement, de Coquin, Fournier, J-P Gilbert, de Loye, H Pelle, Prieuré de St Céols, la Tour St Martin, J Teiller, C and G Turpin.
- White: Stuffed sole.
- White: 2002, 2002, 1997.
- Red: 2–5 years. White: 1–2 years. Rosé: 1 year.

MONTLOUIS

MONTLOUIS LIES ON the west bank of the Loire, directly opposite the *appellation* of Vouvray *(see p226)* and only a few miles east of the center of Tours. The vineyards of Montlouis slope south toward the Cher River and include the villages of Montlouis, Lussault, and St Martin-le-Beau. Once sold under the name of Vouvray, the white wines of Montlouis can be dry, medium-dry, or sweet. The only grape variety used here is Chenin Blanc, known as Pineau de la Loire. In this area, the soils are rich in flinty clays and are quite sandy, resulting in light wines with mineral overtones. As in Vouvray, the best wines produced in Montlouis are the sweet wines that are sold as AC Montlouis Moelleux and the slightly sparkling wines that are sold as AC Montlouis Pétillant.

Olivier Delétang
This producer makes some of the best and longest-lived examples of the subtly appealing Montlouis wines.

Small Estates
Unlike the good-quality wines produced in other *appellations*, most of Montlouis' best wines are made by small estates like this one.

- AC Montlouis.
- White: Chenin Blanc.
- Dry, medium, and sweet.
- C Boureau, P Benoit, des Chardonnerets, F Chidaine, de Cray, Laurent Chatenay, Olivier Delétang, Daniel Fisselle, Christian Galliot, Levasseur, des Liards, Patrick Marne, de la Milletière, Dominique Moyer, Ch de Pintray, la Taille aux Loups, des Tourterelles.
- Pike with butter sauce.
- Moelleux: 2003, 2001, 1999, 1997, 1995, 1990, 1989.
- 5–15 years.

MUSCADET

ONE OF THE BEST-KNOWN white wines in the world, Muscadet entered the 21st century confronting the very real prospect of being unfashionable and unwanted. Unlike wines such as the Chardonnays and Sauvignons that, for the moment, tend to occupy the spotlight, this is not a fruity or oaky white wine, but is instead fairly neutral in flavor.

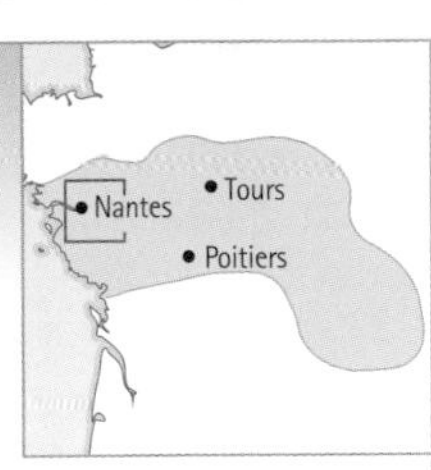

Small Is Beautiful
While big merchants blend and sell much of the wine produced in the *appellation* of Muscadet, there are many small estates that produce, bottle, and try—often with great difficulty—to sell their own wines.

Good Muscadet, like the oysters with which I like to drink it, comes my way all too rarely. The producers in this frost-prone region make their wine from Melon de Bourgogne, a relatively flavorless grape variety that bears none of the muskiness implied by the name Muscadet. This grape, of which the wine growers of Muscadet are so proud, is actually relatively new to the area. In the 17th century the wines made here would have been mostly thin, weedy, and acidic reds. However, when the vineyards were almost wiped out by frost in 1709, the Dutch merchants, who were the grape-growers' biggest customers, encouraged them to plant a second-rate variety from Burgundy. Known as Melon de Bourgogne, this variety could survive the cold weather. The neutral flavor of the wines made from the Melon de Bourgogne was of little concern to the producers. Initially, it was only ever going to be used to make cheap brandy.

Muscadet did, however, have one important distinction. The tradition of being bottled *sur lie,* while still in contact with its sediment, kept the wine fresh and gave it a slight spritz and yeasty roundness. In the mid-20th century, before the world became awash with good Chardonnay and Sauvignon, this tradition gave Muscadet a brief heyday of international popularity. Today, the availability of Chardonnay, Pinot Grigio, and Viognier from warmer regions has led to a Muscadet surplus—and the uprooting of vineyards here.

Muscadet should be bought *sur lie*. Of the four *appellations* available, basic Muscadet (not to be recommended) represents less than a fifth of the total production, the Coteaux de la Loire's wines are generally green and unripe, and the Côtes de Grandlieu, which was created in 1994, covers most of the wine that used to be sold as basic Muscadet. The one to look for is Sèvre-et-Maine—ideally from one of the producers listed below.

- AC Muscadet, AC Muscadet des Coteaux de la Loire, AC Muscadet Côtes de Grandlieu, AC Muscadet de Sèvre-et-Maine, AC Muscadet *sur lie.*
- White: Melon de Bourgogne.
- Steely, dry whites.
- Audouin, Donatieu Bahuand, de Beau-Lieu, de Beauregard, Gilbert Bossard, de la Botinerie, Chéreau-Carré, Ch du Cléray, de Contreaux, Gadais, Ch de la Galissonnière, de la Garnière, de Goulaine, de l'Hyvernière, des Jardins de la Menardière, Christian and Pascale Luncan, Michel Luncan, Métaireau, Clos du Moulin, Ch l'Oiselinière de la Rameé, de la Preuille, de la Ragotière, Dominique and Vincent Richard, Clos St Vincent des Rongères, Sauvion.
- Oysters on the shell.
- 2004.
- 0–2 years.

Château l'Oiselinière de la Ramee
One of a range of excellent wines produced by Domaines Chéreau-Carré, this is a great example of how Muscadet ought to taste: dry, with a refreshing slight fizz and some richness.

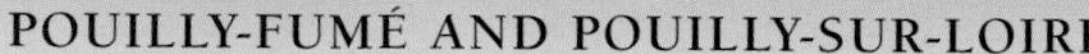

POUILLY-FUMÉ AND POUILLY-SUR-LOIRE

FIRMLY IDENTIFIED WITH the Sauvignon Blanc grape, the *"fumé"* in Pouilly-Fumé describes the wine's somewhat elusive, smoky, gun-flint flavor, brought out by the flinty chalk of the best vineyards in the *appellation*. Wines sold under the less prestigious Pouilly-sur-Loire label are made from the Chasselas grape.

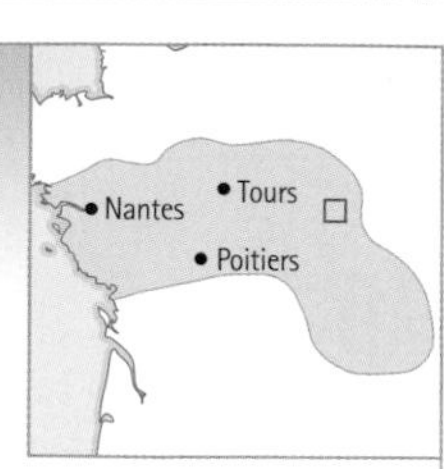

Château du Nozet de Ladoucette
The fairy-tale towers of the Château du Nozet de Ladoucette provide a dramatic contrast to the humble appearance of many other *domaines* in the *appellation* of Pouilly-Fumé.

An area of gently sloping vineyards situated on the eastern bank of the Loire, today the *appellation* of Pouilly-Fumé is most strongly associated with the Sauvignon Blanc grape. Surprisingly, however, it was not until the late 19th century, when widespread replanting of vines became necessary as a result of damage caused by the phylloxera louse, that this variety was grown here at all. Until then, the vineyards here were planted almost exclusively with Chasselas, a popular, sweet table grape traditionally considered to have a great affinity with the soils of the area. With floral aromas and low acidity, the still and sparkling wines made from these grapes are often tired and flabby, and as a result are fast becoming an endangered species. In 1997, only 300,000 bottles of Chasselas wine were produced here, compared to the 7.75 million bottles made from Sauvignon Blanc. Wines made here from Chasselas are sold as *appellation contrôlée* Pouilly-sur-Loire, which covers the same geographical area as the exclusively Sauvignon Blanc *appellation* of Pouilly-Fumé.

The much-vaunted smoky flavor of the wines of Pouilly-Fumé is, in truth, a characteristic specifically associated with wines made from grapes grown in the flinty soil of the *appellation*'s best vineyards. Another arguable piece of received wisdom is that the best wines here have more depth and structure than those of Sancerre *(see p222)* on the opposite bank of the Loire. This may occasionally be true, but more often the wines of the two *appellations* are hard to tell apart.

Some of Pouilly's best examples are made by the innovative producer Didier Dagueneau. By fermenting in new oak, he produces crisp wines with a hint of vanilla, many of which age extremely well. His experimental, late-harvest wines are also fine, but, needless to say, they are not well regarded by the narrow-minded local authorities.

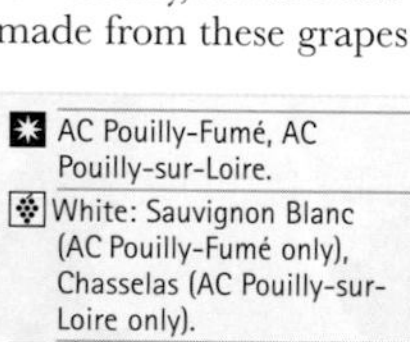

AC Pouilly-Fumé, AC Pouilly-sur-Loire.

White: Sauvignon Blanc (AC Pouilly-Fumé only), Chasselas (AC Pouilly-sur-Loire only).

Crisp, dry whites with smoky grape flavors.

Des Berthiers, Bouchié-Chatellier, Henri Bourgeois, Cailbourdin, Chatelain, Patrick Coulbois, Didier Dagueneau, Jean-Claude Dagueneau, Marc Deschamps, Ch Favray, des Fines Caillottes, Pascal Jolivet, Masson-Blondelet, Joseph Mellot, Ch du Nozet, Roger Pabiot, Caves de Pouilly-sur-Loire, Raimbault-Pineau, Guy Saget, Yvon et Pascal Tabordet, Thibault, Ch de Tracy.

Trout grilled with lemon juice and toasted almonds.

2002, 2001, 2000.

1–4 years.

Château de Ladoucette
This may not be the best wine in Pouilly-Fumé, but it is one of the most reliable. The same estate's Baron de L is finer—and both rarer and decidedly pricier.

QUARTS-DE-CHAUME

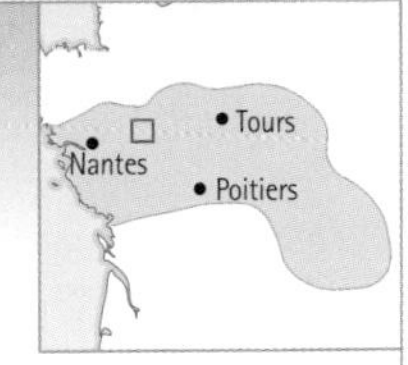

THE GREAT, SWEET WHITE wine *appellation* of Quarts-de-Chaume, on the banks of the Layon tributary, is a tiny plateau of vines in the middle of the much larger Coteaux du Layon *appellation (see p216)*. Occupying around 100 acres (40 ha) of gravelly clay slopes around the village of Chaume, only 100,000 bottles of Quarts-de-Chaume are produced here each year, from very ripe, mainly botrytized, Chenin Blanc grapes. The southern exposure of the vineyards, combined with careful harvesting and a high proportion of old vines, produces low yields of extremely high quality. Lighter and slightly dryer than the wines of nearby Bonnezeaux *(see p214)*, the wines of Quarts-de-Chaume make attractive drinking when young, but after 10 years in the cellar they will develop inimitable and gloriously complex flavors of beeswax, honey, and spice.

Château Bellerive
This is a serious wine that is a pleasure to drink young, but will be even better after a decade of maturation in the cellar.

Waiting Game
Producers in Quarts-de-Chaume must wait patiently for the late-harvest, often botrytized Chenin Blanc grapes that give their rich, sweet flavors to the wines of the *appellation*.

- AC Quarts-de-Chaume.
- White: Chenin Blanc.
- Long-lasting sweet whites, from botrytized grapes.
- Ch. des Baumard, de Bellerive, de la Bergerie, Pierre Bise, de l'Echarderie, de Laffourcade, des Maurières, Papin, du Petit Metris, de Plaisance, Joseph Renou, de la Roche Moreau, de Suronde.
- *Foie gras.*
- 2003, 2001, 1999, 1997, 1995, 1990, 1989, 1976.
- 10–20 years.

QUINCY

UNLIKE IN NEIGHBORING Reuilly *(see right)* and Menetou-Salon *(see p218)*, the vineyards of Quincy, on the western bank of the Auron tributary, are planted exclusively with Sauvignon Blanc. This is a white-only *appellation* and its wines can offer a good-value alternative to those of Sancerre *(see p222)* or Pouilly-Fumé *(see left)*. Despite promising sandy-flint soils, wines here can be green and acidic. Good examples, however, made from old, low-yielding vines, are well worth buying.

Jean-Michel Sorbe
This producer's wines are often similar to those of Sancerre, and just as good.

- AC Quincy.
- White: Sauvignon Blanc.
- Crisp, dry whites.
- Des Ballandors, Godinat, Mardon, Grand Rosières, Jacques Rouzé, Jean-Michel Sorbe.
- Omelet fried in butter with goat's cheese, fresh chives, and tarragon.
- 2002, 2001.
- 1–3 years.

REUILLY

ALL THREE STYLES of wine, red, white, and rosé, are produced from grapes grown on the 75 acres (30 ha) of limestone-rich soils that make up the *appellation* of Reuilly. Whites, made from Sauvignon Blanc, are dry with flavors of grass and nettles. Rosés are distinctive and dry, made from Pinot Gris, while light, fruity reds are made from a blend of Pinot Noir and Pinot Gris. There are bargains here, especially among the reds and rosés, but poorly made efforts tend to be overly acidic.

Reuilly
Best within a year or so of the harvest, white Reuilly is simple and refreshing.

- AC Reuilly.
- Red/rosé: Pinot Noir, Pinot Gris. White: Sauvignon Blanc.
- Light, fruity reds. Crisp, dry whites. Dry, light-bodied rosés.
- Bigonneau, Lafond, Grandes Rosières, Jean-Michel Sorbe.
- Fresh oysters with lime.
- White: 2002, 2001.
- White: 1–3 years.

SANCERRE

SET ON A ROCKY outcrop, the ancient town of Sancerre keeps watch over the vineyards of the *appellation* below. Stretching along the western bank of the Loire to the north of its confluence with the Allier, Sancerre is now world-famous for its dry, aromatic white wines, but the area was well known for excellent red wines as early as the 12th century.

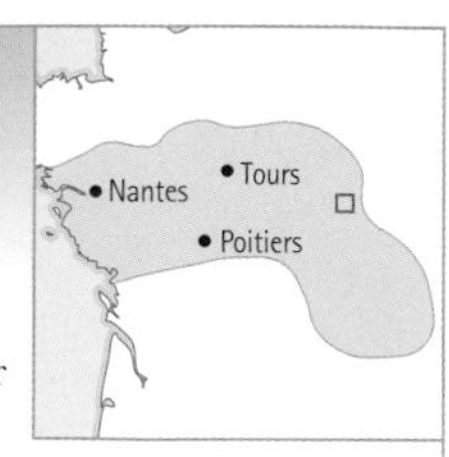

Perfectly situated
In all but the coldest years, Sauvignon Blanc vines flourish in the limestone and gravel soils of the Sancerre hillsides, producing classic wines that are full of the flavors of gooseberries and flint.

Wine has been made in the area around the town of Sancerre for many hundreds of years. One local legend suggests that when the church of St. Martin was rebuilt during a drought in 1040, the mortar was mixed with wine rather than water. By the 13th century, the wine of Sancerre was being praised in poetry as worthy of the royal table. Three hundred years later, King Henri IV declared that the wine of the village of Chavignol, a few miles northwest of Sancerre, was the best he had ever drunk and that its general consumption would bring an end to the currently raging religious wars. This method of pacification is sadly untestable today, however, as the Sancerre enjoyed by Henri IV was almost certainly a deeply colored red, made from a combination of Pinot Noir and Gamay grapes, very different from the much lighter red wines produced in Sancerre today. The first written reference to white Sancerre appears as late as 1816, and the preferred grape for white wine at that time was the sweet-tasting but undistinguished Chasselas. Sancerre as we know it today, made from Sauvignon Blanc, is a product of the *appellation contrôlée* system established in 1935. It was not until 1959 that red wines made from Pinot Noir were included in the *appellation.*

Today the limestone and gravel vineyards of the *appellation* are used to produce some of the finest examples of Sauvignon Blanc in the world. Unfortunately, overcropping and under-ripening also result in large amounts of thin, miserable white wine that is sold far too easily throughout the world. With 16 villages and 440 producers, sorting the good wines from the bad would be easier if Sancerre were to name its best villages and vineyards with a *crus classés* system similar to that in place in Beaujolais *(see pp126–7).* As in the neighboring *appellation* of Pouilly-Fumé *(see p220)*, some interesting experiments have been made here with sweet, late-harvest white wines. Red and rosé Sancerre wines sell well, especially in classy restaurants, but rarely stand comparison with good Pinot Noir produced elsewhere.

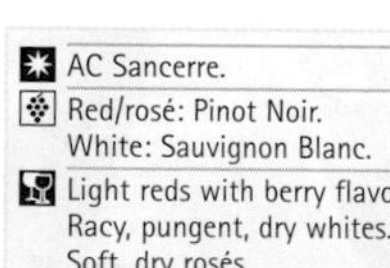

AC Sancerre.

Red/rosé: Pinot Noir.
White: Sauvignon Blanc.

Light reds with berry flavors. Racy, pungent, dry whites. Soft, dry rosés.

Sylvain Bailly, Jean-Paul Balland, Henri Bourgeois, Cotat, Lucien Crochet, Vincent Delaporte, André Dezat, de la Garenne, Gitton, les Grands Groux, Pascal Jolivet, Serge Laporte, Alphonse Mellot, Thierry Merlin-Cherrier, Paul Millerioux, de Montigny, Roger Neveu, du Nozay, Vincent Pinard, Hippolyte Reverdy, Jean-Max Roger, de Saint-Romble, des Trois Noyers, Vacheron, André Vatan.

White: Grilled salmon steaks with a sauce made from fish stock, cream, and crayfish.

White: 2004, 2002, 2001.

White: 1–4 years.

Vincent Pinard
The reliable and innovative producer Vincent Pinard offers characterful individual *cuvées* of the wines he makes in Sancerre.

SAUMUR

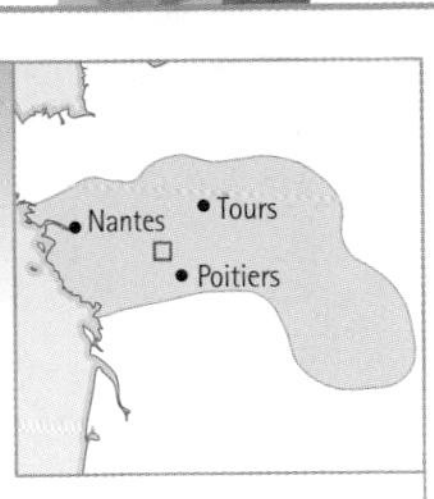

PART OF THE LARGER *APPELLATION* of Anjou, Saumur, also known as the "pearl of Anjou," produces still red, white, and rosé wines, as well as sparkling whites and rosés. Much less well known than sparkling Saumur, the red wines of the *appellation* range from light, fruity Saumur *rouge* to full-bodied, fragrant Saumur-Champigny, the hidden treasure of the *appellation*.

The chalky tufa soils to the south of the town of Saumur are home to Cabernet Franc and Cabernet Sauvignon vines. These are used to produce fresh, light, Beaujolais-style red wines rarely seen outside France, which are sold as red *appellation contrôlée* Saumur. To the east of the town, on the gravelly limestone soil around the confluence of the Loire and Vienne rivers, are the Cabernet Franc vineyards of the Saumur-Champigny *appellation*. These provide some of the Loire Valley's best red wines, as good as or better than the classic wines of nearby Chinon *(see p216)*, Bourgueil *(see p215)*, and St Nicolas de Bourgueil *(see p215)*. The popularity of this wine has led to a huge increase in production and price. There are now more than 10 million bottles of Saumur-Champigny produced every year, and the concentration of flavor and general quality is very variable. For this reason, proceed carefully when buying.

Keeping warm
Oil burners are a necessary feature of the vineyards in Saumur, protecting the vines against hazardous frost.

The cool climate and chalky soils of the *appellation* make this ideal sparkling-wine territory. The white and rosé sparkling wines of Saumur are far better known than the region's reds, and are a popular, if not always reliable, alternative to Champagne, which is invariably pricier. The wines of the two *appellations contrôlées*, Saumur Mousseux and Saumur Pétillant, are made largely from the Chenin Blanc, giving them an aromatic flavor of apples and nuts. This differs from the yeasty flavors of the Chardonnay- and Pinot Noir-dominated wines of Champagne, though the recent addition of Chardonnay grapes to Saumur's sparkling wines has given them a much more Champagne-like flavor. The popularity of both *appellations* is diminishing, however, as producers turn to making wines sold under the generic but more prestigious Crémant de Loire *appellation*.

Made, like the sparkling wines, mainly from Chenin Blanc grapes, the still whites of Saumur are often decidedly undistinguished, with a tendency to taste thin and acidic. A notable exception to this are the semisweet *appellation contrôlée* Coteaux de Saumur late-harvest wines. Full-bodied and deliciously rich, these wines are rare but, at their best, well worth seeking out.

- AC Saumur, AC Saumur-Champigny, AC Cabernet de Saumur, AC Coteaux de Saumur, AC Saumur Mousseux, AC Saumur Pétillant.
- Red: Cabernet Franc, Cabernet Sauvignon. White: Chenin Blanc, Chardonnay.
- Fruity light reds. Dry, still whites. Dry sparkling whites.
- Ackerman, du Bois Mozé, de Bonneveaux, du Caillou, Cave des Vignerons de Saumur, Clos des Cordeliers, Yves Drouineau, Filliatreau, de la Guilloterie, Hospices de Saumur, du Hureau, Joseph, Langlois-Château, René-Noël Legrand, Roches Neuves, Clos Rougeard, Ch de Targé, Ch de Villeneuve.
- Red: Roast goose with chestnut stuffing.
- Red: 2004, 2003, 2002, 1999.
- Red: 2–10 years. White: 1–3 years.

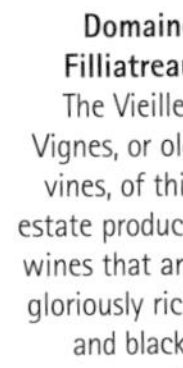

Domaine Filliatreau
The Vieilles Vignes, or old vines, of this estate produce wines that are gloriously rich and black-curranty.

SAVENNIÈRES

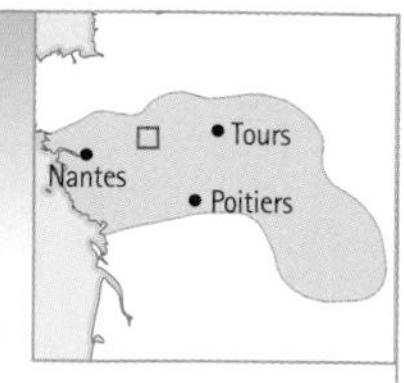

FAMOUS SINCE THE 18th and 19th centuries, when it was a popular sweet white wine, Savennières is now one of the world's most extraordinary dry whites. It is also one of the best examples of the ability of the Chenin Blanc grape to be both ripe and fiercely acidic at the same time. The vineyards of Savennières face southeast across the Loire River to Rochefort, just south of Angers. The mineral intensity of Savennières' wines is attributed to the volcanic debris that lies beneath the soil, while the concentration of their flavor is due to the low yield, one of the smallest of any *appellation*. When young, the combination of honey and tart cooking apples in Savennières deters many modern drinkers, but drink it with creamy food after five years or so and it will live up to its reputation as the world's greatest Chenin Blanc.

Domaine de Closel
Dry Savennières is, for many, the ultimate expression of the appley, honeyed, nutty character of the Chenin Blanc grape.

Coulée-de-Serrant
Nicolas Joly uses biodynamic methods *(see below)* to farm his vines in this beautiful riverside site, where he produces some of the region's best wines.

- AC Savennières.
- White: Chenin Blanc.
- Long-lived, acidic, dry whites.
- Des Barres, des Baumard, Benon, la Bizolière, de Chamboureau, Clos Rougeard, de Closel, Coulée-de-Serrant, Emile, d'Epire, la Franchaie, Laffourcade, aux Moines, Pierre-Bise, de Plaisance, Roche- aux-Moines, P. Soulez, de Varennes.
- Salmon in *beurre blanc* sauce.
- 2002, 2001, 2000, 1997, 1995, 1990, 1989, 1985.
- 10–20 years.

SAVENNIÈRES GRANDS CRUS

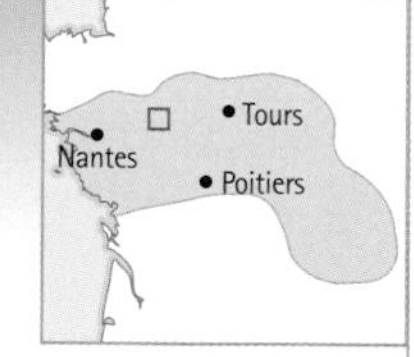

THESE TWO SMALL *GRANDS CRUS* within the *appellation* of Savennières have attracted a cult following for lovers of Chenin Blanc. The three producers all battle against naturally low yields that are further jeopardized by the risk of frost. Nicolas Joly, who owns Coulée-de-Serrant *(see above)* and vineyards in Roche-aux-Moines, is raising the odds by tending his vines and producing his wines according to the strictest biodynamic rules. The procedures, which include timing vineyard work in accordance with phases of the moon and treating the soil with small doses of manure that has been stored in a cow's horn, are, predictably, often mocked. However, this has not deterred Joly and his fellow believers, like Lalou Bize-Leroy of Domaine Leroy in Burgundy, whose wines are good enough to silence the mockery.

Château de Chambourea
At its finest, *grand cru* Savennières like this is one of the most complex, long-lived white wines in the world.

Roche-aux-Moines
The Chenin Blancs of Roche-aux-Moines and Coulée-de-Serrant are complex, honeyed, floral yet mineral wines that go brilliantly with rich fish dishes like salmon.

- AC Savennières Roche-aux-Moines; AC Savennières Coulée-de-Serrant.
- White: Chenin Blanc.
- Long-lived, bone-dry whites with great complexity.
- Coulée-de-Serrant, aux Moines, Ch de la Roche-aux-Moines, Ch de Chamboureau.
- Trout cooked in a foil parcel and served with new potatoes and peas.
- 2002, 2001, 2000, 1997, 1995, 1990, 1989, 1985.
- 10–20 years.

TOURAINE

THE LOIRE REGION COVERS A WIDE RANGE of landscapes as it stretches westward to the sea, and the Touraine *appellation* lies at its heart. Within its borders are examples of most of the reds and the dry and sweet white wines that are produced in the Loire. Between tastings, the spectacular châteaux of this attractive *appellation* are well worth taking time out to visit.

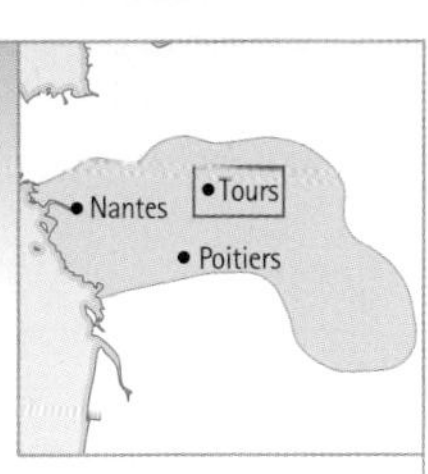

Le Château d'Azay le Rideau
The grandeur and beauty of this famous château reflects the historic importance of this region and its prestige at the royal court. Azay le Rideau is one of France's most breathtaking châteaux, though it faces fierce competition in this area.

Despite the presence of all kinds of other agriculture competing for space, the Touraine *appellation* is huge, producing some 40 million bottles of red, white, and rosé wines. These are made primarily from Gamay, Sauvignon Blanc, and Chenin Blanc, but also from Cabernet Franc and Cabernet Sauvignon, Malbec and Pinots Noir, Meunier and Gris, Grolleau and Pineau d'Aunis. Chardonnay is also present, but its use has been restricted since 1994. Wines range from excellent Sauvignons and Cabernet Francs to dull Chenin Blancs and Gamays that taste as though they were lucky to make it into a bottle—the name of the producer here is crucial. *Coopératives* like Oisly et Thésée and the Cellier Léonard de Vinci in Limeray do well, as do a number of good merchants like Aimé Boucher and Bougrier.

Finer wines are supposedly produced under three separate Touraine *appellations*: Touraine-Mesland, Touraine-Amboise, and Touraine Azay-le-Rideau. In practice, everything here depends on the producer, but visitors to the region will be so dazzled by the beauty of the châteaux and the landscape that they will probably forgive all kinds of faults.

Touraine Azay-le-Rideau produces light-dry and semi-sweet Chenin Blancs and good Malbec and Gamay-based rosés. For red wines, head to Touraine-Mesland, where the reds are dominantly Cabernet Franc and have more character and body than those of Touraine-Amboise. The white wines of both these *appellations* are best avoided in all but the ripest vintages.

Other styles that are worth looking for here are Touraine Pétillant and Touraine Mousseux. The sparkling and semi-sparkling whites and rosés are good value when well made, but the real curiosities are the black-curranty Cabernet Francs, made in Chinon *(see p216)*, Bourgueil and St Nicolas de Bourgueil *(see p215)*.

AC Touraine, AC Touraine-Amboise, AC Touraine Azay-le-Rideau, AC Touraine-Mesland, AC Touraine Mousseux, AC Touraine Pétillant.

Red/rosé: Gamay, Cabernet Franc, Malbec, Pinot Noir, Pineau d'Aunis.
White: Chenin Blanc, Sauvignon Blanc.

Light, often fruity reds. Light, dry whites. Dry or medium rosés. Sparkling reds, whites and rosés.

Bellevue, de la Besnerie, Paul Buisse, la Chapelle de Cray, de la Briderie, les Corbillières, de la Gabillière, Henry Marionnet, Moncontour, Octavie, Oisly et Thésée, Oudin Frères.

White: St Marcellin cheese

White: 2002, 2001, 2000.

Red: 3–8 years.
White: 1–4 years.
Rosé: 1–2 years.

Domaine Bellevue
Fresh and tangy, this Sauvignon has the refreshing bite of wine that is produced from this variety in a cool climate.

VOUVRAY

IF ONE *APPELLATION* IN THE LOIRE had to be chosen to demonstrate the extraordinarily varied potential of the Chenin Blanc, it would be Vouvray. While sweet, dry, and sparkling wines may be made in other parts of the Loire, only Vouvray can produce all three quite so well and, at the same time, demonstrate the aging potential of the Chenin Blanc.

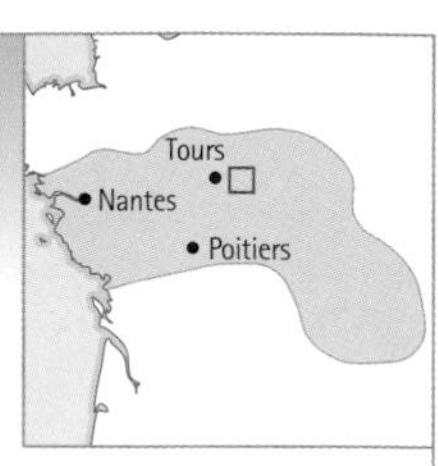

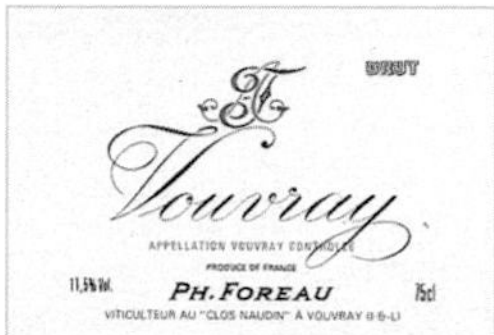

Philippe Foreau
Philippe Foreau is, unarguably, one of Vouvray's top three wine-makers. His estate, Domaine du Clos, is definitely a name to look for.

Few wine regions anywhere have given me more, and less, pleasure than these vineyards on the northern bank of the Loire River. Vouvray has produced extraordinarily old sweet wines that have glorious flavors of apples, honey, and praline, as well as aggressive young wines that are packed full of surplus sulfur dioxide and tooth-stripping acidity. There is nothing new about the minefield character of Vouvray; as the British author Roger Voss points out, Dutch merchants routinely blended other wine into Vouvray from the 15th to the 19th centuries and, during the early 20th century, the Loire grape growers casually used the *appellation*'s name on wines from vineyards scattered throughout other parts of Touraine.

In the 1960s and 1970s, Vouvray was consigned to the role of being the French semidry alternative to poor-quality German wines. Thankfully, in the 1990s, a run of good vintages and the success of quality-conscious producers like the Domaines Huët and des Aubuisières and Clos Naudin have led to a huge improvement in the quality of Vouvray. Most observers tend to focus on its sweet wines that, like any wines that are late-harvested, are the most seductive and long-lived. However, I must confess to being more fascinated by the semidry and dry wines that walk the tightrope between richness and acidity. Fine examples of either style can be complex wines, full of floral and nutty flavors. Be warned when buying Vouvray that many of its wines make no mention on the label of their level of sweetness. As one wine-maker explained to me, "customers prefer to drink semidry wine, but they like to fool themselves that it is dry." Although the quality of Vouvray Mousseux does vary, a well-made example is smooth and creamy.

Winter in the Clos Baudoin
The weather during the period between harvesting the grapes for the late-picked, sweet wines and the budding of the next year's crop can be very tough both on the vines and on the people who tend them.

- AC Vouvray, AC Vouvray Mousseux, AC Vouvray Pétillant.
- White: Chenin Blanc, Arbois.
- Dry-sweet still whites.Dry sparkling whites. Dry-sweet semisparkling whites.
- Des Aubuisières, Bourillon D'Orléans, Marc Brédif, Didier Champalou, Gagneux, Ch Gaudrelle, Huët, Daniel Jarry, Bernard Mabille, Francis Mabille, Vincent Peltier, Clos Baudoin, Pichot, Vaugondy.
- Chicken braised in milk and stock.
- Moelleux: 2003, 2001, 1999, 1997, 1995, 1990, 1989, 1985.
- Still dry: 5–20 years. Still sweet: 7–30 years. Sparkling: 1–3 years. Semisparkling: 0–1 year.

Domaine Huët
The sparkling and still wines of this estate are skillfully produced using strictly organic methods.

OTHERS

As well as the "big name" wines covered on previous pages, the Loire also offers a large number of smaller *appellation* and *VDQS* wines that cover a wide range of styles. Often overlooked by people outside the region itself, these wines are discovered with much delight by visitors, who soon learn to appreciate their fresh, characterful flavors.

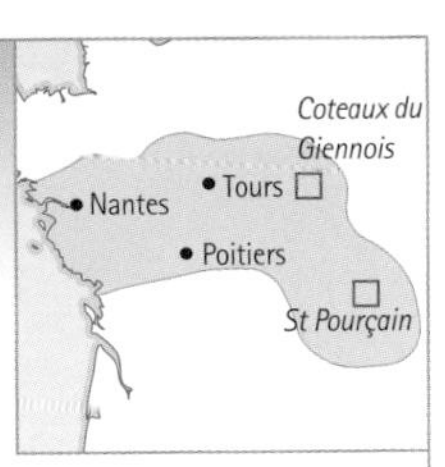

Small Is Beautiful
While there are many large estates in France, most of the vineyards in this region are quite small and are often tended by local farmers who have other crops.

Of the other wines from the Loire, Gros Plant, made from a naturally acidic grape called the Folle Blanche, deserves a passing glance—but that's about all. Although this wine is perfectly acceptable on the Atlantic coast as an accompaniment to seafood dishes when it is well made, young, and preferably bottled *sur lie*, it is not a wine that I would travel too far to drink.

Wines labeled as Rosé de Loire are dry and made from the Cabernet Franc or Sauvignon, Pineau d'Aunis, Grolleau, or Gamay grapes, grown anywhere within the *appellations* of Anjou *(see p214)*, Saumur *(see p223)*, or Touraine *(see p225)*. Not surprisingly, it varies in both style and quality and should be bought with care. Crémant de Loire comes from the same areas as Cheverny *(see p215)*. Wines that carry this label can be white or, sometimes, rosé and are made from grapes that include the Chenin Blanc, Chardonnay, Pinot Noir, Cabernet Franc, and Cabernet Sauvignon.

Mostly known for its light and usually unmemorable reds made from the Gamay, the Coteaux d'Ancenis is a small 740-acre (300-ha) *VDQS* region that also makes inexpensive, and generally similarly unremarkable, wines from the Chenin Blanc, Cabernet Franc and the Pinot Gris, which is known here as the Malvoisie.

Elevated to *appellation contrôlée* status in 1998, the Coteaux du Giennois is a small but growing region of some 370 acres (150 ha) yielding Gamay, Sauvignon Blanc, and Pinot Noir grape varieties. The limestone and silex soil here results in quite serious, if shortish-lived wines.

If a long history has any value, on the other hand, St Pourçain ought to be an *appellation* wine rather than a *VDQS*. Grapes were, after all, first planted here by the Phoenicians in around 1100 BC. The red and the rosé wines are both juicy blends of the Gamay and Pinot Noir grapes, while the dry, grassy white wines are a combination of Chardonnay, Sauvignon Blanc, and the local Tressalier. I predict its elevation to *appellation contrôlée* status before too long.

Other light, Gamay-based wines worth drinking young, and while in the region, are those labeled Côtes du Forez, Châteaumeillant, Côtes d'Auvergne, and Côtes Roannaises. Also of interest are the red wines of the Coteaux du Vendômois. These reds show how wines made mainly from the Pineau d'Aunis can be strengthened and improved by blending with the Gamay or Cabernet Franc.

Les Vignerons Foreziens
This Côtes du Forez estate is one of the very few wine producers to concentrate on the Gamay grape.

PROVENCE AND CORSICA

Provence and Corsica

Among the oldest of France's wine regions, Provence and Corsica have the potential to produce a wealth of wines that are packed with the flavor of the sun.

Sea View
Corsica's wines might not be as famous as those from some other regions, but few could ask for better weather or more breathtaking views of the Mediterranean.

Order a bottle of Provençal rosé in a Parisian restaurant, and you are likely to be presented with a dull, copper-colored wine with about as much freshness as last week's newspaper. Provence does make good wines, but the problem is, people claim, that they just don't travel very well. In reality, as any experienced wine-maker will tell you, a well-produced wine can be carried around the world without suffering any ill effects. Take, for example, all the Australian wines that are enjoyed in countries like Canada, thousands of miles away. The thing that does genuinely suffer from travel sickness and jet lag is our memory. Unexceptional wines that we enjoyed in a little café at the edge of the beach on a sunny, carefree day in Provence simply lose their allure when they are set in the harsher reality of a winter evening in the city.

According to historical records, the wines of Provence appear to have traveled more successfully when the Romans carried them home in *amphorae*. However, those wines, like the region's best today, were almost certainly red. Provence's famous rosé is a relatively modern invention, and most of it is deserving of the contempt with which it is treated. If you want to enjoy wines that really exploit the full potential of this glorious region, head for *appellations* like Bandol *(see p234)*, Cassis *(see p235)*, Palette *(see p236)*, and Coteaux d'Aix-en-Provence *(see p235)*, and the village of Les Baux-de-Provence, within that last *appellation*.

In wine-making, as in so many other things, Corsica seems to be much farther from the rest of France than the 105-mile (170-km) sea journey might lead one to expect. Towns with names like Ajaccio and Porto-Vecchio and estates called Catarelli and Torraccia reveal a strong Italian influence here that also extends to the flavor of the island's wines. In many ways, Corsica seems to have more in common with the Italian islands of Sardinia and Sicily than with the French mainland. Nielluccio, for example, the most widely planted grape variety in Corsica, is actually a close cousin of the Sangiovese of Italy's Chianti region.

REGIONAL OVERVIEW

- 54,000 acres (22,000 ha): 165 million bottles.
- Despite occasional variations caused by the proximity of the Mediterranean, the climate here is generally very warm in both summer and winter. Dry conditions can be a problem for the vines.
- Varied, including granite, sandstone, and occasional outcrops of limestone and flint.
- Red: Nielluccio, Syrah, Grenache, Mourvèdre, Cinsault, Carignan, Sciacarello, Barbarossa.
  White: Ugni Blanc, Grenache.

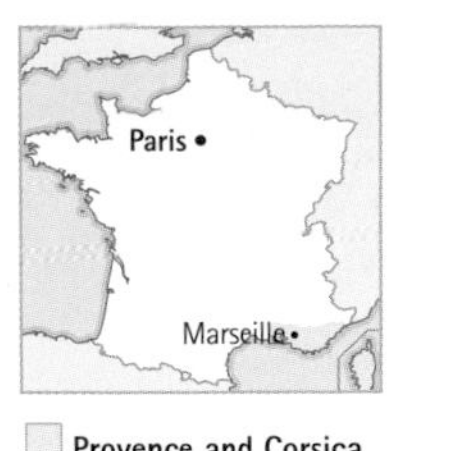

Provence and Corsica regions

KEY

- Ajaccio
- Bandol
- Bellet
- Cassis
- Coteaux d'Aix-en-Provence
- Coteaux Varois
- Côtes de Provence
- Muscat du Cap Corse
- Palette
- Patrimonio
- Vin de Corse
- *Département* boundary

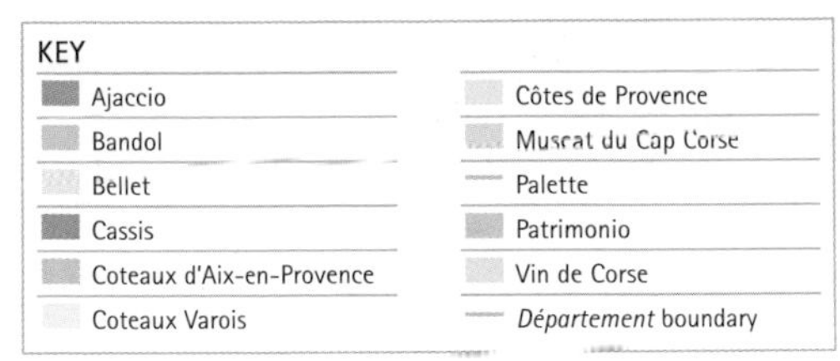

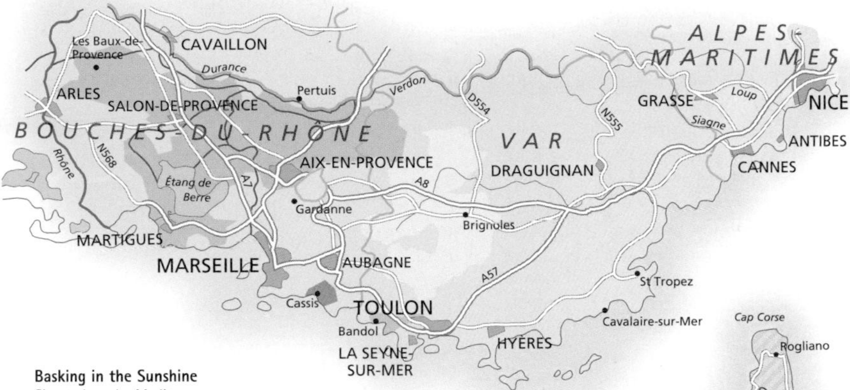

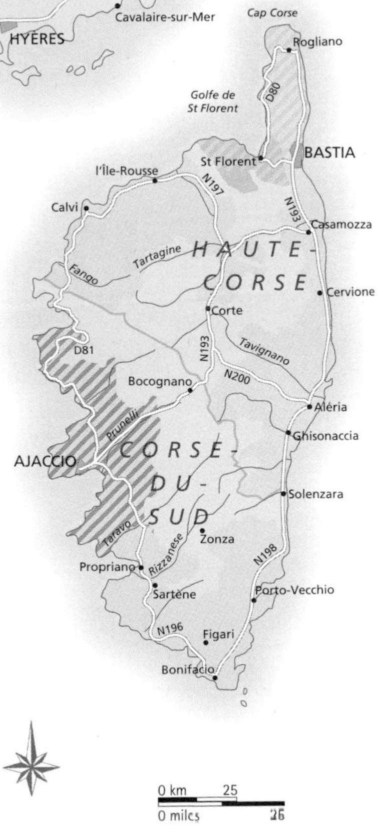

Basking in the Sunshine
Situated on the Mediterranean coast, Provence enjoys a sun-soaked climate similar to that of Corsica, the aptly named Ile de Beauté, which lies just 105 miles (170 km) off the mainland but has very different grapes.

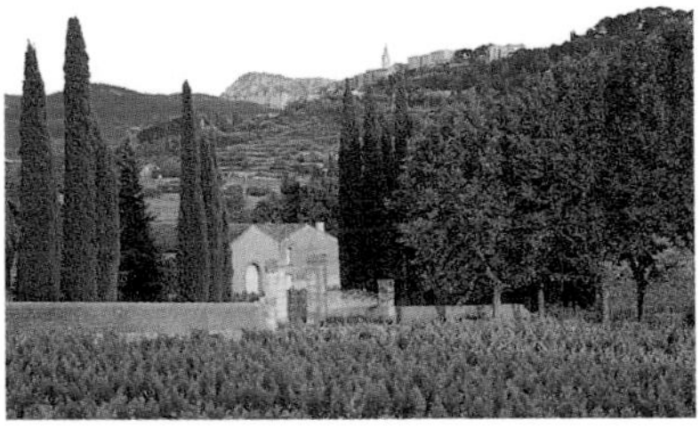

Domaine de Rochebelle
While *coopératives* and merchants have traditionally sold most of the wine in Provence, small estates like this are increasingly developing reputations for their wines.

Until recently, a quick taste of a range of Corsica's wines was enough to show the almost laughably generous way in which the authorities have handed out *appellation contrôlée* status here. Most of the wines offered could be said to have deserved little more than *vin de pays* status. Now, however, a growing number of estates are producing good, characterful wines that truly exploit the potential of the island's grape varieties.

TRAVELING IN PROVENCE AND CORSICA

These two areas share an ancient history and a great climate, but offer very diverse experiences to visitors. Delve a little deeper in Provence and you find a lot more than rosé; explore Corsica and you will encounter dishes and wines unlike any other.

HOTELS & RESTAURANTS

A selection of the region's best establishments, offering good local food and wine and notable, characterful places to stay.

PROVENCE

AIX-EN-PROVENCE

Le Carillon, 10 Rue Portalis
The absence of a telephone number in the details above is no editorial oversight; this bistro happily functions without one, filling its seats with local people who appreciate eating traditional local fare at some of the lowest prices in town.

BANDOL

l'Oulivo, 19 Rue des Tonneliers.
04 94 29 81 79
On the road which, to judge by its name, was once home to Bandol's barrel-makers, this is a good, simple Provençal restaurant with a terrace on which one can eat almost throughout the year.

BORMES-LES-MIMOSAS

Le Bellevue, Place Gambetta.
04 94 71 15 15
FAX 04 94 05 96
W www.bellevuebormes.fr.st
A lovely traditional, modestly priced, family-run hotel with 12 rooms and a great view across to the Iles des Porquerolles. The restaurant, which has a palm-shaded terrace, is recommendable, too.

NICE

L'Auberge des Arts—La Cave, 9 Rue Pairolière.
04 93 62 95 01
In the oldest part of town, this is a great modern version of the old fashioned bistro where wine is sold from the barrel to drink in situ, or to enjoy elsewhere. Those going for the first option will experience great local cooking and knowledgeable wine service at low prices in the vaulted restaurant downstairs.

ST-RÉMY DE PROVENCE

Le Chalet Fleuri, 15 Avenue Frédéric Mistral.
04 90 92 03 62
FAX 04 90 92 60 28
A bargain in this region, for anyone prepared to enjoy staying half-board in a family-owned guesthouse. The rooms are simple but comfortable, and the food flavorsome. But make sure to wander along to La Gousse d'Ail for a more special meal before leaving.

La Gousse d'Ail, 6 Boulevard Marceau.
04 90 92 16 87
This is *the* place to go in St-Rémy for good food and wine at a reasonable price, but precisely what you get may depend on the day of the week. On Tuesday you could enjoy *bouillabaisse*, while on Thursday there's jazz.

CORSICA

BASTIA

Restaurant a Casarella, 6 Rue Ste-Croix.
04 95 32 02 32
Occupying one of of the best locations in the town, this restaurant is in the citadel, close to the old Genovese governor's palace. The food is classic Corsican, though prepared with a light hand. Try a Dégustation menu for a good introduction to local flavors.

PORTO-VECCHIO

Spuntino, Rue Sampiero.
04 95 72 11 63
Definitely not the place to go in search of a wide selection of Corsican wine; there are only two offered. The menu is pretty short, too—painted by hand on a board every day. But the food is some of the best simple, tasty fare on the island, and the terrace is a great place to relax and watch the world wander by.

Le Grilladin, Quai Paoli.
04 95 70 59 75
Close to the water, this restaurant sensibly focuses its attention on fish, much of which is cooked over a wood-fired grill. The wine list is one of the best-chosen on the island, and includes good examples from the mainland.

ZONZA

Hotel-Restaurant le Tourisme, Route de Quenza.
04 95 78 67 72
FAX 04 95 78 73 23
W www.hoteldutourisme.fr
Over a century old, this hotel has something of the feeling of a classic cruise liner. There are plenty of balconies and terraces and a restaurant that serves modern variations on Corsican cuisine, accompanied by a well-chosen range of local wines.

Eating Alfresco
Nowhere in France offers more opportunities to eat well outdoors.

WINE SHOPS

Many of Provence and Corsica's wines can be difficult to find outside the region, so stock up while you're in the area.

PROVENCE

CANNES

La Vinotheque,
14 Rue Marceau.
04 93 99 94 02
Laurent Bonetto offers a huge selection of wines from all over France, but this shop (and the one at 6 Avenue Michel-Jourdan in Cannes-la-Bocca) is one of the best places to go exploring for wines from Provence and Languedoc-Roussillon.

NICE

La Part des Anges,
17 Rue Gubernatis.
04 93 62 69 80
Olivier Labarde is another understandable favorite of *La Revue du Vin de France*, partly for the way he champions organic and biodynamic wines, and partly for the fact that the shop is also a wine bar where wines bought over the counter can be enjoyed for the same price with a plate of local food.

CORSICA

BASTIA

Grand Vin de Corse,
24 Rue César-Campinchi.
04 95 31 24 94
Local wines are a specialty here, but there are plenty of good examples from other parts of France, if you want to set up a comparative tasting.

ANNUAL WINE EVENTS

Provence and Corsica have relatively few wine-specific events, but wine is available at the local food fairs. Ask tourist offices *(see below)* for details.

JUNE

Toulon Les Rencontres Internationales du Rosé—cooking competition and tastings of pink wines

JULY

Hyères and **Ramatuelle** wine festivals

Luri Fiera Di U Vinu—the biggest annual wine event on the island of Corsica, and a great opportunity to taste a wide range of young examples

Montegrosso Fiera di l'Alivu—an olive fair that would be worth attending even if there were no wine offered

SEPTEMBER

Cogolin, **Grimaud**, **St Tropez**, **Cassis**, and **Plan de la Tour** wine fairs

MUSEUMS

Some producers offer vineyard or winery tours. Contact tourist offices *(see below)* for details.

PROVENCE

ANSOUIS

Musee de la Vigne et du Vin,
Château Turcan.
04 90 09 83 33
One of the best-known estates in Luberon has set up this museum, which has displays of old tools and reveals the 12 processes involved in grape-growing and wine-making.

MENERBES

Le Musée du Tire Bouchon,
Domaine de la Citadelle.
04 90 72 41 58
FAX 04 90 72 41 59
W www.luberon-news.com/musee-tire-bouchon.html
In an age when screwcaps are taking the wine world by storm (happily for those who care more about purity of flavor than tradition), this Luberon estate offers a museum dedicated to corkscrews. There are over 1,000 examples, including some that date from the earliest days of the cork, in the 17th century.

ANTIBES

Musée d'Archéologie,
1 Avenue Mézière.
04 92 90 54 35
While taking a break from the more modern objects and paintings on display at Provence's many art museums and galleries, drop in here to see a range of old artifacts, including pottery salvaged from 18th century shipwrecks.

BIOT

Verrerie de Biot,
46 Rue St-Sebastien.
04 93 65 78 00
Of peripheral relevance to wine, but definitely worth a visit, the glassworks here offers the chance to see how glass is blown. Bear in mind, while watching the process, that the modern 75-cl glass bottle is said to owe its size to the lung capacity of early blowers.

WEBSITES

There is a wealth of information relating to both Provence and Corsica online. The best sites for Provence are www.cotes-de-provence.com, www.vinsdeprovence.com, and www.coteauxdaixenprovence.com. For Corsica, try www.corsica-isula.com, www.corsica-online.com, and www.corse.visite.org. For local tourist information, go to www.tourisme.fr and type in the name of any town or village.

OTHER INFORMATION

PROVENCE

LES ARCS SUR ARGENS

Comité Interprofessionnel des Vins Côtes de Provence
04 94 99 50 10
FAX 04 94 99 50 19

CORSICA

AJACCIO

Agence de Tourisme de la Corse
17 Boulevard Roi-Jerôme
04 95 51 00 00
@ info@visit-corsica.com

AJACCIO

AT FIRST GLANCE, THIS LARGE *appellation* on the west coast of Corsica would seem destined to produce thick wines with high alcohol levels. But the temperature here is actually cooler than one might expect, thanks to an altitude of over 330 ft (100 m), and to the moderating effect of the sea. Low temperatures in the spring help to reduce yields and aid in the production of wines with concentrated flavors. The red wines are primarily made from the Sciacarello grape, which does well on the granite soil here. Until recently, the flavor of Ajaccio was often obscured by an excess of tannin and a lack of freshness. Improved wine-making skills and the efforts of ambitious producers have, however, exposed both the peppery character of the Sciacarello and the more herby appeal of the local Vermentino grape that is used for white Ajaccio.

Clos Capitoro One of Corsica's best wines, this Ajaccio is fresh, fruity, and very characterful.

Worth the Detour
Corsica's popularity with tourists both from the French mainland and from farther afield ensures that most of the wine is sold and drunk on the island.

- AC Ajaccio.
- Red/rosé: Sciacarello, Barbarossa, Nielluccio, Vermentino, Grenache, Carignan, Cinsault. White: Ugni Blanc.
- Light, peppery reds and rosés. Dry, if often acidic, whites.
- Clos d'Alzeto, Clos Capitoro, Comte Peraldi.
- Red: Baked eggs with Parmesan.
- Red: 2003, 2001, 1998.
- Red: 3–5 years. White/rosé: 1–2 years.

BANDOL

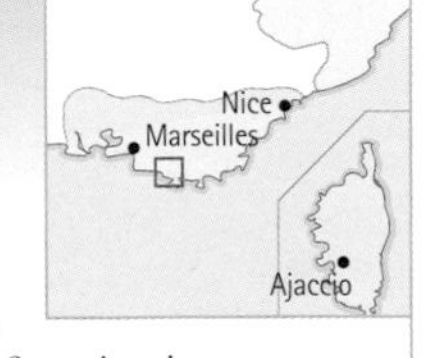

ONE OF THE LONGEST-ESTABLISHED *appellations* in France, Bandol made full-bodied wines that were popular at court in the 16th and 17th centuries and were supposedly credited by Louis XV, who said they provided him with "vital sap and wits." Like Bordeaux *(see p93)*, Bandol benefited from being a port and at one point it no doubt shipped more wine under its name than was produced from its vines. Following replanting as a result of phylloxera, a group of producers fought to restrict the *appellation* to the natural amphitheater of terraced vines. Today, however, the main threat comes from the vacation houses that sell more easily than the wines. Bandol's red wine is made primarily from the Mourvèdre grape, which gives it an intense, spicy flavor. The peppery rosés are also good, but the whites are generally dull.

Domaine Tempier This estate has almost single-handedly established the growing international reputation of the wines of this *appellation.*

The Perfect Setting
The grapes that are produced by these vines ripen reliably in what is one of the finest natural sun-traps in France.

- AC Bandol.
- Red/rosé: Mourvèdre, Grenache, Cinsault. White: Sauvignon Blanc.
- Dark, full-bodied reds. Simple, dry whites. Powerful dry rosés.
- Barthes, Bastide Blanche, Bunan, Frégate, Moulin Costes, Pibarnon, Pradeaux, Romassan, de la Rouvière, Tour de Bon, Tempier, Terrebrune, Vannières.
- Duck with olives.
- Red: 2003, 2001, 1998, 1996.
- Red: 3–10 years. White/rosé: 1–3 years.

LES BAUX DE PROVENCE

THIS SPECTACULAR MEDIEVAL hilltop village, which is now among France's most popular tourist attractions, can add its village name to the vast *appellation* of the Coteaux d'Aix en Provence. Its best reds are deep, dark, chocolatey wines, with notes of plums and cherries, while the rosés can compete with the best of the Rhône. There are some excellent producers here, including a number who use a combination of traditional and organic methods in the vineyards and cellars.

Mas de Gourgonnier
This rich, gamey wine has fruity, berryish flavors.

- AC Les Baux de Provence.
- Red/rosé: Grenache, Cinsault, Mourvèdre, Syrah, Cabernet Sauvignon.
- Full-bodied reds. Dry rosés.
- Terres Blanches, Mas de la Dame, Mas de Gourgonnier.
- Cold beef salad.
- Red: 2003, 2001, 1998.
- Red: 3–10 years. Rosé: 1–3 years.

BELLET

ONE OF FRANCE'S SMALLEST *appellations*, Bellet is situated on the steep hills to the west of Nice. The cooling Alpine winds combine with sea breezes to create a surprisingly cool microclimate. The grape varieties used here are found almost nowhere else. The fragrant reds are made from Braquet (Italy's Brachetto) and Fuella (Folle Noir), while whites are made from Rolle, blended with Ugni Blanc, Pignerol Muscadet, Mayorquin, Clairette, Bouboulenc, and Chardonnay.

Château de Bellet
Cuvée Baron G adds spicy notes of new oak to the flavors of the local grapes.

- AC Bellet.
- Red/rosé: Braquet, Fuella, Cinsault. White: Rolle.
- Full-bodied, earthy reds. Scented, full-bodied whites. Dry, full-bodied rosés.
- Ch de Bellet, de Crémat.
- Sea bass with fennel.
- Red: 2001, 2000.
- Red: 3–10 years. White/rosé: 1–3 years.

CASSIS

ONE OF FRANCE'S OLDEST *appellations*, this fishing village turned arty resort lies to the east of Marseilles. Vineyards compete with tourism and real estate development, allowing wine-makers to command high prices. The rosés are pleasant, but unremarkable, and the dense and deep-colored reds are best drunk young. Cassis' white wines, made from Ugni Blanc, Sauvignon Blanc, Clairette, Doucillon, Marsanne and Pascal Blanc, are more interesting and go perfectly with the local fish dishes.

Clos Ste Magdeleine
Examples of fine Cassis are among the world's most distinctive white wines.

- AC Cassis.
- Red/rosé: Mourvèdre, Grenache, Cinsault. White: Clairette, Ugni Blanc, Marsanne.
- Medium-bodied reds. Dry, perfumed, full-bodied whites. Dry rosés.
- Du Bagnol, Ste Magdeleine.
- Pizza.
- White: 2003, 2002.
- 1–4 years.

COTEAUX D'AIX EN PROVENCE

THE COTEAUX D'AIX EN PROVENCE is a relatively new *appellation*, covering some 50 *communes* spread across Provence from Arles eastward to Rians and from the Durance River south to Marseilles. The area's traditional grapes have been enhanced by the addition of up to 30 percent of Cabernet Sauvignon. This is still too little to allow the inclusion within the *appellation* of the Cabernet-influenced wines of Domaine de Trevallon, the region's top estate.

Château de Fonscolombe
This large 18th-century château makes one of the best wines of the *appellation*.

- AC Coteaux d'Aix en Provence.
- Red/rosé: Grenache, Cinsault, Mourvèdre.
- Medium-bodied, fruity reds. Light, dry rosés.
- De Beaulieu, Calissanne, Fonscolombe, Pigoudet.
- Red: Lamb with garlic.
- Red: 2003, 2001, 1998.
- Red: 2–5 years. White/rosé: 1–3 years.

COTEAUX VAROIS

THIS PART OF PROVENCE was once a vinous no-man's-land. Today, however, quality is improving, thanks to new rules prescribing an increase in the proportion of Mourvèdre, Syrah, or Grenache in red and rosé wines to 80 percent. Good, peppery, red-curranty examples of the rosé are often better than the ubiquitous Côtes de Provence *(see right)*. The reds can have a Rhône-like richness, while the rare whites are dry, aromatic, and good with local specialties such as *poulpe* (octopus) *à la Provençale*.

Dom du Deffends Clos de la Truffière
This wine is a star feature in any lineup of reds from Provence.

- AC Coteaux Varois.
- Red/rosé: Grenache, Syrah, Mourvèdre. White: Vermentino.
- Full-bodied reds. Light- to medium-bodied whites; dry rosés.
- Des Chaberts, du Deffends.
- Red: *steak au poivre*.
- Red: 2001, 1998, 1995.
- Red: 2–5 years. White/rosé: 1–3 years.

CÔTES DE PROVENCE

AROUND HALF OF FRANCE'S rosé wine is made in this, France's largest *appellation*, which covers 45,000 acres (18,000 hectares) of diverse landscape and vines. Reds range from intense Syrah to light, peppery Grenache. Wine-making skills and aspirations vary. Most cheap bistro rosé is dull and disappointing, but there are serious rosés to be had (including the highly priced wines from Domaine Ott), and a growing number of worthwhile reds and whites.

Domaine Richeaume
Domaine Richeaume is one of Provence's pioneer organic producers.

- AC Côtes de Provence.
- Red/rosé: Carignan, Syrah, Cabernet. White: Clairette.
- Full-bodied reds. Crisp, dry whites and rosés.
- La Bernarde, de la Mireille, Richeaume.
- Red: *saucisson sec*.
- Red: 2001, 1998, 1996.
- Red: 2–4 years. White/rosé: 1–3 years.

MUSCAT DU CAP CORSE

UNTIL 1993 THESE classic wines, produced in 17 villages in the rugged north of Corsica, had no *appellation* of their own and no means of finding their way beyond Corsica. Thus they were rarely compared with such Muscats as Beaumes-de-Venise *(see p259)* and Frontignan. The chalky soil and sea breezes contribute to some wonderful, ripe purity of fruit, and fresh, perfumed aromas. These Muscat Blanc à Petits Grains wines are among France's finest *vins doux naturels*.

Domaine de Catarelli
De Catarelli produces an orange-scented wine that would go well with fruit salad.

- AC Muscat du Cap Corse.
- White: Muscat Blanc à Petit Grains.
- Sweet *vins doux naturels*.
- Antoine Arena, de Catarelli, de Gaffory, Dominique Gentile, Leccia, Orenga de Gaffory, San Quilico.
- Chocolate cake.
- 2003.
- 1–3 years.

PALETTE

TODAY, THIS WINE comes from two producers, both taking advantage of the limestone soil and relatively cool climate of the north-facing slopes to the east of Aix. In fact, however, the *appellation* (whose fans have included kings René and Edward VII) owes its existence to just one: Château Simone. Considering Palette's tiny size, the list of permitted grape varieties seems ludicrously long, but there is no doubting the quality of this small area's reds, which can keep for up to 20 years.

Château Simone
A classic of southern France—well worth keeping for a decade or so.

- AC Palette.
- Red/rosé: Grenache, Mourvèdre, Cinsault, Syrah, White: Clairette, Muscat, Ugni Blanc, Sémillon.
- Traditional rich red and whites. Long-lived rosés.
- Ch Cremade, Ch Simone.
- Red: Braised calf's liver.
- Red: 2001, 1998, 1995.
- Red: 5–15 years. White/rosé: 3–7 years.

PATRIMONIO

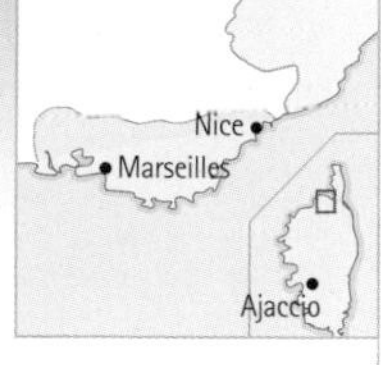

PATRIMONIO IS CORSICA'S OLDEST *appellation* and one of its best. It comprises seven *communes* and is situated just west of Bastia on the island's northern tip. The dominant grape for the reds, Nielluccio, is cited as a native grape, but is almost certainly the Sangiovese of Tuscany, and may be a fairly recent introduction in Corsica. The combination of this and other Italian and Italianate varieties with the local limestone soil contributes to the long-lived, meaty, herby style of some reds, such as Orenga de Gaffory's oak-aged Cuvée des Gouverneurs. The rosés, made from varieties including Grenache, have an herby, peppery style similar to many rosés from Provence, but they are often better-made and better value. The Patrimonio *appellation* also covers whites, which are now made solely from the local Vermentino.

Antoine Arena
This is a perfect chance to try the herby flavors of the Vermentino grape, which gives Corsica's whites their character.

Savage Country
The northern part of the island of Corsica boasts some spectacularly rugged countryside.

- AC Patrimonio.
- Red/rosé: Nielluccio, southern Rhône varieties. White: Vermentino.
- Deep-colored, full-bodied, often peppery reds. Peppery rosés. Light, dry whites.
- Dom Aliso-Rossi, Antoine Arena, de Caterelli, Dominique Gentile, Leccia, Clos Marfisi, Orenga de Gaffory, Pastricciola.
- White: Fish soup.
- Red: 2003, 2001, 1998.
- Red: 3–5 years. White/rosé: 1–3 years.

VIN DE CORSE

THIS GENERIC *APPELLATION* APPLIES to the whole island of Corsica and covers red, white, and rosé wines, many of which do not warrant *appellation* status. Production is centered mainly on the large *coopératives* on the east coast, but smaller estates do make interesting wines, often under the name of smaller *appellations*. For example, Domaine de Torraccia produces red and rosé wines of the Vin de Corse Porto Vecchio *appellation*. The pink is a full-bodied rosé, perfect with *bourride*, the local fish stew, while the red has flavors of berries, herbs, and tobacco. The Vin de Corse Figari *appellation* is close to Bonifacio in the south. Much of its wine is quaffing fare, but Domaine de Tanella and Poggio d'Oro are two quality-conscious names to watch. Other small *appellations* are Vin de Corse Calvi and Vin de Corse Sartène.

Clos Culombu, Corse Calvi
This *cuvée prestige* is one of the best examples of the kind of well-made wines that are now being produced here.

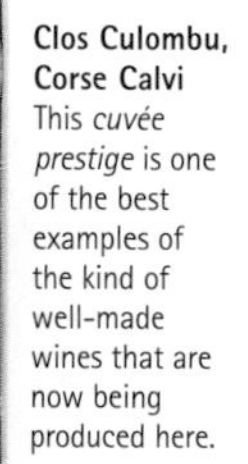

Winter Wonderland
Corsica's snowy hills overlook these sloping vineyards on the east coast. Here, the vines are pictured "resting" before the growing season.

- AC Vin de Corse Coteaux du Cap Corse.
- Red/rosé: Nielluccio, Sciacarello, Grenache, S. Rhône varieties; White: Vermentino.
- Full-bodied, herby reds. Dry rosés. Dry or sweet whites.
- Clos d'Alzeto, Dom de Tanella, Clos Culombu, Clos Landry, Maestracci, Poggio d'Oro, Clos Reginu, de Torracia.
- Rosé: Fish stew.
- Red: 2003, 2001, 1998.
- Red: 2–4 years. White/rosé: 1–3 years.

The Rhône Valley

The Rhône Valley

Of all the red wines produced in France, none offer a wider range of excitingly spicy flavors than those of the long, sun-baked Rhône Valley.

Every time I head south through France, I try to pause, ideally just before dusk, for a few minutes at a small chapel on top of a hill at the end of a winding and bumpy road. The building in question is the former home of a crusader turned religious hermit and has given its name to one of the most famous wines in the world. Jaboulet Aîné's La Chapelle vineyard in the *appellation* of Hermitage *(see p258)* is not only one of the most famous, it is also one of the most gloriously situated. The view across the sinuous river below is spectacular enough, but it is the vertiginous slope of the terraced vineyard itself that always makes me reflect on the extraordinary human effort involved in planting, tending, and picking grapes here. An hour or so farther south you will find another uninhabited building and another, very different, site of vinous pilgrimage. This is the château of Châteauneuf-du-Pape *(see p251)*, the ruined castle that was once the summer residence of the exiled Pope John XXII. There are no spectacular slopes, but walking is still no easy matter because the vineyards are covered with large round pebbles like the ones on inhospitable beaches.

Both these vineyards produce mainly red, with a little white wine. In Hermitage at the northern end of the Rhône Valley, and in the nearby *appellations* of Crozes-Hermitage *(see p257)*, St Joseph *(see p260)*, Cornas *(see p253)* and the Côte Rôtie *(see p256)*, the smoky, blackberry flavor of the reds comes exclusively from the Syrah grape. In Châteauneuf-du-Pape, in Gigondas *(see p257)* and in the villages making wines sold as Côtes du Rhône *(see pp254–5)*, the flavors are more varied, depending on the proportions in which a cocktail of grape varieties are used. Although Syrah still features here, the leading player is Grenache. Wines from this variety vary enormously depending on how they are made, but they are all marked out by the instantly recognizable and deliciously incongruous smell and taste of freshly ground pepper.

Life at the Top
The vineyards of the Rhône Valley are far more often planted on steep slopes than those of Bordeaux or Burgundy.

For centuries, these Rhône reds were used to improve weedy wines from Bordeaux *(see pp80–111)* and Burgundy *(see pp112–159)*. At one time, the practice was so acceptable that higher prices were charged for Médoc wines *(see p99)* that had been "*hermitagé*"—that is, dosed with Hermitage. Today, such mixtures are illegal—and unlikely—since wine drinkers are willing to pay as much for the finest wines of the Rhône as they do for the best wines of other regions.

REGIONAL OVERVIEW

- 173,000 acres (70,000 ha): 450 million bottles.
- Continental climate in the north with warm summers and cool winters. More Mediterranean-influenced in the south, where the seasonal variation in temperature is less marked.
- Varied, with granite plus sand and chalk in the north, becoming limestone and pebbles in the south.
- Red: Syrah, Grenache, Mourvèdre, Cinsault, Carignan. White: Marsanne, Roussanne, Viognier, Grenache Blanc, Clairette, Muscat.

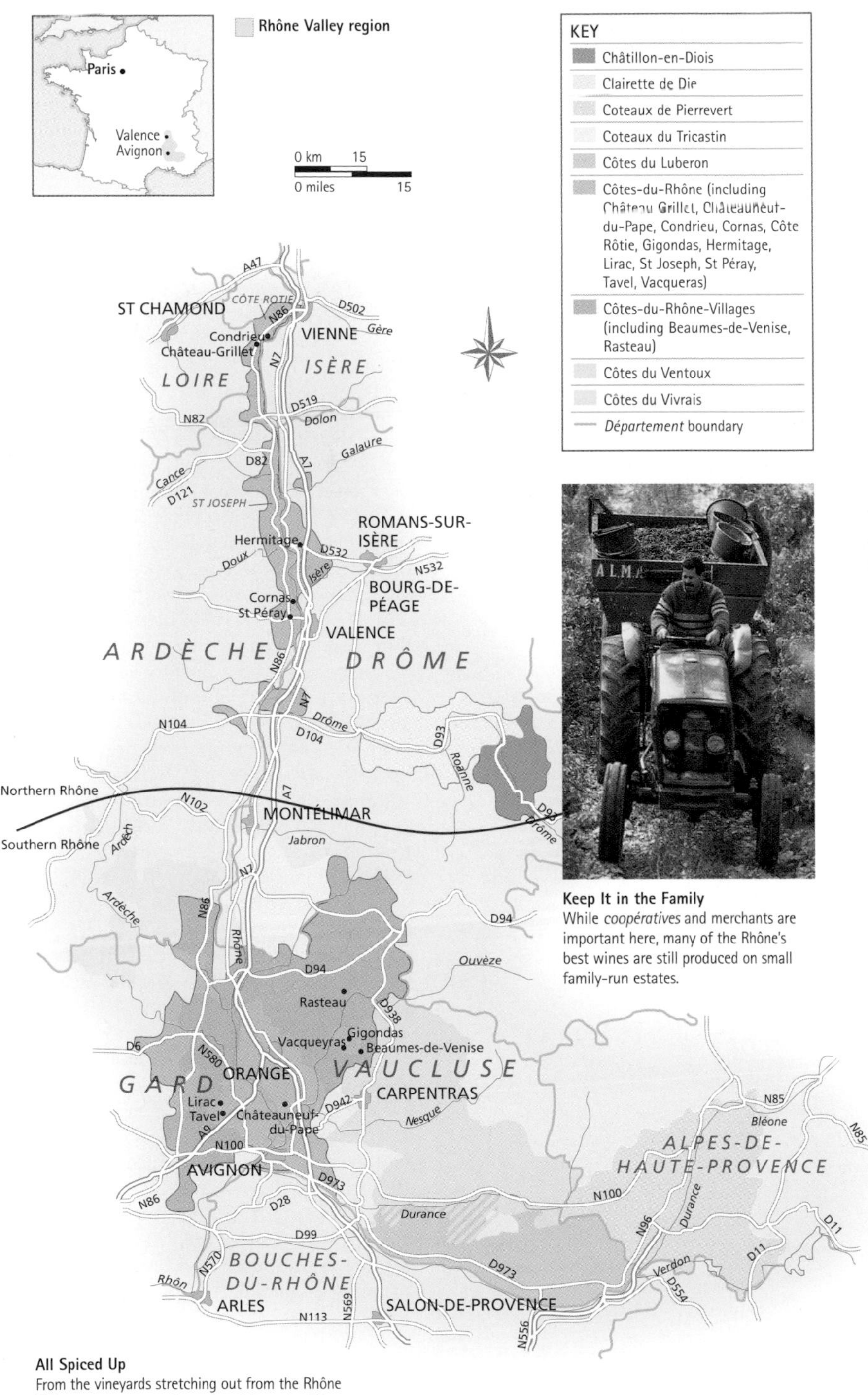

Keep It in the Family
While *coopératives* and merchants are important here, many of the Rhône's best wines are still produced on small family-run estates.

All Spiced Up
From the vineyards stretching out from the Rhône Valley come a range of sweet and dry red, white and rosé wines whose common characteristic is their rich and often spicy flavors.

The History of the Rhône Valley

The Rhône Valley has inevitably played a huge role in the history of France, serving as a principal artery between the north and south. But it has also been a source of fine wine, from the vineyards that were established 2,000 years ago in the northern part of the region, to those farther south at Châteauneuf-du-Pape that gained their fame 1,300 years later.

In the early days of the Roman Empire, no river in France was more important to traders than the Rhône. We know that during the first century BC, wine from Rome and Provence was carried up the river valley and used as currency by the tribes who were struggling for supremacy in Gaul. Even before Julius Caesar and his troops arrived in Chalon-sur-Saône, in what is now part of southern Burgundy, the wine business was thriving enough for two enterprising Romans to have already set up shop as merchants.

The first quality wines said to have originated in the Rhône were the red wines that were made in the vineyards of Hermitage *(see p258)* and the Côte Rôtie *(see p256)* by a tribe called the Allobroges. These wines were evidently good enough for Pliny to note in 71 AD that the red wines of Vienne were sold at a premium. They were also considered fine enough to be exported to Rome and even across the Channel to the new colony of Britain. Historians still argue over whether the grape variety grown by the Allobroges was Syrah or Pinot Noir. The quality of these wines lay in the ripeness of their flavors, but the flavor of the grape may well have been hard to discern behind the pine resin that was used to preserve the wine on its travels. As elsewhere in France, monasteries in the Rhône region grew vines and made wine in the 12th and 13th centuries, but none of the wines they made gained the reputation enjoyed by their counterparts farther north in Burgundy. Recognition of the region's potential first arrived in 1305, when Pope Clement V temporarily moved his palace from Rome to Avignon. Although the papal preference was apparently for Burgundy, most of the wine drunk at the papal court was from local vineyards. Pope John XXII unknowingly gave the name to the Rhône's most famous wine, Châteauneuf-du-Pape, when he built himself a summer home in a flattish, pebbled region near Avignon.

Châteauneuf-du-Pape
In the 14th century, Pope John XXII built a new castle, the Châteauneuf-du-Pape, and planted the vineyards that produce one of the most famous wines of the Rhône.

In the 15th and 16th centuries, the region began to prosper as Lyon became an important trading center for silk. Rivalry with the Burgundians, however, who banned all Rhône wines from passing through Dijon on the grounds that they were "*très petits et povres*"(very small and poor), prevented the wines from being sold in northern France, Britain, and the Low Countries. Rhône wines finally began to develop a following among wine drinkers in Paris and London in the 17th and 18th centuries. At this time, they were also popular among merchants, who used Hermitage to improve the quality of red Bordeaux.

The Rhône
The banks of this 125-mile (200-km) river are lined with vineyards, from Valais in Switzerland to the Bouches-du-Rhône just west of Marseilles in southern France.

Ironically, it was not long before the wines of another Rhône *commune* found themselves to be the focus of attention among blenders and vinous fraudsters. When the vineyards of Châteauneuf-du-Pape were replanted at the beginning of the 20th century after having been destroyed by phylloxera, unscrupulous merchants and vine-growers used this famous name on wines that had nothing to do with its pebbled vineyards. In response to these threats to the prestige of their wines, a group of quality-conscious Châteauneuf-du-Pape producers, led by Baron Leroy *(see p37)*, the owner of the finest domaine in the region, drafted a set of laws that dictated the boundaries within which Châteauneuf-du-Pape could be made. These rules covered a range of stipulations, including vine varieties, pruning, training, and ripeness, and even the health of the grapes. Thus it was that Châteauneuf-du-Pape became the true birthplace of the *appellation contrôlée* system.

These efforts, and the wine-making success of the region's best growers and merchants, helped to keep the key *appellations* of the Rhône firmly among France's more respected wines, but it was the rare exceptions, such as Jaboulet's Hermitage La Chapelle, that were ranked alongside the top reds of Bordeaux.

This changed in the 1980s and 1990s, with the arrival on the scene of the American wine guru Robert Parker. Like the Romans of 2,000 years earlier, Parker relished the naturally ripe and "voluptuous" style of the region's top wines, and treated them as seriously as he did the classic wines of the Médoc *(see p99)* and St Émilion *(see p105)*. As wine-makers throughout the world tasted recent vintages from the Rhône and wines made from the same grape varieties in Australia and California, they began to question whether they ought to be planting Syrah, Grenache, and Viognier grapes instead of Cabernet, Merlot, and Chardonnay. No French wine region entered the 21st century better placed than the Rhône Valley.

Home Away from Home
Paul Signac's painting of the Palais des Papes in Avignon evokes the mood of the castle in which the exiled popes established themselves when they decamped from Rome.

A Driving Tour of the Rhône Valley

This short tour takes you southward, past the Syrah-dominated vineyards of the northern part of the Rhône Valley, through evocatively named and often spectacular appellations *that include Côte Rôtie, Hermitage, and Condrieu, famous for the unexpectedly exotic white wines produced from the Viognier grape.*

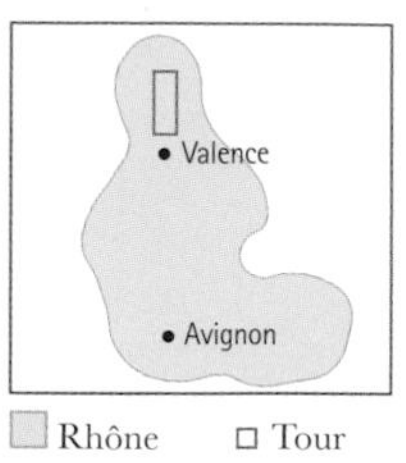

Château Grillet
This tiny *appellation* uses the Viognier to make good but overpriced white wines.

VIENNE TO AMPUIS

It is worth pausing in Vienne ① to visit some of the city's churches and Roman monuments, including La Pyramide, an 82-ft (25-m) obelisk that is said to mark the tomb of Pontius Pilate. Then follow the river southward for a few miles before crossing to the west bank and the small but illustrious Côte Rôtie *appellation*. In Verenay ②, stop to visit producers like Clusel-Roch and Jean-Michel Gérin before turning left and following the steeply sloping vineyards toward Ampuis ③. This quiet town is just beginning to wake up to the recent explosion of interest in Côte Rôtie and Condrieu wines. The merchant Marcel Guigal, maker of some of the best, most expensive wines of the Côte Rôtie, has cellars here. Among Guigal's very best wines is one named after the imposing Château d'Ampuis, visible in the distance but not open to visitors.

CONDRIEU TO ST PIERRE-DE-BOEUF

Near Ampuis is the town of Condrieu ④, surrounded by the vineyards of its namesake white wine *appellation*, where the Viognier grape shows what it can do when used on its own. If you pass through at harvest time, look for actor Gérard Depardieu, who owns a vineyard here. Turning right onto the D34 at the village of Vérin, you will reach the spectacular punchbowl vineyard and château that make up the tiny *monopole* of Château Grillet ⑤. The setting is worth a look, but this rather overpriced wine is not sold at the château. Offering better value, Condrieu producers well worth visiting include André Perret and Yves Cuilleron at Verlieu ⑥, and Alain Paret, whose cellars are at St Pierre-de-Boeuf ⑦.

ST PIERRE-DE-BOEUF TO ST DÉSIRAT

The wines of the St Joseph *appellation* are made in *communes* spread over 37 miles (60 km) between Condrieu and Hermitage. Head for the 16th-century village of Malleval ⑧—to get there, turn off the N86 at St-Pierre-de-Boeuf on the D503, through the Gorge de Malleval, and past the Saut de Laurette waterfall, taking the D79 to Malleval. Its medieval salt market, the château and the cellars of Pierre Gaillard are worth visiting. Returning to the N86, some of the best-value wines in the area can be found at the *coopérative* of St Désirat ⑨, one of the most highly regarded in France.

CROZES-HERMITAGE AND TAIN L'HERMITAGE

Cross the river at Sarras and follow the N7 before turning left onto the D163, which takes you up through the vineyards of Crozes-Hermitage ⑩. Michel Martin is a producer worth visiting in Crozes-

Hermitage, and there are plenty of good estates in nearby villages, such as Chanos-Curson. Back on the N7, you will soon reach Tain l'Hermitage ⑪, which faces its twin town of Tournon-sur-Rhône across the river, and takes its name from the single hillside that makes up the *appellation* of Hermitage. These great granite vineyards cover an area of 311 acres (126 ha) on the east bank of the Rhône. All face due south, overlooked by the famous chapel that stands in the vineyard of Hermitage La Chapelle. You can reach the chapel by following the narrow road that climbs the hill near the *cave coopérative.* My favorite producer here is Gérard Chave of Domaine Jean-Louis Chave, who can be found in the nearby village of Mauves ⑫. All of the wine-makers listed on p214 are also worth a visit.

CORNAS TO ST PÉRAY AND VALENCE

The village of Cornas ⑬ lies at the heart of the small, underrated *appellation* of Cornas. The vines, sheltered from the mistral winds, produce unusually ripe grapes. For a fine view of the vineyards and river, head up the narrow road to St-Romain-de-Lerps, returning to pick up the N86 that leads to the sparkling-wine village of St Péray ⑭ and on to the town of Valence ⑮, where the vineyards are increasingly being encroached upon by housing developments.

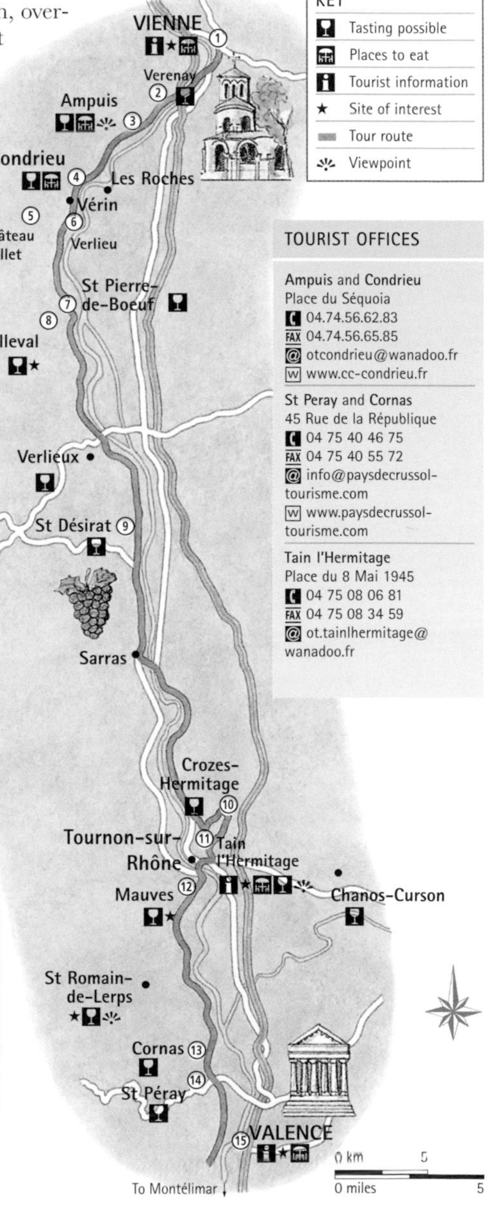

Riverside Terraces
On the western bank of the Rhône, these Cornas vineyards produce wines that are magnificently dark and powerful.

The Food of the Rhône Valley

Like the Loire Valley, the Rhône Valley is made up of several regions connected by one great river. Inevitably, there are huge differences between the cuisine of Lyon, in the heart of the country, and Châteauneuf-du-Pape, which is closer to the Mediterranean. But, like the red wines of the Rhône, the traditional dishes here share a single quality in their intense flavors.

If you were to ask a number of French gourmets to name the city where they would most like to spend a few days, Lyon would no doubt be among the most popular choices. Situated right on the border between the Rhône Valley and Burgundy, this has long been the home of a number of great restaurants, not to mention some of the finest *charcuteries* in France. Traditionally Lyonnaise, the spiced, dry, salami-style sausages *rosette* and *saucisson de Lyon* are now famous all over France and are made by charcuteries in other regions. Harder to find outside this city, however, is *saladier lyonnais*, once prepared with sheep's testicles, but now more commonly made with sheep's feet and chicken livers, and *cervelas lyonnais*, a brioche filled with boiled sausage mixed with pistachio nuts and truffles.

Throughout the northern part of the region, veal is cooked in white wine to make *blanquette de veau*. The main ingredient here, however, is the onion, which goes into *soupe à l'oignon* (onion soup) as well as *sauce soubise*, a simple onion sauce that is often served as an accompaniment to sausages.

Peppers
Farther south in the Rhône Valley, the cuisine adopts a Mediterranean flavor, and peppers, tomatoes, and olives are more commonly used.

Poulet à la Demi-Deuil
To make this dish, also known as *poularde à la Lyonnaise*, the chicken is poached in white chicken stock and stuffed with truffled forcemeat. Small pieces of truffle are also inserted under the skin and the dish is served with vegetables cooked in the chicken broth.

Pike fished from inland rivers is used as the basis of *quenelles de brochet*, fish mousse sausages, a delicious appetizer served with crayfish sauce.

As you move south, the focus shifts toward Mediterranean flavors: of ratatouille and tapenade, of wild herbs, saffron, tomatoes, peppers and olives. Whereas the northern part of the region cooks with butter, here olive oil is far more common.

Rosette de Lyon
Made of meat from leg of pork and served in chunky slices, *rosette de Lyon* is the most famous of Lyon's sausages.

The river is also the source of eel, used to make *matelote,* a fish stew from Barthelasse island on the Rhône River near Avignon. But the best fish come from the sea. There is *rougets grillés aux feuilles de vigne*, red mullet cooked with grape leaves and fennel, and all kinds of fish soup, the most famous being *bouillabaisse* served with *rouille,* a mayonnaise made with oil, garlic, chili peppers, and stock. Just as interesting, though, is *bourride,* a fish stew that comes with garlicky *aïoli* mayonnaise.

The Rhône Valley isn't a haven for the sweet-toothed, but it is the place to find nougat, *bugnes lyonnaises* (lemon fritters) and almondy bread tarts.

Clafoutis
This cherry flan is made with locally grown dark cherries covered in a dough and laced with *Kirsch*, a cherry liqueur.

REGIONAL CHEESES

When cheese lovers refer to the Rhône, they are usually thinking of the Rhône-Alpes in the eastern and northern part of the region, where a variety of often quite pungent cheeses are made. Among those associated with the region are the various Fourmes from Forez, the goat's milk Chevrotins, the Grataron d'Arèches from Savoie, and the rich, creamy, but relatively low-fat cow's-milk Tommes, made in small farms in the Alps. These cheeses all go well with light Rhône reds and, more particularly, whites.

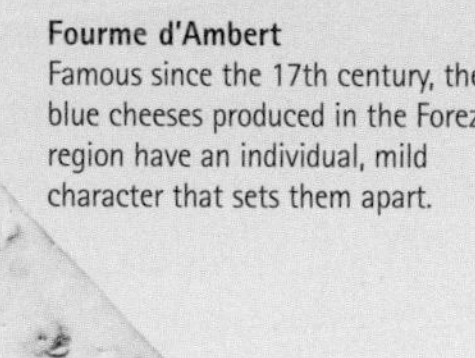

Fourme d'Ambert
Famous since the 17th century, the blue cheeses produced in the Forez region have an individual, mild character that sets them apart.

Chevrotin des Aravis
Similar to the more famous Reblochon, this goat's milk cheese comes from Savoie, but is popular in the Rhône, where it goes well with white wine.

TRAVELING IN THE RHÔNE VALLEY

Too many people speed through this region on their way to the south of France. Leave them to zoom along the autoroute *while you turn off at Vienne and follow the river at a more leisurely pace. Apart from some of France's most spectacular vineyards, the Rhône Valley has a wealth of historic villages and lots of great places to sleep and eat.*

HOTELS & RESTAURANTS

A selection of the region's best, combining good local food and wine with notable places to stay.

AVIGNON

L'Europe, 12 Place Crillon.
04 90 14 76 76
FAX 04 90 14 76 71
W www.hotel-d-europe.fr
Napoleon stayed here in 1799 and, despite the discreet addition of the conveniences expected of a top-class hotel, it feels much as it would have done then.

CONDRIEU

Le Beau Rivage, Rue de Beau Rivage.
04 74 56 82 82
One of the most attractively situated restaurants in the region, the Beau Rivage offers the chance to enjoy a leisurely lunch and some great local wines while watching the river.

Hotel-Restaurant La Réclusière, 14 Route Nationale.
04 74 56 67 27
FAX 04 74 56 80 05
Popular with wine merchants looking for a base from which to explore the Northern Rhone, this restaurant boasts an unusually well-stocked cellar.

CROZES-HERMITAGE

Le Bistrot des Vins, La Place du Village.
04 75 07 18 03
Don't come here expecting a wide-ranging menu; there is just one well-executed main course, which changes daily depending on what is available at the market. However, little can compete with the experience of drinking a wine among the vines from which it has been produced.

Michel Chabran, Avenue du 45ème Parallèle, Route Nationale, Pont de l'Isère.
04 75 84 60 09
Situated between Tain l'Hermitage and Valence, this 12-room hotel is light and airy, with a great restaurant offering a really good range of wines from local producers.

PIOLENC, NEAR ORANGE

L'Auberge l'Orangerie, 4 Rue de l'Ormeau.
04 90 29 59 88
FAX 90 29 67 74
W www.orangerie.net
There are only half a dozen rooms here, but they all boast reproductions of classic paintings by the patron. The restaurant and wine list are first class. Book well in advance.

LES ROCHES

Hôtel Bellevue, Quai du Rhône.
04 74 56 47 56
The spectacular view over the Rhône River and the great food are just two of the reasons to spend a night at this surprisingly reasonably priced hotel.

TAIN L'HERMITAGE

Reynaud, Rue Président Roosevelt.
04 75 07 22 10
A good restaurant that also offers a dozen bedrooms with river views.

VALENCE

Pic, 285 Avenue Victor Hugo.
04 75 44 15 32
Top wine-makers take their best customers here, both for the food and for the choice of wines.

VIENNE

La Pyramide, 14 Boulevard Fernand Point.
04 74 53 01 96
This great restaurant has the rare distinction of being situated on a boulevard named after the chef who made it famous. It is still a mecca for food- and wine-lovers.

WINE SHOPS

Some Rhône Valley wines that are widely available here can be more difficult to find at home, so don't forget to stock up.

LYON

La Vieille Reserve, 59 Avenue Foch.
04 78 89 15 17
1 Place Tobie-Robatel.
04 78 28 69 98
Monsieur Morel and his son run this pair of shops, which offer fine wines from the Rhône Valley and from Burgundy to the north.

MONTÉLIMAR

Saveurs & Millésimes, 97 Rue Pierre-Julien.
04 75 90 96 97
A favorite of *La Revue du Vin de France*, this shop offers a well focused range of Rhône Valley wines.

Summer Delights
In the summer, explore the local whites and rosés of the Rhône Valley.

TAIN L'HERMITAGE
Compagnie de l'Hermitage, 7 Place Taurobole.
04 75 08 19 70
Within a short walk of the best vineyards in the Rhône Valley, this friendly shop stocks the wine they produce, and those of every other corner of the region.
Des Terrasses du Rhône au Sommelier, 13 Rue Joseph-Péala.
04 75 08 40 56
The other place in this small town to offer a terrific range of wines from across the Rhône.
VINSOBRES
Cave du Prieuré, Avenue de Nyons.
04 75 27 60 11
In the heart of the Côtes du Rhône, a shop selling 100 wines from nowhere but here.

MUSEUMS

Some producers offer vineyard or winery tours. Contact tourist offices *(see below)* for details.

CHÂTEAUNEUF DU PAPE
Le Musée des Outils de Vignerons, Musée du Père Anselme/Caves Laurent Charles Brotte.
04 90 83 70 07
Set up by a big producer, this museum focuses on the tools used over the years by vine-growers and wine-makers.
RASTEAU
Le Musée du Vigneron, Route de Vaison.
04 90 83 71 79
This well-laid-out space, centered, again, around the tools of the trade, is the work of Paul Coulon of the Domaine de Beaurenard.

ANNUAL WINE EVENTS

Almost all the wine-producing villages of the Rhône Valley hold one or more festivals during the year. Celebrations of the vine are often combined with events that are dedicated to music. Dates and venues do vary, so it is always worth checking in advance.

JANUARY
Ampuis wine fair

FEBRUARY
Tain-l'Hermitage, Orange and **Lauris** wine fairs

MARCH
Bons en Chablais wine fair

APRIL
Vinsobres wine fair and agricultural show
Vaison-la-Romaine spring festival
Châteauneuf-du-Pape festival of St Marc
Malleval wine festival

MAY
Tain l'Hermitage Caves en Caves—tastings
Apt Pentecost cavalcade
Vaison-la-Romaine fair
Salmagne wine fair
Rasteau wine fair

JUNE
Vacqueyras, La Vraie Croix wine fairs

JULY
Visan, Vacqueyras Cecile-Les-Vines, Jonquieres, Cairanne and **Bollène** music among the vines
Beaumes de Venise, Violes, Cairanne and **Bedoin** wine fairs

JULY/AUGUST
Various villages music among the vines

AUGUST
Rasteau, Séguret, Maurice sur Eygues, Chatillon-en-Diois, and **Valréas** festivals
Châteauneuf-du-Pape Veraison celebration—festivities including jousting
Puymeras and **Rasteau** wine evenings
Seguret music among the vines

SEPTEMBER
St Peray, Die (Clairette de Die), Voyer, and **Beaufort sur Gervanne** wine fairs
Avignon Ban des Vendanges—the beginning of the year's harvest festivities
Tain-l'Hermitage vintage festival, including a parade featuring Bacchus

NOVEMBER
Avignon baptism of the new vintage of Côtes du Rhône
Crozes-Hermitage, Cornas, Vaison-la-Romaine, Nyons, and **Avignon** wine fairs

DECEMBER
Marignier, Grignan, and **Seguret** wine fairs

WEBSITES

There is a website for the whole region at www.vins-rhone.com, and the Ban des Vendanges des Cotes du Rhone operates a site at www.banvendanges.com. Pages relating to specific *appellations* can be found at www.clairette.com, www.rasteau.com, www.tavel.tm.fr, www.cotes-ventoux.com, and www.vacqueyras.tm.fr. For tourist information, go to www.tourisme.fr and type in the name of a town or village.

OTHER INFORMATION

Office de Tourisme, Parvis de la Gare, Valence.
04 75 44 90 40
There are tourist offices in most towns, but this one has plenty of general information.
Inter Rhone, 6 Rue des 6 Faucons, Avignon.
04 90 27 24 00
Maison@inter-rhone.com
The office of the Rhône region's wine fraternity.

CHÂTEAU GRILLET

Vienne
Valence
Avignon

SURROUNDED BY VINEYARDS belonging to the *appellation* of Condrieu *(see p252)*, this unusually tiny, single-estate *appellation* faces southeast, providing perfect ripening conditions for the low-yielding Viognier vines. Extravagantly praised by 18th-century connoisseurs, the delicate white wines of Château Grillet have traditionally been considered some of the best in France, but vintages in the 1980s and early 1990s were disappointingly dull and over-sulfured. More recent efforts have shown a marked improvement, and at their best these wines can develop remarkably with time. Prices are still very high, and my advice for anyone looking for great apricot-scented Viognier wines is to consider the best wines of Condrieu before indulging in the wines of Château Grillet, which come with rather more extravagant price tags.

Château Grillet
The brown bottle and distinctive label make it easy to recognize the wines of Château Grillet.

Faded Glory
Gloomily imposing, the once-great Château Grillet overlooks its vineyards, which nestle comfortably in a natural granite amphitheater.

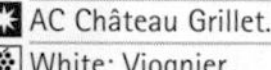

- AC Château Grillet.
- White: Viognier.
- Opulent, perfumed, dry.
- Château Grillet.
- Fresh black truffles baked in a puff-pastry case with *foie gras* and smoked bacon.
- 2003, 2001, 1999, 1997, 1996, 1995, 1994.
- 5–20 years.

THE VIOGNIER REVIVAL

Chardonnay is the most widely planted white-wine grape variety in the world, and its apparent ubiquity has prompted some of the more experimental wine-makers to search for an alternative. Having dismissed Riesling, Sauvignon Blanc, Sémillon, Chenin Blanc, and Pinot Gris, a number of producers, including the prominent Beaujolais *négociant* Georges Duboeuf, have turned their attention to the Viognier grape. This fragrant but low-yielding grape was once widely planted along the northern part of the Rhône Valley. Its tendency, however, to give small crops, and to make wines that go flabby a few years after bottling, led to a decline in its popularity. By 1968 there were just 35 acres (14 ha) of Viognier vines under cultivation. As part of the grape's recent revival, Georges Duboeuf has planted significant Viognier vineyards in the Ardèche, and there are now more than 370 acres (150 ha) of Viognier vines farther south in Languedoc-Roussillon. The variety's greatest success, however, is most evident in the vineyards of the recently rejuvenated *appellation* of Condrieu *(see p252)*. Often made with nearly 100 percent Viognier grapes, the exotically perfumed and perfectly balanced white wines made here are some of the most exciting in the Rhône Valley.

Challenging but Rewarding
Deliciously fragrant but temperamental and low-yielding, Viognier is a difficult grape variety to grow.

CHÂTEAUNEUF-DU-PAPE

THE *APPELLATION* OF Châteauneuf-du-Pape is situated in the sun-baked southern reaches of the Rhône Valley, where the Mediterranean climate allows a great number of grape varieties to flourish. These well known vineyards are famous as much for their unusual covering of glacier-scoured stones as for the spicy, long-lived red wines that they produce.

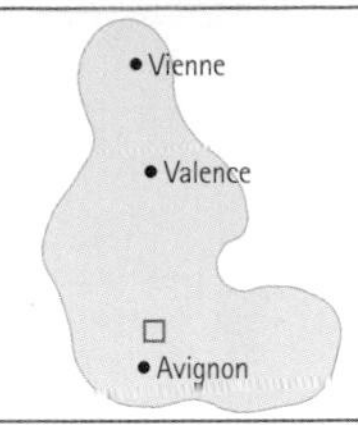

Shingle Vineyards
It is the pebbles in Châteauneuf-du-Pape that set its vineyards apart from wine-growing land elsewhere in France. At night, the stones give off heat that has been stored during the day.

Dominating its namesake village, the now-ruined 14th-century château at Châteauneuf-du-Pape was built for Pope Jean XXII as a summer retreat from the papal court in the nearby city of Avignon. By the second half of the 14th century, flourishing walled vineyards had been established here. They produced popular red and white wines that were sold throughout the region, until the latter part of the 18th century, under the name of *vin d'Avignon*.

Classified under the rules of the *appellation contrôlée* system in 1935, the *terroir* of Châteauneuf-du-Pape is unusually varied, with soils ranging from sand through to gravel and alluvial deposits.

As a result, producers here are entitled to combine 13 different grape varieties, from Grenache and Syrah to Mourvèdre, Terret Noir and white Bourboulenc. Despite this freedom, most wine-makers use a mixture of only three or four grape varieties, with Syrah, Mourvèdre, and Grenache the most widely used. Another famously unusual feature of most parts of the *appellation* are the large, cream-colored pebbles that make the vineyards look like pebble beaches, storing heat during the day and reflecting it onto the vines at night.

In recent years, most of the the red wines produced here have become much less light and fruity than they used to be, and are richer and more gamey and long-lived. White wines are often dull, though better use of the Roussanne grape is helping to make a growing number of intriguingly aromatic wines.

Château Rayas
This is one of the very best estates in the *appellation*. Unusually in Châteauneuf-du-Pape, the wines here are made entirely from a single grape variety, Grenache.

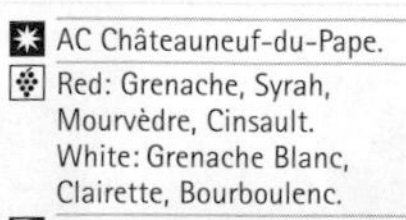

- AC Châteauneuf-du-Pape.
- Red: Grenache, Syrah, Mourvèdre, Cinsault. White: Grenache Blanc, Clairette, Bourboulenc.
- Full-bodied dry reds. Small amounts of dry white.
- Pierre André, Ch de Beaucastel, Beaurenard, Bosquet des Papes, Cabrières, les Caillous, Chapoutier, la Charbonnière, Clos du Mont Olivet, Clos des Pâpes, Delas, Font de Michelle, Fortia la Gardine, Guigal, Jaboulet, Janasse, Mont-Redon, la Mordorée, Nalys, la Nerthe, du Pegaü, Ch Rayas, Réserve des Célestins, de la Solitude, Tardieu-Laurent, du Trignon, Vieux Télégraphe, Villeneuve.
- Red: Leg of lamb in pastry.
- Red: 2003, 2001, 2000, 1998, 1995, 1994, 1990, 1989.
- Red: 5–20 years. White: 3–5 years.

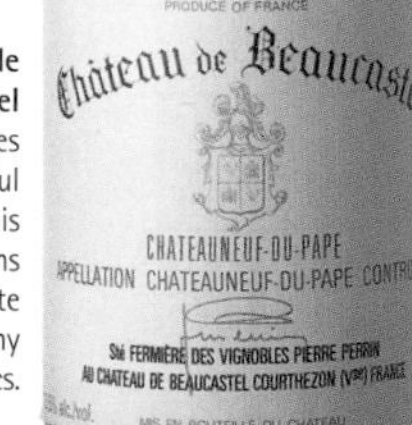

Château de Beaucastel
Producing wines of wonderful character, this estate remains the favorite of many French critics.

CLAIRETTE DE DIE

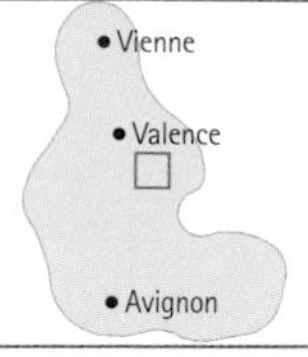

HUGGING THE SLOPES OF the Drôme Valley, about 25 miles (40 km) to the east of the Rhône, the sparkling white-wine *appellation* of Clairette de Die is something of an anomaly in a region better known for full-bodied red wines from *appellations* such as Côte Rôtie *(see p256)* and Crozes-Hermitage *(see p257)*. The area covered by the Clairette de Die *appellation* produces two contrasting styles of sparkling wine. The first is a dry, neutral-tasting wine made entirely from the Clairette grape and known, since a recent name change, as Crémant de Die. The second is the deliciously ripe and peachy Clairette de Die Méthode Dioise Ancestrale. Made from a mixture of Clairette and Muscat grapes, this unusual wine is bottled during its initial fermentation, to trap the carbon dioxide bubbles.

Vincent Achard
This fine producer makes fruity, semi-sweet Méthode Dioise Ancestrale, sold until 1999 as Clairette de Die Tradition.

Windswept Slopes
In contrast to the red-wine Rhône Valley *appellations* to the north, the bleak, windswept slopes of the Drôme Valley are best suited to the production of white sparkling wines.

- AC Clairette de Die Méthode Dioise Ancestrale, AC Crémant de Die.
- White: Clairette, Muscat à Petits Grains.
- Dry and sweet sparkling whites.
- Vincent Achard, Cave Cooperative de Die, Didier Cornillon, Magord, Jean-Claude Raspail, Union des Jeunes Viticulteurs (Chamberan).
- Clairette de Die Méthode Dioise Ancestrale: Raspberry and strawberry tart.
- 2002.
- 1–2 years.

CONDRIEU

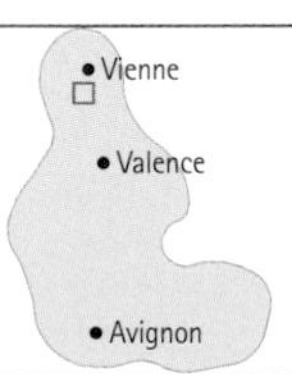

DRY AND RICHLY ALCOHOLIC, and with a wonderful, unexpected perfume of peach blossom, apricots, and violets, the white wines of Condrieu are the best in the Rhône and have recently acquired almost cult status. Originally planted during the first few centuries AD, the south-facing vineyards around the town of Condrieu in the eastern part of the *appellation* have long been used to to produce semi-sweet, often botrytized, late-harvest wines; a style that is being successfully revived. Planted, as today, with the fragrant but temperamental Viognier grape *(see p250)*, by the 1960s the vineyards of Condrieu covered only 25 acres (10 ha). Today, however, thanks to the recent Rhône boom, global Viognier fever, and some talented young producers, the area has risen to 259 acres (105 ha).

Yves Cuilleron
This Condrieu producer makes fragrant, late-harvest sweet wines as well as the usual apricot-scented dry ones.

Picking in Condrieu
Yields are low and harvesting is hard in the steeply sloping vineyards of Condrieu, two explanations for the high prices paid for the hugely popular wines of the *appellation*.

- AC Condrieu.
- White: Viognier.
- Full-bodied, highly-perfumed dry. Occasionally sweet.
- Ch d'Ampuis, P. & C. Bonnefond, Louis Chèze, Gilbert Chirat, Clusel-Roche, Y. Cuileron, Delas, Pierre Dumazet, P. Faury, Pierre Gaillard, J-M. Gerin, Guigal, A. Perret, G. Vernay, F. Villard.
- Crab bisque with a garnish of deep-fried sage.
- 2003, 2002, 1999, 1997, 1996, 1995.
- 2–8 years.

CORNAS

AN AREA OF STEEPLY TERRACED south-facing granite vineyards on the western bank of the Rhône, the tiny *appellation* of Cornas covered only 130 acres (53 hectares) in 1975. Since then, however, the increasing international popularity of wines from the Rhône has given the full-bodied, somewhat rustic red wines of Cornas a new lease on life, and the area under vine has now risen to 210 acres (85 hectares). Improved vineyard practices have increased yields, while techniques such as destemming grapes before fermentation and the use of new oak barrels for maturation have produced smoky wines that are fruitier and less tannic than the ones traditionally made here. Old-school wines made by producers such as Auguste Clape offer top quality, but they need time.

Vienne
Valence
Avignon

Auguste Clape
Bucking the modern trend in Cornas toward a lighter, fruitier style, these more traditional wines are attractive and robust.

Sun-Trap Slopes
The terraced south- and southeast-facing vineyards on the hillsides of the Cornas *appellation* are perfectly positioned to soak up every available ray of sunshine and are ideal for Syrah.

- AC Cornas.
- Red: Syrah.
- Full-bodied, deep-colored reds that are very tannic when young.
- Thierry Allemand, Guy de Barjac, Chapoutier, Auguste Clape, Jean-Luc Colombo, Courbis, Jaboulet, Jean Lionnet, Robert Michel, Rochepertuis, de Saint-Pierre, Tardieu-Laurent, Noël Verset, Alain Voge.
- Partridges braised with cabbage.
- 2003, 2000, 1999, 1998, 1995, 1990, 1989, 1988.
- 8–10 years.

COTEAUX DU TRICASTIN

SPREADING OUTWARD from the eastern bank of the Rhône just south of Montélimar, the little-known hillside vineyards of Tricastin were awarded *appellation contrôlée* status in 1973. Several varieties are grown here, but many of the red and rosé wines of the *appellation* are made from a blend of Syrah and Grenache. The red wines in particular can offer excellent value, but so do the whites, which are often made from a blend of Viognier, Marsanne, and Roussanne.

Domaine de Grangeneuve
This light, fruity-peppery wine offers good value and easy drinking.

- AC Coteaux du Tricastin.
- Red/ rosé: Grenache, Cinsault, Syrah, Carignan.
  White: Clairette, Viognier, Roussanne, Marsanne.
- Spicy reds. Dry, crisp whites, rosés.
- Grangeneuve, des Rozets, du Vieux Micoulier.
- Cold roast beef.
- 2003, 2001.
- 1–4 years.

CÔTES DU VENTOUX

CLOSE TO THE POINT where the Rhône Valley meets Provence is Mont Ventoux, venerated in local folklore as the source of the bitterly cold, high-speed *mistral* wind that whips down the Rhône Valley every winter. The limestone vineyards of the surrounding Côtes du Ventoux *appellation* are used to grow varieties such as the Grenache, the Cinsault, the Mourvèdre and the Syrah, producing fruity, light, early-drinking reds. Smaller amounts of unmemorable white and rosé are also made here.

Château Unang
In contrast to many Rhône wines, the Côtes du Ventoux are fresh and fragrant.

- AC Côtes du Ventoux.
- Red/ rosé: Grenache, Syrah, Cinsault, Carignan.
  White: Clairette.
- Light, scented reds. Dry whites. Dry rosés.
- Des Anges, Michel Bernard, Jaboulet, Ch Pesquié.
- Roast partridge.
- 2003, 2001.
- 1–4 years.

CÔTES DU RHÔNE

OF ALL THE LARGER, SO-CALLED generic *appellations* in France, it is the Côtes du Rhône, stretching along the banks of the Rhône River from Vienne to Pertuis, and the Côtes du Rhône-Villages with its 16 named villages, that would get my vote for the greatest improvement in wine-making in recent years, and some of the very best value for money.

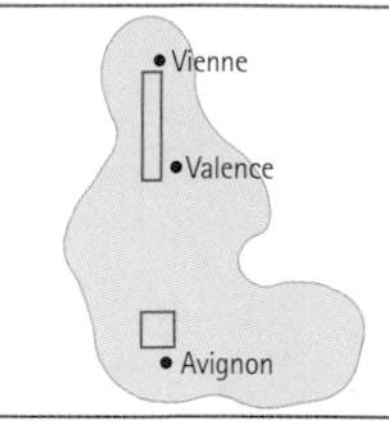

Domaine de la Cantharide
This wine from Visan is peppery when young, and develops an extra richness with age.

Officially, a bottle of wine labeled *appellation contrôlée* Côtes du Rhône could come from any part of a large swath of vineyards between Vienne and Pertuis—in other words, from anywhere along the Rhône Valley. In practice, the geography of the region means that the contents of such bottles have almost certainly been crushed from grapes grown in the southern Rhône. Between them, 10,000 wine-makers produce around 300 million bottles of *appellation contrôlée* Côtes du Rhône each year. Both the soils and the grape varieties grown here are diverse, with the dominant Grenache followed closely by Syrah, Mourvèdre, and Cinsault. As for the whites, these include a mixture of varieties from the dull Clairette to the fragrant Roussanne. Further variety is guaranteed by the ways in which the wines are made. Many of the reds are now made by the *macération carbonique* method *(see p26)*, which makes for light, juicy wines that are easy to sell within months of the harvest. At the same time, the trend among more ambitious producers is to use more traditional techniques to make wines with a firmer structure and greater longevity.

In theory, the finest wines of the Côtes du Rhône are found among the 20 million bottles labeled as Côtes du Rhône-Villages. Many of the best of these are produced in the villages listed on the right, each of which is named on the label (after Côtes du Rhône in the case of the first 16, before it in the case of Brézème). While named village wines quite justifiably command the highest prices, many good wines are also sold under the more basic Côtes du Rhône *appellation*, made by well-known *négociant* firms including Jaboulet Aîné and Guigal, and on estates throughout the southern Rhône Valley such as Château Mont-Redon in Châteauneuf-du-Pape *(see p251)*.

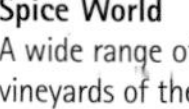

Spice World
A wide range of grape varieties are grown in the hillside vineyards of the Côtes du Rhône, producing a similarly varied range of excellent red wines that are notable for their distinctively rich and spicy flavors.

- AC Côtes du Rhône, AC Côtes du Rhône-Villages.
- Red/rosé: Grenache, Syrah, Carignan, Mourvèdre. White: Clairette, Grenache Blanc, Bourboulenc, Viognier.
- Light- to medium-bodied reds. Dry rosé. Dry white.
- Denis et Daniel Alary, d'Ameilhaud, de Beaurenard, des Bernardins, Berther-Raynède Cabasse, Cave de Cairanne, Chapoton, Cave de Chusclan, du Colombier, de Fonsalette, les Goubert, Guigal, Jaboulet, de la Janasse, de Lindas, Jean-Marie Lombard, Mont Redon, de la Mordorée, Ogier, de l'Oratoire St Martin, Rabasse-Charavin, Marcel Richaud, Ste Anne, Ste Gayan, St Maurice, la Soumade.
- Red: Sautéed potatoes with *saucisson* and melted cheese.
- Red: 2003, 2001, 2000.
- Red: 2–5 years.

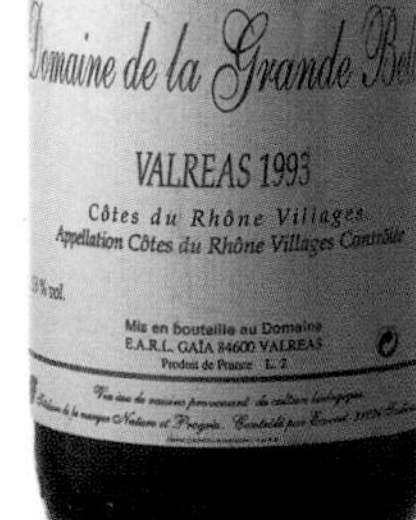

Domaine de la Grande Bellane
This is a really good single-estate wine from the village of Valréas, packed full of rich, spicy fruit flavors.

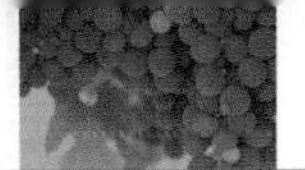

GREAT WINE VILLAGES OF THE RHÔNE VALLEY

The first 16 villages belong to the *appellation* Côtes du Rhône-Villages and print their name after the name Côtes du Rhône. Listed at the end is Brézème, which has its own *appellation.*

Beaumes-de-Venise *(see p259)* Best known for its fortified wines made from the Muscat grape, this village also produces good, light but juicy, peppery reds. Best producers include Domaine de Fenouillet and Château Redortier.

Cairanne One of the star villages of the region, home to several ambitious producers making some seriously good, spicy wines.

Chusclan The wines to buy here are the rosés, which can be better than those of nearby Tavel *(see p261).* The reds are attractive, too, but they are less worth keeping.

Laudun Producers here make unusually good white wines, as well as some of the region's finest Grenache-dominant reds. The best wines will improve with a year or two in the bottle.

Rasteau *(see p260).* This village and Beaumes-de-Venise *(see above)* are noted as the only two *communes* in France that include both fortified *(vin doux naturel)* and unfortified wines.

Roaix The *commune* of Roaix shares a wine-making *coopérative* with the neighboring village of Séguret *(see below)*, producing intense reds that repay three or four years' aging.

Rochegude Although once famed for its whites, this *appellation* now covers only red wines, which are light and peppery.

Sablet Competing with Cairanne *(see above)* and named for its sandy soil, this is a dynamic *commune* known for its light reds, but increasing use of the Syrah grape variety is producing longer-lived wines.

St Gervais This *commune* is increasingly well regarded, thanks partly to the efforts of producer Guy Steinmaier at Domaine Ste Anne. The Mourvèdre and Syrah grapes both perform well in this southern region, as does Viognier, which contributes to some fine whites.

St Maurice-sur-Eygues Most of the unexceptional wines of this village are produced by the local *coopérative.*

St Panteléon-les-Vignes and **Rousset-les-Vignes** The coolest climate in the Rhône explains the lightness of the wines made in these two neighboring villages.

Séguret These are some of the most serious and tightly structured wines in the Côtes du Rhône, and deserve to be kept for four years or more before drinking.

Valréas This *commune* produces some of the most attractively fruity, floral reds in the Rhône.

Vinsobres The red wines from this *commune* range from light and easy-drinking to slow-maturing and intense.

Visan Delicious when young, many of the wines from this *commune* also age well, and are worth keeping in the bottle for a few years.

Brézème Lying midway between the northern and southern Rhône and to the north of the Villages, Brézème labels its wines Brézème-Côtes du Rhône. The reds here are distinguished in that they are made only from the Syrah grape.

Intense Wines
In the shadow of brooding hills, the Grenache vineyards of Vinsobres produce the varied range of red wines sold as Côtes du Rhône-Vinsobres.

CÔTE RÔTIE

THE CÔTE RÔTIE, or the "roasted hillside," where the grapes are often literally roasted in the sun, produces red wines that live up to their evocative name, being deep-colored, luscious, and powerful. Covering the steep slopes behind the village of Ampuis, the vineyards form a bridge between Burgundy to the north and the Rhône Valley to the south.

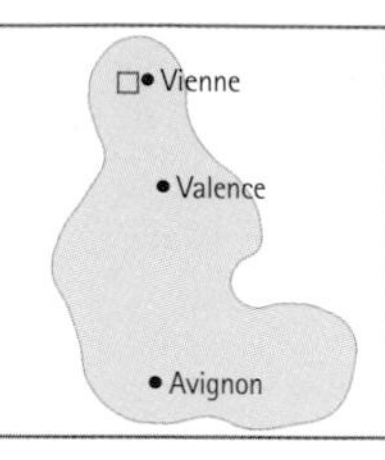

Château d'Ampuis
Many of the finest wines of the Côte Rôtie come from producer Marcel Guigal's collection of vineyards, including his illustrious recent acquisition, the Château d'Ampuis, whose wines bear the name of the château.

Despite a vinicultural history dating back nearly 2,000 years, a large proportion of the vineyards of the Côte Rôtie were not replanted following the devastating late-19th-century epidemic of the vine louse phylloxera. Vines gave way to fruit trees and, for the first three-quarters of the 20th century, the wines of the Côte Rôtie were almost forgotten. While a small number of wine-makers have always persevered on the steep and challenging slopes here, credit for the rescue of the *appellation* has to go largely to the gifted producer and *négociant* Marcel Guigal. Not only is Guigal a tireless promoter of high-quality Côte Rôtie, he has also revealed the potential of several individual estates by producing and bottling their wines separately. Today, Guigal's single-estate wines, produced from grapes grown in the vineyards of La Landonne, La Mouline, La Turque, and the Château d'Ampuis, are undoubtedly the very best of the *appellation*, and command prices that are some of the highest in France. Guigal also produces a wine known as *Brune et Blonde*, made from a blend of grapes grown on two of the best-known slopes of the Côte Rôtie, the Côte Brune and the Côte Blonde. Popular legend has it that the vineyards, with their different-colored soils, were named after the hair color of the two beautiful daughters of the local landowner.

This is quintessential Syrah country, producing great wines with complex berry flavors and an unmistakable smoky note. Increasingly, producers are adding up to 20 percent white Viognier grapes to the Syrah, giving the wines an exotic violet and apricot perfume.

Côte Blonde
Naming an individual vineyard is common practice in Côte Rôtie. The chalky-sand soil of the Côte Blonde produces early drinking wines.

- AC Côte Rôtie.
- Red: Syrah. White: Viognier.
- Full-bodied reds with an opulent bouquet.
- Ch d'Ampuis, Pierre Barge, Michel Bernard, de Boisseyt, Patrick et Christophe Bonnefond, Bernard Burgaud, Champet, Chapoutier, Clusel-Roch, Yves Cuilleron, Delas, Philippe Faury, Gaillard, Jean-Michel Gérin, Marcel Guigal, Jean-Paul et Jean-Luc Jamet, Robert Jasmin, la Landonne, Bernard Levet, Gabriel Meffre, les Moutonnes, Michel Ogier, René Rostaing, Georges Vernay, Vidal-Fleury, François Villard.
- Leg of lamb roasted with fresh rosemary and whole garlic cloves.
- 2003, 2000, 1999, 1998, 1997, 1996, 1995, 1994, 1991, 1990, 1989, 1988.
- 10–15 years.

La Landonne
Single-vineyard wines from La Landonne have contributed to the prestige of this *appellation*.

CROZES-HERMITAGE

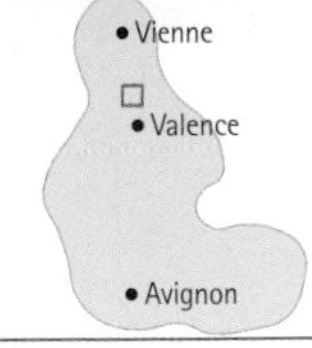

COVERING AN AREA OF 2,470 acres (1,000 ha), this large *appellation* spreads out around 11 villages to the north and south of the town of Tain-l'Hermitage. Like the *terroir*, the wines of Crozes-Hermitage are very varied, but at their complex, full-bodied, fruity best, they offer fantastic value. The finest estates, including Les Chassis and Domaine de Thalabert, lie to the north of Tain-l'Hermitage on south-facing slopes along the banks of the Rhône. Farther east the land is flatter, yields are higher, and the wines more ordinary. Ninety percent of the wines are red, made mainly from Syrah mixed with small amounts of Roussanne and Marsanne. White wines are made from the delicate Roussanne, either alone or mixed with Marsanne, and are often fresh and elegant.

The Brothers Chapoutier
The largest landowners in Crozes-Hermitage, the Chapoutier brothers produce a variety of fine wines.

Hidden Treasure
Some of the best vineyards in Crozes-Hermitage are tucked away just behind the slopes used to produce the more expensive wines of neighboring Hermitage *(see p258)*.

- AC Crozes-Hermitage.
- Red: Syrah.
  White: Roussanne, Marsanne.
- Full-bodied reds. Full-bodied, shorter-lived dry whites.
- Belle, Chapoutier, les Chassis, Chave, des Clairmonts, Colomber, Combier, Delas, des Desmeure, Entrefaux, A Graillot, Jaboulet, E Pochon, Remizières, M Sorrel, Caves de Tain-l'Hermitage, Tardieu-Laurent, de Thalabert, Vidal-Fleury.
- Chicken sautéed with basil.
- 2003, 2000, 1999, 1997.
- 5–8 years.

GIGONDAS

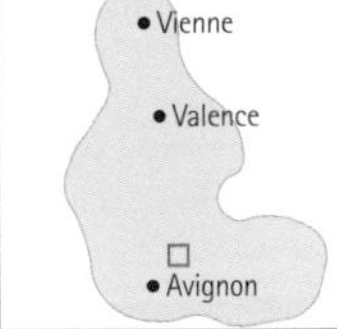

THE VILLAGE AND THE surrounding vineyards of the *appellation* of Gigondas are situated in the spectacular Dentelles de Montmirail mountains to the east of the small town of Orange. In the early 1950s, the *commune* was granted *appellation contrôlée* Côtes du Rhône-Villages status, and in 1971 its wines were promoted to *appellation contrôlée* Gigondas. At their best, the reds of Gigondas are plummy and rich, dominated by the mellow flavors of the Grenache, carefully combined with smaller amounts of the tannic Syrah and the aromatic Mourvèdre. A great alternative to the more expensive vintages of nearby Châteauneuf-du-Pape *(see p251)*, these wines will develop well for up to a decade. Dry, peppery rosé wines are also made here, and are well worth looking for.

Domaine du Cayron
Strangely underrated, the peppery, long-lived wines of Gigondas offer some of the best value in the region.

Mountains of Lace
Small but poetically named, the "lacy" Dentelles de Montmirail mountain range forms a stunning backdrop to the vineyards of Gigondas.

- AC Gigondas.
- Red/rosé: Grenache, Syrah, Mourvèdre.
- Full-bodied, sometimes rustic reds. Dry, peppery rosés.
- Des Bosquets, Brusset, De Cabasse, Cayron, Delas, Espiers, les Goubert, Gour de Chaule, Guigal, Jaboulet, de Montmirail, Piaugier, Raspail-Ay, St Gayan, Ste Anne, Santa Duc, Tardieu-Laurent, des Tourelles, du Trignon, Vidal-Fleury.
- Ragout of lamb.
- 2003, 2001, 2000, 1998.
- Red: 3–10 years.

HERMITAGE

THE VINEYARDS OF Hermitage lie deep in Syrah country on the steep slopes of the Rhône Valley between the *appellations* of Crozes-Hermitage *(see p257)* and St Joseph *(see p260)*. Flourishing here as almost nowhere else in the world, the Syrah, with its spicy, smoky flavors, is the only grape variety used in the complex, long-lived red wines of the *appellation*.

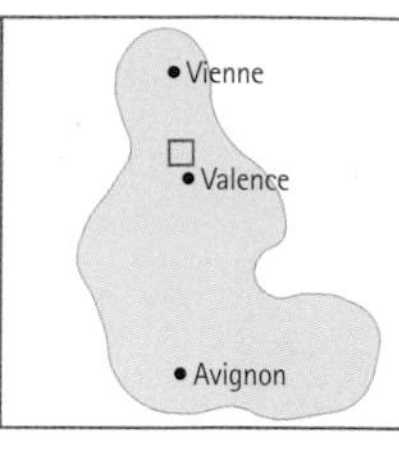

Writ Large
The stone walls that hold the steeply terraced vineyards of Hermitage in place are often used as billboards by *négociants* eager to publicize the locations from which they make some of their finest wines.

Producing classic, inky-black wines, the unique vineyards of Hermitage have been famous for more than 500 years. By the 19th century, the wines of Hermitage were commanding higher prices than the wines of the best Bordeaux estates. Fanning out around the town of Tain-l'Hermitage, this is a hillside *appellation* of rocky vineyards, distinguished by a mushroom-shaped underlying granite outcrop and a southern exposure, which allows the ripening grapes to catch every ray of sunshine.

Unlike most Syrah-based *appellations*, including nearby Crozes-Hermitage and St Joseph, which use small amounts of various white grape varieties to add perfume and lightness to their wines, the reds of Hermitage include nothing except the richly tannic Syrah. Although packed with the flavors of raspberries, blackberries, pepper, and smoke, these wines can be somewhat tough and inaccessible in their youth. A decade or so in the cellar, however, gives them a wonderfully gamey complexity. Extending over 380 acres (154 ha), the single south-facing slope that makes up the Hermitage *appellation* includes a number of subtly different environments, and wines here traditionally have been made from a blend of grapes selected from several sites. Increasingly, however, producers are choosing to make their wines from grapes grown on single, named plots of land. The best of these include Paul Jaboulet Aîné's well-known La Chapelle. Other excellent single-estate wines to look for include Les Bessards and Les Greffieux.

The white wines of Hermitage, once as highly regarded as its reds, are now produced in only tiny quantities, but in two distinct styles. First, with its own *appellation*, but rarely produced, is the unusual wine known as *vin de paille*. Made by drying the grapes on straw before pressing, the best of these wines are crisp and honeyed. More common are rich, dry white wines made from a mixture of Marsanne and Roussanne grapes, which often improve for as long as 10 years in the bottle.

- AC Hermitage, AC Hermitage Vin de Paille.
- Red: Syrah. White: Marsanne, Roussanne.
- Powerful, tannic reds. Full-bodied, herb- and peach-scented whites.
- Albert Belle, Michel Bernard, Chapoutier, Bernard Chave, Jean-Louis Chave, Gérard Chave, du Colombier, Delas Frères (Marquise de la Tourette, les Bassards), Faurie, Ferraton, Grippat, E Guigal, Guyot, Paul Jaboulet Aîné, des Remizières, St Jemms, Marc Sorrel, Cave de Tain l'Hermitage, Tardieu-Laurent, De Vallouit.
- Roast pheasant with a sauce of red wine, shallots, and wild mushrooms.
- 2003, 2000, 1999, 1996, 1995, 1990, 1989, 1988.
- Red: 10–20 years. White: 8–15 years.

Jean-Louis Chave
The wines produced by Jean-Louis Chave are some of the very best of the *appellation.*

LIRAC

KNOWN UNTIL RECENTLY as an unsuccessful emulator of the rosé wines produced by its southern neighbor, Tavel *(see p261)*, today the *appellation* of Lirac is more famous as a producer of fast-improving red and white wines. Set on the west bank of the Rhône just north of Avignon, the producers of Lirac use a classically varied southern Rhône combination of the Grenache, Syrah, Mourvèdre, and Cinsault grape varieties to make red wines that are medium-bodied, smooth, and spicy. At their best, these represent excellent value. The dry white wines made here are losing their reputation for dullness and have been vastly improved by the inclusion in 1992 of the Marsanne, the Roussanne, and the fragrant Viognier on the list of permitted grape varieties, and many are now attractively floral.

Domaine Pélaquié
Deliciously rich and peppery at their best, the little-known red wines of Lirac can offer excellent value.

Grenache Vines
Skillfully combined with other grape varieties, the mellow flavors of the Grenache are an important component in the red and rosé wines of Lirac.

- AC Lirac.
- Red/ rosé: Grenache, Carignan, Mourvèdre, Syrah. White: Clairette, Ugni Blanc, Marsanne, Roussanne, Viognier.
- Medium- to full-bodied reds. Dry whites. Dry rosés.
- Ch d'Aquéria, les domaines Bernard, de Devoye Martine, la Fermade, Maby, de la Mordorée, Chapelle de Maillac, Pélaquié, St Maurice, St Roch.
- Red: Saddle of hare.
- 2003, 2000, 1998, 1997.
- Red: 2–5 years. White/ rosé : 1–3 years.

MUSCAT DE BEAUMES-DE-VENISE

ALTHOUGH IT PRODUCES high-quality red wines that are sold under the Côtes du Rhône-Villages *appellation*, the village of Beaumes-de-Venise, to the east of the town of Orange, is more famous for its apricot-gold *vins doux naturels (see p31)*, made from the fragrant Muscat grape. Most of the Muscat wines here are made at the Coopérative des Vins et Muscats, famous due to its hugely successful 1970s marketing campaign, which sold the wine throughout northern Europe as a dessert wine to be enjoyed by the glass, thanks to its screw-top bottle. The *coopérative's* top wines are comparable to the single-estate wines made by individual producers. The best efforts of this *appellation* are rich and peachy, achieving a perfect balance of sweetness and acidity.

Domaine de Durban
The best wines here are made by individual producers like this one, rather than in the local *coopérative*.

Provençal Sun
The sun-baked vineyards around the village of Beaumes-de-Venise are used to grow two varieties of the Muscat grape, named for its distinctive musky fragrance.

- AC Muscat de Beaumes-de-Venise.
- White: Muscat Blanc à Petits Grains, Muscat Rosé à Petits Grains.
- Fragrant *vins doux naturels*.
- Beau Mistral, de Beaumalric, Cave Coopérative des Vignerons de Beaumes-de-Venise, des Bernardins, Chapoutier, de Coyeux, de Durban, de Fenouillet, Paul Jaboulet Ainé, la Soumade, Vidal-Fleury
- Three-chocolate mousse.
- Mainly non-vintage.
- 1–5 years.

RASTEAU

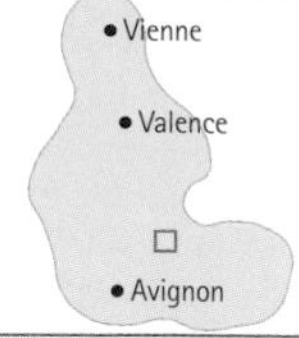

THIS CÔTES DU RHÔNE-VILLAGES *commune* offers both fortified and unfortified wines. The grapes for the former are 90 percent Grenache (Noir, Gris, or Blanc) from the villages of Rasteau, Sablet, and Cairanne. Fortification is carried out by adding brandy during early development. The fortified wines are in *rancio* style—that is, they are purposely maderized by storing the wine in oak casks, which are later exposed to air and sunlight. The wines vary with the quality of grapes, the cleanliness of casks, and the degree of maderization. Some are like thick, sweet sherry; others have a delicate, Madeira-like quality. Rasteau's red table wines, though possibly less exciting, tend to be reliable, peppery Rhônes. The whites can be dull and are almost always best drunk young.

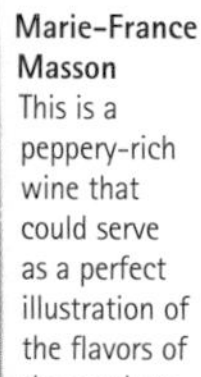

Marie-France Masson
This is a peppery-rich wine that could serve as a perfect illustration of the flavors of the southern Rhône.

Cave des Vignerons
As in some other parts of the Rhône, the smaller *coopératives* to be found in these communes produce some of the best—and best-value—wines.

- AC Rasteau, AC Rasteau Rancio.
- Red/white/rosé/tawny: Grenache Noir, Grenache Gris, Grenache Blanc.
- Peppery red wines and cask-aged sweet *vins doux naturels.*
- Des Coteaux des Travers, des Girasols, de la Grangeneuve, Masson, de la Soumade, Francis Vache, Cave des Vignerons de Rasteau.
- *Vin doux naturel:* Chocolate tart.
- Red: 2003, 2000, 1998.
- 3–10 years.

ST JOSEPH

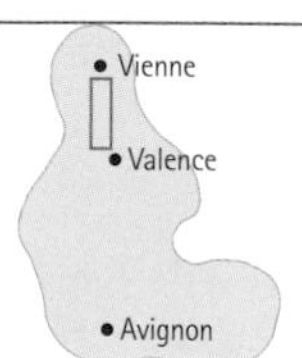

ONCE CALLED Vin de Mauves after the *commune* of that name, St Joseph became an *appellation* in 1956. It then grew to six times its former size, stretching south down the west bank of the Rhône to Valence. Many of the new plantings took little account of the character of the original vineyards, with the effect that buying St Joseph today is a hit-or-miss business—wines range in style and quality from basic Côtes du Rhône *(see pp254–5)* to junior Hermitage *(see p258)*. The best vineyards are on the sandy and gravelly granite slopes behind and around Tournon. Grapes ripen less well than they do in Hermitage, and wines are less intense. Even so, they can be first-class, blackberryish reds for relatively early drinking. Small quantities of Marsanne- and Roussanne-based whites are also produced.

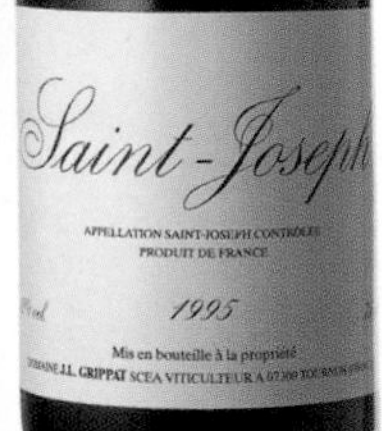

Jean-Louis Grippat
Classy reds like this can sometimes age more successfully than feeble examples of supposedly classier Hermitage.

Mauves
The village that once gave its name to the entire region is now a quiet *commune* almost hidden among the vines, and still producing good wine.

- AC St Joseph.
- Red: Syrah. White: Marsanne, Roussanne.
- Soft, fruity reds. Fragrant, richly flavored dry whites.
- Cave St Désirat, Cave de Tain-l'Hermitage, Chapoutier, Chave, Chèze, Courbuis, P. Coursodon, Y. Cuilleron, Pierre Gaillard, Graillot, J-L. Grippat, Jaboulet, Perret, G. Vernay, Villard.
- Red: Wood pigeon with onions, red wine, and ham.
- Red: 2003, 2000, 1999.
- Red: 3–10 years. White: 1–3 years.

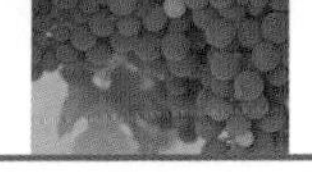

ST PÉRAY

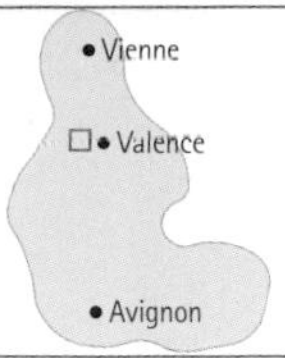

THIS *APPELLATION* IS SITUATED on the Rhône's west bank, opposite and now almost within the sprawling outskirts of Valence. The fight against competition from developers is not made any easier by the undistinguished character of these light, often quite acidic wines. St Péray's style makes it an anomaly in this area of rich, meaty Syrahs and full-bodied Viogniers. Conditions for grape growing are affected by a cooler climate and the richness of the soils. Most of the grape harvest goes to make rustic *méthode traditionelle* sparkling wines, which are jointly produced by the *caves coopératives* of Tain-l'Hermitage and St Péray, and mostly sold within the region itself. For a taste of what this *appellation* can produce when given more individual care and attention, try the wines of Jean Lionnet and Marcel Juge.

Jean Louis et Françoise Thiers
Thiers offers an increasingly rare example of gently floral, dry sparkling wine made from traditional Rhône grape varieties.

Threatened Territory
Vines in St Péray are giving way to houses and apartment buildings that will accommodate the growing population of nearby Valence.

- AC St Péray, AC St Péray Mousseux.
- White and sparkling: Marsanne, Roussanne.
- Still and sparkling dry whites.
- Cave de Tain-l'Hermitage, J.-F. Chaboud, Auguste Clape, Bernard Gripa, Marcel Juge, Jean Lionnet, Jean-Louis et Françoise Thiers, Alain Voge.
- Still: Shoulder of veal cooked with white wine, leeks, onions, and capers.
- Still: 2002.
- Sparkling: 1–3 years. Still: 1–4 years.

TAVEL

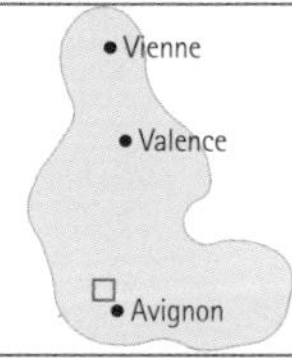

A FAVORITE WITH BOTH Louis XIV and the novelist Honoré de Balzac, this is the most famous rosé in France, and the only Rhône *appellation* to produce exclusively pink wine. In the past, although it often tasted stale and dull, it was praised for its bronze color and lauded as the only rosé wine to improve with age. This reputation helped to swell the vineyards to nearly 2,500 acres (1,000 ha). There is no disputing the potential of Grenache, Syrah, and Mourvèdre to make good wine on Tavel's sandy, clay-alluvial and pebbly soils, and modern wine-growers and critics respectively produce and praise much fresher, more violet-hued wine. Good Tavel should be both fragrant and fruity, yet full-bodied and bone-dry. It is an excellent food wine that can accompany *charcuterie*, fish in sauce, or white meats.

Domaine de Valéry
Despite its traditional bronze color, this is an example of Tavel whose rich, peppery flavors will not displease modern drinkers.

Rosé Prospects
Better wine-making and vine-growing are belatedly improving the prospects of the rosé-producing vineyards of Tavel.

- AC Tavel.
- Rosé: Grenache, Cinsault.
- Potentially refreshing, peppery, dry rosé.
- Ch d'Aquéria, de la Forcadière, de la Genestière, Guigal, Jaboulet Aîné, de la Mordorée, Prieuré de Montezargues, Ch de Trinquevedel, de Valéry, Vieux Moulin de Tavel, du Vieux Relais.
- Squid stuffed with onions and garlic, stewed in squid ink and white Côtes du Rhône wine.
- Rosé: 2004
- 2–5 years.

VACQUEYRAS

EIGHTEEN YEARS AFTER GIGONDAS *(see p257)* became the first of the named Côtes du Rhône-Villages *(see p255)* to get its own *appellation*, this village achieved similar recognition in 1990. Its best reds rarely match good examples of Gigondas and do not always outclass wines from Côtes du Rhône-Villages *communes* such as Cairanne. The reds contain Grenache (a minimum of 50 percent) plus Syrah, Mourvèdre, and Cinsault. At their best, they are deep-colored, spicy wines, though after three or four years in the bottle they lose some of their rustic character and gain complexity. The rosés are good; whites are less so, partly because of their high content of Grenache Blanc, Clairette, and Bourboulenc. An increased proportion of Marsanne, Roussanne, and Viognier would improve them dramatically.

Château des Tours
Serious examples of Vacqueyras like this *réserve* can compete well with—and outlive—Châteauneuf-du-Pape.

Vacqueyras Vineyard
Grenache grapes from vineyards such as this one produce some of the most peppery red wines in the Rhône region.

- AC Vacqueyras.
- Grenache, Syrah, Mourvèdre, Cinsault.
- Rustic, full-bodied red. Less impressive white and rosé.
- Dom des Amouriers, Burle, Clos de Cazaux, la Fourmone, Jaboulet, de Montmirail, de Montvac, Sang des Cailloux, Tardieu-Laurent, Ch des Tours.
- Roast lamb with garlic, herbs, zucchini, and tomatoes.
- Red: 2003, 2000, 1998, 1997.
- Red: 2–10 years. White: 1–4 years.

GRAPE VARIETIES OF THE RHÔNE

Four varieties are well known for the role they play in the wines of the Rhône Valley. First there is the leading player, Syrah, from which are made the rich, dark, smoky, blackberryish red wines of Hermitage *(see p258)*, Côte Rôtie *(see p256)*, Cornas *(see p253)*, St Joseph *(see p260)* and Crozes-Hermitage *(see p257)* in the northern Rhône. Second is Grenache, the mainstay of the strawberry-cherryish, peppery-red Côtes du Rhône *(see pp254–5)* and Châteauneuf-du-Pape *(see p251)* of the southern Rhône. Third is Muscat, which produces the unashamedly grapey wines of Beaumes-de-Venise *(see p259)*, and fourth is the newly fashionable Viognier, found in the perfumed white wines of Condrieu *(see p252)* and Château Grillet *(see p250)*. The Rhône is also the traditional home of a large range of other, less well-known grapes. Some, such as Grenache Blanc, Bourboulenc, and Clairette, are decidedly dull, and depend on good wine- making to produce white wines with any degree of flavor. Then there are the far more characterful Roussanne and Marsanne, which are used to make some of the world's most fascinatingly floral dry whites. The spicy Mourvèdre and Cinsault, though usually better in blends than as soloists, can contribute quite significantly to the flavor of red Châteauneuf-du-Pape and a range of other red wines.

Mourvèdre
One of the unsung heroes of the Rhône Valley, this spicy variety is a component of many Châteauneuf-du-Pape wines.

Marsanne
Often underestimated, this variety is the mainstay of many Rhône whites, with its distinctive combination of spicy and floral aromas and flavors.

OTHERS

AMONG THE OTHER WINES of the Rhône, some are dull and old-fashioned, while others offer some of the best value in France. Among those most worth seeking out are light, juicy reds that compete well with Beaujolais; spicy, fuller-bodied Côtes du Rhône-style reds; and the extraordinary sweet whites that are now being made from partially dried grapes.

Côtes du Vivarais
While this region is best known for its fairly priced wines, its orchards are also the source of a wide variety of fruits that, like the grapes, ripen well in the climate here.

One Rhône Valley wine that I would dispose of quickly is Coteaux de Die, which gained an *appellation* in 1993 as part of the redefinition of the sparkling wines previously called Clairette de Die. Under the new arrangements, less of Die's *appellation* bubbly is now made from the dull Clairette grape variety—and instead of consigning the now-obsolete Clairette grapes to *vin de pays* blends, the authorities generously encourage producers to turn them into a still wine that they can sell under this *appellation.*

Similar generosity was shown in 1998 when the Coteaux de Pierrevert were promoted from *VDQS* to *appellation contrôlée.*

Châtillon-en-Diois is a small *appellation* that celebrated its 25th birthday in 1999. The white is made from two Burgundy grape varieties, Chardonnay and Aligoté, while the red is made from Gamay with some Pinot Noir and Syrah.

Côtes du Lubéron owes its *appellation* status to the efforts of Jean-Louis Chancel, who, during the 1970s and 1980s, invested part of a fortune made from vegetable oil in relandscaping and planting 400 acres (160 ha) of pebbly vineyards and in building his showcase Val Joanis wine estate. The quality of the Val Joanis Grenache-Syrah reds has not always justified the creation of the *appellation,* and the whites have been downright dull, but the rosés have been good and a number of other producers, such as La Vieille Ferme, Châteaux de l'Isolette and Canorgue, and Domaines de la Citadelle and de Fontenille, make attractive, fairly lightweight wines in all three styles.

One region that can offer good-value reds is Côtes du Vivarais. Still a *VDQS,* it produces a growing range of good light reds, rosés, and even whites, thanks to recent moves to outlaw duller grape varieties such as Carignan and Ugni Blanc. The best villages (whose names are permitted to feature on labels) are St Remèze and Orgnac.

Finally, Hermitage Vin de Paille is a glorious, ancient style that, like its counterpart in Alsace, has been revived by a number of top producers, including Chave, Chapoutier, Grippat, and Guigal. The drying process, which allows the grapes to lose three-quarters of their water content, produces glorious, sweet wines with extraordinary longevity.

Domaine de la Citadelle
Here is the proof that the Côtes du Lubéron can make reds worthy of its recently won *appellation* status.

SOUTHWEST FRANCE

Southwest France

This region is an ideal hunting ground for anyone who wants unusual flavors or good-value alternatives to Bordeaux made from the same grapes in similar conditions.

The southwest is an area where frontiers have been drawn up with more regard for convenience than logic. There are several *appellations* here that grow the same grape varieties used in neighboring Bordeaux *(see pp80–111)*, and that might, but for an accident of geography and history, be classified as part of that region. Bergerac *(see p270)*, for example, was an important wine region long before the Médoc *(see p99)* began to earn its reputation. Indeed, the second-class status of Bergerac today owes more to the efforts of Bordeaux merchants to discriminate against it than to the quality of its wines. Though never great, when made with care and skill the wines of Bergerac can compete easily with many pricier wines from Bordeaux. The same is true of wines from the sweet white *appellation* of Monbazillac *(see p274)*, and of more expensive wines from *appellations* such as Saussignac and Pécharmant *(see p275)*.

A Taste of the Past
Many vineyards in the Southwest region are small and family-owned, like this one run by the three Laplace brothers. Using the traditional Tannat grape, the brothers make rich red wines that are distinctive and attractively old-fashioned.

REGIONAL OVERVIEW

- 32,400 acres (13,000 ha): 220 million bottles.
- Very varied in this large region, but the Atlantic Ocean to the west and the Mediterranean to the southeast give most of the area a maritime climate that keeps winters warm and summers cool.
- Ranging from the gravelly clay of Cahors to the sandy soils of the Côtes de Duras and Tursan.
- Red: Cabernet Sauvignon, Merlot, Cabernet Franc, Fer, Tannat, Malbec, Gamay.
  White: Gros & Petit Manseng, Picpoul, Clairette, Ugni Blanc, Colombard, Sauvignon.

Even more interesting, to my mind, are a number of *appellations*, including Gaillac *(see p272)*, Cahors *(see p271)* and Irouléguy *(see p275)*, that make their wines from local grape varieties such as Tannat, Fer, Gros and Petit Manseng, and Len de L'Elh, which are grown almost nowhere else in the world. These wines are often resolutely unfashionable, and stand out like hand-thrown pots in a shop full of machine-made crowd pleasers. Although varied, the reds tend toward the rugged and tannic, made to accompany the hearty stews for which this region is known. The whites, at their best, have a fresh and gently tangy character all their own. Perhaps inevitably, the so-called real world of international commerce and technical innovation has begun to make an impact on these wines in recent years. While Cahors, for example, has traditionally produced intense, inky-dark wines, modern techniques are now being used here to make light and medium-bodied reds, too. So, until you pull the cork, there is often no way to know whether the contents of the bottle will be richly tannic and best drunk with a *cassoulet*, or light and fruity to go with a plate of cold meats. Throughout the

Paris •
• Toulouse

Southwest region

KEY

- Bergerac
- Buzet
- Cahors
- Côtes de Duras
- Côtes de St Mont
- Côtes du Frontonnais
- Côtes du Marmandais
- Gaillac
- Irouléguy
- Jurançon
- Madiran (including Pacherenc du Vic-Bilh)
- Pécharmant
- *Département* boundary
- Other AOC and VDQ areas (including Monbazillac, Marcillac, Montravel, Tursan)

0 km 50
0 miles 50

MONTRAVEL MONBAZILLAC DORDOGNE BERGERAC D933 Dordogne Dordogne Cère D660 Dropt LOT N122 Lot A61 Garonne GIRONDE LOT-ET-GARONNE Lot Cahors D911 Aveyron MARCILLAC Eyre LANDES D933 AGEN TARN-ET-GARONNE D922 Viaur N112 N10 MONT-DE-MARSAN D932 Gers MONTAUBAN Gaillac Tarn Midou Douze GERS Tarn Garonne N88 Dadou N124 TURSAN Baïse Arrats TARN Gabas Luy de France Arros AUCH Gimone TOULOUSE Girou N124 N126 CASTRES Agout Adour PACHERENC DU VIC-BILH Adour D929 Gers D632 HAUTE-GARONNE MAZAMET Thoré BAYONNE A64 N21 Save Gave d'Oloron Saison PAU N117 N117 Hers N113 A61 Canal du Midi TARBES CARCASSONNE PYRÉNÉES-ATLANTIQUES HAUTES-PYRÉNÉES Salat Aude AUDE ARIÈGE Ariège

Southwest France
Despite the high quality of its wines, this diverse region has historically been overshadowed by neighboring Bordeaux, where merchants often took steps to prevent rival wines from reaching overseas markets.

Southwest region, a new generation of wine-makers has responded to the demands of the international market-place by learning new ways to bring out the best qualities of their vineyards and local grape varieties, and to replace rusticity with refinement. It is no coincidence that, after centuries of disdain, the grandees of Bordeaux have recently begun to consider including both Bergerac and Monbazillac within their *appellation*.

New Shades of Black
The tough, tannic "black wine" from the Cahors vineyards may be a rarity these days, but there are delicious modern versions to be found by anyone prepared to seek them out.

TRAVELING IN SOUTHWEST FRANCE

Traditionally, the country to the east of Bordeaux and to the northwest of the Languedoc was far too often overlooked. But in recent years its discovery by Britons looking for a place to spend the summer and its rediscovery by Parisians have helped to clear the way for a growing number of first class hotels and restaurants.

HOTELS & RESTAURANTS

A selection of recommended establishments in southwest France, combining great local food and wine with notable places to stay.

CAMBO-LES-BAINS

Hôtel-restaurant Euzkadi, 285 Karrika-Nagusia, Espelette.
05 59 93 91 88
FAX 05 59 29 28 57
If you want to explore traditional Basque cooking, and what happens when talented cooks put a modern spin on it, this is the place to come. Try the Elzekaria vegetable soup with a glass of Jurançon or the Tripotxa black pudding with an Irouleguy. Stay overnight and you can spend the next day by the pool.

BERGERAC

L'Enfance de Lard, Rue Pélissière.
05 53 57 52 88
FAX 05 53 57 52 58
@ lenfancedelard@yahoo.fr
In the heart of this town, and hidden away above a shop in a 12th century house, this is a tiny room that feels as though it is more part of an eccentric private residence than a restaurant. Meat grilled over vine twigs is a specialty. Wines are first-class, too, and include one made nearby by novelist William Boyd that you won't find elsewhere.

DURAS

l'Hostellerie des Ducs, Boulevard Jean Brisseau.
05 53 83 74 58
If you want to discover the wines of Duras and the traditional cuisine of the region in luxury, though at affordable prices, this converted convent is the place to head for. It's best to make reservations well in advance and allow yourself a few hours to work off the meals in the pool, or to sleep them off on the terraces.

FOURCÈS

Château de Fourcès.
05 62 29 49 53
FAX 05 62 29 50 59
In the heart of the charming little village of Fourcès, this 12th-century chateau has been very well converted into a luxury hotel with a classy restaurant. When the weather is fine, spend some time enjoying the gardens and swimming pool.

GAILLAC

La Verrerie, 1 Rue de l'Egalité.
05 63 57 32 77
FAX 05 63 57 32 27
W www.la-verrerie.com.
As the name suggests, this hotel and restaurant are situated in a converted 19th century glass factory. Prices here are modest, both for the rooms and for the well-prepared local foie gras.

LAGARDE FIMARCON

Castelnau des Fieumarcon.
05 62 68 99 30
FAX 02 47 32 02 52
W www.lagarde.org
@ fcoustols@lagarde.org
Close to Condom and the heartland of Vin de Pays des Côtes de Gascogne and Armagnac, this is quite simply a 13th century walled village in which 12 houses have been sympathetically restored to include kitchens, but no telephones or televisions—making the views over what Stendhal called France's Tuscany all the easier to appreciate.

LARESSINGLE NEAR CONDOM

l'Auberge de Larressingle.
05 62 28 29 67
FAX 05 62 68 33 14
W www.auberge-de-larressingle.fr
A few minutes along the D15 from Condom, this is a pretty old hotel and restaurant close to the gorgeous castle and offering good local cooking. There are also well chosen

A treasure trove for those looking for something different
The restaurants of the southwest offer an unusually wide ranges of wines, thanks to the varied list of grapes the wine makers have at their disposal.

examples of Vin de Pays des Côtes de Gascogne and Côtes de St Mont.

MERCULÈS

Château de Mercuès, 46090, Mercuès, Lot.
05 65 20 00 01
FAX 05 65 20 05 72
@ mercues@relaischateaux.com
This medieval turreted castle overlooking a swath of vines was once the place where the bishops of Cahors used to spend their summer. Today, it is both a wine estate, and a luxury hotel and restaurant where truffles and *foie gras* are well handled. Be sure to visit the cellar before dining, and stay overnight to enjoy the sensation of waking here in the morning.

TOUZAC

Hostellerie la Source Bleu, Moulin de Leygues.
05 65 36 52 01
FAX 05 65 24 65 69
@ sourcebleue@wanadoo.fr
W www.sourcebleue.com
Beautifully set in a trio of old mills, dating from the 11th, 12th, and 17th centuries, with a rustling stream and a peaceful lake, this 15-bedroom family hotel is a perfect place from which to explore the country around Cahors.

ANNUAL WINE EVENTS

There are plenty of wine festivals throughout the southwestern region, sometimes combined with celebrations of local dishes and ingredients. Look also for musical events like l'Eté Musical (which is held every year in several villages and towns in the Lot Valley), the terrific Marcillac jazz festival in August, Cahors' blues festival, and Vinojazz in Bergerac in the spring. Contact tourist offices *(see below)* for further details.

MARCH
St-Mont wine festival centered around the region's reds

MAY
Albas wine festival—a good chance to sample young vintages of Cahors
Bergerac Vinojazz—a festival that reflects the popularity of jazz in this area

JULY
Eauze wine festival
Bergerac Cyrano festival
Cahors blues festival

AUGUST
Buzet wine festival
Madiran Fete du Madiran
Fronton Frontonnais food and wine Festival
Gaillac wine festival
Cahors, Belaye, etc. L'Eté Musical dans la Vallée du Lot

SEPTEMBER
Donzac world grape-picking championship
Moissac Chasselas festival

OCTOBER
Sigoulès harvest festival

NOVEMBER/DECEMBER
Jurançon harvest festival

DECEMBER
Eauze Concours des Vins Blancs—a white wine competition

WINE SHOPS

Wines from the southwest can be difficult to find back home, so it's worth visiting a good shop while you're in the area.

AGEN

Plaisirs du Vin, Allée de Riols, ZAC Agen Sud.
05 53 66 76 42
Agen is best known for its prunes, but it also lays claim to one of the best wine shops in the southwest.

MUSEUMS

Some producers offer vineyard or winery tours. Contact tourist offices *(see below)* for details.

BERGERAC

Musée du vin de la Batellerie et de la Tonnellerie, 5 Rue des Conférences.
05 53 57 80 92
Barrel-making is as much of a focus as vines and wines here, which adds to the interest of the museum.
Maison des vins—Cloître des Recollets, 1 Rue des Récollets.
05 53 63 57 55
FAX 05 53 63 01 30
A small promotional center and regional museum in an old cloisters, the Maison des Vins is worth dropping into as you wander around Bergerac.

WEBSITES

The first stop for this region is www.vins-du-sud-ouest.com. Other (more specific) sites worth visiting include www.plaimont.com, www.vignerons-buzet.fr, www.montus-madiran.com and www.vins-jurancon.fr—the last of these is a particularly good site devoted to the old but often overlooked region of Jurançon. There is also some very useful information about Bergerac and the surrounding area at www.bergerac-tourisme.com.

OTHER INFORMATION

Conseil Interprofessionnel des Vins de la Région de Bergerac, 1 Rue des Récollets, Bergerac.
05 53 63 57 57
FAX 05 53 63 01 30
@ contact@vins-bergerac.fr
The place to go for information on Bergerac and its wines.

BERGERAC

Bordeaux
Bayonne
Toulouse

THE WINES OF BERGERAC have for a long time been kept in the shadows, with Bordeaux *(see p93)* across the Dordogne taking the limelight. Vines have been cultivated in this picturesque region since Roman times, with exports of wine to England recorded as early as 1250. Today, Bergerac is the biggest *appellation* in the southwest. The wine produced here is sufficiently similar to Bordeaux for it to have been suggested in the late 1990s that it might one day be accepted as part of that region. Another *appellation*, the Côtes de Bergerac, exists for red wines with a higher minimum alcohol content (11 rather than 10 percent), but some top producers prefer not to use it, focusing attention instead on Bergerac and on the names of their estates.

Château Tour des Gendres
Good white Bergerac, like this, easily outclasses wines like Entre-Deux-Mers *(see p95)* and basic white Bordeaux.

Bergerac
A magnet for thousands of fans of the play "Cyrano de Bergerac," Bergerac is a small, pleasant, country town that is only now beginning to gain a good reputation for its wines.

- AC Bergerac, AC Côtes de Bergerac, AC Bergerac Sec.
- Red: Merlot, Cabernet Sauvignon, Cabernet Franc. White: Sauvignon Blanc, Sémillon, Muscadelle.
- Medium-bodied reds. Dry or sweet whites. Dry rosés.
- Ch Belingard, Court-les-Mûts, des Eyssards, de Gouyat, Grinou, Jaubertie, le Raz, Richard, Ch Tour des Gendres.
- White: Grilled carp.
- Red: 2003, 2001, 2000.
- Red: 3–5 years. White: 1–3 years.

BUZET

Bordeaux
Bayonne
Toulouse

FORMERLY KNOWN AS THE Côtes de Buzet, the vineyards located between the towns of Agen and Marmande date back to Roman times. As with many *appellations* in this area, Buzet suffered when the importation of wine into Bordeaux *(see p93)* was banned following the Hundred Years' War. More recently, however, Buzet's wines were blended with the wines of Bordeaux, until *appellation* laws made this illegal. Today, this region's red wines are better than some more expensive Haut-Médoc *(see p99)* and St Émilion *(see p105)*. Those of Châteaux de Gueyze, Baleste, du Frandat, and de la Tuque can all be recommended and are made by the local *coopérative*, which produces most of Buzet's wines. Sadly, its rosés and whites are decidedly less interesting.

Les Vignerons de Buzet
Wines like this illustrate how efficient *coopératives* can compete on level terms with small estates and merchants.

Buzet Vineyards
Despite its lack of international prestige, Buzet benefits from vineyards that can, in good years, provide grapes as ripe as those found in most parts of Bordeaux.

- AC Buzet.
- Red: Merlot, Cabernet Sauvignon, Cabernet Franc.
- Bordeaux-like reds that often benefit from being aged in small oak barrels.
- Ch Baleste, Ch du Frandat, Ch de Gueyze, Pierron, Sauvagnères, les Vignerons de Buzet (whose wines are sold under the names of individual estates such as Ch du Bouchet and de la Tuque).
- Lamb casserole with spring vegetables.
- Red: 2003, 2001, 2000, 1998.
- 4–8 years.

CAHORS

Bordeaux
Bayonne
Toulouse

THE ONCE FAMOUS "BLACK WINE" of Cahors takes its name from the Malbec grape that, prior to phylloxera, produced dark, inky-colored wine. This is said to have been enjoyed in London since the 13th century, but the merchants of Bordeaux *(see p93)* banned its sale in Great Britain after the Hundred Years' War. The producers responded by selling their wine in Holland, where drinkers preferred it to the paler efforts of Bordeaux. Today's Cahors is more approachable, but varies in quality, from the light and dull examples sold cheaply in supermarkets to the rich, delicious wines stocked by specialized merchants and good restaurants. Fans of traditional Cahors should head for the limestone flats, while those seeking lighter, plummier reds will prefer wines from the sand and gravel hillsides.

Clos la Coutale
Although this Cahors is not "black," it does have some of the depth traditionally associated with this *appellation.*

Pont Valentré
With its imposing towers, the fortified bridge over the Lot River illustrates the importance the town enjoyed in the Middle Ages, when it was a trading center for a wide variety of goods.

- AC Cahors.
- Red: Malbec, Tannat, Merlot.
- Dark, tannic, long-lived traditional reds. Supple, fruity, modern reds.
- Ch de Caix, la Caminade, Ch du Cèdre, Clos la Coutale, Clos de Gamot, Côtes d'Olt Coopérative, Gautoul, de Hauterivem, Haute-Serre, Lagrezette, Lamartine, Latuc, Paillas, Rochet-Lamothe, Clos Triguedina.
- Bayonne ham.
- 2002, 2000, 1998, 1996, 1995, 1990, 1989.
- 5–15 years.

CÔTES DE DURAS

IF BORDEAUX *(see p93)* ever wanted to expand the boundaries of its region, the wine-makers could quite easily join up with the Côtes de Duras, whose slopes carved out by the Dourdèze River are actually an extension of the Entre-Deux-Mers *(see p95)*. Even the grape varieties used here are primarily the same as those used for Bordeaux. As for the quality of its wines, while there are no Côtes de Duras wines that provoke excitement, there are plenty of decently made reds and whites.

Moulin des Groyes
A classic, dry white, this example of Côtes de Duras could pass for Bordeaux.

- AC Côtes de Duras.
- Red: Cabernet Sauvignon, Cabernet Franc, Merlot. White: Sémillon, Sauvignon Blanc, Muscadelle.
- Bordeaux-like reds. Dry or sweet whites.
- Amblard, des Groyes.
- Red: Lamb in brioche.
- Red: 2003, 2001, 2000.
- Red: 2–5 years. White: 1–3 years.

CÔTES DU MARMANDAIS

SURROUNDED BY ENTRE-DEUX-MERS *(see p95)*, the Côtes de Duras and Buzet *(see p270)*, this *appellation* for red, white and rosé wines extends over both sides of the Garonne River. The often rustic reds are prevented from being too Bordeaux-like *(see p93)* by the stipulation that the three main Bordeaux grape varieties (Cabernet Franc, Merlot and Cabernet Sauvignon) can only make up 75 percent of the blend. The whites are mainly mixtures of Sauvignon Blanc, Sémillon, and Ugni Blanc.

Château de Beaulieu
Local grape varieties help to give Côtes du Marmandais a "gamey" character.

- AC Côtes du Marmandais.
- Red/rosé: Cabernet Sauvignon, Cabernet Franc, Merlot, Abouriou, Fer. White: Sauvignon Blanc.
- Light reds. Dry whites. Dry rosés.
- Ch de Beaulieu, Cave de Beaupuy, de Cocumont.
- Red: Game casserole.
- 2003, 2002, 2001, 2000.
- 3–5 years.

GAILLAC

ONE OF FRANCE'S MOST ANCIENT wine regions, Gaillac is enjoying a renaissance due to a growing interest in traditional grapes and styles. Gamay, used to produce Gaillac's feebler red wines, is on its way out and local varieties, like Duras and Fer, are being encouraged. For whites, Mauzac, Ondenc, and Len de l'Elh are making a similar comeback. Luckily, the authorities have recognized that these grapes produce better wines if blended with varieties such as Syrah and Sauvignon Blanc. Gaillac produces a wide variety of wines, from light reds and pale rosés to appley, perfumed, dry and honey-sweet whites. Gaillac's appley, sparkling wines are its most interesting product and are sold as Méthode Gaillaçoise and Méthode Gaillaçoise Doux.

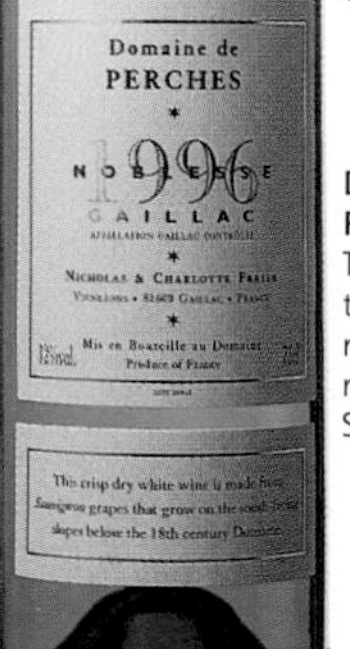

Domaine des Perches
This is a lovely, tangy example of new wave Gaillac made from the Sauvignon Blanc.

Pattern of Life
Gaillac's vineyards, some of which are among the oldest in France, are grown alongside a wide range of other crops because wines can be hard to sell.

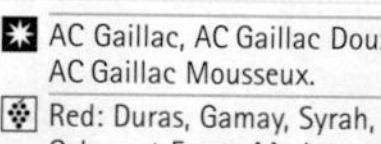

- AC Gaillac, AC Gaillac Doux, AC Gaillac Mousseux.
- Red: Duras, Gamay, Syrah, Cabernet Franc, Merlot. White: Mauzac, Sauvignon Blanc, Sémillon, Ondenc.
- Soft reds. Still, sparkling whites.
- De Bouscaillous, de Gineste, de Labarthe, Lastours, Mas d'Aurel, Perches, R.. Plageoles, René Rieux, Clement Termes, Terrisses, Très-Cantours, Vayssette.
- Veal brisket stuffed with Swiss chard.
- Red: 2004, 2002.
- Red: 3–5 years.

JURANÇON

PROPONENTS OF MODERN VIEWS against giving alcohol to children presumably dislike the legend that drops of Jurançon were placed on Henri IV's lips at his baptism in 1553. Jurançon is one of France's oldest *appellations*, and its delicate white wines have always been fiercely protected. Planted in the foothills of the Pyrenees around the town of Pau, most of the vines are at an altitude of 1,000 ft (300 m), and they are often trained on trellises to avoid frost damage. The local grape varieties are Gros Manseng, Petit Manseng, and Courbu. In the best dry and sweet wines, these produce a tangy bouquet of pineapples and peaches, and a combination of richness and acidity that comes from the underrated Manseng. The *appellation* has good producers and deserves to be better known.

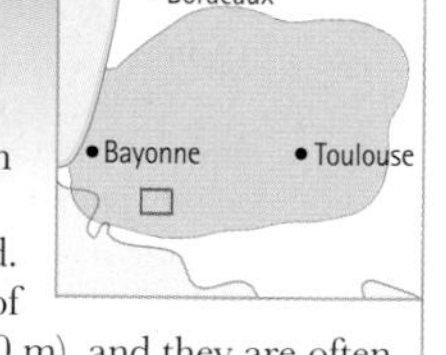

Domaine Cauhapé
This producer is well worth remembering for both its dry and sweet Jurançon wines.

View from the Top
Some of Jurançon's best vines are grown on the very steep hillside slopes of the *appellation*, while other crops are grown on the flatter land beneath.

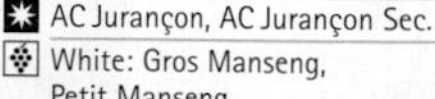

- AC Jurançon, AC Jurançon Sec.
- White: Gros Manseng, Petit Manseng.
- Fresh, dry, and lusciously sweet whites.
- Bellegarde, Jean-Pierre Bousquet, Brana, Bru-Baché, Cauhapé, Clos Guirouilh, Clos Lapeyre, Clos Uroulat, Cru Lamouroux.
- *Roquefort* cheese and walnut tart.
- Sweet: 2003, 2001, 2000, 1999, 1998.
- 3–6 years.

MADIRAN

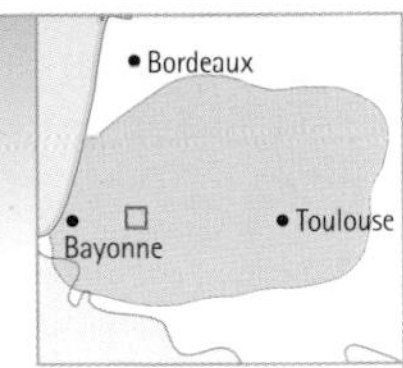

ONE OF THE ONLY *appellations* to produce red wines made from the Tannat grape, this region has a distinctive, old-fashioned character. Dating back to Roman times, Madiran's wine-making heyday was in the Middle Ages, when its reds were relished by pilgrims en route to Santiago de Compostela. The vineyards of this *appellation* are mainly on clay and limestone soils and the climate is tempered by the Atlantic to the west. The use of Tannat and Fer gives the wines of Madiran a rustic character that can take a long time to soften. Although Tannat must now represent 40 percent of the blend, Cabernet Franc and Cabernet Sauvignon are also used to soften the wines, providing a fruitiness they might not otherwise have shown in their youth.

Domaine Pichard
The toughness of the Tannat grape variety is beautifully balanced by the fruitiness and richness of this Madiran red wine.

Château Bouscassé
One of the best, most progressive producers in the area, Alain Brumont produces first-class barrel-matured Madiran at this château.

- AC Madiran.
- Red: Tannat, Fer, Cabernet Sauvignon, Cabernet Franc.
- Full-bodied, traditional, tannic reds.
- Aydie, Barréjat, Berthoumieu, Bouscassé, Brana, la Chapelle, Crampilh, Ducourneau, Lanestousse, Lafitte-Teston, Lenclos, Montus, Moureou, de Peyros, Pichard, Cave de Plaimont.
- Roast pigeon in Armagnac.
- 2002, 2001, 2000, 1998, 1997, 1996.
- 5–10 years.

MARCILLAC

THE SAVAGE AUVERGNE COUNTRYSIDE is one of the few places in which the Fer, or Mansois, grape is found. It produces reds and rosés that tend to be fiercely tannic when young, becoming peppery and almost perfumed with age. Once there were thousands of acres of Fer vines in this *appellation*, but today there are only a scant hundred left. If the authorities had not elevated Marcillac's status from *VDQS* to *appellation contrôlée* in 1990, the area's producers might even have given up wine-making altogether. Recent regulations require a minimum of 90 percent of Fer, with Merlot, Cabernet Sauvignon, or Cabernet Franc making up the balance. The young reds are now more approachable, but the rosés still tend to be fairly dull.

Domaine du Cros
Domaine du Cros' peppery, perfumed wines are some of the most characterful and reliable of the wines produced in Marcillac.

Sun-Baked Terraces
The vines of Marcillac are planted on steep slopes, where grapes ripen and develop thick skins that can give toughness to the the red and rosé wines.

- AC Marcillac.
- Red/rosé: Fer, Cabernet Sauvignon, Cabernet Franc, Merlot.
- Peppery, ideally aromatic, but often toughly tannic reds. Dry, full-bodied, peppery rosés.
- Du Cros, Lacombe Père et Fils, Cave du Vallon-Valady.
- Chicken stuffed with eggs, ham, and chopped garlic and cooked with tomatoes and herbs.
- Red: 2003, 2002.
- Red: 3–5 years. Rosé: 1–3 years.

MONBAZILLAC

Bordeaux
Bayonne
Toulouse

MONBAZILLAC, WHOSE VINEYARDS were originally planted on the hill of Mont Bazailhac 900 years ago, enjoyed its heyday in the 16th and 17th centuries, when its main customers were Dutch wine merchants. Later, following the impact of phylloxera, Monbazillac was relegated to producing "poor man's Sauternes" *(see p110)*. Generally, the grapes used to make excellent sweet wines are best picked by hand, but here they were often machine-harvested. However, in 1993 the producers decided to pay more attention to quality, and as a result machine-picking was outlawed. Today, emphasis is placed on harvesting genuinely nobly rotten grapes in successive pickings; the resulting wines should be deep golden in color, often with an orange tinge.

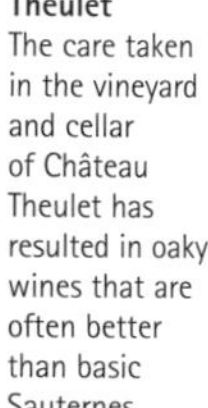

Château Theulet
The care taken in the vineyard and cellar of Château Theulet has resulted in oaky wines that are often better than basic Sauternes.

Château de Monbazillac
One of the most imposing châteaux in Monbazillac, this is also the source of some of the best, longest-lived wines produced in the *appellation*.

- AC Monbazillac.
- White: Sémillon, Sauvignon Blanc, Muscadelle.
- Botrytized, dessert whites.
- Ch Belingard, la Borderie, la Brie, Fonmourges, Grand Marsalet, Lajonie, les Marnières, Ch de Monbazillac, de Pecoula, Septy, Theulet, Tirecul la Gravière, Treuil de Nailhac.
- *Foie gras* with Monbazillac jelly.
- 2003, 2001, 1999, 1997, 1996, 1995.
- 5–15 years.

MONTRAVEL

THIS AMBITIOUS SMALL REGION follows the Dordogne River westward from Ste Foy-la-Grande to the border between the Gironde and the Dordogne *départements*. Boasting three separate *appellations* for its white wines, Montravel produces crisp wines mainly from Sémillon and Sauvignon, while Côtes de Montravel and Haut-Montravel cover semi-sweet, medium-sweet, and late-harvest whites. Red Montravel from top estates often outclasses Bordeaux and red Bergerac *(see p270)*.

Château Pique-Serre
This white wine, with its dry, peachy flavor, is typical of Montravel.

- AC Montravel, AC Côtes de Montravel, AC Haut-Montravel.
- White: Sémillon.
- Dry or sweet whites.
- Ch du Bloy, Ch de Bondieu, Ch Pique-Serre, De la Roche-Marot, Viticulteurs de Port Ste Foy.
- Grilled trout.
- 2003, 2002.
- 2–4 years.

PACHERENC DU VIC-BILH

ONE OF THE LITTLE-KNOWN gems of the French wine world, Pacherenc du Vic-Bilh has an unusual Gascon name and comes from 247 acres (100 ha) of vines to the west of Auch and north of Pau. The dry, medium-sweet, and sweet whites are made from the local Ruffiac, Petit Courbu, Petit Manseng, and Gros Manseng varieties, better known for their role in Jurançon *(see p272)*, as well as Sémillon and Sauvignon. The best Pacherenc du Vic-Bilhs have a fruity flavor, with an occasional touch of oak.

Plaimont
A fine, honeyed example of Pacherenc du Vic-Bilh from the Plaimont *coopérative*.

- AC Pacherenc du Vic-Bilh.
- White: Gros Manseng, Petit Manseng, Ruffiac, Petit Courbu.
- Dry or sweet whites.
- Ch Berthoumieu, du Boucassé, Brumont, Capmartin, des Crouseilles, Laffitte-Teston, Plaimont.
- Grilled *foie gras*.
- 2003, 1999, 1997, 1996.
- 5–10 years.

PÉCHARMANT

THE RED WINES OF PÉCHARMANT, an *appellation* covering 445 acres (180 ha) to the east of the town of Bergerac, put many Bordeaux *(see p93)* reds to shame. The Cabernet Franc, Cabernet Sauvignon, and Merlot vines grow on the banks of the Dordogne, where the soil's high iron content contributes to the rich structure, flavor, and longevity of the wines. A number of estates are exploiting the region's potential and making ideal accompaniments to traditional Perigord cuisine.

Château de Tiregand
This fine old estate produces subtle and supple wines.

- AC Pécharmant.
- Red: Merlot, Cabernet Franc, Cabernet Sauvignon.
- Medium- to full-bodied reds.
- Ch de Biran, Champeral, des Costes, Grand Jaure, de Tiregand.
- Pigeon with turnips and morels.
- 2003, 2000, 1998.
- 5–8 years.

TURSAN

MOST OF THE WINES MADE in this small *VDQS* to the west of Armagnac are produced by the local *coopérative*. The often tough, berryish reds and fruity rosés are mainly made from Tannat, but must contain at least 25 percent Cabernet Franc, Fer, or Cabernet Sauvignon. Tursan's Baroque-based whites are traditionally dull, but the local Michelin-starred chef Michel Guérard's Domaine de Bachen wines benefit from the use of Sauvignon and Gros Manseng.

Cave de Tursan
Tasty, robust reds like this are ideal when served with strongly flavored dishes.

- VDQS Tursan.
- Red: Tannat.
  White: Baroque.
- Tannic reds. Aromatic whites.
- De Bachen, Cave de Tursan.
- White: Grilled shad or herring.
- Red: 2003, 2000, 1998.
- Red: 3–7 years.
  White: 1–4 years.

OTHERS

• Bordeaux
Côtes du Frontonnais
• Bayonne
• Toulouse
Irouléguy

AMONG THE OTHER WINES of the southwest are Irouléguy's richly spicy if tannic reds, made from a blend of Tannat and Cabernet grapes. These are easy to spot on the shelf: their Basque names tend to include unexpected consonants as with the excellent Cuvée Bixintxo. Rosés can be fair, but the whites are dull. The reds of the Béarn *appellation*, made nearby from similar blends, are lighter and less interesting, though the young whites and rosés can be aromatic. The Côtes du Frontonnais reds—sold as Fronton or Villaudric, depending on the village in which they were produced—are characterful country wines with the spicy, berryish flavors of the Negrette grape, which must make up at least 60 percent of the blend. Saussignac and Rosette are sweet wines worth watching. Saussignac is made from Sémillon, Sauvignon Blanc, Muscadelle, and Chenin Blanc and must have a minimum of 18 g (0.6 oz) per liter of residual sugar. At its best, it is full-bodied with a rich flavor. Rosette must contain between eight and 54 grams (0.3–2 oz) per liter of residual sugar and is softer than Saussignac. Produced near Bergerac *(see p270)*, under whose name their reds are sold, these are good alternatives to Sauternes *(see p110)*.

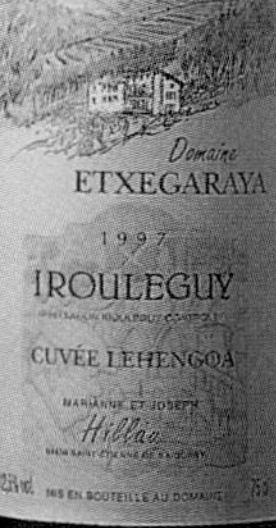

Domaine Etxegaraya
Berryish, red Irouléguy like this is delicious served with Basque dishes made with tomatoes and herbs.

Irouléguy
The picturesque countryside around Irouléguy is some of the moodiest and most beautiful in this part of southwestern France.

Vins de Pays

France's vins de pays, *or country wines, are increasingly the unexpected driving force behind the French wine industry.*

In the early 1990s, a reliable way of bringing a disdainful look to the face of a Parisian wine snob would have been to utter the three words "*vin de pays.*" California, Australia, and South Africa were, he might grudgingly have conceded, starting to make palatable country wines. But in France, to get something worthwhile, you had to choose from the *appellations contrôlées*.

The *vins de pays*, he would argue, are merely 140 or so designations created in the 1970s for areas that had previously turned out basic *vins de table.* This wine was either sold by the liter in plastic or returnable glass bottles, or poured directly into the European wine lake. Admittedly, the *vins de pays* were subject to legislation that dictated where they could be made and which grapes could be used, but the rules were far looser than they were for *appellation* wines. *Vins de pays* could be made by combining grapes that were never blended elsewhere, and fruits from vineyards hundreds of mies apart were often blended in the larger regions.

In a sense, the snob's dismissal of the *vins de pays* was, and still is, largely valid. While there have been occasional exceptions to the rule, such as the Vin de Pays de l'Hérault made by Aimé Guibert at his Mas de Daumas Gassac estate, most of the wines sold under this designation are still basic fare, carelessly produced by ill-equipped *coopératives* from badly tended grapes grown on poorly sited land. However, behind the scenes, this picture has begun to change.

Coteaux d'Aix-en-Provence
Most of the red *vin de pays* produced in the *département* of Bouches-du-Rhône comes from the area of Coteaux d'Aix-en-Provence.

Pioneers like Yves Grassa in Gascony and Robert Skalli have introduced New World wine-making methods and marketing techniques, and have begun to play the New World producers at their own game by producing smartly packaged, modern, fruity wines in France. Throughout the Vin de Pays d'Oc vineyards of Languedoc-Roussillon, dull Carignan and Grenache Blanc vines have been replaced by Chardonnay, Sauvignon Blanc, Merlot and Cabernet Sauvignon, all of whose names feature on *vin de pays* labels in the same way as they do on bottles from California and Australia. Another influence has been the arrival of outside investors and "flying wine-makers," who, like vinous mercenaries, have been sent into French *coopératives* by British supermarkets to make the modern wine that their customers demand.

Vins de pays now represent over a quarter of all French wine and a growing proportion of France's vinous exports. They are classified by region, *département*, and zone. Although there is no official quality difference between the three, zonal *vins de pays* often show more individual character than those from regions or *départements*. There is still room for improvement, but the best examples not only easily outclass the least distinguished efforts from *appellation contrôlée* regions like Bordeaux and the Loire, they are also commanding higher prices for their quality.

Hérault
This *vin de pays département* produces more than 11 million cases of wine a year, with red accounting for more than 85 percent.

HOW THE VINS DE PAYS WORK

Vins de pays have a hierarchy all of their own. At the lowest level are the four regional designations, Vin de Pays du Jardin de la France, Vin de Pays du Comté Tolosan, Vin de Pays d'Oc and Vin de Pays Comtés Rhodaniens. Next come the 39 *vins de pays départements* that are responsible for the production of nearly half of all *vins de pays* and are named after the *département* in which the wines are made— unless this is part of the name of an *appellation contrôlée*. Finally, there are nearly 100 zonal *vins de pays*. Between a quarter and a third of the total, they can be smaller than some *appellations*.

Corsica
The island of Corsica is not a *département* but a *vin de pays* zone.

BOUCHES-DU-RHÔNE

THE *DÉPARTEMENT* of Bouches-du-Rhône stretches from the peaks of the Alpilles to the marshlands of the Camargue, and from Marseilles to the port of Aigues-Mortes. Most Bouches-du-Rhône wines come from the Coteaux d'Aix en Provence area, with 80 percent being reds made from Merlot, Carignan, Grenache, Syrah, Cinsault, and Cabernet Sauvignon. Many Bouches-du-Rhône rosés are in fact better than a lot of Provençal *appellations contrôlées* examples.

Domaine des Gavelles
This rich red wine tastes better than many an *appellation contrôlée*.

- Bouches-du-Rhône.
- Red/rosé: Carignan, Syrah, Grenache, Cinsault, Merlot, Cabernet Sauvignon. White: Clairette, Ugni Blanc
- Soft, reds. Dry whites. Dry rosés.
- De Beaulieu, des Gavelles, Mas de Rey, de Trévallon.
- Lamb with garlic.
- Red: 2003, 2001, 2000.
- Red: 1–7 years.

COTEAUX DE L'ARDÈCHE

ALTHOUGH THIS AREA comes under the regional category of Comtés Rhodaniens, most wine-makers here prefer to sell their wines as Coteaux de l'Ardèche. The Burgundy merchant Louis Latour's Grand Ardèche Chardonnay is made from grapes grown in the limestone soil here, and the Beaujolais merchant Georges Duboeuf, who has planted grapes in partnership with 120 grape growers and seven *coopératives*, helped to put the area on the map.

Vignerons Ardèchois
Wine makers Ardèchois produce attractive, peppery, light red wines.

- Coteaux de l'Ardèche.
- Red/rosé: Syrah, Grenache, Cinsault. White: Marsanne, Ugni Blanc, Roussanne, Viognier.
- Peppery reds. Dry rosés.
- Ardèchois, la Clapouze, Combelonge , Louis Latour.
- Red: Pigeon with olives.
- White: 2002.
- 1–5 years.

CÔTES DE GASCOGNE

UNTIL THE 1970s, this region produced little but Armagnac. Thanks to the efforts of the Domaine du Tariquet and the Plaimont *coopérative*, Colombard and Ugni Blanc are now used to make fruity, dry wines. Modern methods of fermentation and the addition of Sauvignon Blanc and Manseng to the blend have given the whites a more lifted, aromatic quality. Wines from many warmer regions farther south, however, are giving the Côtes de Gascogne a lot of competition.

Domaines Grassa
This dynamic producer has greatly improved the reputation of this region.

- Côtes de Gascogne.
- Red: Gamay, Cabernet Sauvignon and Franc, Duras, Tannat. White: Colombard, Ugni Blanc, Chardonnay, Gros Manseng
- Light- to medium-bodied reds. Crisp, dry whites.
- Grassa, Plaimont.
- White: Cheese tart.
- White: 2004, 2003, 2002.
- White: 1–3 years.

HÉRAULT

THE REPUTATION OF THIS huge *département* was given its biggest boost by the success of the Mas de Daumas Gassac estate to the north of Montpellier. Aimé Guibert, the man behind this enterprise, planted an eccentric mixture of vines on steep slopes of fine, volcanic soil close to the village of Aniane, which subsequently attracted the likes of Robert Mondavi and Gérard Dépardieu. Plots of land like this are rare, but the area's vine-growing and wine-making skills are improving fast.

Mas de Daumas Gassac
This eccentric blend is produced by one of the best estates in southern France.

- Hérault.
- Red: Carignan, Cinsault, Grenache, Syrah. White: Clairette, Ugni Blanc Macabéo, Grenache Blanc.
- Medium- to full-bodied reds. Dry whites. Dry rosés.
- De Bosc, Capion, Mas de Daumas Gassac.
- Red: Beef casserole.
- Red: 2002, 2001, 2000.

ÎLE DE BEAUTÉ

THE GENEROUS WAY IN which *appellation contrôlée* designations have been allocated here leaves little room for wines to be labeled *vins de pays*. However, there are interesting experimental wines being produced here, including a number of promising early attempts with the Pinot Noir grape variety. Although Pinot Noir has been used with success, the designation encompasses local varieties as well as Italian ones, making it very hard to generalize about the overall quality.

Producteurs Réunis
This attractive wine has the herby, Italian character of most Corsican red wines.

- Île de Beauté.
- Red/rosé: Nielluccio, Cabernet Sauvignon, Pinot Noir. White: Vermintino, Muscat.
- Herby reds. Light, fruity whites. Herby rosés.
- Laroche, Producteurs Réunis, Sette Piana.
- Red: Mixed pork meats.
- Red: 2003, 2001.
- 1–3 years.

VAR

THE *DÉPARTEMENT* OF Var stretches west from St Raphael to Bandol and north to the Provençal Alps and Lac St Croix. Here, the predominantly rosé wines are primarily made using the *saignée* method, and range in color from pale *vins gris* through to deep coral. The whites are of little interest, but good reds include spicy blends of Grenache, Mourvèdre, Cabernet Sauvignon and Syrah. Within Var, the zonal Coteaux de Verdon is the source of Louis Latour's Pinot Noir red.

Nicolas Thiais
This light, fruity, and spicy red is a typical example of wine from this region.

- Var.
- Red/rosé: Grenache, Syrah, Mourvèdre. White: Ugni Blanc, Clairette, Roussanne.
- Soft, fruity reds. Dry whites. Dry rosés.
- Du Deffends, Rabiega, de Valmoissine (Louis Latour).
- Red: Pizza.
- Red: 2004. 2003.
- Red: 1–4 years.

VIN DE PAYS D'OC

THE HUGE REGION of Oc takes in the *départements* of Pyrenées Orientales, Aude, Hérault, and Gard and produces most of the best *vins de pays* in southern France. These wines have done particularly well outside France, partly due to the easy recognition of the name and because of the quality and "international" style of producers here: Skalli Fortant de France and Domaine Virginie; Australian companies such as Penfolds; and "flying wine-makers," employed by British retailers.

Fortant de France
This red wine is made by one of the region's most ambitious producers.

- Vin de Pays d'Oc.
- Red: Merlot, Grenache, Syrah, Cabernet Sauvignon. White: Sauvignon Blanc, Chardonnay, Marsanne, Viognier.
- Medium- to full-bodied, fruity reds. Dry whites.
- De la Baume, Fortant.
- Red: Mixed pork meats.
- Red: 2003, 2001.
- Red: 1–6 years.

OTHERS

COMPARED TO OC, the three other main *vin de pays* regions seem fairly insignificant. The Jardin de la France designation runs from the mouth of the Loire River at Nantes to Auxerre, taking in 14 *départements*. Although it is best known for dry whites, most of its wines are in fact red. Comté Tolosan, which follows the Garonne, Lot, and Tarn rivers and takes in the Pyrenees and Auvergne, makes mainly red wines, from a wide range of varieties. Comtés Rhodaniens, which encompasses eight *départements*, stretches south from Mâcon to the Ardèche and east into the Alps; this name can only be given to wines that are already zonal *vins de pays*. Outside these three regions lie the *départements* of Dordogne and Puy de Dôme and, between Champagne and Alsace, the *département* of Meuse.

Clos de Cray
The Jardin de la France in the Loire Valley can make delicious Chardonnay like this.

GENERAL RESOURCES

France offers innumerable opportunities to sample and buy wine—and plenty of places where one can learn about wine in general, or improve one's knowledge of a particular region. In these pages, we have picked out recommendable examples, including some that fall outside the regional sections covered in the rest of this book.

BUYING WINE

Apart from the wine retailers listed elsewhere in this book, France offers plenty of other sources of wine, including the Nicolas chain—which has branches in most towns. There are, however, few other big chains; most companies have one or, at most, two shops. When visiting producers, it is a good idea to ask for recommendations of retailers who sell their wine, or take advice from *sommeliers* in restaurants that have particularly good wine lists.

SUPERMARKETS

France's big supermarkets—*les Grandes Surfaces*—are a mixed blessing for wine-lovers. Generally, the focus will be on wines from nearby vineyards, but far too many shelves are filled with wines bought on the name of their *appellation* and price. Look closely to find finer examples among the dross. These same chains also buy wines such as top Bordeaux, and offer them at fair prices, at *Foires aux Vin*—Wine Fairs—where they are used to entice shoppers into the stores. Do take careful note of vintages, however. The supermarkets do much of their shopping in years when other customers are less enthusiastic. Canny wine lovers go the *Foires àux Vins* armed with a magazine or a book detailing which producers did best in each vintage.

Parisian wine shop
In France, most fine wine is sold by small, independent shops with no more than one or two outlets.

WINE FAIRS

There are opportunities to buy wine at all of the regional fairs listed elsewhere in this book. In addition to these, there are also national fairs—usually held in and to the north of Paris—at which small-scale producers (*Caves Particulières or Viticulteurs Indépendants*) from throughout the country present their most recent vintages. Even if you are not looking for large quantities of wine, these events offer a unique opportunity to taste your way around the whole of France, to see how different regions fared in the same vintage and which wine-makers offer the best value for money. The biggest and best of these is held in Paris in November. For details, visit www.vigneron-independant.com.

BUYING ONLINE

A growing number of firms now offer good French wines online, although not all of them deliver outside France. I would particularly recommend three: www.savour-club.com, www.chateauonline.com and www.wineandco.com. Do also look at other online retailers, however, since prices can vary quite considerably from one website to another.

FINDING INFORMATION

Given the confusing nature of France's wines and the natural variation between vintages, it is worth doing a bit of research before pulling out your wallet. There are magazines, newsletters, books, and plenty of information on the Internet.

BURGHOUND

W www.burghound.com

The other side of the Robert Parker *(see below)* coin. Allen Meadows loves and understands Burgundy, and his subscription-based website is well respected by readers across the globe who share his passion. It is available in English only.

LE CLASSEMENT DES MEILLEURS VINS DE FRANCE

Editions de la Revue du Vin de France is responsible for producing this annual guide, which unfortunately is published only in French. Over the 10 years of its existence, it has become the equivalent of a *Guide Michélin* for wine. The founding authors, Michel Bettane and Thierry Desseauve, stepped down in 2005, but it is worth looking for other works by these writers.

DECANTER

W www.decanter.com

The UK's oldest wine magazine. The website has a good news section and information on international auction prices.

LE GUIDE HACHETTE

Hachette's annual guide appears in French and English, and covers the full range of France's wines and producers. Its *Coups de Coeur* ("love at first sight") wines are always worth watching for.

INTERNATIONAL WINE CELLAR
W www.internationalwinecellar.com
Stephen Tanzer's newsletter is a good US-based alternative to Robert Parker's *(see below).*

LA REVUE DU VIN DE FRANCE
☎ 03 44 03 26 17
Published only in French, this is the one wine magazine that is taken seriously in France.

ROBERT JOSEPH
W www.robertjoseph-online.com
The author's own website, which incorporates a wine school.

JANCIS ROBINSON
W www.jancisrobinson.com
The British editor of the *Oxford Companion to Wine* offers a first class subscription-based site, which gives an impartial view on wines of every kind.

THE WINE ADVOCATE (ROBERT PARKER)
W www.eRobertParker.com
The newsletter that turned its author and publisher Robert Parker into the world's leading wine guru. You don't have to agree with his taste or opinion, but ignoring them is a little like going sailing without checking the weather forecast.

WINE INTERNATIONAL
W www.wineint.com
An English-language monthly magazine, launched in 1983 by the author of this book.

WINESEARCHER
W www.wine-searcher.com
An English language site that should be on every wine lover's list of favorites. Type in the name of a wine and vintage and you will see what it is being sold for worldwide, including at auction. It reveals, for example, that one firm charges as much for a 75-cl bottle of Bordeaux as another asks for a magnum.

WINE SPECTATOR
W www.winespectator.com
A US-based biweekly competing with Robert Parker's newsletter *(see above)* for global influence. The website has a good news section.

FRENCH WINE COURSES

PARIS

Britt Karlsson, 51 Rue du Chevalier de la Barre, Issy-les-Moulineaux.
☎ 06 80 45 35 70
Courses for beginners and enthusiasts, with a focus on food-and-wine matching.

Centre d'Information, de Documentation, et de Dégustation, 45 Rue Liancourt.
☎ 01 43 27 67 21
FAX 01 43 20 84 00
A dozen courses are available on request, as well as dinners and lectures by producers.

Grains Nobles, 5 Rue Laplace.
☎ 01 43 54 93 54
FAX 01 43 25 19 54
A cellar in which top critics and producers host tastings and courses (in French) in a very convivial atmosphere.

Maison de la Vigne et du Vin de France, 21 Rue François 1er.
☎ 01 47 20 20 76
FAX 01 47 23 07 21
Courses are offered to groups in an attractive old building close to the Champs Elysées.

Musée du Vin, Rue des Eaux.
☎ 01 45 25 63 26
FAX 01 40 50 91 22
The cellars of this medieval abbey now house a museum, restaurant, and wine bar offering wine courses.

BORDEAUX

L'Ecole du Vin, 1 Cours du 30 Juillet, Bordeaux.
☎ 05 56 00 22 66
FAX 05 56 00 22 82
This establishment conducts courses in several languages.

Lesparre Château Loudenne Ecole du Vin, St-Yzans-de-Médoc.
☎ 05 56 09 05 03
FAX 05 56 09 02 87
This beautiful Médoc château is a perfect spot to learn about wine-making and tasting.

L'Ecole du Bordeaux, Chateau Cordeillan-Bages, Pauillac.
☎ 05 56 59 24 24
FAX 05 56 59 01 89
This school, launched by the owners of Chateau Lynch-Bages, hosts courses at the luxurious Cordeillan Bages hotel in Pauillac, and in the heart of Bordeaux.

Institut d'Oenologie de l'Université de Bordeaux, 351 Cours de la Libération, Talence.
☎ 05 56 84 64 58
FAX 05 56 84 64 68
One of the world's most respected faculties opens its doors to students seeking brief introductions to wine and to Bordeaux.

BURGUNDY

L'Ecole du Vin du Bureau Interprofessionnel des Vins de Bourgogne, 12 Boulevard Bretonnière, Beaune.
☎ 03 80 24 70 20
FAX 03 80 24 69 36
Good courses and vineyard visits are offered at various levels, but only in French.

THE LOIRE VALLEY

Bouvet Ladubay, St-Hilaire-St-Florent, Saumur.
☎ 02 41 50 11 12
FAX 02 41 50 24 32
One of the most respected of the larger Loire Valley producers hosts wine courses taught by a contributor to the *Guide Hachette.*

THE RHÔNE VALLEY

Université du Vin, Château de Suze, Suze-la-Rousse.
☎ 04 75 04 86 09
FAX 04 75 98 24-20
Situated between Valence and Avignon in an imposing chateau, this establishment offers weekend courses in French and English.

GLOSSARY OF TECHNICAL TERMS

Appellation Contrôlée/Appellation d'Origine Controllée The top quality designation, guaranteeing a wine's origin, grape varieties, and production methods.

Caves Coopératives Vineyards and wineries owned jointly by a number of members are known as *caves coopératives*. More than half of all French vineyards are currently collectively owned, but numbers are declining.

Climat Specific vineyard site, defined by its climatological and geographical characteristics. The terms *climat* and *terroir* are interchangable.

Commune French for village or parish.

Cru Classé The best wines of Bordeaux's Médoc district are split into five *crus*, from *premier cru classé* (best) to *cinquième cru classé*, with an additional sixth, *cru Bourgeois*.

Dégorgement (**Disgorgement**) Following *remuage*, this is the final stage in *méthode traditionelle* sparkling wine production: the removal, by freezing, of yeast deposits.

Grand Cru Literally "great growth," this classification is awarded to the finest vineyards and the wines they produce. Specific meanings vary from region to region.

Grand Vin The best wine of an estate.

Méthode Traditionelle Method used to make all high-quality sparkling wines, involving, among other things, a second fermentation in the bottle.

Phylloxera Aphid that has periodically devastated French vines, killing them by feeding on their roots.

Premier Cru Quality indicator applied in Burgundy to wines classified just below *grand cru*, and used in various ways in Bordeaux and elsewhere.

Remuage (**Riddling**) In the *méthode traditionelle*, the shaking process by which dead yeasts are moved to the neck of the bottle after the second fermentation.

Vin de Table Quality classification applied to the lowest level of French wines.

Vin de Pays One step above the *vin de table* quality classification, and one below *VDQS*, these are mostly simple country wines with a regional character.

Vin Délimité de Qualité Supérieur (VDQS) Quality classification for wines better than *vin de pays* but not as good as those of *appellation contrôlée* status.

SUPPLIERS

BOSTON

Federal Wine and Spirits
Tel: (617) 367 8605

Marty's Liquors
Tel: (617) 782 3250

CHICAGO

Sam's Wine and Spirits
Tel: (312) 664 4394

Wine Discount Center
Tel: (773) 489 3454

DALLAS-FT. WORTH

Centennial Fine Wines & Spirits
Tel: (214) 361 6697

Sigel's
Tel: (972) 387 9873

DETROIT

Merchant's Fine Wine
Tel: (313) 563 8700

Village Corner
Tel: (734) 995 1818

HOUSTON

Richard's Liquors and Fine Wines
Tel: (713) 523 7405

Spec's Warehouse
Tel: (713) 526 8787

LOS ANGELES

Wally's Wines & Spirits
Tel: (310) 475 0606

Woodland Hills Wine
Tel: (800) 678 9463

MINNEAPOLIS-ST PAUL

Haskell's
Tel: (612) 342 2437

Surdyk's
Tel: (612) 379 3232

NEW YORK

Astor Wines & Spirits
Tel: (212) 674 7500

Zachys
Tel: (800) 723 0241

PHOENIX

Epicurean Wine Service
Tel: (480) 998 7800

Sportsman's Wines
Tel: (602) 955 7730

SEATTLE

McCarthy & Schiering
Tel: (206) 524 9500

Pike & Western Wine Shop
Tel: (206) 441 1307

TAMPA

Bern's Fine Wines and Spirits
Tel: (813) 250 9463

The Wine Warehouse
Tel: (727) 839 5601

WASHINGTON, DC

MacArthur Beverages
Tel: (202) 338 1433

Schneider's of Capitol Hill
Tel: (202) 543 9300

GENERAL INDEX

D

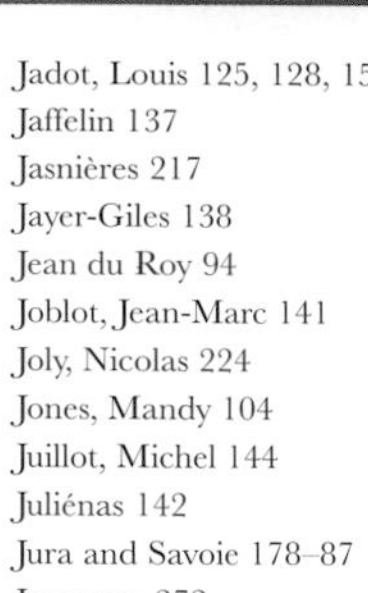

R

S

T

V

W

Z

ACKNOWLEDGMENTS

The Publisher would like to thank the following people, whose contributions and assistance have made the preparation of this book possible:

Proofreader Gary Werner
Indexer Hilary Bird
Picture Research Sarah Hopper, Carlo Ortu
Picture Library Richard Dabb

Original Project Editor Marcus Hardy
Original Art Editor Tessa Bindloss
Original Editors Nancy Jones, Jane Bolton, Edward Bunting
Original Designers Catherine MacKenzie, Tim Mann
Original Managing Editor Francis Ritter
Original Managing Art Editor Derek Coombes
Original DTP Designer Sonia Charbonnier
Original Picture Research Brigitte Aurora
Maps James Anderson
Illustrations Claire Littlejohn
Wine Photography Steve Gorton
Original Production Manager Julian Deeming
Additional Photography Max Alexander, Andy Crawford, Phillip Dowell, Andrew Holligan, Paul Kenward, Neil Lukas, Ian O'Leary, Neil Mersh, Stephen Oliver, John Parker, Guy Ryecart, Kim Sayer, Alan Williams

Picture Credits
t: top, tl: top left, tlc: top left center, tc: top center, trc: top right center, tr: top right, cla: center left above, ca: center above, cra: center right above, cl: center left, c: center, cr: center right, clb: center left below, cb: center below, crb: center right below, bl: bottom left, b: bottom, bc: bottom center, bcl: bottom center left, br: bottom right, d: detail.

The Publisher would like to thank the following individuals, companies and picture libraries for permission to reproduce their photographs:

AKG-images: 69 (br), 69 (tr). **Alamy Images**: Philippe Roy 55. **Ancient Art & Architecture Collection**: 206 (bc). **Anthony Blake Photo Library**: 47(br). **www.bridgeman.co.uk**: 85 (br); Biblioteca de Catalunya, Barcelona, Spain 84 (bl); British Library, London, UK 13 (br); Buhrle Collection, Zurich, Switzerland, 12 (bl); Centre Historique des Archives Nationales, Paris, France, Lauros / Giraudon; 84 (ca); Musee d'Orsay, Paris, France, Giraudon; 243(br); Musee National du Moyen Age et des Thermes de Cluny, Paris, Peter Willi; 14 (b); Museo dell' Opera del Duomo, Florence, Italy, Giraudon; 12 (ca); Private Collection, Roger-Viollet, Paris 17(b); Staatliches Museum, Schwerin, Germany 13 (t); Victoria & Albert Museum, London, UK, 68 (clb). **Cephas Picture Library**: 210(cfr), 243(t); Mick Rock 168 (cra), 187 (ca), 207 (b), 207 (tl); Nigel Blythe 206 (cla), 264-265; Pierre Hussenot 49 (br); Stockfood 46 (bl); TOP/Pierre Hussenot 46 (br); TOP/Tripelon/Jarry 72 (cfr), 120 (cfr); Wine Magazine 41 (tr). **Corbis**: Chris Lisle 60-61 VineyardandDove. **Institut National des Appellations d'Origine (INAO)**: 36 (ca), 37 (br). **The Interior Archive**: JP0002/001/01 51 (tr). **Jean Loup Charmet**: 15 (tl). **Robert Joseph**: 201 (br); E.T. Archive: Cathedral Treasury 14(ca). **Retrograph Archive**: 165(br). **Scope**: 37 (tr), 230 (cla), 253(ca), 266 (cfl); Charles Bowman 52 (br); Francis Jalain 29 (br), 146 (bc); Frederic Hadengue 23 (cfl); Jacques Guillard 261 (cb); Jacques Guillard 6 (tc), 7 (ca), 7 (car), 7 (cbr), 7 (cfl), 7 (cl), 16 (ca), 17 (tl), 19 (tr), 20 (bcr), 22 (ca), 22 (ca), 23 (tr), 28 (bl), 28 (tr), 30 (bl), 30 (ca), 31 (tl), 40 (cra), 48 (cra), 50 (ca), 54 (tr), 59 (tr), 66 (cra), 70 (bl), 76 (bc), 77 (bc), 77 (ca), 78 (ca), 79 (br), 79 (ca), 102 (cla), 116 (cla), 117 (tl), 118 (bl), 119 (br), 119 (tl), 132 (cla), 133 (bl), 133 (tl), 134 (clb), 135 (cla), 137 (cla), 138 (ca), 139 (ca), 142 (bc), 145 (cla), 147 (clb), 148 (cra), 149 (cla), 150 (ca), 150 (crb), 151 (clb), 152 (clb), 153 (cla), 154 (bc), 156 (bc), 157 (clb), 158 (cr), 159 (cla), 164 (b), 167 (c), 176 (bl), 177 (cla), 180 (cra), 181 (br), 184 (cla), 186 (cb), 187 (cb), 188 (ca), 204 (cfl), 208 (cla), 209 (br), 209 (tr), 214 (bc), 214 (ca), 215 (ca), 216 (bc), 216 (ca), 217 (ca), 218 (bc), 218 (ca), 219 (cla), 220 (cla), 221 (ca), 222 (cla), 223 (clb), 224(bc); 225 (cla), 226 (clb), 231 (clb), 234 (cb), 240 (cra), 242 (bl), 244 (cfl), 245 (bl), 250 (bl), 250 (ca), 251 (cla), 252 (bc), 252 (ca), 254 (clb), 255 (bl), 256 (cla), 257 (ca), 257 (cb), 258 (cla), 259 (bc), 259 (ca), 260 (ca), 260 (cb), 261 (ca), 262 (ca), 262 (clb), 262 (crb), 276 (bl); Jean Guillard 124 (cla), 125 (ca), 125 (cb); Jean- Luc Barde 141 (ca); Jean-Luc Barde 6 (br), 6 (cbl), 18 (bl), 19 (tcl), 20 (bl), 25 (bl), 26 (b), 27 (bc), 32 (ca), 41 (br), 47 (tr), 52 (ca), 53 (tl), 58 (tl), 82 (cla), 88(cfr), 96 (tl), 99 (ca), 104(bl), 109 (clb), 109 (crb), 111 (bl), 114 (clb), 126 (cfl), 127 (bl), 127 (tr), 129 (tl), 130 (br), 130 (cra), 131 (cb), 131 (cla), 139 (bc), 140 (cla), 142 (ca), 143 (cfl), 144 (bc), 146 (ca), 148 (bc), 185 (ca), 190 (clb), 191 (br), 195 (cla), 195 (clb), 196 (bc), 196 (ca), 197 (bc), 197 (ca), 198 (ca), 198 (cb), 199 (ca), 199 (cb), 201 (ca), 263 (cla), 267 (br), 270 (bc), 270 (ca), 271 (ca), 272 (ca), 272 (cb), 273 (ca), 273 (cb), 274 (ca), 275 (bc), 277 (tr); Jean-Luc Sayegh 15 (br); JLB112863 34 (ca); Michel Guillard 16 (bl), 18 (br), 23 (bl), 24 (bl), 25 (tr), 26 (ca), 27 (tl), 29 (tr), 31 (br), 40 (bl), 44 (tl), 50 (bl), 54 (bl), 76 (ca), 86 (cfl), 92 (bl), 92 (ca), 93 (cla), 95 (cb), 98 (tl), 99 (bc), 100 (cla), 101 (bl), 101 (tr), 103 (cla), 104 (ca), 105 (cla), 106 (cla), 106 (clb), 107 (cla), 108 (cla), 109 (ca), 110 (cla), 136 (bc), 141 (bc), 155 (ca), 234 (ca); Michel Plassart 36 (b), 39 (tcl), 39 (tcr), 39 (tl), 39 (tr), 78 (cb), 117 (bl), 138 (bc); Noel Hautemaniere 46 (ca), 194 (ca), 200 (cla); Philipe Blondel 217 (br), 227 (cla); Philippe Beuzen/Iles Images 237 (ca); Philippe Blondel 22 (bl), 237 (bc); Sara Matthews 59(br). **Stephen Lenthall**: 8 (tr).